SOCIETY AND ECONOMY
IN COLONIAL
CONNECTICUT

SOCIETY AND ECONOMY IN COLONIAL CONNECTICUT

Jackson Turner Main

PRINCETON UNIVERSITY PRESS
PRINCETON, NEW JERSEY

CONTENTS

GRAPHS AND TABLES

APPENDIXES

GRAPHS AND TABLES

INTRODUCTION

This book originated over a dozen years ago when I began a survey of colonial probate estate inventories in order to plot the distribution of property over time and place. Such an outline would enable someone working in local history to place a particular society within the general framework, purging intensive local studies of their principal bias.

At the same time broad generalizations about the nature and direction of change in colonial society and economy needed testing. The most popular interpretation posited a comparatively democratic, equalitarian, near-subsistence society, beginning in the seventeenth century, and sometimes associated with cooperative attitudes, at least in New England. These communal qualities gradually retreated before a process of Anglicanization, characterized by the emergence of a wealthy, powerful upper class dominating a poor, often servile proletariat. This change occurred partly because small-scale subsistence agriculture gave way to large landed estates raising staple crops with a heavy investment of capital (especially in labor), or to trading and financial centers dominated by merchant-capitalists. The evidence for this interpretation derived at first primarily from the "Tidewater" South and the northern cities, presently supported by studies of New England towns that indicated an economic decline, Malthusian pressure on the land, a hardening of class lines, and the same growing inequality.

An alternative hypothesis originated with the conviction that the colonists became increasingly unlike the Europeans, more American, for a variety of reasons including the frontier environment, the tradition of dissent in religion, an emphasis on liberty in politics, and the belief in the individual's ability to rise from poverty to wealth. In general the proponents of this view argued for economic and social progress, for increasing wealth available in some degree to a majority, rather than stagnation or decline. Thus they viewed colonial society favorably and optimistically, with the Revolution tending to affirm the march of progress and democracy.

Further to complicate matters, occasional dissidents suggested that no evolution in either direction occurred, but that the society and economy moved either cyclically, in a straight line, or (as in a multiple-choice question) all of the above. By the mid-1970s we seemed to confront anarchy. Each hypothesis was supported by data and seemed valid for at least some times and places. A scientific approach required that we either test each of these hypotheses or discard the whole lot and proceed empirically with a large-scale accumulation of data. So I began, but when I reached Connecticut I found such riches of then untapped sources that I never left. What follows constitutes not the intended large framework but a progress report.

At first I took notes only on what seemed important categories of contents within the inventories, along with the name, title, residence, and age of the decedent. Halfway along, the need for information on family status appeared. A little later I learned about the significance of consumer goods, and the first draft revealed that I needed to work out the requirements for various standards of living at different stages in the life cycle. Little guide to these topics then existed in the literature and as a result I was obliged to retrace my steps and enlarge my coverage. Also, because my initial purpose was limited I did not bother to enter any of the data on a computer. Ultimately my data bank grew until a computer would have been very handy indeed, but by then I had already completed most of the tables.

The study as originally designed consisted of Chapters Two to Four and bits of the rest. Even as expanded it still excludes subjects that we are coming to expect in a book on social history and skims over topics that merit fuller treatment. Indeed, each of the chapters and even some parts of chapters could well become monographs with a little more research, such as the social and economic history of the colony's ministers or the characteristics of the first settlers. Women scarcely appear in my account, though the sources furnish a quantity of information. In this case the need for a full treatment was so evident that for me to include a few pages would be almost insulting, and I leave that book for someone else. The same is true of Indians. Blacks receive a little more attention only because most of them enter the probate records as property. The book indeed consists of a series of related essays, not a definitive treatment of social history. However, I think it does accomplish the objective of an accurate general guide to the social and economic history of the period, a foundation for the more detailed research of future scholars.

My primary professional obligation is owed to the courteous, capable, and intelligent staff of the Connecticut State Library in Hartford. Financial support has come from the Research Foundation of the State University of New York and the National Endowment for the Humanities, which provided a fellowship to the Center for Advanced Study in the Behavioral Sciences during 1980-1981 supplementing a sabbatical from SUNY Stony Brook. Many of the Fellows at the Center were extremely helpful. Above all I thank my beloved wife Gloria and my three children.

Boulder, Colorado
July 1984

SOCIETY AND ECONOMY
IN COLONIAL
CONNECTICUT

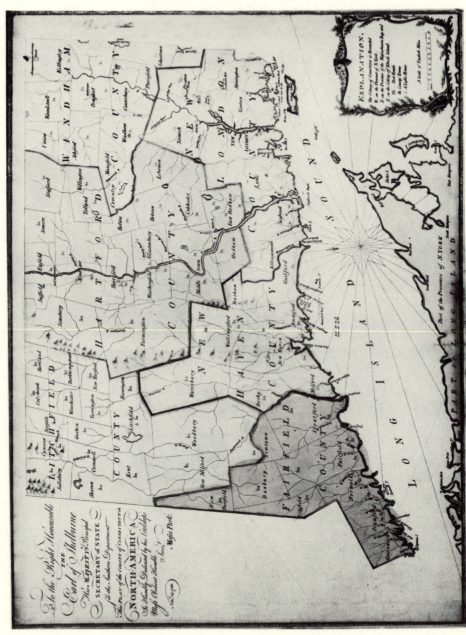

Moses Park 1766 map of Connecticut (Courtesy Yale University Map Collection)

ONE

On Population

This chapter exists quite by accident. I was trying to discover how many of the men who died in early Connecticut turned up in the probate court, in order to judge the reliability of the records. Using the published estimates of population and a commonly assumed death rate, I found that, until 1720, we seemed to have inventories of the estates of almost nine out of ten.[1] Indeed, during one decade the proportion exceeded 100 percent! Something was wrong: either the death rates were higher than we had supposed or the colony contained more people than the published estimates indicate. A fresh start on the problem was called for before I could proceed.

Tax lists for almost any time and place show a lot of people with little or no property, and we need to know whether such men were young, in which case their poverty was a (perhaps) temporary condition, or middle-aged. Partly for this reason we cannot interpret data on the distribution of wealth until we know the age structure of the society. Also, using estate inventories—our most important source—requires a knowledge of the age structure of both the "decedents" and the living population, because the former are much older. Half the men featured in the probate records had reached the age of fifty, whereas half of those still alive were in their twenties and early thirties. Older men are wealthier because they have been accumulating property for a longer time than average. So, to discover the wealth of the living by extrapolating from the wealth of the dead we must discover the age structure of both groups and adjust for the difference.[2] Moreover, we

[1] Including those without inventories but leaving wills, we seemed to have all but 7 percent. Evarts B. Greene and Virginia D. Harrington assembled data from the published *Colonial Records* in their *American Population before the Federal Census of 1790* (New York, 1932). These give the number of taxables living in the town. See J. H. Trumbull and Charles Hoadly, eds., *The Public Records of the Colony of Connecticut . . .* 15 vols. (Hartford, 1850-1890). To find the adult male population one subtracts men under twenty-one. I am arguing that we must add back a considerable number for those excused or accidentally omitted, so that the adult males were more numerous than commonly supposed and probate coverage accordingly less.

[2] For this adjustment see Gloria L. Main, "The Correction of Biases in Colonial American Probate Records," *Historical Methods Newsletter* 8 (1974-1975), 10-28.

should follow the changing situation of the people of colonial Connecticut as they move through a typical life cycle, from the child to the young single person to the newlywed, then the parent of youngsters, of teen-agers, of grown children, of grandchildren, and into old age. Social history demands that we study every sort of people with equal respect and in the same detail, especially if four-fifths of the population—the women and children—are almost excluded.

These reasons, and others as will appear, compelled an extensive though selective investigation of the colony's demography. Flaws in the sources kept enlarging the scope of the investigation. Thus where dates of birth were lacking a date of marriage or of a first-born might serve, but only if the average age at marriage was known for at least some of the people, so that fact had to be determined. Changing patterns of population over time required study of the demographic shifts during the whole period. The search for answers, far from being dull, was like a detective story, a piecing together of the evidence to solve a whole series of problems, the enterprise made the more fruitful because of the contrasts that appeared between the characteristics of colonial Connecticut's demography and those of other times and places. And some interesting facts emerged.

I started with the earliest settlers, to determine their ages upon arrival, estimate their number, discover the dates of their deaths, compute their life span and death rate, and compare the number of deaths recorded in probate with the actual frequency. These data would yield, among other inferences, the solution to our very first problem: why we find an unexpectedly large number of inventories. For this undertaking the records furnish reasonably complete lists of the settlers resident about the year 1640 for five of the eleven towns: New Haven and Stamford on the coast and Hartford, Windsor, and Wethersfield up the Connecticut River.

The first colonists of New Haven landed in 1638.[3] The town contained some seventy "free planters" by the next June and in 1640 confirmed its survival with the erection of a meetinghouse. By 1645 about 340 men had resided in the town at least briefly. Of these, one-third simply disappear, probably among the two out of five immigrants known to have left the colony. The settlement reminds one of the early Ches-

---

[3] Lists of early settlers in C. J. Hoadly, ed., *Records of the Colony and Plantation of New Haven*, 8 vols. (Hartford, 1857), 1:91-93; genealogies and notices in Donald Lines Jacobus, *Families of Ancient New Haven*, 9 vols., 1922-1932 reprinted in 3 vols. (Baltimore, 1974). This is a work of exceptional value, complete and accurate. I treat New Haven and its neighbors as part of Connecticut though actually they remained independent until 1664.

apeake ventures or of a mining town. It was mostly male and among those whose ages we know, more than half were in their twenties and another couple of dozen were still teen-agers. If we classify the latter as men, 64 percent had not reached the age of thirty, leaving aside those who vanished. Few had married and no doubt the great majority were poor laborers.

Genealogists have spent a good deal of time on such of the survivors as founded families, but have discovered the exact birth dates of only forty-three, with approximations for another twenty-six. These dates enable us to estimate the men's average age at marriage, usually assumed to be twenty-five for the seventeenth century. New Haven's was thirty, reflecting the later age at marriage in Old England, where some men had already wed, but especially the shortage of women in the new colony. Using this figure, or the consequent assumption drawn from the birth date of a first child, we arrive at the following age structure of adult men in 1640: age twenty to twenty-nine, 59 percent; age thirty to thirty-nine, 24 percent; age forty to forty-nine, 12 percent, and over fifty, 5 percent. None had reached the age of sixty.

Since so many of the early settlers simply vanish, it may seem presumptuous to comment on the average age at death or the life expectancy of men at particular ages. However, we might forget about the transients and focus on those who remained to buy land, become permanent residents, and, in most cases, marry and die in the colony—the founding fathers of New Haven. Among these the age at death was high because they had already survived for nearly thirty years. We know the death dates for 130 individuals present in 1640, among whom the median age at death was fifty-eight, varying with the date of birth as follows: born before 1600, sixty-nine; born 1600-1609, sixty; born 1610-1620, fifty-five. The last figure records the life expectancy of men aged twenty to twenty-nine in 1640. It seems high, considering the problems of a new settlement, exceeding that of Maryland by a dozen years, but, as we will discuss later, Plymouth settlers apparently outlasted them.[4] We cannot tell anything about the death rate at this point because of an excessive number of missing men. During the 1650s the death rate of those adult men we do know about was only eighteen per thousand. Of course most men were still young,

---

[4] Immigrants into seventeenth-century Maryland who reached the age of twenty-one would live only twenty-three more years, compared to thirty or more in New Haven. See the discussion by Russell H. Menard, "The Immigrants and Their Increase: The Process of Population Growth in Early Colonial Maryland," in *Law, Society, and Politics in Early Maryland*, ed. Aubrey C. Land, Lois Green Carr, and Edward C. Papenfuse (Baltimore, 1977), pp. 88-110.

which keeps the figure down. Since some of the transients surely died without record, we must suspect a higher death rate and a shorter life expectancy.[5]

The first New Haven settlement, then, reminds us of the Chesapeake colonies in that both contained mostly young single men who either died soon or left the colony. From 1638 to 1645 only a little more than a hundred women aged sixteen or more had arrived (that we know about), being outnumbered almost 3.5 to 1 by the male immigrants. In the latter year, since some men had left, the sex ratio was 2.2 to 1. Although some of these women had already produced children and the rest married young—under twenty—their small number prevented a boom in population. Worse, the town was an economic failure, and so many men gave up and left that the population was not growing at all. This situation began to change, however. Most of the men who survived married eventually, the proportion of men who died single declining from 37½ percent in the 1640s to 25 percent in the 1660s. The young girls soon became mothers and many children survived. Thus the unstable village dominated by young males gave way to permanent families, and New Haven came at last to resemble not her Chesapeake predecessors but her sister villages up the Connecticut River.

The lists of early settlers in Hartford, Windsor, and Wethersfield come from "taxables" in 1654-1655, an estimate of 150 "settlers" for Hartford in 1639, genealogies in extensive histories of Windsor and Wethersfield and a more limited one for Hartford, together with additions from probate records.[6] These sources permit a reconstruction of the population in 1640. By that date the three communities, founded in 1634 and 1635, included nearly three hundred adult men. Forty percent were in their twenties and the median age was thirty-three. Only a little over half of the earliest settlers had married. The young bachelors of Hartford had to wait until they were over thirty, on the average, before they found wives, though in Windsor they married at twenty-eight and in Wethersfield at twenty-seven. In the last, there was only one woman over sixteen for every two men. The situation was

[5] Probate records furnish inventories for twenty-four. Jacobus (*Families of Ancient New Haven*) adds five who died without inventories and three more may also have died there during the decade. The adult male population in 1655 was about 170. Boundaries for the death rate per thousand men are 17.1 and 18.8.

[6] Greene and Harrington, *American Population*, p. 52n; Henry R. Stiles, *History and Genealogy of Ancient Windsor*, 2 vols. (Hartford, 1891-1892); Lucius B. Barbour, *Families of Early Hartford* (Baltimore, 1977); Henry R. Stiles, *The History of Ancient Wethersfield*, 2 vols. (New York, 1903).

alleviated, however, by the removal of many of the men. One-fourth of the early emigrants into the three towns left the colony, usually headed north into Massachusetts, and another group moved to found new communities in Connecticut, so that their society was almost as mobile as that of New Haven.[7]

So far we are struck by the resemblance between the colony's early settlers and those of the Chesapeake. Relatively more women had arrived, to be sure, but not nearly enough to go around, and young men, almost all with little property, predominated. But one big demographical difference appears: far more of them survived and their children, too, lived to have families of their own. In Maryland the young male—and presumably female—immigrant of twenty-one lived for another two decades or a bit more. The life expectancy in the West Indies was probably even less. In contrast, the New Haven women who reached age twenty-one survived into the fifties and their Wethersfield sisters even longer, while the men lived for thirty years after their arrival. The median age at death in Hartford was 62½ years and in Windsor, fully 70. These men, being mature when we meet them, would of course greatly exceed the population as a whole in longevity, but the figure is impressive, exceeding that in New Haven by a decade. The peculiar age structure helped to keep down the annual death rate, which during the 1650s was seventeen per thousand for adult men in Hartford and only thirteen in Windsor.[8]

The pioneers of Connecticut, then, did not all arrive in family groups. Over half of even the adult men were single. It was a young population with over 40 percent in their twenties and only one-fifth having reached the age of forty. The shortage of mature women raised the men's average age at marriage to thirty. Unlike the British settlers in the Chesapeake and the West Indies, they did not die young of disease, malnutrition, or Indian attacks. Collectively they lived to be over sixty and

[7] Linda Auwers Bissell shows nearly half of the Windsor men leaving that town. "From One Generation to Another: Mobility in Seventeenth-Century Windsor, Connecticut," *William and Mary Quarterly* 31 (1974), 79-110. My figures differ slightly but we reach the same conclusion. The total in my sources was 285, with a median age of thirty-four, but there was a great deal of moving in and out of the town and I guess at an additional 5 percent of young bachelors. In Harford I find that 28 percent left Connecticut and 16 percent moved to another town. The basic source is a "mill rate" list for 1655, which included transients, supplemented by data identifying grants of lots and rights to temporary inhabitants.

[8] In Hartford, twenty-two estates entered probate during 1650-1659, three did not, and one additional person probably died, out of 170 adult men present in 1654. Windsor that year contained about 145 men. Fourteen estates entered probate and four other men probably died also.

the man or woman of twenty-five would survive another thirty-five years. While over one-fourth left the colony soon after arrival, those departures helped to dispose of young single men for whom wives and perhaps even jobs were lacking. Settlers who remained fared well.[9]

The next adequate set of records comes a generation later, about 1670, when we can draw, first, on eight tax lists;[10] second, data on New Haven from Jacobus; third, a modern census for the colony assembled from the foregoing and other records;[11] fourth, the number of taxables reported to the legislature by the towns; and finally, probate records. Each of these contains flaws but all are essential sources.

The tax lists by law omitted some men: ministers, men over seventy, and soldiers on active service. The towns forgave others their rates, notably paupers, and also an occasional skilled worker whom the town wished to attract. Elisha Hart of Windsor never appeared on the lists although he lived there for many years, because he was both insane and poor.[12] Also the names of servants, slaves, and males age sixteen through twenty do not appear, their rate being paid for them by their masters or fathers or guardians. The same was true of older men if they remained or became dependent on someone else. Furthermore, although the assessors tried to catch the migrants they sometimes failed. Thus the number of persons taxed, the so-called "polls" or heads that the towns reported to the legislature fell considerably short of the total population.[13] In addition, from a colonywide point of view, newly established towns sometimes obtained an exemption for a few years.

[9] For detailed data see Appendix 1A.

[10] Elizabeth H. Schenck, *History of Fairfield, Fairfield County, Conn.*, 2 vols. (New York, 1889-1905), 1:334; Guilford and Middletown lists in the Connecticut State Library, Hartford; Richard Anson Wheeler, *History of the Town of Stonington*, . . . (Mystic, Conn., 1966), p. 67; Stiles, *Wethersfield*, 2:912-14; Edwin Hall, *The Ancient Historical Records of Norwalk, Conn.* (Norwalk, 1847), p. 61; E. B. Huntington, *History of Stamford, Connecticut from Its Settlement in 1641, to the Present Time* . . . (Stamford, 1868), 25-26; and *Some Early Records and Documents of . . . Windsor, Connecticut 1639-1703* (Hartford, 1930), pp. 87-89.

[11] Jay Mack Holbrook, *Connecticut 1670 Census* (Pamphlet, Holbrook Research Institute) (Oxford, Mass., 1977).

[12] Charles William Manwaring, comp., *A Digest of the Early Connecticut Probate Records*, 3 vols. (Hartford, 1904-1906), 1:320.

[13] The degree to which the tax returns were deficient determines the multiplier that the historian should use to determine the total population from the polls. If, for example, the town reported 100 polls, and if one subtracts one-fifth for men under twenty-one, multiplying the remainder by 5 equals 400. Historians have generally used such a formula: polls times 4 equals total. But we must add all those persons whom the collectors missed—at least 10 percent and perhaps twice that number because of migration, varying with the town. The true multiplier therefore becomes 4.5 or even 5.0, as used here.

My revised data suggests a total for Connecticut in 1655 of 1,200 men, or presumably 6,000 persons.[14] Considering the number of men who supposedly had entered the colony during its first decades, probably not far from 1,000, the number seems low, with a growth rate of only 1.2 percent annually despite some continued immigration. The failure to grow between 1640 and 1655 reflected considerable emigration and a lopsided age structure, since many immigrants were young single men who did not produce adult sons for over twenty years. More seriously, women of marriageable age were in short supply.

Beginning about 1660, however, the second generation began to appear as taxables, emigration lessened after a brief exodus to East Jersey and Long Island, and a few more settlers arrived. The recorded adult male population abruptly spurted. New Haven town furnishes an exaggerated example. About 230 men were present in 1647 but only 170 remained ten years later, including relatively few young men. By 1668 the total had recovered to 219 (including Wallingford), the proportion of men in their twenties jumped, and there were numerous boys in their late teens. The same was true of women: the colony was ready for a population boom.

The course of this explosion is revealed not only by the taxables reported to the legislature but—in a sort of inverse way—the deaths recorded in the probate court.[15] By the last third of the century these had become so numerous as to equal if not exceed the number predicted by the male population as indicated by the polls. We have now explained this miraculous completeness: there were more men than the tax lists indicate. Still, the probate court reported a very high proportion of the deaths, at least four out of five during the half-century after 1660.[16] The researcher finds the appointment of an administrator or executor, the posting of a bond, the probate of a will, an inventory of the person's property, the settlement or distribution of an estate. From a demographic point of view, we can add to the population men not

[14] In 1654 the reported taxables totaled 777 but that did not include the towns in New Haven's jurisdiction—Guilford, Milford, Branford, and New Haven itself, nor did it include the district of New London. If they grew at the same rate as those for which we do have data, they contained 566 taxables, so that the whole adult male population totaled about 1,315, minus boys of sixteen to twenty (one-sixth of the men aged sixteen and up), plus those exempted from taxation, and wanderers.

[15] Microfilms of probate court records are located at the Connecticut State Library, which also contains the originals for the Hartford and some other districts. Selections from the Hartford records to 1750 appear in Manwaring, *Early Connecticut Probate Records*, which also contains a list of all the districts and all the towns, with the dates of their founding and the districts to which they belonged. Most of the records for the New London district prior to 1700 have been destroyed.

[16] See Appendix 1B.

appearing on the tax lists, and by discovering the birth date of the decedents learn the longevity of the population. Thus the combination of probate records, assessment lists, and collective genealogies enables us to analyze the population of Connecticut during the late 1600s.

By 1670 the age structure of the colony's people had stabilized. At first, as we saw, young men predominated and old men scarcely existed. The population remained quite young—the high birth rate saw to that—but the median, among adult men, rose from thirty-two to nearly thirty-six and men over sixty now became common, though still scarcely one in twelve. The relative decline of men under forty reflected a continuing emigration of that age group, the diminished immigration, and the trend toward a "normal" age distribution as native-born residents replaced newcomers. The much larger proportion of older men resulted from the survival of the first settlers, since a man of thirty in 1640 would have reached seventy in 1670. A further slight increase in the septuagenarians, coming, so to speak, at the expense of men in their fifties, would presently complete the change in pattern.

The large population on this set of tax lists and other sources, with considerable information concerning the dates of death of these men, permits a discussion of how long Connecticut's settlers lived. If we consider only the people on the lists, the general age at death would be rather high because the men were in their thirties to start with. Those in 1640, taken together, lived to be over sixty—about thirty years for the "average" man (not for someone just turned twenty-one). This figure is certainly higher than the reality because so many youngsters vanished, some of whom must have died; an age at death of fifty-nine is more likely. By 1670, as the population aged, it had risen to sixty-three.

TABLE 1.1

Age Distribution of Adult Men, Seventeenth Century (percentages)

	21–29	30–39	40–49	50–59	60–69	70+	Total	Median	N
Five towns, 1640	42.2	34.9	15.8	5.5	1.6	0	100.0	32.3	493
Nineteen towns, 1670	35.8	25.4	15.7	15.4	5.4	2.1	99.8	35.6	1,451

NOTE: Many ages must be inferred from the age at marriage, assumed to be twenty-eight to thirty in 1640 if it occurred in the colonies (depending on the town), twenty-five if in England or on the 1670 list. "Unknowns," consisting of men for whom we have no clue, are numerous. They are incorporated into the table by assuming that they were single, and allocated among the age groups accordingly. In 1640 about 10 percent of the men vanish and may have left before that date. I guess that half were still present.

In 1670 probate records and genealogies add 20 percent to the men on tax and other lists. If we depended entirely upon such lists for 1670 and excluded the unknowns in both years, the proportion of men aged twenty-one to twenty-nine would drop to 35.6 in 1640 and to 29.7 in 1670. The medians would become 33.9 and 37.4.

A better measure is the life expectancy of each age group. Probate records furnish this information because the death of every man who reached the age of twenty-one appeared there potentially, so that our population, or pool, should consist of all adult men. Actually, as we have seen, 15 or 20 percent of the estates did not enter the court, but these were spread over the entire age spectrum.[17] There remains a catch: as entries in the probate records begin the data is distorted by the youth of the population. During the 1640s the median age at death was barely forty (N = 51) and if anything probably less, since half of the "unknowns" were single and only one is known to have left children. During the next decade the figure rose by three years, but not until the 1670s did the age distribution of the population raise the age at death to forty-nine, after which it stabilized at about fifty.[18]

The ample information furnished by the sources allows us to trace the life expectancy by cohorts. Thus we can identify over 400 men who had reached the age twenty-one to twenty-nine by 1670, the "cohort" of the decade 1641 to 1649. These lived for thirty-three more years, so that a man of twenty could expect to reach fifty. The new-lywed of twenty-five survived until his late fifties, while the average person in his mid-thirties would nearly celebrate his sixtieth. From a

TABLE 1.2
Life Expectancy of Adult Men
Living in 1670

Age group	Years to live	N
21–29	33	454
30–39	24	313
40–49	19	208
50–59	13	198
60–69	12	71
70–79	8	19

[17] The probate records, like tax lists, omit some men about whom we know almost nothing. I reduced probate coverage by 4 percent to allow for them and incorporated them into the age structure. They probably died at a younger age than other men: I know this to be true of servants, and the general situation of obscure men would tend to an early death. If so, the age at death of all the men age twenty to twenty-one becomes just fifty instead of fifty-three, the same as the median age at death shown by probate records (see Appendix 1C); and for men of twenty-five, about fifty-five years.

[18] Eliminating the deaths attributable to King Philip's War would send the age back up to fifty-three, counteracting the adjustment for omissions. But I think fifty a fair estimate.

practical point of view, the Connecticut man would almost always live long enough to marry, could normally expect to see his children enter their teens, would commonly preside over their marriage, and had a nearly fifty-fifty chance of becoming a grandfather.

How many years one has yet to live on this earth is an important matter to us as individuals and for historians as well. It affects men's ability to acquire property, to care for their children and assist them as they marry. It supplies or deprives a society of leaders experienced and wise. A long life expectancy influences the number of children and the growth of population. It is, in short, an excellent index of the health and welfare of a society. How does Connecticut compare with her sister colonies of Massachusetts Bay and the Chesapeake? Our men and women[19] lived for at least ten years longer than those in Maryland but perhaps not as long as their neighbors to the north. We will elaborate the point presently after discussing trends during the eighteenth century, but we pause to comment on the factors affecting life expectancy in the seventeenth.

During the earliest years the average immigrant did not live quite as long as the colonial-born group that followed. In New Haven the settlers born from 1610 to 1619 who were still alive in 1640 lived to be fifty-five, but since some would have died before that date (remember that the town was founded in 1638) the true figure is probably closer to fifty.[20] Some may have been in rather poor condition when they immigrated, though the men in charge of the movement would certainly have preferred a healthy group. More importantly, the trip and the new environment, especially the winters, would have injured even the best-treated. We will see in Chapter Five that servants died earlier than the sons of established families. It is common knowledge that sailors, laborers, and migrants do not live as long as men more sedentary and enjoying an above-subsistence standard of living. Men with these characteristics continued to arrive throughout the seventeenth century, though in much smaller numbers, and the society itself always produced a class of poor or otherwise disadvantaged, including

[19] New Haven's native-born women of the first generation lived until their mid-sixties, actually a bit longer than the men. The median age at marriage had risen from eighteen to twenty-two. Only one-sixth died during childbearing age eighteen to thirty-nine. The data here is based on 94 out of 150 women, the age at marriage being known for 35. The sex ratio of men to women was 113:100 or, excluding women under twenty-one, 123:100.

[20] We know of only two individuals out of eighty-two dying in their twenties. The true figure is surely between eight and twelve.

servants and slaves. Other factors that killed men before their prime included the dangers of sailing, the hazards of farm life, and war.

Counteracting these were several decided advantages of residence in Connecticut. Wars were infrequent. The diseases of the Chesapeake were almost absent and, indeed, the first really serious pestilence did not occur until 1689. After the mid-1640s the overwhelming majority of the people were born in the colony. Finally, that great majority were not servants, slaves, mariners, migrants, or occasional laborers but farmers, craftsmen, and others of like situation whose standard of living was usually well above the subsistence level.

We now turn to a survey of Connecticut's population during the century after 1670. From fewer than 10,000 settlers in that year the number of people exploded to 200,000 by the time of the Revolution.[21] That growth might have been achieved by doubling every twenty-five years—an annual rate of nearly 3 percent. But in fact the rise proceeded unevenly. Between 1675 and 1715 the annual increase was only 2.5 percent because of the various wars and their attendant losses through deaths on the campaigns and epidemics brought back by soldiers and sailors.[22] After the close of Queen Anne's War, however, the colony boomed both economically and in population. The West Indies furnished a market for exports and plenty of good land remained. The annual growth of 2.5 became fully 3.5 for a period of forty years, at least among adults. Newcomers continued to enter, especially from Massachusetts, while emigration slowed (if New Haven's experience is typical). Virtually all of the women married, at an average age of twenty-

[21] Bruce C. Daniels makes it 15,800 by working backward from the census of 1756 and assuming an annual growth rate of a little under 3 percent. *The Connecticut Town: Growth and Development, 1635-1790* (Middletown, Conn., 1979). We both agree that the colony contained more people than commonly supposed (notably in 1730), but we differ on the early population. I have started with 1,450 men in towns other than the New London district (increasing Holbrook's figures by 22 percent) and adding the latter to obtain 1,874 adult men (Holbrook's 347 plus my 22 percent). Multiplying the result by five yields 9,370, by 5.5, 10,307. Incidentally, if we apply a growth rate of 3 percent annually the polls reported to the legislature in 1676 (less Rye) equals the number of men almost exactly. I think this correct, and that one should multiply the number of polls by 5, not by 4, as in Greene and Harrington (*American Population*, p. xxiii).

[22] If the proportion of decedents' estates entering probate remained stable and if polls equals adult men, then estate inventories as a percentage of men fluctuated between a low of only 11 percent during the period 1700-1709 to over 20 percent during the 1680s and 1710s, the deaths in the latter decade being heavily concentrated during 1712 and 1713. The epidemic killed between 5 and 8 percent of the men, depending on one's count. The year 1689 took a comparable toll. After 1713 probate coverage declined, and the figure of 13.7 percent as a proportion of the men during the 1720s ought I think be increased by a fifth or even a fourth, since another epidemic occurred in 1727.

two, and overcame infant mortality so as to double the population every twenty years. By 1730 it had reached 50,000, by 1740 65,000, and by mid-century, when several Massachusetts towns were annexed, nearly 100,000.[23]

After 1756 the rate of growth abruptly slowed to 0.015 annually, according to a census of 1762, picked up to 0.026 through 1774, and then dropped again to 0.014 between 1774 and 1790. The first and last of these numbers owe something to war, but the years of peace also registered a reduced rate of growth compared with the earlier period. We will discuss the reasons in some detail presently. The major factor was a rising tide of emigration that not only dampened growth by the removals but, because the emigrants were young, reduced the number of births.

The death rate among adult men remained about the same during the entire century after 1670, varying with wars, peace, and pestilence. In the 1670s it had been eighteen per thousand. A good set of assessment lists about 1730 indicate the same level.[24] Another set covers the years 1751 to 1773, from which we extract a rate of twenty-two, the war years accounting for most if not all of the difference.[25] As we have seen, all of these estimates involve an uncomfortable amount of guesswork, but Connecticut's death rate was clearly stable unless a slight rise occurred at the very end of the colonial period.

The age structure of the men we can determine from tax records, comparing the 1670 population with those of about 1730 and 1770.

[23] The starting point in 1708 presupposes that polls still equaled adult men. The evidence comes from assessment lists in Norwalk (1687), Windsor (1702), Stamford (1701), Greenwich (1694-1696), and a reconstruction of Wethersfield's population in 1700. Hall, *Norwalk*, p. 172; "Taxes under Andros," *New England Historical and Genealogical Register* 34 (1880), 371-82; Windsor list in Connecticut Historical Society, Hartford; Huntington, *Stamford*, pp. 173-76; Charles Henry Stanley Davis, *The History of Wallingford, Conn.* . . . (Meriden, 1870), pp. 429-30; Stiles, *Wethersfield*; Daniel M. Mead, *A History of the Town of Greenwich*, . . . (New York, 1857), pp. 54-55. Daniels furnishes an excellent discussion of the question. *Connecticut Town*, chap. 2.

[24] The tax lists are in the Connecticut State Library except that of Waterbury, for which see Joseph Anderson, *The Town and City of Waterbury*, . . . 3 vols. (New Haven, 1:303-309. The others are for Wethersfield, Glastonbury, East Guilford, Groton, Torrington, and Bolton. All these include the number of polls for which each taxpayer was responsible, so that we can search for such dependents, usually sons but sometimes an elderly father, a servant, or a slave. Reconstruction of the adult male population becomes easier with lists of that type though they are never complete.

[25] They consist of Goshen (1741, 1751), Milford (1768), Wethersfield (1771-1773), Glastonbury (1768), and a series for Bolton, most importantly that of 1769, all in the Connecticut State Library, and Durham (1766), in the *Conn. Hist. Soc., Collections* 21 (1924), 190-99.

TABLE 1.3
Age Distribution of Adult Men, 1670–1770 (percentages)

	21–29	30–39	40–49	50–59	60–69	70+	Total	Median	N
1670	36	25½	16	15½	5½	2	100½	35½	1,451
1730	35	28	16	12	7	2	100	35	1,360
1770	32½	26	15½	12	9	5	100	37	2,084

Age structure shows very little change during the first sixty years. The population remained young, as one would expect from its exceptional growth during the years before 1730, and such limited emigration of young men as took place was probably counteracted by immigration from Massachusetts into the northern towns. By 1770, however, this stable situation had changed in two ways: fewer young men were living in the colony and considerably more people were older.

We would expect age at death to show corresponding slight variations. The men of Holbrook's 1670 census as supplemented from other sources, including men of all ages, died at a median age of about sixty-three. The median age at death of men on the 1730s set was sixty-five and that of the final tax lists reached sixty-six as we would predict. The probate records reveal the median age at death for a different pool, consisting of every adult reaching twenty-one. Between 1670 and 1740 it had varied around fifty-one. A combination of economic depression and wartime deaths then reduced the figure to forty-eight until the return of peace in the early 1760s, after which it shot up to fifty-three and then to fifty-six and a half.[26] The first figure is reasonable as a rebound from the war (the same high level appeared after King William's War) and reflects also the older age structure displayed by the tax lists. The second figure, however, is far too high and we must either investigate some new bias in the probate records or discover a major demographical change.

Such a change might consist of an increased life expectancy of different age groups—of cohorts. We had found that men born during 1641-1649 who survived until 1670 lived another thirty-two or thirty-three years after reaching age twenty-one. Probate records indicate that this life expectancy for men in their mid-twenties remained virtually the same over a period of eighty years, men born during 1710-1719 surviving only a little longer than the cohort of 1640-1649, that is, to age fifty-eight. The probate records, as we speculated, may miss a few

[26] See Appendix 1E.

15

drifters who would lower the average, but nothing suggests a change over time.[27]

Other sources confirm a general stability. In New Haven, men born during the 1640s and 1650s, if they attained their majority, died at sixty and a century later they had improved upon that by two years.[28] Wethersfield's twenty-one-year-olds seem to have gained more—from fifty-nine to sixty-three, but the sons of the colony's leaders lost a year and a half, from sixty-four to sixty-two and a half. The age at death of men on tax lists, who to repeat had already reached their mid-thirties, rose from 62.4 in 1670 to 63.3 a generation later, 64.9 in 1730, and 66.4 at the close. All of these sources contain an upward bias because they exclude migrants and occasional residents such as slaves and childless men, and the leaders' sons were obviously favored by the environment. We therefore return to the probate records. Here we find a fundamental continuity: men of age lived for some thirty years, with fluctuations but no secular change until the final decade. From all this we conclude that the life expectancy for men who reached age twenty-one was as low as thirty-one years for the immigrants, but improved to thirty-six or -seven for those born in the colonies between 1640 and 1690 and at most another two years thereafter, depending upon our adjustments to the town genealogies. This table summarizes these results, except that the very earliest settlers did not live quite as long:

	20	30	40	50	60
Seventeenth-century	36	30	24	18	13
Post-1700	38	32	25	20	14

This survey raises two problems: the situation at the end of the period, and this life expectancy, which differs from that commonly accepted for New England. Modern estimates for seventeenth-century Massachusetts predict that men of twenty-one years would survive for another forty-four to forty-eight years. Our figure for Connecticut is at least ten years lower, actually as close to the expectancy for Maryland's native-born whites (twenty-six years) as to that of Massachusetts. So also our average man of thirty, prior to 1700, will live to be only sixty, ten years less than that for the Bay colony, and so on through every age group.[29]

[27] See Appendix 1F.

[28] See Appendix 1G.

[29] Massachusetts life expectancies are summarized in Maris Vinovskis, "Mortality Rates and Trends in Massachusetts before 1860," *Journal of Economic History* 32 (1972), 198-99. See also Daniel Scott Smith, "The Demographic History of Colonial New England,"

Are we to suppose a less healthy environment along the Sound and up the Valley? It seems unlikely. Instead, certain methodological differences may be responsible. First, the procedure followed here included deaths found in probate records and widened the investigation to include not only residents of the towns but also migrants. Our survey of particular towns yields a result much closer to the Massachusetts communities in question, especially in the case of Windsor. Secondly, the Massachusetts towns were all primarily rural and agricultural whereas many in Connecticut were not, or much less so, such as New Haven, Hartford, and Wethersfield. All of these contained an above-average number of young sailors, laborers, and servants. Finally, the Connecticut probate data covered the entire colony, or a large and typical part of it, and the tax lists of 1670 and 1730 included a good sample. These two sources yield a lower life expectancy than studies of particular towns, the probate records in particular incorporating men who are underrepresented by other sources and who died younger.[30] The data for Salem in the eighteenth-century shows a life span below that for Connecticut, and presumably Bostonians died even younger. Connecticut did not contain a Boston or even a Salem but in a sense duplicated them through a dozen lesser trading centers. Probably a general survey of Massachusetts would yield lower estimates for the colony as a whole and life expectancies close to ours.

The other problem arises from the records for the final decade of the colonial period, which show some demographic changes for the first time since the earliest years. First, tax lists indicate a population older by two years, a rise for the proportion of men over sixty equaling a decline in those under forty. Second, the age of men whose estates were inventoried in the probate court rose by three years during 1765-1769 and three more years after 1770. Again the number of older men rose sharply while the younger declined, a change substantially greater than that of the tax lists. Third, a considerable reduction occurred in the growth of population, beginning before 1756 and continuing for twenty years. These new developments might have several causes: fewer births beginning about 1725 or at least by 1730; a longer life expectancy (though this would not slow the rate of growth); substantial emigration of the young; or some new bias in our sources.

An examination of the tax lists does not show any distortions other

---

ibid., 165-83. The life expectancy in Massachusetts at age 40 was 31 more years, at 50, 23½ years, and at 60, 16 years compared with Connecticut's 24, 18, 13.

[30] The life expectancy before 1700 for a servant reaching age twenty-one was only thirty-two and for poor orphans thirty-four to thirty-five more years compared with the thirty-six for men generally (perhaps thirty-seven without the servants and orphans).

than those already considered and allowed for. The probate records are another matter: they are now biased against the young, with too many older men. The true median age at death was 52.5 rather than the 53 of 1765-1769 and the 56.5 of the next five years.[31] The records err, but correcting them still leaves an older population: that was real. The death rate seems to have risen a little, as one would expect with a changing basic age structure. We are left with fewer young men and a diminished growth in population.

Was there a reduced number of births? New Haven data does show a decrease[32] and the replacement rate of Connecticut's leaders diminished late in the colonial period. A depression during the 1730s and 1740s may have contributed, as is often the case; but we need detailed research to be certain. Be that as it may, the movement out of Connecticut into other colonies is well known. Again the New Haven data furnish a case study. The proportion of first-generation native men born 1640-1649 who left the colony averaged 3 percent, which remained essentially unchanged until those born after 1730. At that point it rose to 9 percent and then reached 11 percent for the cohort of 1740-1749.[33] This exodus may have reflected declining opportunity in Connecticut but that is doubtful, for reasons we will discuss later. The attractions of other areas are, however, unquestioned. Victory over the French and their Indian allies encouraged a movement north and northwest into Massachusetts, New Hampshire, and New York, to land much cheaper and in some cases better than any remaining in Connecticut, while some pioneers penetrated into northern Pennsylvania. Many of those who died outside the colony waited until after the Revolution to move (Jacobus gives the place of death but not the date of emigration), but the men born 1730-1749 would probably have left during their twenties and thirties, meaning for most of them

[31] The six assessment lists cited above and Jacobus's genealogy of New Haven together with various other records furnish over 600 deaths for the period. These supply a distribution and a median of 52.5 years. They also show a slight increase in the death rate, consistent with an older population.

[32] The decrease was not due to more single women or an older age at marriage. A trial run into Jacobus's *New Haven*, letters A through C, shows no reduction in the proportion of women who married among those born 1710-1719 compared with the cohort of 1680-1689; almost all did. The median age of those who married during 1700-1709 was 22 and thirty years later it was 21½. N = 39 and 80.

[33] The Ns for the last two cohorts are 398 and 523. The total number leaving the town averaged 20 percent of a given cohort until those of 1730-1749, when it rose to 25 percent. At first over half of the migrants simply shifted to a nearby town and one-fourth left for a farther place in Connecticut. By the final period, however, three-fourths removed some distance and half left the colony entirely.

before 1776, not after 1783. Even if we take only half of the increase in emigration shown by the New Haven figures, those departing would account for the older population, lower rate of growth, and fewer deaths of young men revealed in the tax, census, and probate records.

We conclude, then, that during the closing years of the colonial period the character of Connecticut's male population began to change, featuring fewer young men and more older ones. This may have been accompanied by a small increase in the life expectancy and slightly fewer births. Primarily the change resulted from the emigration of young men and women after the French and Indian War.

By the end of the colonial period the thousand men who immigrated to Connecticut had grown to nearly forty thousand, principally through the efforts of the residents themselves, for total emigration probably equaled immigration. This growth began quite modestly because the first generation did not consist exclusively of husbands and their fertile wives, as we commonly believe. Instead, not far from half of the men arrived unmarried and the settlements contained only half as many women as men. The population was young and died at an earlier age than their successors. By 1660 circumstances were improving. Many of the single men died or left and a new generation of native-born residents was coming of age, so every man might find a wife. Life expectancy increased by several years and the political settlement in England combined with the West Indies trade improved the people's prospects. Population then increased rapidly until about 1675.

At that point the rate of growth slowed again to a more moderate though perfectly respectable rate. We will see later that a sharp economic downturn during the 1680s did not entirely end for several decades. A series of wars, and epidemics following some campaigns, cost lives and property and limited geographical expansion. After 1713, however, a period of peace and prosperity inaugurated a spectacular increase, as far as population is concerned, until the Seven Years' War, when the rate of growth reverted to a more sedate level. Meanwhile the age distribution of the population, at first so very young, had reached an equilibrium that endured, testifying to the colony's famous stability, until the same war. After that event the modest emigration out of the colony increased. The loss of young men and women not only slowed population growth and shifted the age structure upward but also meant that their children would be born outside the colony, to the same effect. At the same time a slightly longer life expectancy also resulted in an older population.

Yet that life expectancy was less than we have previously believed. Some years ago a highly reputable genealogist asserted emphatically that New Englanders commonly reached their seventies, and, in fact, we have noted that several modern studies found that a man of thirty (though not of twenty-one) might do just that. The flaw in our genealogist's statement arose from the fact that the people she was studying left descendants and therefore had married. Subtract single men from our equation and the chances of a long life do indeed jump. The reality in Connecticut and probably in New England generally is more modest and did not remain entirely stable. The original settler at age twenty-one reached fifty but little more; the second generation added a few years, and the next may have also improved a bit, until by the end of the colonial period a young man might expect to live until age sixty—but not seventy—and his wife survived still longer. Insofar as a long life indicates a good one, the people of Connecticut fared well. For more evidence on that we turn to a study of their property.

Demographical Characteristics of Adult Men in 1640

AGE AT MARRIAGE

Date born	Under 25	25–29	30–34	35–39	Median	Total
Pre-1600	10	16	17	13	30	56
1600–1609	8	21	18	22	31	69
1610–1619	25	54	21	15	27	115
Total	43	91	56	50	29	240

AGE AND MARITAL STATUS

Age in 1640	Single	Married	Uncertain	Total	Probable % of men
21–29	113	24	4	141	42.4
30–39	32	105	8	145	34.9
40–49	4	69	2	75	15.8
50–59	0	27	0	27	5.5
60+	0	8	0	8	1.6
Unknown	55	4	11	70	

AGE AT DEATH (PERCENTAGES)

Age in 1640	21–29	30–39	40–49	50–59	60–69	70+	Total	Median	N
21–29	4.0	11.9	29.8	16.6	17.9	19.9	100.0	53	151
30–39	—	6.3	23.2	24.2	25.3	21.1	100.0	58	95
40–49	—	—	15.6	28.9	24.4	31.1	100.0	63	45
50–59	—	—	—	25.0	31.3	43.7	100.0	68	16
60–69	—	—	—	—	50.0	50.0	100.0	—	2

SOURCES: New Haven (see note 3), Windsor, Hartford, Wethersfield (see note 6), and Stamford, for which see E. B. Huntington, *History of Stamford, Connecticut from It. S . . .*

The Coverage of Probate Records

During the 1640s and 1650s few wills or inventories appear in the probate records as might be expected from a very young population, a good deal of emigration, and perhaps inadequate agencies of enforcement. From 1660 to 1669 ninety-four inventories were entered for the towns of New Haven, Hartford, Windsor, Stamford, and Wethersfield. From other sources we can add nine more men who certainly died during those years and another seventeen whose year and place of death are doubtful, so that the proportion for whom we have inventories falls between 78 and 91 percent. Since some of the unknowns surely survived the decade or moved away almost at once to a place unknown, the most likely proportion is a midpoint of 85 percent. The annual death rate for adult men would then be about eighteen per thousand and the median age at death forty-eight years, both reflecting a still-young population.

Exceptionally full data for the 1670s permits a second test using Holbrook's "census" and genealogies. Excluding the New London district, for which probate records are missing, the adult male population in 1670 totaled about 1,470. Of that number 74 removed themselves from the pool by leaving the colony and vanishing, so our population at risk is approximately 1,400. We know that 182 left inventories within ten years and 27 died without them. Forty-five disappear from the records without trace. Therefore the proportion of decedents who left inventories ranged from 90 down to 72 percent. How many of the unknowns should we expect to have died before 1680? Their age was young—at least one-third and probably half were under thirty. Judging from what we know about the age of men at death, they would normally contribute less than 15 percent to the total even with a war, and King Philip's War caused little loss of life in Connecticut, mostly among men who were under twenty-one in 1670. We need only a dozen for them to meet their quota, so to speak. Once again the midpoint seems fair, namely 81 percent.

Finally, to complete this discussion for the seventeenth century, the tax lists for Norwalk (1687), Windsor (1686), Derby (1681), Lyme (1688), Middletown (1679), and, to trespass a little, Windsor (1702), Stamford (1701), and New Haven (1704) show 319 men dying during the decade after the date of the tax of whom 274, or 86 percent, left inventories. In addition, 62 are unaccounted for of whom 18 probably died also (based upon their ages), so that once again the coverage for inventories was 81 percent, and a few more left wills or other traces in the probate data. No age bias appears, incidentally.

APPENDIX 1C

Age at Death, Men with Probated Estates, 1640–1659

Age	1640–1649	1650–1659
21–29	9	8
30–39	16	39
40–49	13	40
50–59	8	19
60–69	4	10
70+	1	5
Single	5	12
Married	4	1
Old	1	0
Total	61	134

Age at Death, Adult Men, from Tax Lists

1655 set	21–29	30–39	40–49	50–59	60–69	70+	Total	Median	Left/ Unknown
New Haven	6	17	26	36	40	39	164	58½	12
Hartford	1	6	18	29	32	44	130	63½	6
Stamford	1	3	11	11	11	11	48	58	4
Windsor	0	4	15	22	40	47	128	64	6
Wethersfield	2	6	18	17	17	25	85	59	1
Total	10	36	88	115	141	166	556	62.1	29
1670 set									
Branford	1	5	5	9	9	6	35	57	2
Fairfield	4	11	14	21	27	29	106	61	3
Farmington	1	3	10	11	20	25	70	62	5
Greenwich	0	0	4	3	7	7	21	—	7
Guilford	2	5	8	22	27	13	77	60	5
Haddam	0	5	2	7	8	6	28	59½	2
Hartford	1	6	23	35	33	61	159	64½	8
Middletown	—	1	7	12	14	22	56	66	0
Milford	2	5	10	14	26	23	80	64	1
New Haven	4	9	15	27	51	50	156	64	4
Wallingford	0	3	3	2	5	22	35	72	3
Norwalk	1	2	12	14	7	19	50	60	6
Stamford	3	2	13	17	14	14	63	58	5
Stratford	0	5	9	19	29	18	80	62½	2
Wethersfield	3	11	13	27	25	33	112	61	6
Windsor	2	12	19	31	49	53	166	64	2
Total	24	85	167	266	351	401	1294	63	61
1700 set									
Norwalk	3	2	13	11	11	23	63	63	17
Derby	1	2	4	5	8	8	28	63	2
Lyme	1	5	8	8	9	23	54	66	7
Windsor	4	21	20	31	56	131	269	69	24
Greenwich	2	4	8	14	17	15	58	62	4
Stamford	4	12	19	20	18	25	98	58	17
New Haven	7	21	39	65	96	163	391	66½	0
Wallingford	3	10	9	14	25	59	120	69	2
Total	25	77	126	168	240	447	1083	66	73

1730 set	21–29	30–39	40–49	50–59	60–69	70+	Total	Median	Left/ Unknown
Waterbury	1	2	18	14	18	48	101	67	6
East Guilford	0	5	11	19	20	39	94	66	10
Groton	4	10	22	36	44	100	216	68	45
Glastonbury	4	7	23	22	35	49	140	64	8
Bolton	2	5	12	10	18	31	78	65	18
Wethersfield	9	19	35	50	66	147	326	67½	32
Total	20	48	121	151	201	414	955	66.8	119
Final set									
Glastonbury	12	20	39	48	55	144	318	67	21
Goshen	2	14	13	11	9	44	93	67	11
Bolton	8	27	27	51	66	156	335	68	57
Milford	12	30	50	75	101	206	474	67	32
Durham	2	12	18	30	25	74	161	67½	16
Wethersfield	24	41	66	98	137	268	634	66½	71
Total	60	144	213	313	393	892	2015	67.1	208

SUMMARY, AGE AT DEATH, PERCENTAGES

	21–29	30–39	40–49	50–59	60–69	70+	Total	Median
1655 set	1.8	6.5	15.8	20.7	25.3	29.9	100.0	62.1
1670 set	1.9	6.6	12.9	20.6	27.1	30.9	100.1	63.0
1700 set	2.3	7.1	11.6	15.5	22.2	41.3	100.0	66.0
1730 set	2.1	5.0	12.7	15.8	21.0	43.4	100.0	66.9
Final set	3.0	7.1	10.5	15.5	19.5	44.3	99.9	67.1

NOTE: The Windsor list used for the 1700 set is that of 1702. The 1730 data for Bolton combines names of 1731 and 1738. In the final set, the Goshen figures uses lists of 1741 and 1751 and Bolton those for 1756 and 1769. Nearly half of the unknown group had left the colony about whom I had no information. As a test, I kept track of the men who left New Haven during the late colonial period and found that they lived longer than those who remained. Probably that information is biased but certainly I have no reason to believe that they survived for any shorter time than the men who remained, so I have eliminated them without prejudice. The reader should remember that the population at risk includes adult men of all ages, not men as they reached twenty-one.

To the men named on the tax lists I have added others from probate records and genealogical sources.

Age at Death, Men with Probated Estates, 1670–1774 (PERCENTAGES)

Birth Cohort	21–29	30–39	40–49	50–59	60–69	70+	Total	Median	N
1670–1679	21	14	13	28	13	11	100	51	206
1680–1689	10	16	20	15	21	18	100	53	415
1690–1699	13	18	24	21	12	12	100	47½	468
1700–1709	15	16½	16	19	20½	12½	99½	51	490
1710–1719	11	19	22½	16	17½	14	100	50	908
1720–1729	13	18	17	20	14½	17	99½	50½	827
1730–1739	13	22½	14	18½	15	17	100	49½	443
1740–1749	14	16	19	14	17	20	100	51	657
1750–1764	19½	19	17½	17	13	14	100	46½	1,609
1765–1769	11½	16	17½	17	17	21	100	53	612
1770–1774	11½	14	12	18½	18½	25	99½	56½	717

NOTE: The table starts with the 1670s when the age structure had become nearly normal. The data through the 1720s come from the entire colony, for 1730–1764 from the Hartford, Fairfield, and Middletown probate districts only, and thereafter from about two-thirds of the colony. Declines in the medians reflect wars.

Age at Death, All Towns (PERCENTAGES)

Birth Cohort	21–29	30–39	40–49	50–59	60–69	70+	Total	Median	N
1640–1649	4½	10	20½	17	25½	22	99½	58½	159
1650–1659	8	12	15	21	18	26	100	57½	214
1660–1669	11	9	16	17	18	31	100	58	287
1670–1679	5	19	15	16	16	30	101	57	330
1680–1689	11	11	16	18	18	26	100	57	334
1690–1699	8	9	13½	17	16	26	99½	61	249
1700–1709	8	13	16	18	15	30	100	57	344
1710–1719	6	15	16½	18½	14½	30	100½	58	305

SOURCE: Probate records.

New Haven Age at Death (PERCENTAGES)

Birth Cohort	21–29	30–39	40–49	50–59	60–69	70–79	80+	Total	Median	N
1640–1649	6	12	16½	12	27½	16½	9	99½	61½	98
1650–1659	6	13	10	22½	18	21½	9	100	59	99
1660–1669	10½	10½	24	13½	13½	18	9½	99½	54	95
1670–1679	6	12	10	14	20	25	13	100	65	141
1680–1689	8	10	15½	8	19	18	21	99½	64	122
1690–1699	12	13	10½	11	25	10	18	99½	58	169
1700–1709	13	13	11½	17	14	17	15	100½	57½	235
1710–1719	10	9	14	13	18½	20	16	100½	62	260
1720–1729	13	13½	10	12½	16	22	13	100	62½	309
1730–1739	16	12	8	11	18	22	12½	99½	62	294
1740–1749	12	12	12	12	17	18½	17½	100½	61½	384

SOURCE: See note 3.

NOTE: Numbers italicized emphasize the two periods of abnormally numerous deaths due to wars and their associated epidemics. The median age at death runs two years higher than that for the probate population probably because the latter included more migrants.

TWO

On Property and Status

We might study the people of Connecticut in several ways, according to their various activities or roles. They themselves valued religion highly and distinguished men and women by their relative virtue. Military ability also meant more to them than to us because they fought, as they saw it, defensive battles against mortal enemies and because their wars involved at first almost everybody and later a high proportion of the young adult men. We might alternatively focus on politics, if we understand that word to include local governments, for most critical decisions grew out of town meetings and people judged others, in part, by their political talent. We will return to these subjects when we consider status, but first we will discuss income and property.

To say that income was vital does not deny the importance of morality, courage, or qualities of leadership but only to remind ourselves that one can't exist without it. Leadership in politics, the military, the church assumed that one possessed enough food, clothes, and shelter; status followed economic independence. Their Old World experience taught the settlers the value of acquiring enough productive property to assure a livelihood. In Europe, that most often meant land, and the prospect of owning a farm was a major reason for moving to the New World. Land quickly came to form two-thirds of the people's wealth and to produce fully that proportion of their income. That income enabled Connecticut's residents to achieve a generally adequate standard of living, with variations that both influenced and reflected their status.

From an economic point of view we can categorize the colonists in two significant respects: by their occupation and by relative wealth. Most numerous were the farmers, especially if we define them broadly. Indentured servants and other immigrants of low status, if asked their occupation, generally claimed some skill that would elevate their standing, most often "farmer," and doubtless in the colonies the farm boys thought of themselves as farmers too. We will here require the ownership of land, identifying farm laborers, even those older hired hands with experience, simply as laborers. We will admit tenants, an inconsistency that in Connecticut does not matter greatly because a man

28

could acquire land easily, as we will see; nor will we exclude those whose fathers withheld technical title to the land while allowing its use. One qualification does arise from the almost universal practice among men who could do so of buying real estate, sometimes for future gain but commonly as a genuine farm, to produce food and wood or even a cash profit. Thus the skilled craftsman even in the largest towns normally owned a few acres and in more rural areas a good many—a farm; while traders and professional men often purchased substantial properties in the country. For us, farmers earned their primary income from their own land. Otherwise they did not constitute a single economic group, varying greatly in the amount of property they owned and the incomes they derived from it.

The income of other occupational groups does not flow so obviously from articles of production and capital. Craftsmen such as millers and tanners did possess conspicuous property but coopers and smiths derived their incomes from their skills. So also professionals and traders might prosper greatly even with rather little visible property. We must infer the true economic position of these groups from other evidence, such as the value of their consumption goods or their money, which luckily appear as part of estate inventories.

The same is true for our last occupational group—laborers. We define these as men who had not yet acquired the land, shops, or craft tools—the articles of production or capital goods—necessary to the full-fledged farmer or artisan. They owned little property and depended upon others for their livelihood, whether that took the form of wages or of maintenance such as sons or servants would receive. Here again we cannot judge their income or prospects except by inference from known wage scales or from inventories of their estates.

An alternative method to this classification by occupation is a division of Connecticut's people into wealth classes. We can distribute these along a spectrum from rich to poor on the basis of their income, if we can discover it, and of property, with particular regard to the requirements of various levels of living in the colony. This approach does not require the imposition of modern theories or attitudes but reflects the actual situation and in some respects the values of the people. Take the case of ministers. The towns paid them an annual salary considerably in excess of the average for a family man, gave them a house (the manse) and a lot typically including an orchard and garden along with some pasture and plowland (the glebe), in addition to occasional gifts such as firewood, all tax-exempt. Thus they freed their spiritual leader from money worries, bestowing on him the material comfort that they themselves had to strive for.

Obviously the individual and the family required a minimum simply for survival, and, indeed, if they did not possess considerably more than that minimum their poverty led not only to an unpleasant life for the adults but an inferior start for the children. Below this subsistence level one depended on someone else, as the child on the parent, the aged on their children, the pauper on charity. Everyone tried to acquire property or learn a skill adequate for financial independence, what we today call a minimum level of health and decency, which would enable a man to support a family. That minimum did not bring comfort, did not permit the purchase of amenities; so the couple would strive for a higher level of income to reach what we would call a middle-class standard of living. Above that stretched the alluring prospect of an even better life, of becoming well-to-do or, at the top, living in luxury. In concrete terms a house, lot, and some skill sufficed for a single man or a craftsman, but a young married farm couple needed at least forty acres. Eighty acres was adequate for a yeoman and his family, while true comfort required at least a hundred.[1]

This approach divides the people of Connecticut into economic strata, identifies their standard of living. The strata were constant but the people involved differed. Most man progressed through a series of steps, starting with little property and so dependent for subsistence upon others, usually a parent, improving to an adequate independence at marriage and achieving comfort by middle-age. The twenty-one-year-old farmer's son and his unmarried sister might have to share a room with siblings in the parental house, and work for the family's benefit without pay. They owned almost no property, but most of them wore decent clothes and ate well. Marriage commonly (we will be more precise later) meant moving into a little house with a simple, even crude bed, scanty household furnishings, minimal work clothes, plain food, and perhaps a little barn on a small farm with a few live-stock. Over the years the couple would add to their estate roughly in proportion to the increased size of the family (up to a point), adding a larger building, one very good bed, superior cooking utensils and fireplace equipment, comforts such as chairs and nice clothes, a big barn, and more land than necessary, to provide for the children. The same sequence characterized men other than farmers as they progressed through the ranks of their occupations. Obviously some men remained at the bottom level and a few enjoyed luxury from the start, but most followed this typical pattern. Property was thus primarily

---

[1] Later chapters will amplify the relation between marital status and the life cycle. See also my article in *Journal of Economic History* 43 (1983), 159-65.

responsible for the quality of one's life, and a prime indicator of success.

The status order, relative prestige, interlocked with but was independent of wealth. Prestige derived from or was evidenced by one's position on various ladders, such as religion or relative piety, the military, and politics. At the bottom of society were those who refused to accept the dominant ethic and theology, who neglected to attend or were expelled from church, or whose behavior deviated from the norm—drunkards, criminals, the lazy, the dissolute, or nonconformists. Slaves belonged to the same species, by the whites' definition, or a bit higher if they conformed. Above them came those who attended church but never became members; members ranked higher, and at the top were the deacons and ministers. So also the lowly expendables served as common soldiers in the war, while the respectable family man belonged to the militia but rarely fought. These chose the company officers, whose titles earned them universal respect. A political hierarchy ranged from the disenfranchised poor or disreputable to the freeman who could vote and hold office on up through various levels of officialdom. Finally, remnants of the social structure of the Old World survived in the use of titles, especially during the seventeenth century: no title for the lowly, "mister" for the respectable, "gentleman" for him who need not soil his hands—a little more often assumed than conferred.

The status order interlocked with age as well as with property. Young adults to some extent reflected the status of their parents, but possessed no rank of their own. These young men performed the bulk of the labor along with drifters or immigrants without family connections, servants, and slaves, who collectively formed what people then sometimes called the "inferior sorts." With marriage usually came an independent property, sufficient income, the right to vote, the duty to hold office, membership in a church, and relief from combat duty. From that point, one might move up toward the top, become a captain or a deacon or a selectman, enjoying honor as well as material comfort. Only toward the end of a man's life might the association of economic rank with status reverse, for the latter would remain even if the former declined, eroded by the next generation. Property, then, was not equivalent to status, but the two moved together, and we study the measurable with the intangible.

With this brief introduction, we consider first property and then status in more detail. Property consisted and consists of two forms, real and personal. Real property, like our "real estate," primarily meant land and buildings, but also included certain manufacturing establish-

31

ments of a fixed nature such as mills and tanneries. The two general categories of land were improved and unimproved. The latter, which the colony did not tax, consisted primarily of wilderness tracts, unused and not even fenced. It had only a potential or speculative value, and might indeed be quite worthless until the Indians vacated it and until roads made it accessible, meaning, for much of the colony, after 1700. Even then it cost but a few shillings per acre (a shilling being worth, crudely, £10, 1980 money).[2] A lad who saved his wages over and above subsistence could buy thirty such acres in a year. "Improved" meant made use of, not necessarily bettered. It included woodland with fences, swamp or marshland, and pasture of varying quality, on up to the relatively valuable meadow, plowland, orchard, and the home lot on which the house stood. At first the towns granted small plots (two or three acres) as home lots to settled inhabitants, which generally meant that a man received a home lot upon marriage, and in the early years sometimes much larger amounts in "divisions."

We learn about real estate from several basic sources. Town or proprietary records inform us about the first grants. Deed books reveal later purchases and sales. These rarely include prices but usually do state the acreage. At the least we can tell who was buying real estate or who was selling out; thus we can study upward and downward mobility, arrivals and departures, and when a father turned over his farm to his sons. Assessment lists, if they itemized the taxable property (which was rare), omitted unimproved land and valued the rest according to the price set by the legislature, not the actual worth at a sale. Doing so tends to magnify the estate of the poor and underestimate that of the rich, except of course for their unimproved holdings. The most serious deficiency of the tax lists as a source for landholding, however, is the fact that they do not include property outside of the town. Thus Alexander Allin's 1702 assessment in Windsor showed almost no land, but his inventory six years later included 150 acres in that town worth £100 or so, another 155 acres valued at £40, 88 in Suffield at £110, plus £213 worth, acreage unknown, in Windsor and Enfield. He also owned about £300 invested in buildings, which would not show up on tax lists at all.[3]

---

[2] The multiplier from colonial pound to current dollar varies so much from one article to another that no single figure serves. The median farmhouse during the seventeenth century was valued in estate inventories at £20, rising gradually to £45 by 1770. The most common daily wage for a farm laborer was 2 shillings, a bushel of wheat 4½ shillings, adequate food for a man per day 5 pence. Ministers earned £100 per year plus perquisites amounting to 50 percent more.

[3] The most common type of tax list simply listed the taxpayers and the sum owed.

As Allyn's case indicates, the best source by far consists of estate inventories. They have defects, of which more later, but they do furnish prices of all sorts of lands and, if carefully handled, yield data on distributions. As just one more example, the inventory of an early Hartford settler, Thomas Bunce (ca. 1612-1683) lists his house and 1-acre home lot at £65; another house with its home lot and 11 acres valued at £190; three meadow lots totaling 21 acres for £193; 8½ acres of upland, clearly improved, at £4 per acre; two 40-acre tracts of upland, each at £1 per acre; 90 more worth only £5; and finally 36 acres worth £4. Thus he left, all told, almost 250 acres and two houses in his home town, plus another 80-acre farm in Wethersfield.[4]

Land values passed through several stages. During the seventeenth century the towns gave land to residents, who needed only to improve it for use. Undeveloped land might be valued for as little as £5 or £10 per 100 acres, much less than the dollar per acre charged by Congress after independence. Once improved, the price rose to an average of £2 per acre (cash), varying greatly from one tract to another but not a bad return for one's efforts. A newcomer could buy a forty-acre farm, adequate as a beginning, for £80, the equivalent of a year's labor by a skilled worker or twice that by a farmhand. This price remained almost the same for nearly a century, partly because vacant or undeveloped land still existed in many older towns but primarily because new towns were being established in Connecticut and adjacent colonies. This stability even characterized the valuable meadowland, although its limited quantity did create a price increase of some 50 percent between 1680 and 1750. About the latter year a general advance began that by the close of the colonial period had raised the average for all land to £3½ and a farm with its buildings came to £4 per acre. Within a few years the same sum that would buy 50 acres in Connecticut would purchase 640 in Ohio.[5]

Real estate also included mills, tanneries, ropewalks, distilleries, iron manufactories, and like establishments. The inventories list not only the building and land (or the dam, quarry, mine, etc.) but also equipment forming a fixed part of it. On the other hand, movable tools belonged with personal property, so that the mill itself appears in the

---

Only rarely do we find a "grand list" that itemized every article. The Windsor list of 1702 is in the Connecticut Historical Society. For his inventory, Hartford district probate records, 7:199-204 and 11:231-32. "Silver reckoned at 8/ the ounce."

[4] Ibid., 4:139. Money is country pay.

[5] See Table 2B appended to this chapter. The data derives from all of the probate records to 1730 and then for a few districts only until 1765, when the coverage becomes 60 percent of the colony.

records with the land but associated implements are separated. In either case these articles escaped taxation (except as related to "faculty," described later) and most of our knowledge about them comes from probate records.

Real estate in colonial Connecticut was important economically, socially, and politically. It formed about two-thirds of the total wealth, and acquisition of land was the principal way by which parents could provide for their children and their own old age. This was not a form of speculation but a safe investment. In addition, ownership of a farm carried with it the same connotations as in the Old World: it conferred prestige, proved one's ability, and testified to permanence; anyone who did not own land presumably lacked some essential attribute—health, intelligence, or diligence. The landless tended to migrate instead of settling, and became undesirable, consigned to the "inferior class." Land, as we said, enabled one to vote and hold office, and the colony often rewarded military or political service with grants, just as the towns provided the minister with a house and land. Ownership of a farm became nearly synonymous with virtue, and almost every freeman, regardless of occupation, acquired one if he could.

Three varieties of property composed personal wealth: consumption goods (a bed), capital (an ox), and financial assets. The first item interests us because it reveals the standard and style of living—both the level of comfort and the cultural choices of the people.[6] One can identify or even define class by the value of consumption articles, ranging from almost nothing on up to luxury. The poor man would not own a bed at all: slaves and servants might sleep on a sort of mattress made from straw or rushes and some old clothes. As a first step up, one acquired a "flock bed" of wool and a corded wooden bedstead, then a featherbed with more elaborate furnishings such as curtains for privacy, and finally these became works of art, or ornate and ostentatious depending on one's point of view. The student of family history would ask questions not answered in these essays, such as the number of beds per person and the incidence of sheets, while anyone interested in the lives of women and their daughters would inquire about cooking utensils and the like, all subjects I reluctantly leave to others. I will, however, consider the value of men's clothing, which reveals much about

[6] The chapters in this book touching on consumption depend heavily on the path-breaking work of other historians. See in particular Lois Green Carr and Lorena S. Walsh, "Inventories and the Analysis of Wealth and Consumption Patterns in St. Mary's County, Maryland, 1658-1777," *Historical Methods* 13 (1980), 81-104, and Gloria L. Main, *Tobacco Colony: Life in Early Maryland, 1650-1720* (Princeton, 1982).

standards of living and preferences; and books, for their cultural significance.

The data for articles of consumption come almost entirely from probate records, especially inventories of estates, though wills and accounts of administration help. They were not taxed, and literary sources tell us little about them except for cultural items such as books and paintings, and these not systematically; nor do physical remains provide as much information as we need, being biased toward the well-to-do. Probate records, however, often list everything with its price.

The principal component of "capital" was livestock, which made up one-fifth of the total personal wealth in this rural economy. Livestock in turn consisted of pigs and cattle, which furnished both food and profit, and oxen; horses primarily for transportation; sheep more for wool than meat; poultry, geese, rarely turkeys, goats locally, and bees, which we have to place somewhere. Grains, along with such other crops as flax, hay, fruit, and vegetables produced income for the family either directly by sale or exchange or indirectly by supplying what otherwise must be bought. In the same way the farm provided leather, wool, and feathers. Tools fall into two categories: one for household use and so part of consumption goods rather than capital, and those generating profit such as husbandry implements, smithy tools, and weavers' looms.

Ships included everything from oceangoing vessels down to canoes. In the late colonial period newspapers listed arrivals and departures of the larger type, which appear also in British customs records and ship registers. Inventories of estates tell us about prices, and accounts of administration sometimes report the cost of construction by way of a claim against the estate. The value of rigging and of other equipment usually formed part of the total price.

Capital also included articles that people offered for sale. Even ordinary farmers might produce some surplus in addition to extra provisions, for example if they turned out shingles or yarn, but most such marketable commodities came out of the shops of artisans, such as barrels from the cooper, furniture from the joiner, and leather from the tanner, or the goods for sale in the stores of shopkeepers and merchants. The last owned by far the largest proportion of this form of property. Finally, servants and slaves may belong here too. In Connecticut they accounted for only 1 percent of all personal wealth during the seventeenth century and even at their most numerous they formed only 5 or 6 percent. Except for the slaves, our best source for information about capital goods still comes from the probate court records. Tax lists include only the older cattle and horses and other types of capital not at all, though the owner of a male slave of sixteen and over had to pay a poll tax. Literary sources do cast some light on the servants and slaves, though not very precisely, consistently, or reliably.

"Financial assets" consisted of cash, debts receivable, and—arguably—articles of silver and gold or jewelry. The last appear in estate inventories and perhaps belong under "consumption." They took the form most often of silver spoons, more rarely of some silver dish or goblet, possibly a luxury article such as a silver watch, ornaments like the shoe buckles worn by men in the eighteenth century, or the rings, necklaces, and other jewelry treasured by women. The silver could readily be transformed into cash and probably during much of the colonial period such articles served as a form of savings rather than for everyday use. Ownership of money—coins or after 1700 paper currency—was not taxable, so we learn about it from the estate inventories. Until the government began issuing promissory notes during the wars with France, money and silver articles combined equaled only about 3 percent of all personal wealth, after which that figure doubled. We know the quantity of paper money circulated by the government but have no source other than inventories for the amount or distribution of gold and silver coin.

Finally, "debts receivable" refers to the money owing to someone at a given time, usually in our case at the time of his death. These sums, like their opposite "debts payable," were widespread and considerable, averaging one-eighth of all personal wealth during most of the colonial period and over one-fifth toward the end. They originated in many ways, most of them well-known. The estate of a large merchant listed the credits advanced to local customers or the sums owed to him as profits of foreign trade. Occasionally such an individual, with capital at his disposal, acted as banker to the community, but this was rare. Rather, most people purchased goods and services on credit from storekeepers, craftsmen, and professionals such as doctors, whose account books recorded these transactions. Estate inventories contain a great deal of information about this type of capital. The evaluators listed each such debt owing to the estate: thus the assets of a soldier or sailor might consist largely of wages due to him. The administrator was responsible for the collection of these obligations. Sometimes at the end he reported to the judge those debts still outstanding as "sperate"—hopeful—and "desperate"—hopeless.

The administrator also paid out the debts owed by the estate. These originated in the same way as those mentioned above, and another worth adding: family obligations. A man sometimes willed his farm to

36

a son, who paid his siblings their share over time out of the farm's profits. The death of the son in turn, or that of a daughter's husband, revealed the existence of this debt, still owed by the son, now to be settled. In general, debts cast much light on the economic activities of the period, the transmission of property from one generation to another, and the distribution of wealth among the people.

Before presenting the information about the distribution of all this property, which begins in the next chapter, we must evaluate the sources for our generalizations, primarily tax lists and probate records. So-called literary evidence contains many deficiencies. Most seriously, it tells us nothing at all about many subjects crucial to our investigation, such as the proportion of poor and rich, the median wealth, the general standard of living, what sorts of people owned slaves, servants, or books, or became deacons. Also, almost all literary sources come from the educated upper class, colonial or foreign, reflecting the biases of that class, and pertain principally to people of the same type in the larger towns, whereas we are interested in all sorts of people everywhere. Another bias arises from the special situation of the writers, as in the case of the governors in their reports, who habitually lied to royal officials, or the letters of businessmen, who pretended to face bankruptcy. Finally, it is sparse: for example, Connecticut lacked newspapers for the first century and few diaries or travel accounts remain or ever existed except during the final decades of the colonial period. We can use this material with benefit but cannot write accurately or completely from it.

The great advantage of the tax lists is their naming of the taxpayers. As noted in Chapter One, not everyone paid a tax, some being relieved by the legislature, others by the town. Also, the head tax of a dependent was paid by whoever was responsible, so dependents did not appear on the list. That applied to every male aged sixteen or over who had not become independent (a "householder"), including slaves, servants, and most unmarried men. A few men remained in that category all their lives. We learn about the existence of such individuals from "grand tax" lists that itemized every article being assessed. These furnish the number of polls subject to the tax; so if, for example, a man paid for three polls we can search for two others, or if a woman paid one we must look for a male. The list that simply names the taxpayer and the total amount paid is much less useful. If we know his age we can guess whether unmarried sons or other men of age might be living with him and undertake research to identify them.

All these lists, however detailed, omit an uncertain number of migrants. Furthermore, many species of property do not appear because they were not taxed. Young livestock and all sheep are missing, as are both consumption articles and financial assets. Thus of personal wealth only productive goods were taxed, and not all even of these: tools, stock, and (until late) ships were omitted. The poll tax partly compensated for this, for it essentially defined every man's labor as a productive asset worth £18 annually net of expenses—four-and-a-half times as valuable as an ox. However, since every man was assessed for the same £18, it does not distinguish between rich and poor except insofar as the former might own servants or slaves.

Also, men deriving their income from a nonfarm occupation paid a "faculty tax" on their labor that yielded an otherwise invisible return. A lawyer or doctor might own little taxable property yet enjoy a high standard of living, so the faculty tax tapped the profits earned from his practice. The faculty might be rated at only a pound or two in the case of a poor shoemaker and ranged up to £50. That sum fell far short of the actual incomes of the most prosperous professionals and merchants, who even in Connecticut might earn hundreds of pounds annually. Moreover, about half of the nonfarmers and such farmers as supplemented their income through another occupation were not so assessed.

Real estate, as we previously noted, appears on the tax lists up to a point. Undeveloped land remained exempt, the definition broadening to include woodlands. Worse, the legislature might even exclude some improved land, as it did in 1677 when it decreed that whoever cleared and enclosed land need not declare it for four years.[7] Finally, buildings were not included, although at the end of the colonial period the colony did tax chimneys.

Even apart from their numerous omissions, tax lists are defective as a source for our purposes. To begin with, few have survived and most of those that exist simply give the names of the taxpayers and the amount of the tax paid, whereas we need to know all the articles on which the tax was based. Instead of the name Simon Couch and his tax of 17/ (the slash mark stands for a shilling, a lazy person's *s*), we need Simon Couch, four persons £72, a three-acre house and lot £3, eight acres of upland £4, two oxen £8, two cows £6, one two-year-old £2, a swine £1, two horses £6, total £102, on which he paid the shillings tax.[8] From this, we can identify him as a quite ordinary farmer with three dependents, who we discover were sons. Such detail is,

[7] J. H. Trumbull and Charles Hoadly, eds., *The Public Records of the Colony of Connecticut . . . ,* 15 vols. (Hartford, 1850-1890), 2:327-28.

[8] Glastonbury Grand List, 1730, Connecticut State Library. The rate equals $\frac{1}{120}$.

unfortunately, rare. Thus the tax lists are too few and when they survive are too skimpy. We cannot rely on them without extensive research elsewhere. We have to fill in the names of missing men somehow; we learn nothing about houses and their contents, or money, debts, trading stock, or much of the land, especially that held outside the town's boundaries. The laws defined the value of the taxable articles arbitrarily and stuck to the decision. Horses, for instance, rose in value over time and differed greatly from one person's animal to another, but the tax lists rated all equally. Some house lots and meadowland far exceeded in value that of other tracts even in the same town, to say nothing of the difference between a farm in the hills and that in a rich valley, yet all were taxed the same until well along in our period. If the sales price of property rose or fell we could not know it from these records. Tax lists yield at best rough approximations, not accurate data.

Finally, these lists are regressive, understating the estates of the rich relative to those of the poor. In general, the true value of an individual's property, as evaluated in probate court, was eight times the assessment (£75 versus £587) including the poll tax or, adjusting for the lapse in time between the date of the tax and that of death, in this case two and a half years (at £20 per year), seven times. But the multiplier for the largest estates is about twenty-five.[9] This means that the true wealth of the colony was, as usual, vastly in excess of that taxed, and distributed much more unequally. As to the underassessment of the largest properties, we may quote the Duke de la Rochefoucauld-Liancourt, who informs us, at a later date to be sure, that the listers of taxes could not prevent cheating: "Several of the wealthiest persons in the state, have owned to me, that the taxation which they actually pay, is not above a sixth part of what they ought to pay. One mode of evasion, commonly practised in Connecticut, is, by placing in the lowest class, land that, on account of its situation, its quality, its produce, ought rather to be ranked in the highest."[10]

The complete assessment or "grand" lists, however, have great value for certain purposes. In our first chapter we showed their demographic importance. They indicate the minimum number of the propertyless or very poor in a town at a given moment, although we must distinguish among various types of the poor. They show how many men,

[9] N = 169. The mean of assessments was £79, of inventories £449. In addition twenty-eight men whose estates were inventoried paid no tax. Their mean worth was £143. Source: Twenty-one tax lists from nineteen towns.

[10] *Travels through the United States of North America* . . . 2 vols. (London, 1799), 1:553-54.

at that point, lacked land or possessed oxen; the faculty tax reveals part of the nonfarm population. By making proper adjustments we can study the relationship between wealth and age. A series of lists—very rare indeed—enables us to observe geographic mobility and changes in wealth. They also serve as an essential check on the biases in our most important source of all: probate records.

These records consist of some or all among various documents concerning the disposition of a "decedent's" estate. They included a will if the person died testate, the inventory of the property, the court's naming of an administrator if that seemed necessary, his or her subsequent report, and the ultimate distribution of the estate. First in point of time came the will, usually written or dictated by someone who expected to die soon.[11] The more property one owned the more likely one was to make a will, so that if only wills survived, and never inventories, we would have to counteract a strong upward wealth bias.[12] However, wills from all wealth groups do exist in sufficient number for us to use them. Thus young Henry Hollstead in June 1692 left his tiny property of £20 country pay to his "kind and loving Master," except for his Bible, willed to his master's son John, an iron pot given to John's sister Mary, and an iron kettle to another sister, Sarah.[13]

As this shows, wills can tell us a great deal about the "testators," their families, and often their friends. Hollstead, for example, introduced us to the family of John Meekins, Sr. Meekins's own will, ten years later, identifies his wife, Sarah, and two other sons, Joseph and Samuel. He refers to property given by his father-in-law John Bidwell. Daughter Mary had married a Belden, Sarah a Spencer, and the family also included two unmarried daughters. John, he informs us, had al-

---

[11] For much more detail on what follows, see Gloria L. Main, "Probate Records as a Source for Early American History," *William and Mary Quarterly* 32 (1975), 89-99.

[12] Thus in the Hartford probate district 1700-1709, the distribution of inventories by percentages was:

Net worth	Wills (N=55)	No will (N=90)
Under £100	14	39
100-199	15	22
200-499	44	32
500-999	24	4
1,000+	4	2
	101	99

Three men with small estates left noncuptative wills. Two men in the £1,000 class left wills but no inventories and two, probably with average or little property, left neither, but the death was otherwise noted by the court.

[13] Hartford district probate records, 5:144.

ready built a house. Thus at least three children had married, so we may safely infer his age as at least fifty, and probably above sixty, in 1702. We also learn, from specific bequests, of his house, barn, orchard, garden, and land, quantity uncertain but including both meadow and unimproved. He had already given property to the married daughters and now adds £20 each. The two unmarried daughters each received £40. If this represented their share of the estate, then the six children inherited £240 plus another £40 for the eldest's double share, and the widow's third would be £140 for a total of £420, at the least, for he ought to have allowed for the costs of probate, the funeral, and possible debts. Actually his inventory three and a half years later came to £480, so the will accurately predicted his wealth.[14]

We might therefore reconstruct a pretty good picture of colonial society from wills alone, since probably a third of the men left them, and we could allow for the bias. But probate records include much more. When someone died, either the wishes of the decedent were carried out by executors of his choice (Meekins chose his wife and eldest son) or the court appointed administrators, sometimes the wife and a son, or a reliable citizen, who would account to the court for the disposition of the property and his care of the family. The first step was to inventory and evaluate the estate, item by item. Two knowledgeable neighbors would move from room to room, usually listing first the clothing of the deceased, his gun if any, and money, then everything else in the house, item by item. This process may enable us to reconstruct the houses, for the appraisers sometimes announced the names of each room in turn and its contents, so that the student can infer what each room looked like and the spatial distribution of articles such as beds. We can also study, as we have seen, what kinds of property the person owned, his books or silver, the number of beds, sheets, and blankets per person, perhaps the presence of chamber pots, mirrors, window curtains, or clocks. Out of doors the appraisers noted the oxen and other livestock, the barn and small outbuildings, the crop, and the land. They were supposed to value each article, so we can derive a price series and determine relationships among types of property. If we are lucky, we may read, "two acres of wheat £4" and, "two bushels of wheat 8/," from which we know that wheat was worth 4 shillings per bushel and since the two acres produced 80 shillings' worth they grew twenty bushels, or ten bushels to the acre, a valuable bit of information for the student of agriculture or farm income.

14 Ibid., 93-94.

Can we rely on these inventories? Yes and no. First, the prices are based upon local values and money. If the appraisers rate a yoke of oxen at £10 in 1690—a little under the average—we may accept this as fact, since we find that in any given year in the seventeenth century the price of oxen will vary from £7 or so (generally with an adjective like "poor" or "small") on up to £15: the appraisers were carefully distinguishing by quality. Also, when the administrators sold part of an estate at auction, they realized about as advertised; besides, other sources support the inventories.[15]

However, we must remember that these prices record *local* opinion based on the experience of the particular town, and were expressed in the money of the time and place. The usual currency until after 1700 was "country pay," the definition of which everybody knew, but which we are obliged to discover and relate to other monetary systems. Prices in country pay during the seventeenth century were 50 percent higher than those in silver money. The Spanish silver dollar, which became the basis for our own dollar, was worth 4½ shillings in English money (sterling) and 6 shillings in Connecticut. This money was called "cash," "merchantable price," or "money," and the appraisers sometimes used the 6-shilling standard when the value of the inventory, or some part of it, needed to be expressed in terms of external money, as in the case of foreign debts. Thus in 1673 an estate of £182.19.2, appraised "according to common valuation between man and man in ordinary dealing," meaning country pay, was reduced to £160.4.2 because both some pork and most of the debts were payable at "merchantable prices."[16]

During the eighteenth century, the colony gradually increased the quantity of money in circulation because of wartime spending, and

[15] E.g., the homestead farm of Jonathan Arnold of Hartford (d. 1719), valued at £250, sold the next year for £278, an orchard appraised for £120 brought exactly that, and his meadow, priced at £50, went for £45. During the depression following the Revolutionary War land and sheriff sales brought less than the inventory price, as the people were complaining. Some appraisers also became overly optimistic about the price rises during the 1760s and 1770s. The New Haven records trace the sale of Josiah Robinson's large farm of 173 acres (inventory, or 168 as sold) which fell short by 30 percent of the evaluation, though his £219 in personal wealth sold for exactly that. Abraham Terrill's estate sold for 13 percent under the inventory and a Guilford property in 1769 was short by 28 percent. However, even at that uncertain time some appraisers hit the value on the button: e.g., Thomas Vose of Derby, and William Booth of Colchester (New Haven district probate records, 11:97; Cochester district probate records, 4:132-33). Earlier sales and appraised values coincided closely and we have as many instances of property bringing more than expected, as less.

[16] New Haven district probate records, B:46.

this raised prices. Also, the legislature interfered with the monetary system by fixing certain prices for tax purposes and attempting to regulate the value of the new money. Between about 1700 and 1712, some inventories were expressed in the old country pay and some in "money." After several years of confusion the appraisers essentially melded the two, and we find estates presumably in the latter actually equivalent to the former, after which they reflected the general inflation, except that estate values lagged behind values in silver, either a memory of country pay surviving, or the appraisers being unable to absorb the changes.

By the early 1750s, prices had risen ten or twelve times that of the 1700 "pay" base, seven or eight times the earlier "cash." Then, obeying a royal proclamation, the colony abruptly returned to values as of 6 shillings to the Spanish dollar. For example, one finds oxen appraised in 1700 at £11 pay or £6.14 cash, rising to £84 in 1754 and then suddenly plummeting to £7.10 in obedience to the law. Theoretically it ought to have stayed there, but it shot up to the old "country pay" level during the war years, around which it fluctuated thereafter. Clearly the appraisers genuinely tried to identify the true market value of each article, and clearly we must interpret these estimates, working out a table by which we can translate the prices of inventories into some common denominator. In our case, we will use country pay as our standard, following actual practice, until 1700, after which we will reduce everything to "cash," and for comparing the two periods multiply country pay before 1700 by 0.7, the difference between it and "cash."[17] We will discuss some details presently.

The prices, then, are honest, though complex. What about the articles being evaluated? Omissions and biases do appear, but not such as to invalidate the reliability of the inventories. The defects occurred for several reasons. First, where the will disposed of certain items, the heirs sometimes carried them off promptly and the appraisers simply shrugged. If creditors existed, however, they would demand payment by the estate before any distribution to the heirs. In that case the administrators would insist upon a complete accounting and the addition of any assets that appeared after the original inventory, such as a crop just harvested. Moreover, other members of the family would protect their own interests. Therefore this defect seldom occurred, involved small amounts, and ran consistently in the same direction.

[17] Thus pre-1700 oxen, averaging £10 for a yoke, becomes £7. By 1754 the multiplier was 0.085, so the inflated value of £84 becomes £7.3. From that point on, the currency stabilized and a figure of £7.10, a year or two later, indicates a genuine increase in prices unrelated to monetary inflation.

Second, many articles did not form part of a man's estate but by long custom belonged to other members of the family or were considered of no value. The clothing, toys, and other private possessions of children appear very rarely, evidently only when a child had recently died and no one could make use of them. So also the wife's clothing, jewelry, or other personal items were inventoried only if the man had been widowed. One learns about them from the estates of widows. The inventories of heads of families thus consistently fall short of the actual amount owned by, or available to the household. In addition, one does not find any dogs, cats, or (with rare exceptions) poultry, and the appraisers often omitted perishables such as most food.

Third, the wife's property is sometimes missing. Marriage contracts might specify that her dowry, other inheritances, or gifts remained her own or at any rate reverted to her upon the husband's death, so that an apparently landless man may actually have enjoyed the use of land while he lived. The wife occasionally claimed whatever she had brought at marriage, most often household goods. These would include her beds and bedding, kitchen utensils, and fireplace equipment, so that the absence from inventories of such consumption articles does not prove that the estate never contained them. In sum, inventories *understate* the person's property, especially of consumption articles.

Fourth, we must remember that an older man might have given a large part of his property to his married children, which would therefore be omitted from the inventory, usually without notice. Many men who seem poor actually had once owned considerable estates: those with grandchildren, even excluding the group who had given away much of their wealth and virtually retired, left 16 percent less property than fathers with grown children but not grandchildren. This factor also tends to minimize the person's true worth. A similar distortion occurs when a fire had destroyed some of the decedent's property and occasionally himself.

Fifth, the inventory figures contain various human errors. The appraisers inadvertently omitted assets, counted them twice, misjudged the value, or wrote the price incorrectly or sloppily so that 20 pounds becomes 20 shillings. The historian usually works with clerks' copies, which are inaccurate, add columns wrongly, or don't add at all. Pages are missing, torn, or illegible. We ourselves copy or add incorrectly. The numbers in one's notes exceed or fail to reach the supposed total. Fortunately, the errors are not cumulative but random. They do not introduce any consistent tendency except for a downward bias, as described above, applicable to a small proportion of the whole and probably constant over time.

Sixth, we must deal with a consistent upward bias arising from the greater age of the decedents as compared with the living, as our first chapter described. The median age at death exceeded by fifteen years the median of the living adult population, during which additional time the men would be adding property at an average rate of £10 per year, mostly in houses and land. We must therefore reduce the means and medians and revise the distributions to counteract this. If, for example, 9 percent of the inventories come from men aged twenty-one to twenty-nine who, however, number 36 percent of the adult population, we must multiply the average wealth of that age group by four as a first step toward recalculating the actual total and other data. The process requires a knowledge of the age of every decedent, or a reasonable approximation. This bias makes the others seem minor, but luckily we can correct for it.

Seventh, since not all estates entered the probate court and some probated estates were not inventoried, we must ask whether the missing ones deviated from those included, in particular as to age and wealth, that is, do the inventories represent equally the men who died regardless of age and property?[18]

TABLE 2.1

Converting Probate Population to Living Population

	Inventories			Living population		
Age group	% of men	Mean £	Total £	% of men	Mean £	Total £
21–29	9	40	360	36	40	1,440
30–39	15	200	3,000	28	200	5,600
40–49	25	400	10,000	18	400	7,200
50–59	20	500	10,000	12	500	6,000
60 +	31	400	12,400	6	400	2,400
Total			35,760			22,640
Mean			358			226

[18] The literature on this point is considerable. One group of historians has argued that the problems are so serious as almost to prohibit use. See, for example, Harold B. Gill, Jr. and George M. Curtis III, "Virginia's Colonial Probate Policies and the Preconditions for Economic History," *Virginia Magazine of History and Biography* 87 (1979), 68-73. Their warnings are well taken. The only probate court in all of South Carolina was located in Charleston, effectively discouraging wills or inventories at any distance from the center. On the other hand, Alice Hanson Jones demonstrated that one could still rely on the inventories by hard work and careful procedure in her *American Colonial Wealth: Documents and Methods*, 3 vols. (New York, 1977) and Gloria L. Main explained how to solve the problems in *Historical Methods Newsletter* 8 (1974), 10-28. Her work

We have already examined part of this threefold question. We discovered that until after 1700 the proportion of estates escaping the probate court was not great enough to cause any problem, nor did we detect any bias except perhaps in the underrepresentation of migrants. We guessed that about 5 percent of the men show up only rarely on either tax lists or probate records. Most of these were surely young and the correction just described accounts for them, except that their inclusion might lower the mean wealth of the men aged twenty-one to twenty-nine. Since that forms only a small part of the total wealth, the mean will remain almost the same, a few pounds less, and the median unaffected. During the eighteenth century probate coverage gradually diminished, but no additional age bias existed until the final decade before independence, when the proportion of decedents aged twenty-one to thirty-nine among probated estates falls below the actual deaths by 3 percent and that of men over fifty exceeds the true number. The correction for this bias lowers the wealth of the people and changes the distribution in that there were more small properties and fewer large ones than the inventories show.

As to a bias toward including more poor or more rich decedents in the probate population than among actual deaths, we will start with two general observations. One might expect that the probate court would entrap the helpless poor and excuse the rich. But the court's purpose was not to punish or tax, only to settle the estate fairly, making sure that creditors, children, and widows were all cared for. People might indeed prefer privacy and forestall an inventory by making a will (which seems to have run in the family, by the way), but such a desire would correlate only weakly with property because inventories exist for almost all estates, with or without wills.

TABLE 2.2
Distribution of Debts, New Haven
Probated Estates

Total value of estate	% with debts	% with liabilities
Under £100	46.6	49.1
£100–399	47.2	57.5
£400–999	48.0	41.2
£1,000+	69.2	53.8

and that of many others have successfully exploited the probate records in Maryland, where coverage is exceptionally complete, like that of Connecticut during its first century.

The most important function of the probate process relevant to the question of wealth bias is that it assured the collection of debts owed to and the payment of obligations by the estate. Now, men had or owed debts regardless of class. In the seventeenth-century New Haven district, for example, we find the same proportion of creditors in every wealth class of decedents—just under half—except in the largest estates above £1,000. Similarly, those owing money appear equally distributed. Therefore, as far as debts are concerned the estates of the well-to-do would be a little *more* likely to enter probate rather than the reverse, but the bias will be quite small and would simply cancel the slight tendency for well-to-do men to leave wills but not inventories.

The reason for this presence of debts owed or owing in estates of all sizes arises from their various origins, as we have already noticed. The poor laborer might have borrowed, but since he worked for wages he often had money coming to him. Soldiers and sailors frequently had not yet collected their back pay. Craftsmen, professionals, and men in trade kept accounts listing what others owed to them, but they often were debtors, too. Men of large property loaned and borrowed just as did others, only on a larger scale, and faced insolvency as often as the poor. Thus the merchant and governor Stephen Goodyear (d. 1658) left property worth £804 with debts of £2,404; the trader Nicholas Auger's estate of £1,639 in 1678 included credits of £1,093 but he also owed £357; while Jonathan Frisby (d. 1695) had £250 in assets and £380 in liabilities.[19]

In sum, we cannot predict any inherent class bias in the probate records and must proceed pragmatically. First we test the hypothesis that the men who died poor were less likely to leave inventories than the well-off. The principal source of information concerning the properties of men who died without inventories comes from the tax lists, inaccurate though they are. When these are missing we can derive inferences from deeds, positions held, family property, or hints in wills. We need to know which men on a given list died within a few years, in order to minimize radical changes in wealth between the date of the list and the time of death and yet yield enough people to form a useful sample. As we discussed earlier, we can obtain the death dates of most men during the seventeenth century, but our knowledge diminishes for the later period, especially with respect to the young and poor, thus jeopardizing any conclusion. However, we must use what we can,

---

[19] New Haven district probate records, 1:76, 285, 305; for Auger, 1:177; for Frisby, 2:166. All values country pay. New Haven's records are by far the best for a study of debts.

TABLE 2.3
Probate Coverage, Mean on Tax Lists

	Lowest quintile			Second quintile			Middle quintile			Fourth quintile			Highest quintile			Total		
	yes	no	% yes	yes	no	% yes	yes	no	% yes	yes	no	% yes	yes	no	% yes	yes	no	% yes
Seventeenth century																		
	31	6	83.8	19	6	76.0	15	3	83.3	22	8	73.3	27	7	79.4	114	30	79.2
Early eighteenth century																		
	47	19	71.2	25	22	53.2	31	11	74.8	38	20	65.5	56	19	74.4	197	91	68.4
Later eighteenth century																		
	42	21	66.7	40	28	58.8	52	32	61.9	49	24	67.1	80	29	73.4	263	134	66.2
Revised later eighteenth century																		
	42	34	55.3	40	34	54.1	52	34	60.5	49	24	67.1	80	29	73.4	263	155	52.9

NOTE: See Appendix 2C.

and derive Table 2.3. The "Later Eighteenth Century" line presents data without including men whose date of death remains uncertain, and who may have died within the ten-year period. Appendix 2C explains why we must add some of them and why most of them were poor. Doing so gives us a revised set of figures for the "Later Eighteenth Century." We find a considerable bias in favor of large properties. Some 30 percent of the inventories drew from the top quintile, as many as from the bottom two combined, whereas the true proportion was 26 percent. In conclusion, we can trust the probate records until the final decade, when we must subtract 15 percent from the top quintile (3 percent of the whole number), adding these to the bottom quintiles. Doing so has the additional happy advantage of correcting for age bias as well.

We return now to a discussion of the records' content. Many estates required considerable labor before a final settlement, and we gain a great deal of valuable information from the accounts of administration. In these the executors reported to the court the various charges brought against the estate and their payment as well as the debts they collected, additions to or corrections of the inventories, and agreements with the heirs. Charges included the funeral expenses, sometimes itemized, the court costs, and the services of appraisers and administrators. Also interesting are the bills submitted by the doctor or for nursing, men helping with the crop or rounding up the livestock, and the widow for household expenses, sometimes over a period of several years.[20]

For example, the widow of Deacon Samuel Smith of Hartford (1659-1707) reported that during the three years after his death she had spent £61.4.1 "for the support and service of the family, and stock of creatures," itemizing the cost: "200 bush: Indian corn 2s p^r," "six swine 4^1/7^s" "blew wool 3^s/9^d" (they had seven children). Again, the estate of Captain Amos Chappell of Sharon (d. 1773) paid out £27.6 for boarding, clothing, and schooling little Julius from two and a half years until six years old, at 3 shillings per week, and £6.15 for sister Matilda from four and a half years until six, which means that she cost only about ⅛ or ⅑ weekly.[21] An account of 1682 tells us that it cost £1.4 to weed, hill, gather, and husk six acres of corn, and another 10

---

[20] The clerks often (the word may be usually) did not copy the accounts into their big volumes but only entered the amount owed. If the original dockets survive they should contain the itemized bills, often in the hand of the claimant. One must ask the archivist.

[21] For Smith, Hartford district probate records, 8:16. For Chappell, Sharon district probate records, D:345, F:32.

shillings to thresh it and take it away. Finally, a bill itemized the cost of building a house in 1710—£35.17.6.

As a last step in the probate process, the estate as inventoried might be divided under judicial supervision, item by item, to assure equitable treatment. The widow received one-third during her lifetime, and each child an equal share of what remained except for the eldest son's double portion. The administrators tried to preserve enough of the estate intact to provide an economically viable unit—a working farm, so that all of the real property, together with essential tools and livestock, might go to one son, with the other personalty divided and, if insufficient, supplemented by future payments out of the farm's profits. A daughter might thus receive some consumption goods, which would be useful when she married, plus an I.O.U. payable later by her brother, forming a valuable source of credit for her husband. The court especially guarded the widow's welfare, setting aside necessities for her use if the husband's will did not so provide. Eventually the legislature ordered that in cases of insolvency her minimal needs took precedence over the claims of creditors.[22] In closing we may add that when the value of the estate fell short of its debts, the administrator sold parts of it (with the assent of the court) and prorated the assets among the creditors, thus providing us with information about debts and prices.

We can use probate records, then, in a great variety of ways from their beginning in the 1640s until as late as we wish. Even if we confine our attention to the seventeenth century, however, we must cope with variations in the price level, which may create inaccuracies, while during the eighteenth the changes can entirely invalidate our conclusions about trends. We must devise a table with which to adjust the prices so as to permit reasonably accurate comparisons over time. Insofar as changes simply reflected the value of money, we could take as par the most reliable such series, that for the price of silver assembled by John McCusker.[23] His figures reflect the values established by the transatlantic trade as recorded particularly at Boston. We might prefer to modify this table by developing one from Connecticut sources, where we find the price of silver lagging behind that in Boston. Another approach requires us to obtain the value of specific articles, common enough to possess some significance and qualitatively stable, such as a bushel of wheat, since wheat itself did not change during our period. Several of these might be combined in some proportion so as

[22] *Pub. Rec. Conn.*, 4:438 (1714).

[23] John J. McCusker, *Money and Exchange in Europe and America, 1600-1775: A Handbook* (Chapel Hill, 1978).

to produce a single table. The trouble with this method lies in the changing quality of some components, as in the case of horses, in the uncertainty about both quantity and quality, and in long-term price trends unrelated to inflation, as was true of land. Appendix 2A presents the median values as reflected in estate inventories of several commodities about which we have ample information. I have simplified by combining years. The total observations for oxen, to 1765, was 2,737, so the evidence is not scattered, but the variation in quality and even from one part of the colony to another prevents any exactitude, and besides the government kept intervening, especially by setting prices for the guidance of tax assessors.

The reader will perceive that no single deflator will serve for all of these items, and I have chosen to adopt, as par, the value established by the government for the last twenty years of the colonial era. When this "cash" came into effect gradually after 1700 it ought to have forced a reduction by one-third in the inventory prices, which had remained stable for a quarter-century, the Spanish dollar now being evaluated at 6 instead of 9 shillings. In practice some appraisers at first evaluated the estate according to the country pay that they knew and then did indeed reduce by exactly a third. Others could not quite bring themselves to so drastic a decline in the familiar prices and the difference between the inventories in the two currencies, even in the same year, was not quite the one-third that a law required. I have therefore selected 0.7 instead of 0.667 as the multiplier by which to adjust pre-1700 inventories. Since 0.667 is 95 percent of 0.7, no great error is involved anyway.[24]

The table in Appendix 2A reveals a different price history for the various items during the half century after 1700. That for oxen and cows had risen slightly but horses doubled in value, a real change in the quality of the animals. Sheep had actually declined, yet clothing was valued at a substantially higher price, whether because men dressed better or the prices had risen I do not know.

---

[24] If we multiply the late seventeenth-century value of oxen, sheep, clothing, wheat, and silver by 0.7 and match these against the cash ("proclamation") prices of 1754-1755, we see that 0.7 usually lowers the early values below the later. Multiplying by 0.667 would make matters worse.

	Oxen	Sheep	Clothing	Wheat	Silver
Pre-1700	£7.14	6/4	£4.4	3/2	6/4
1754-1755	£8.10	4/0	£6.0	3/9	6/8

Late seventeenth-century prices were a little depressed, but on the whole I think a general price rise had occurred and am sticking to 0.7.

In the case of land, the average price taking one acre with another over the whole colony but excluding the remote unimproved tracts was £2.5 before 1700, equal to £1.10 cash. During 1700-1714 it rose slightly to £1.16 cash and again to £2.5 by 1729. There it remained until the early 1750s when it crept up to £2.10, by which time the price had nearly doubled since the late seventeenth century. It then jumped sharply to £3.10 during the 1760s where it stayed (see Appendix 2B). We therefore must employ a different set of deflators for real estate.

All these adjustments are intended not as an intellectual exercise but to enable us to study the distribution of property over time, and to investigate the economic basis for Connecticut's society. Wealth alone, however, did not determine the colony's social order. Property conferred status but status did not depend exclusively upon property. Fairfield in 1671 listed the town's inhabitants with their ratable estates and the acres granted to them proportionate to those estates. The lists included a major, an ensign, a sergeant, one "goodman," and five "misters." The major was the town's richest man but the next two wealthiest (Thomas Staples and John Wheeler) bore no title; and while three of the "misters" owned property above the median, two fell below, one indeed in the bottom decile. The sergeant rated among the top economically but the ensign, who outranked him, belonged near the middle. Mr. Harvey probably derived his title of respect by being a doctor while Mr. Pell, also a doctor and a trader, was the brother of an English minister whose son founded Pelham Manor in New York.

Similarly, Wethersfield's rate list of 1673 distinguished its militia officers by their titles, the minister by a "mister," and also recognized various other "misters" one of whom, Eleazar Kimberly, belonged there by virtue of his education, serving as a schoolmaster. Probate as well as other records also honored men whose estates fell below the median and whose status therefore derived from achievement along non-economic lines, some now mysterious. Mr. John Maltby of New Haven (ca. 1641-1676) left an inventory of only £58, evidently deriving his repute from his well-to-do alderman father. Mr. Thomas Powell of the same town owned only £140 worth of property in 1681, and being the father of five daughters would seem to confer no distinction. Milford's young Richard Hollingsworth (1661-1683) must have inherited his "mister." That relative wealth did not necessarily confer a title is attested throughout these sources. Thus in Lyme the ten largest taxpayers of 1688 included the captain, the lieutenant, the most respected official with his "mister," and his son, but six lacked all such status symbols, including the town's second wealthiest man (Thomas Lee, presently to become an ensign and the founder of a prominent family).[25]

The most obvious and familiar status orders in colonial Connecticut were religious, military, and political. Which took precedence surely varied with the situation and probably over time. Nonchurchgoers certainly did not win much respect even in the eighteenth century, when the laws removed some restrictions on nonconformists. The spread of population into areas distant from the original town center discouraged the removers from regular church attendance—a dislike of which may have contributed to the removal—just as it limited their appearance at town meetings. That ought not to have been held against them, but in practice they probably suffered some disfavor. They could, to be sure, ride their horses and spend the day in church or in the adjacent little houses where one bought rights. The expense of this must have biased churchgoing in favor of the larger propertyowners, thus associating economic with religious status. Construction of churches in such more distant areas would solve the problem temporarily but divisions always lagged behind the need. The loss of interest on the part of many people aroused the ministers to complain, as did the decline in their salaries during the period of inflation. One cannot take their jeremiads at face value, but church membership and contributions did fall off. When in 1679 the people of Middletown were asked to contribute to a meetinghouse bell, the list of donors was very impressive, including 80 percent of the men, whereas the towns of the eighteenth century struggled to collect their rates. The reputable continued to attend, and the enthusiasm of the Great Awakening attracted the most support from the less respected. Thus we see a hierarchy from the unchurched through regular attenders to full church members. The last, and only they, chose the elders or the more numerous deacons, who handled most church affairs. These we will discuss in a later chapter, but will here note that the position brought with it or acknowledged high status, for it required ability, piety, and the Christian virtues professed by the community. Finally, at the top of this prestige order came the ministers, selected from a colonywide pool consisting almost entirely of college graduates. Most churches hired only one person, combining the functions of teacher with those of the minister (who attended to the more mundane matters), but the larger ones supported two. The people paid them a bonus immediately, granted them a substantial salary, provided them with a house and farm, and

[25] New Haven district probate records, 1, part one: 175 (Maltby), 188 (Powell), and part two: 118 (Hollingsworth).

tried to free them from economic burdens. In this way the ministers commonly formed part of the economic upper class, but that came as a result of their religious status, not a requirement for it.

The bottom of the military hierarchy consisted of the town's expendables, who did most of the actual fighting. These were men who never would be missed, such as Indians, free blacks, recent immigrants, or other poor single men. With them served the extra farm boys whose brothers could perform their jobs. In time of need, others might join them, even young fathers, but the pay was so low and survival so uncertain that most married men with skills did not volunteer: their families and indeed the town would suffer from their absence. Married men formed a sort of military middle class, supposedly armed and trained to fight by the militia units, but remaining at home except in emergencies such as King Philip's War.

The militia consisted of able-bodied men aged sixteen to sixty, except for those explicitly exempted (ministers always). They selected out of their number the company officers: in order, corporals and sergeants, ensigns, lieutenants, and captains. The last three technically were appointed by the legislature, one for each company, but in practice the delegates ratified the wishes of the soldiers, mediating in case of disputes.[26] These officers, like the deacons, came from the community and possessed the talents requisite to their tasks such as courage and strength, rather than holiness. Higher-ranking officers commanded units that combined companies of several towns, and so gained their rank from the legislature. Like the ministers they drew from a colonywide, rather than a local pool. In their way, these officers were just as important to the colony as were the church leaders and the higher-ranking among them earned similar awards, especially grants of land, which elevated their economic position proportionately.

The parallel political hierarchy does not need elaborate explanation.[27] At the bottom were the disenfranchised, which during the early decades meant primarily nonchurch members and later those with little property. The latter requirement excluded mostly the men who remained dependents, notably young sons, but some older sons too, and many newcomers. The independent man at once was assessed for £18, as we noted earlier, still not enough to allow him to vote, but the acquisition of a home lot and a few farm animals sufficed. The elements of a farm or craftshop, when combined with marriage, meant that the boy had settled down as a stable member of the community.

[26] *Pub. Rec. Conn.*, 4:82, 162.

[27] Edward M. Cook, Jr., *The Fathers of the Towns: Leadership and Community Structure in Eighteenth-Century New England* (Baltimore, 1976).

Almost at once the young citizen would share political and legal responsibilities such as jury duty, various lesser town offices, or committee work. With age, experience, evidence of ability, and proof of character, he might aspire to the more important and prestigious offices: to become a selectman, honored as a moderator, or sent to the legislature whereupon, by the way, he would be referred to as "mister" if he had not earned another title. A slightly different path led to an appointment, by the legislature, as justice of the peace, supposedly requiring some legal knowledge and certainly good judgment. That brought with it an "esquire." Election to the Council, or upper house of the legislature, conferred an "honorable" and usually a judgeship. Only the first step of this particular ladder involved property, and that simply as an evidence of stability. Since the qualities that enabled one to prosper attested to one's ability, economic success and political progress proceeded together, not essentially connected, but correlated.

Finally, Connecticut's men can be divided into social ranks apart from the preceding hierarchies but reflective both of them and an amorphous, subjective prestige. In the very early days, class distinctions carried over from Europe, and we find a few men distinguished by a "sir" or "gentleman," as was Gentleman John Robbins of Wethersfield and Captain Rene Grignon, Gent., of Norwich. At the same period, as we observed earlier, men who belonged to that class but did not possess a title were addressed as "mister." This attested to one's education, since we find even poor schoolteachers thus complimented, to family background, or to non-economic achievement, notably election as a delegate. About one-fourth of Connecticut's citizens, if they lived long enough, earned a title of respect, and we may suppose that the status also extended to their immediate family.

During the eighteenth century the dividing line may have dimmed, for we find that tax lists and other sources either used the "mister" for everybody or omitted it entirely. The continuation of social class distinctions, however, is shown by the presence of titles and by other evidence such as newspaper notices. The *New London Gazette*, for example, recognized the marriages only of the local elite, usually complete with title or identified as part of the economic upper class by the noun "merchant." The same class, with the addition of the very old, earned obituaries, and where an identification is missing we can ourselves generally supply it. Thus in 1768 the death of Mrs. Susannah Richards, wife of Mr. John, recorded the passing of a member of one of the town's wealthiest families. Education received its due with the notice of the death, at age twenty-six, of a Yale tutor; and business is represented by John Lester, "noted innkeeper." Others so honored included a merchant (at St. Croix), a colonel, an "honorable" judge, two deacons, a captain, a captain's wife, and the son of a minister. The following year, incidentally, the *Gazette* reported the demise of Benjamin Uncas, sachem of the Mohegan Indians (of consumption). We should point out, however, that the obituaries noticed men whose passing would have been ignored in a truly aristocratic society, like the innkeeper above, and later a "noted tailor," the keeper of a "house of entertainment" (a retired ship's captain), a doctor's son, and a blockmaker. The line between the ordinary respectable citizens and the social upper class was always blurred, since one-third or more of the latter came from the former, but the line did exist.

Similarly and lastly we can distinguish a line or a band between the reputable middling sort and those below. Most obviously, the servants and slaves lacked any prestige. In addition, every tax list included men who had newly arrived or were passing through the town, unrelated to any known family, almost without property, nearly always young and single. The probate court caught them too: John Baker, who died in Milford in 1684 leaving £3; Joseph Dickinson of New Haven, a weaver, who was worth £18 at his death in 1683; or Thomas Napp of Hartford, who drowned in the river leaving an estate of £5. A little above them came the much larger number of local men who were either too young to have earned respect in their own right or who belonged to life's failures. Examples of the first group include John Robinson, who died at age twenty-three in Guilford, worth £15, one of eight children, and Joseph Pritchard of Milford, killed in King Philip's War, leaving £43. Representative of the second and far smaller category are Daniel Garrett of Hartford (1613-1688), who was appointed prisonkeeper to help support him, and James Hodge of Wethersfield (ca. 1670-1713), a former apprentice who died in his forties, still single, worth only £37.

The process by which members of the lower or laboring class could achieve higher status, and those of the respectable middle class attain eminence, involved a combination of economic improvement, aging, marrying and having children, and proof of personal attributes, occurring not separately but in unison and interdependently. If we find a man without property we can lay long odds that he is young, single, and at the bottom of the various status orders. Someone with a title— say lieutenant—will have a family, own at least average wealth, belong to a church, and hold local political offices. Property alone did not make the man, but men made property, and we can therefore study the data on wealth with the confidence that we are also learning about Connecticut's society.

Price Changes in Connecticut

	£ Oxen	£ Horses	s Sheep	£ Clothing	s Wheat	SILVER McCusker	Conn.	Multiplier
1640–1659	14.10	10	24/	6	4/6			.7
1660–1669	12.10	6.16	11/	6	4/6			.7
1670–1674	11.10	2.17	8/	6	4/6			.7
1675–1699	11.	2.10	9/	6	4/6	6/8	9p	.7
1700–1709	11p				5/	7/ to 8/		.7p
	7.10c	2.7	5/3	4.10	6p			1.0c
1710–1714	8	2.10	5/3	6	4/c	8/6	7/6	.9
1715–1719	10	3.10	6/	6.10	4/6	10/	8/	.75
1720–1723	10.10	3.14	7/	8	5/	13/	10/	.7
1724–1726	11.10				6/	16/		.6
1727–1729	13	4.16	7/	8.10	7/6	17/6	15/	.5
1730–1734	17	5.10	12/	11	8/	20/	18/	.44
1735–1739	21	8.3	15/	15	10/	28/	30/	.4–.33
1740–1744	30	15	18/	17	12/	30/		.25–.22
1745–1747	41	26	27/	30	15/	42/	42/	.20–.15
1748–1749	60			37	36/	57/	54/	.13–.11
1750	66							.11
1751	69							.11
1752	77	40	33/	50	38/	64/		.10
1753	80						73/	.10
1754	84			6c		69/		.09
1755						74		.085
1755–1758	8.10	4.0	4/	5.10	3/9	6/8	6/8	1.0
1759	10.10							1.0
1760	12.6							1.0
1761	12							1.0
1762	11.8							1.0
1763	11.6	4.12	6/4	6	4/6			1.0
1764	11.10							1.0
1765	10.12							1.0
1766–1768	10	5.4	5/8	6	3/9			1.0
1769–1770	9.8							1.0
1771	9.16							1.0
1772	10.18	6.7	5/3	6	4/6			1.0
1773	11.11							1.0
1774	11.14					6/8	6/8	1.0

NOTE: c = cash value; p = country pay.

Prices of Real Estate (MEAN £)

	House	Barn	All bldgs.	Meadow	Other improved	Miscel- laneous	Total	Remote	"Farm"
1660–1674							(3,468 acres)		
Hartford							2.10		
New Haven							1.5		
Fairfield							2		
All							2		
1675–1699							(22,741 acres)		
Hartford	20	14	35	4.10	3.0	16/	2.5	5/	
New Haven	21			3	1.10	1.0	1.10	4/	
Fairfield				5	3.10	2	3	5/	
All	20	14?	40?	4.10	3	1	2.5	5/	2 +
1700–1714							(42,648 acres)		
Hartford	18	14	44	5	3	18/	2	5/	2
New Haven	24	14	40	4.5	3	1	1.17	10/	1.10
Fairfield	30	14	50	4.8	3.12	1.7	1.16	6/	
New London (South)	30	15	45	3	2.10	1	1.5	7/	1.10
New London (North)						15/	17/	3/	
All	25	14	45	4.5	3	1	1.16	6/	2
1720–1729							(55,782 acres)		
Hartford (part)	40?	13?	45	5	3.6	1.2	2	11/	2.10
New Haven	24	12	40	5	3.16	1.10	2.5	13/	
Woodbury	20	12	35	4		17/	1	5/	3
Guilford				5	4	1.12	2.5	22/	
Fairfield	31	15	50	7	5	2.10	4	10/	
New London	25			5	3	1.12	2	8/	2.10
Northeast				2			15/	10/	2
All	30	14	45	5	3.10	1.10	2.5	12/	2.10
1750–1754							(29,728 acres)		
Hartford	36?	12	50	5.8	3.10	1.5	2	10/	4
Fairfield	30	10	60	5.10	5.8	3	3.4	13/	5

	House	Barn	All bldgs.	Meadow	Other improved	Miscel- laneous	Total	Remote	"Farm"
1750–1754									
Windham	35	7	45			2.15	2.10	11/	3.10
All	35	10	50	5.10	3.10	2	2.10	12/	4
1765–1769							(59,324 acres)		
Hartford*	50	15	80	9	5	2	3.5	12/	3.10
New Haven	35	10	55	6	5.3	2.14	3.14	20/	4.10
Guilford	42	9	55	8	5.13	3	3.8	13/	4.10
Fairfield	50	12	66	6.12	8.5	4.4	5.3	18/	
New London				4	5	2	2.10	16/	4
Windham				7	5	2.4	3		4
All	45	12	65	7	5.10	2.10	3.10	15/	4

NOTE: Medians and means are almost identical because the larger estates, while containing much valuable land, contain proportionately more of miscellaneous varieties.

All money figures, here and elsewhere, are given in pounds and shillings, not decimals. Thus £2.5 equals two pounds, five shillings, not two and a half pounds. "Remote" land refers to tracts at a considerable distance from the place of residence, almost always speculative and undeveloped.

Some inventories lumped all real estate, both buildings and land, providing only the total value, called a "farm." Thus one reads "100 acre farm, £400" which of course means £4 per acre including the buildings. The practice and word were most common in the northeast (Windham County), but I have used the term elsewhere whenever inventories did not itemize real property but did furnish the acreage.

*Includes Colchester, Middletown, Sharon, Farmington, and Simsbury districts.

APPENDIX 2C

Determination of Bias in Probate Records

We illustrate our procedure in studying bias by the case of Wethersfield, whose assessment list of 1730 (Connecticut State Library) reported 410 polls including, as we reconstruct the situation, 363 white men plus certainly a few black slaves. The age structure of these does not indicate that we have missed any, though the median of thirty-five may be a touch low for a diversified and prosperous economic center.

We then try to discover who died within ten years of the tax, starting with the probate records, which of course furnish the names of those leaving inventories, and Stiles's *Wethersfield*, supplemented by other genealogical sources, which inform us of men whose estates did not enter probate. Of those identified, fifty-one left inventories and twenty did not, or about 73 percent coverage. This seems too high because as nearly as we can estimate the population of the colony at that point, and guessing at a general death rate of eighteen (using other tax lists for the guess), only about two-thirds of the estates were inventoried. Moreover, the death rate for Wethersfield would be only seventeen, which seems a bit too low for a trading center. We did not discover the death dates of forty-five, so we must now try harder to learn how many of them died within the decade. If a man bought or sold land, fathered a child, or otherwise left a mark after the ten years, we can eliminate him. That leaves us with fifteen. We could assort these according to age and apply our knowledge about age-specific death rates to estimate their probable fate, or we can simply assume that the man died shortly after the last record of him. Luckily both procedures yield the same result, adding eight to the above twenty dying without inventories. The revised death rate then rises to nearly nineteen, probate coverage declines to 64 percent, and the age structure of the decedents falls within the expected range. No age or wealth bias appears:

	21-29	30-39	40-49	50-59	60-69	70+
% inventoried	62.5	61	91	58	43	62

	Tax under £30	£30-100	Tax over £100
% inventoried	60	71	60

Further evidence for the seventeenth century comes from our analysis based on the 1670 "census," which did not permit a study of wealth bias but did show the absence of age bias and a probable 83 percent coverage of decedents in the inventories, a proportion maintained during the rest of the century. For 1750-1754, a study based on New Haven and Wallingford using Jacobus showed no age or wealth bias at that point, with a probate coverage of 65.5 percent. A comparable test using the same materials for the years 1765-1774 again did not reveal any age bias and a wealth bias the reverse of that indicated above, but without a tax list the property of those men who did not leave inventories can only be guessed at. The coverage was 58 percent.

Finally, I traced the largest estates on the tax lists to see what proportion entered probate. For those taxed on an assessed value of over £200, the result is as follows: men dying before 1700, 83 percent (12-2), 1700-1729, 83 percent (5-1), 1730-1769, 67 percent (10-5), and 1770-1789, 55 percent (10-7). Adding the next largest (£150+) group yields the following series: 75 percent, 95 percent, 69 percent, and 56 percent. The first two combined (N=67) equal 83.6 percent. The last is higher than for the population generally and confirms the bias that we are investigating.

THREE

The Distribution of Property in
the Seventeenth Century

The first settlers of Connecticut during the great migration and their children after them established a society and economy that would remain fundamentally the same for the next century. They founded within thirty years a score of towns from Stonington on the Rhode Island border to Greenwich, and indeed beyond the New York line to Rye. At the same time they settled from Eastern Long Island to the northern Connecticut Valley, where Windsor touched Massachusetts, and overflowed beyond into the sister colony. After this explosion, expansion slowed, then ceased until after King Philip's War, which indeed drove back some of the outlying settlers; and, as we observed earlier, population growth remained only moderate by colonial standards. Four new towns had been founded just before that war, but then none for ten years, and but seven more by the end of the century.[1]

These movements accompanied changes in the amount and distribution of wealth. The very general outlines are as follows. The immigrants consisted of two broad types, those who brought property with them, sometimes a lot of it, and those who had none. The presence of the former created a high average wealth in personal property, of the latter, a low median. The combination resulted in a temporary inequality. The earliest years brought prosperity to those first arrivals who had enough capital to begin farming and other enterprises, for continued immigration created a demand for food, housing, and services. Prices were relatively high. Yokes of oxen, which later averaged £11, sold for £14.10 during the 1640s, horses were worth £7 or more, sheep 26 shillings each—three times that during the eighties—and cows as much as £5, while the legislature was obliged to limit the price of grain.

This prosperity ended with the English Civil Wars. Capital and settlers ceased to flow in and some of the prosperous colonists, as well as many of the poor, returned home. The New Englanders had not

[1] See the discussion in Bruce C. Daniels, *The Connecticut Town: Growth and Development* (Middletown, Conn., 1979).

discovered markets for such surplus as they produced and farm prices began to slide. The Restoration slowed the decline and began a short-lived recovery. A wave of new immigrants arrived, and the people established new farms and towns. Migration into Massachusetts continued and, with the defeat of the Dutch, New Englanders entered not only New York but New Jersey. Land values doubled.

The decline resumed within a few years, primarily because the West Indies market had collapsed along with the price of sugar. King Philip's War deepened the depression. The price of land abruptly dropped and did not fully recover for fifty years. Connecticut had failed to discover a truly profitable staple, without which no real economic growth could occur. Fortunately, by 1690 the gradual increase of trade with the West Indies and internal expansion halted the decline and, though no economic boom occurred until the next century, the situation stabilized. The low price of land enabled the third generation to obtain farms, so that if on the one hand the larger propertyowners suffered economic losses, thus lowering the mean wealth from its initial level, the poor usually acquired property, so maintaining the median, the combination lessening the earlier inequality. From a purely economic point of view, Connecticut in 1699 was more democratic than in 1640.

Let us begin with a snapshot of the people during the late seventeenth century, using the tax lists for three dissimilar towns: Fairfield, Windsor, and Middletown. The first represents the coast along the Sound, blessed with good soil and a relatively moderate climate, though not yet flourishing.[2] Windsor, one of the earliest settlements on the northern border, had attracted some men with large estates and had prospered,[3] while Middletown, settled later than the other two, remained a farming community.[4]

At this time the population of all three towns was quite young because of their newness, because they continued to attract immigrants, and because the sons of the first settlers were just reaching maturity.

[2] Fairfield's list of 1670/1 names the "inhabitants" with the total value of their estates, assembled in order to distribute land. Elizabeth H. Schenck, *History of Fairfield, Fairfield County, Conn.*, 2 vols. (New York, 1889-1905), 1:334. Nearly one-third additional men were present, mostly but not all young dependent sons. See Donald Lines Jacobus, *History and Genealogy of the Families of Old Fairfield*, 2 vols., 1930; reprinted in 3 vols. (Baltimore, 1976). I omit women and nonresidents here and hereafter.

[3] The 1686 tax for Windsor states the number of polls and itemizes the taxable property, enabling us to determine occupations. It does not give the total value of the estates, only that part subject to taxation. Connecticut Historical Society.

[4] The Middletown lists of 1670 and 1673 name proprietors and their estates. So also one recording the contributors to a meetinghouse bell in 1679. Connecticut State Library.

These new arrivals and young sons either remained dependent or were just beginning to establish themselves, so they appear on the lists as almost propertyless if their names are there at all. Therefore, about a third of the adult male population consisted of poor laborers. They did not, however, constitute a single class nor a permanent proletariat because over two out of three were local boys who could expect to succeed their fathers in due time, and would almost certainly become independent propertyholders upon marriage. The others, poor outsiders and generally young, were only a tenth of the men. Chapter five discusses them at greater length. Considering their disadvantages they seem not to have fared badly. A fourth left and cannot be traced. The rest divided into three equal groups: the poor, those who prospered, and the ones in between.

Another group of taxpayers consisted of men whose economic circumstances must have been marginal, enabling them barely to support themselves and their families. Perhaps one out of four men belonged to this category (tax lists are not very precise). Thus in Fairfield one-fourth of the men owned property assessed for between £50 and £100. Of this group, some were single men who needed only a small income and most of the rest had not reached age forty, with a family of young children. The older men commonly belonged to the higher economic category unless they remained single. For example, in Fairfield the median for men in their twenties was £28, for those in their fifties £220. In Windsor so many of the young men were dependent polls or independent but entirely propertyless that their median value on the tax list was only £1 against £85 for men aged fifty to fifty-nine.

The top wealth-holders, then, consisted mostly of older married men, at least in their thirties, nearly half over fifty at a time when only one-fifth of the men had reached that age. This upper class did not possess truly large estates, as far as these lists reveal the situation; they were simply comfortable, at best well-off, generally farmers together with a handful of traders and professional men. Among them were most of the town's leaders. The most prosperous tenth owned no more than 30 percent of the assessed wealth even though we added, at the bottom, a considerable number who did not appear on the lists. Despite the numerous laborers and a few men of substance and rank, the society may fairly be called equalitarian. Half of the men were ordinary farmers, and the laborers were their sons or other local lads, except for the small group of migrants, many of whom would soon merge into the community.

We introduce a few of the taxpayers, not as typical but as representative of the several types. Windsor's Isaac Thayre was assessed for his poll in 1686 and vanishes. Every list includes men like that. Since they had not married they were probably young, though the outsiders who became residents did marry eventually, a few years later than the norm of twenty-five. The Connecticut records are good enough so that if Thayre had remained and married we would almost certainly know about it. Conceivably he died and the probate court missed him, but in all probability he left the colony.

Joseph Patchen and his family illustrate the failures. Born in 1610, he immigrated to Roxbury, where in 1642 he married. Some time after 1645 he proceeded to Fairfield where in 1670 his estate was worth only £60, not enough to support his family. As a result his eldest son Joseph, though age twenty-seven that year, does not appear on the list, being still unmarried and either living with his father or as a servant. Joseph Junior died in 1689, still single and impoverished. His younger brother John, who lived to be about seventy, had been a servant for upwards of thirty years to his neighbor Deacon Isaac Wheeler, dying single and poor. We should add, however, that Joseph Senior, by a second, late marriage, had a son who acquired a farm, joined the church, served as tax collector, married, and died at age eighty-six in Wilton.

Middletown supplies us with two young married men of average property in 1670. The estate of Samuel Collins (1636-1696) was evaluated at £58 that year when he was already the father of three young children. That property might barely suffice. Three years later, now a sergeant, he increased it by 50 percent and thereafter held his own as a small farmer and artisan of some sort—he had an apprentice when he died. David Sage, a few years younger but with a little more property, had not added much in 1673 but at his death in 1703 he had accumulated the good estate of £753 (pay). His eldest son had already received most of his share and the second son part of his, but Sage only now gave the latter the lot upon which he had built a house. Two married daughters tripled their previous dowry and the two young single sons, Jonathan and Timothy, came into their inheritance. The youngest daughter Mercy was to receive part "when she needs it" and part when her mother died. No doubt she would remain at home to help her mother and two brothers. I am sorry to say that Mercy died a few years later, as did Jonathan, now married but childless, and David Junior. The elder Sage had come a long way, for he ended his life with 91 improved acres and 654 unimproved, on which he had built three houses and a barn and kept twenty-one head of cattle. He had also sent six bushels of peas to Boston.[5] None of his sons equaled his prosperity, the youngest indeed dying insolvent, but a grandson acquired a considerable estate in trade and sired a general (Comfort) for the Revolutionary War.

The great majority of men in seventeenth-century Connecticut fit the descriptions of Thayre, the Patchens, Collins, and the Sages. Others, generally older at the time of our lists, possessed more property and were more apt to found what by colonial standards might be called a dynasty, though that did not always follow. Fairfield's Nathan Gold (ca. 1620-1694), a relative newcomer to the colony, was already a major, judge, and assistant in 1670 when his estate was valued at £460, the town's highest. He had more than tripled this at the time of his death and his son Nathan (1663-1723) maintained the family's wealth as well as its status through his sons Reverend Hezekiah and John, Esquire.[6] On the other hand, the largest assessed estate in Middletown belonged to William Harris (ca. 1620-1689), who lost ground three years later, and did not leave a son, so his property apparently benefited his brother Daniel.

These tax lists serve only as a very general introduction to the people and their property. To answer the questions promised by the title of this chapter we must turn to estate inventories. Let us begin at the highest level of aggregation, combining all seventeenth-century inventories (except for a few in the New London district) expressed in country pay. The property owned by the living population fell considerably short of that shown on Table 3.1. The mean personal wealth of all

TABLE 3.1
Value of Probated Estates, Seventeenth Century

		Personal wealth		Real wealth		Total wealth	
	N	£	Mean	£	Mean	£	Mean
New Haven	450	71,005	158	68,699	153	139,704	310.5
Fairfield	386	51,286	133	72,275	187	123,561	320.0
Hartford	650	105,820	163	139,295	214	245,115	377.0
Total	1,486	228,111	153	280,269	189	508,380	342.0

[5] Charles William Manwaring, *A Digest of the Early Connecticut Probate Records*, 3 vols. (Hartford, 1904-1906), 2:109, 214-15 and for the inventory, Hartford district probate records, 7:56-58.

[6] For Gold's estate, Fairfield probate district records, 4:179; for the family, Jacobus, *Fairfield*, 1:228-31, 371-73.

adult men was £110, the real estate £164, and the total, of course, £274, so that wealth per capita in sterling over the whole century was roughly £25. This is almost exactly the same as the figure for Maryland at the same time.[7] The table also reveals regional differences in wealth and a surprisingly high proportion of personal property in a society primarily agricultural. These facts call for investigation, and we need also to examine the distribution of this property by age and marital status as well as over time.

We begin with real property—land, buildings, and other "improvements." During the early years before 1660 the value of real estate remained low, less than half that of personal wealth. There was plenty of land, but the whites could not make much use of it. The towns might vote "divisions" to inhabitants as they came of age,[8] but most men huddled together and farmed nearby fields that the Indians or nature had cleared for them. Two out of five owned none at all—no land and not even a hut. These were primarily the numerous young single laborers living with employers or masters, plus a few squatters and renters. Older men with families generally acquired some good "meadow" for pasture or tillage and also larger tracts, at first almost valueless but which the owners might gradually fence and clear.

After 1660 land values rose very slowly to about £2 per acre overall. Unimproved tracts could still be had for the asking and were valued at only a few shillings per acre. Real wealth increased but still did not equal personal. The major change saw the proportion of landless men drop to one-fourth, partly because towns continued to grant lots to residents as they married and settled down and partly because many young men left the colony without being replaced by immigrants. The presence of Indians continued to limit territorial expansion: thus people in such towns as Middletown, Wethersfield, Hartford, and Wind-

[7] This figure is derived first by using a multiplier of 0.72 for personal wealth and of 0.80 for total property, which result from adjusting for the difference in the age structure of the two populations; second by dividing the figures in half to obtain a sterling value; and finally by assuming that one multiplies by 5.5 to obtain the total population from the adult males. If one uses 5.0 instead, the sterling total per capita becomes £27.8 instead of £25. For Maryland I used Gloria L. Main's figure of £34.68 (decimals) adjusting downward for the lower levels earlier. *Tobacco Colony: Life in Early Maryland, 1650-1720* (Princeton, 1982), pp. 54, 93.

[8] Some towns distributed all their land at once, and then, of course, a new head of household could not obtain a free lot. Other towns divided the land gradually, but probably the quality declined, for we find some young grantees selling at once at a low price and then leaving. The land deeds contain information on sales and purchases. They are extensive and I have used them only for some limited purposes.

sor, on the west bank of the Connecticut, scarcely ventured across the river.

The white victory in King Philip's War permitted a major advance into new areas even though the price of livestock and crops did not promise great profits. The colony's real wealth at last exceeded personal. Land values reached £3 per acre of improved land. By the 1690s only 13 percent of the men lacked at least a little land and almost all married couples possessed enough for food; indeed, their median was eighty-eight acres even including the landless. Those holding less then the desirable forty were usually artisans or others who did not depend entirely upon a farm.

In another society this acquisition of land might have resulted in the appearance of great estates. In Connecticut that rarely occurred. Despite the low cost no more than one out of five men between the age of forty and sixty left as much as 200 acres at their death, which means that only 6 percent of the men did so. New England was not a prosperous commercial farming area, and the farmers saw little advantage in purchasing a labor supply other than their own sons. In favored locations a few individuals bought several hundred acres but very rarely actually used over a hundred. Rather, most men gradually added to and improved their modest farms in order to support their families comfortably and to provide for the children's future. Since the proportion of landless men diminished over time and no really large properties appeared, the ownership of real estate did not become concentrated. Before 1659, when many settlers lacked land, 10 percent of the adult men owned 54 percent of the total value, but by the end of the century their share had dropped to only 40 percent—not an absolute equality but well toward that end of the spectrum (see Appendix 3A). Furthermore, those who did not possess land or had too little of it to support themselves were young, single, or artisans, so that either they needed little real property or could look forward to acquiring some by

TABLE 3.2
Acres Owned, Men Aged Forty to Sixty

								Median	
	None	1–39	40–79	80–119	120–199	200+	Total	All	Owners
Pre-1660	4	8	3	5	3	3	26	50	79
1660–1679	12	11	19	9	9	12	82	67	79
1680–1689	9	11	20	11	6	15	72	75	80
1690–1699	4	25	26	24	18	22	119	88	92

inheritance, grant, or purchase. Landlessness in seventeenth-century Connecticut was a temporary, not a permanent status for most men.

We turn now to personal property. As we have seen, its value greatly exceeded that of real estate during the first quarter-century, and indeed personal wealth per capita would never again be so great.[9] To some extent this resulted from the exceptionally high price of livestock arising from its scarcity relative to demand. But this accounts for only a part of the high level, which reflects mainly the capital brought by the settlers. By 1660 this wealth was diminishing. The first generation of well-to-do immigrants found the cost of colonization greater than the profits. Some returned to England, others died bankrupt, and few men of property replaced them. The expansion of Connecticut into Long Island, southern New York, and East Jersey did not serve to establish profitable colonies but may even have drained capital from the older towns. Trade with the West Indies opened only slowly, and meanwhile the people had to absorb the losses from King Philip's War, the difficult years of the Andros Administration, and the costly King William's War. Personal wealth per adult man dropped by 40 percent and even the less sensitive median fell from £80 to a low of £45 during 1680-1689. A partial recovery followed. Although the wealth of the richer men did not return to the early level, thus limiting the increase of the general mean, the median did so. This fact, taken with the upward trend in real property, suggests that by the end of the century most of Connecticut's people had regained their prosperity. We must, however, test that by more detail, in particular by examining the distribution of personal property by age groups and wealth classes, using estate inventories.

During the period 1640-1659 the colony, as we have stressed, was dominated numerically by young men, mostly single and poor, owning less than one-tenth of the total personal wealth. At the top, men possessing over £500 (country pay) were few in number but had more than a third of the total, and the top 10 percent of wealth-holders owned not far from half. These, and the next highest group, were almost always married men whose property increased with age so that the fifty-year-olds averaged £250 apiece (the median), quite a comfortable sum.

The downturn that followed does not appear in the estates of young men, who indeed had little to lose. Such remained but they were dif-

[9] The mean per adult male, judging from estate inventories, was £179 currency or £152 after adjusting for high livestock prices. That is still a bit higher than for any subsequent time period and considerably above that for the rest of the century.

TABLE 3.3
Distribution of Personal Wealth by Age Group,
Living Population, 1640–1659

£ (country pay)	21–29	30–39	40–49	50–59	60+	N	Total £
1–19	12	1	1	0	0	14	140
20–49	12	3	0	1	0	16	560
50–99	9	11	4	2	1	27	2,025
100–199	2	7	3	1	1	14	1,960
200–499	5	5	6	6	1	23	6,900
500+	0	1	3	1	1	6	6,360
Total	40	28	17	11	4	100	17,945

ferent persons and fewer. We see the depression rather in the reduced circumstances of young fathers in their thirties, who had been the single laborers earlier, and now, instead of improving their position, were often disappointed. This was especially true during the 1680s when the poor twenty-year-olds of the seventies frequently became poor thirty-year-olds. The same depression decade severely affected men over forty. Thus the "typical" male in his early twenties, beginning with personal property valued at £37 about 1660, was worth £90 a decade later, but in 1680, when he should have reached his maximum wealth, he had actually slipped. So, too, a young father beginning with £95 and improving to £143 before King Philip's War, instead of continuing to gain in his fifties suffered a loss to £120. Young men were normally poor, but in the New World they could reasonably expect to earn a decent living, especially with all that land. They would look around them during the years 1660-1679 and see the young fathers of thirty-odd years owning a personal estate almost certainly worth over £50, plus land as we have seen; yet during the eighties two out of five would not have that much. The dashing of great expectations affected every age group (except men over seventy) and disposed them to blame anybody, especially an Andros; that they did not seek out witches we may attribute to their ownership of land and the fact that few suffered extreme poverty.

The final decade redeemed the century economically, perhaps in other ways as well. Every age group gained in wealth. Perhaps most dramatically, the thirty-year-olds of the pre-1680 years, who had suffered a collective median decline of 15 percent as they reached their forties instead of the usual gain, now doubled their property; in particular the proportion of them owning less then £50 in personal wealth, which

70

as been 12.7 percent before 1680 and had risen to 29.3 percent thereafter, now shrank to 9.8 percent. The revolution that had enthroned William and Mary seemed glorious indeed.

We can also trace the changes over time by dividing men into wealth classes. Table 3.4 shows the poorest one-fifth simple holding their own. The middle three-fifths all experienced the decline from the earliest years to the nadir of the eighties. The top group did not, though that is in some degree a demographic accident: two wealthy merchants who died during that decade ought to have lived longer and made the trend unanimous. In that case the top 10 percent of wealth-holders, whose share of the total had declined to 40 percent, would have returned to the early level—as it may in fact have done.

Before we leave the subject of changes in personal property over time we should glance at certain components of wealth. As we have seen, the value of livestock was reduced by half after 1660, accounting for some of the reduction in wealth and presumably income, insofar as beef and pork were exported. During the 1680s a sharp decrease in debts receivable accounted for more of the loss in inventoried wealth than did livestock. This suggests a reduction of investment capital. The people's small store of hard money also diminished.

Three components did increase over time: the value of servants, tools, and consumption goods rose with every time period. The first remained insignificant. The value of tools doubled, exceeding £6 by 1700. Most interesting was the relatively stable value of consumption goods. Older men did own less during the 1680s but the younger actually had more, probably because those older men were passing on to their children what could be spared during the hard times. By the end of the century the general level of consumer's goods per person had reached a new high.[10]

TABLE 3.4

Distribution of Personal Wealth, Probate Population (country pay)

	Lowest quintile	Second quintile	Middle quintile	Fourth quintile	Highest quintile
Pre-1660	13	46	76	170	508
1660–1679	13	40	73	133	345
1680–1689	12	37	61	118	313
1690–1699	14	44	85	133	300

NOTE: Means adjusted for living population.

[10] Since the value of consumption goods did not vary much, their proportion of total

Having artificially separated personal from real wealth—the cattle from their pasture and the furniture from the rooms—we should reunite them. Since the level of personal property began high and declined while real estate followed the opposite course, the sum of the two shows less change than either. The fact that Connecticut's young men became landowners by purchase, inheritance, or gift, together with the rising value of their land as they improved and built upon it, meant an increase in wealth that overshadowed the losses in personal property, certainly in the long run. It meant that most adult and almost all married men owned enough land to feed their families and to become settled members of the community; it limited the inequality of wealth; and it cushioned the severe depression of the 1680s.

The distribution of wealth among the people varied, then, over time. The different occupational groups owned types and quantities of property typical of their circumstances. In addition, inheritance affected both economic and social position. Chapters Five through Nine consider these two factors. Equally important were one's stage in the life cycle and place of residence. We now examine the relationship between these variables and the distribution of different kinds of property, beginning with a brief general discussion of the property itself.

Personal wealth consisted of several components: first, the collection of articles that we have combined under the heading of consumption, or consumer goods; and next, items of production including liquid capital (money, silver articles, debts receivable), tools, trading stock, ships, and bound labor.

The quantity and value of consumption articles remained remarkably stable over time (see Appendix 3B). The mean of the inventoried

TABLE 3.5
Distribution of Total Wealth, Adult Males (country pay)

	1–49	50–99	100–199	200–499	500+	Mean	Median	Share top 10%
Pre-1660	28	20.5	18	26½	7	216	110	42.2%
1660–1679	27	11	27	24	11	241	146	42.3
1680–1689	29	10	19	25	17	280	155	41.8
1690–1699	15½	16½	19½	35	13½	290	192	37.2

personal wealth fluctuated widely with the economic cycle. Before 1660, 27 percent of the people's personal property was in that form. The percentage reached 46 during the 1680s, another clear sign of depression, for the people ought to have been increasing their income-producing goods. It finally settled down at about 40 percent.

consumer goods rose gradually from £52 before 1660 to £63 by 1700. Over the same period it composed an increasing proportion of personal wealth, from 30 percent to 42 percent by the 1680s, but this reflected primarily the decline in the prices of livestock. As a rule of thumb men of all age groups except the oldest invested 40 percent of their personal wealth in consumer articles but those over seventy, while losing or divesting themselves of other property, retained most of their household goods and clothing so that for them such articles formed about 60 percent of the personal wealth. For men younger than seventy the value of this kind of property rose with age, because age brought wealth, and they invested a part of their increased income to raise their standard of living, as the following table shows:

	21-29	30-39	40-49	50-59	60-69	70+	All ages
Median £	15	30	50	60	80	50	40
Mean £	25	55	70	85	90	70	50

Very roughly, the "average" man in Connecticut, in his mid-thirties with several young children, needed as a minimum upwards of £15— say £20—and for comfort £50 worth (we will go into detail later). We can therefore set up a crude table showing the relationship between consumer goods and personal wealth, with distributions. Men with under £20 in property by this definition never owned enough in consumption articles to get by, though actually single men needed less. Those owning slightly larger properties, but still less than £50, commonly did not either. Beginning with that sum, which as we know most married men did possess, they had an adequate amount of indeed, those with over £100 in personal wealth commonly lived comfortably. The relationship for the whole period was roughly as follows:

Personal wealth	Consumption	% in consumption
£1-19	£10	50
20-49	15	45
50-99	36	45
100-199	70	50
200-499	115	35
500+	170	25

Appendix 3B presents the data from estate inventories and translates these into the living population. These data show clearly the improvement during the period 1660-1679 both in a larger proportion of the people with over £100 in consumer goods and notably in the reduction of men owning too little for maintenance. The depression of the next decade halted the advance, but on the whole the people did not suffer any real loss of household necessities, and the nineties saw more comfort than ever before. Among men aged forty to seventy, whose possessions affected almost everyone, we find that before 1660 more than a fourth lacked what they probably needed to furnish their homes decently. That shrank to one out of five but reached a peak of a third during the eighties. By the last decade the proportion with less than the desirable amount dropped to below a fourth. These are maximums: we must subtract a handful of permanent bachelors, a few with very young children, many more whose children had grown and gone, and those whose wives claimed some of the items as their own, brought with them upon marriage, the total collectively numerous enough to reduce our figures by nearly a third. Still, the trend is clear enough. Except during the very early years and the later depression a great majority of the men who needed considerable amounts of consumption goods possessed enough, and no overall decline occurred.

Two components of consumption deserve special treatment: clothing and books. The remarkable feature of the distribution of men's clothing was the stability of the median value, which remained at about £6 country pay during the entire century.[11] The reader will not be stunned to learn that the value of clothing varied with wealth. A minimum seems to be £3 worth, judging from the estates of men leaving £100 or more, who could presumably dress as necessary. Half of the men with under £40 in personal property owned fewer or poorer clothes than desirable; men with £160 and up dressed well; those worth £200 invested three times the minimum; and anyone whose personal wealth exceeded £500 could attend to display if he so desired.

TABLE 3.6
Clothing of Married Men, Seventeenth Century (country pay)

Personal wealth	£1–2	3–4	5–7	8–11	12–19	20+	Median
£1–39	84	50	37	11	10	1	3
40–99	72	120	92	44	20	2	4½
100–159	15	53	90	69	27	2	6
160–199	1	8	38	33	27	5	8½
200–499	0	11	35	68	94	39	12
500+	0	0	3	5	9	35	22
Total	172	242	295	230	187	84	6

SOURCE: Estate inventories.

[11] See Appendix 3C. The data omits men whose inventories listed no clothing but it includes those with only a pound's worth.

One's marital status mattered little, for bachelors often spent much of their small incomes on their persons: John Pardee, a sailor who died in 1683 with an estate of only £26, had clothes valued at £19.[12] Perhaps more significant than the relationship between wealth and the cost of clothing was that of occupation and status. Three-fourths of those with £20 or more bore titles attesting to their station in society. Men in trade and the professions, commonly ministers, made up half of the best-clad, along with some of the well-to-do artisans such as millers. However, most craftsmen, almost all farmers, and men of ordinary position dressed in work clothes with at best one good suit. Conspicuous display was virtually unknown.

The ownership of books also distinguished men of economic wealth, social position, and, in this case, education. Later we will discuss differences by occupation and now ask three questions only: what proportion of men with inventoried estates had books, did that change over time, and to what extent were private libraries correlated with wealth class and age.

During the seventeenth century about three out of five estate inventories mention books, with only a slight increase over time. However, the presence and value of books owned varied greatly with age, so in order to discover the situation among the living population we must, as usual, remove the effect of age bias. For the earliest period, before 1660, the distribution for the probate and living populations is shown in Table 3.7. Slightly over half of the men, at this point almost all immigrants, owned books. With age, men added to their collection,

TABLE 3.7
Value of Books Owned, Pre-1660 (country pay)

Marital status	None	Under £1	£1	£2	£3–5	Over £5	Total	N
Probate Population								
Single men	63	30	4	4	0	1	101	27
Young fathers	40	28	19	8	4	1	100	79
Older fathers	20	28	20	16	4	12	100	25
Retired & misc.	53	21	11	14	0	0	99	21
Living Population								
Single men	28	13	2	1	0	0	44	
Young fathers	17½	12	8	3	2	½	43	
Older fathers	2½	4	2½	2	½	1½	13	
Total	48	29	12½	6	2½	2	100	

[12] For Pardee, New Haven district probate records, 1:185.

75

often by inheritance (especially the family Bible), until a man of fifty without a book was rare, though the median value did not exceed one pound.

We skip now to the final period, 1690-1699, to obtain the same two distributions of the probate and living populations. Few changes had occured. Slightly more men had acquired at least one book and at the upper end we find a few larger libraries, but the same generalizations remained valid: most young men owned none, while the elders had several.

Obviously the value of books owned also varied with wealth, and we need furnish specifics only to allow comparison with other societies and to measure the extent of class differences. Appendix 3D supplies actual numbers over time. Table 3.9 condenses the final two decades and translates into percentages. Clearly only a few even among men

TABLE 3.8

Value of Books Owned, 1690–1699 (country pay)

Marital status	None	Under £1	£1	£2	£3–5	Over £5	Total	N
Probate Population								
Single men	62½	34	0	3½	0	0	100	56
Young fathers	33	36½	18	5½	4½	2	99½	188
Older fathers	28½	28	24	3½	7	8½	99½	159
Retired & misc.	40	34	26	5	1	4	100	104
Living Population								
Young single	21	11	0	1	0	0	33	
Young fathers	12	13½	7	2	2	½	37	
Older fathers	9	9	7½	1	1½	2	30	
Total	42	33½	14½	4	3½	2½	100	

TABLE 3.9

Gross Personal Wealth by Value of Books Owned, 1680–1699
(country pay)

	None	Under £1	£1	£2–5	Over £5	Total	Median	N
£1–19	67.4	28.4	3.2	1.0	0	100.0	0	95
20–29	46.4	45.2	6.0	2.4	0	100.0	+	168
50–99	36.5	45.8	12.6	5.1	0	100.0	+	214
100–199	27.2	38.6	23.5	8.1	2.8	100.2	16/	272
200–499	14.6	21.0	33.8	19.8	10.8	100.0	1	157
500+	4.8	9.5	9.5	42.9	33.3	100.0	4	21

of large property could afford or cared to acquire real libraries. Some of these, however, were sizable, almost always the minister's.

A few of the books were secular in nature, useful to men in public office such as justices, or in business—"physic" books, dictionaries, lawbooks—and we encounter a few in Latin, but the overwhelming majority of those identified were Bibles and others of a religious nature, their value reflecting more the worth of a particular Bible than the number of volumes on the shelves. Thus the books of Daniel Pratt of Hartford, who died in 1691, greatly exceeded the usual value, but they consisted only of a "church Bible" worth £3.10, another Bible at 12/, and six divinity books at £1.10. Therefore we are not perceiving a major disparity in wealth or education, except for the ministers and a few others, but differences in the degree of piety, which led some men to purchase very nice Bibles and a few related works while others were content with an old one or none at all.[13]

Fully as important to the people as books, clothing, and other articles of consumption that established their standard of living were the items of production that provided income. Chief among these, land aside, were the farm animals. We will devote more time to them when we discuss the farmers, and here only make a few general remarks. The Windsor tax list of 1686 shows that men who owned farms, some of whom were not primarily farmers, almost always had a yoke of oxen, especially if they were over forty, and the exceptions could call upon other members of the family. John Drake, Senior, did not, but his son Job took care of that, and John's two brothers had six. So also John Loomis, Junior, used his father's and Joseph, Senior, his son's, as did Thomas, Senior, and Nathaniel, Senior. One per inventory was a general average, and five cattle the median for all inventories. That understates the true situation because men most often died during the winter after the surplus had been sold or killed for food, and before calving, Cattle contributed nearly two-thirds of the value of livestock generally.

Horses were less important than in the South, partly because oxen did the plowing and hauling and because the people lived closer together, thus needing a horse only occasionally instead of habitually. About a third of the inventories contained none at all, and people who

---

[13] The question about the reading habits of the people requires more attention than we can give it here. Appendix 3D presents the books owned by the people living in different kinds of towns. Newly settled communities seem to have contained almost no real "libraries," and only a few shillings' worth of books per man, surely handicapping anyone of an intellectual bent. On the other hand the trading centers and even older country towns provided at least a few sizable collections and the community's holdings would suffice to start an education for the ambitious.

did own them seldom had more than three, typically a horse, mare, and colt. Seventeenth-century New Englanders rarely purchased a specialized saddle horse, and largely for that reason the price remained stable, about the same as a cow. As remarked earlier, horses often ran wild, which not only impaired their quality but also indicates the low value placed on them. Diaries often refer to hours, if not days, spent in searching for errant animals, and accounts of administration report losses that the executor subtracted from the inventory. The value per estate, by 1700, was £5.5, compared with £21 for cattle.

Sheep and pigs each averaged £4 per inventory. Acutally most inventoried estates contained no sheep at all, which means that few of the living population owned any either. Particularly before 1680 wolves prevented anyone from keeping sheep unless they were especially cared for, so that one finds them mostly in the estates of a few specialists, or on islands. William Gibbons of Hartford owned 300 when he died during the fifties, half of the entire number for the extensive distriet before 1680, but Gibbons was a merchant rather than a farmer.[14] In the seventies, nobody in the area had more than nineteen at his death except Reverend Joseph Haynes. Their number increased very slowly and the value remained quite low, at 10 shillings per sheep. Similarly in the New Haven district along the coast among the heads of households dying before 1660 a majority owned none and three individuals had half of the total number. By the end of the century large flocks disappeared from the inventories. Those that remained obviously just provided local wool for clothing and bedding, and not nearly enough of it for the people's needs.

Our material on sheep is fairly reliable because their owners did not habitually kill them for food. Slaughtering was, however, the fate of most pigs, and we know that more existed than the inventories show. There were only a few more pigs than sheep, but the distribution was quite different, for the former were widely kept in small numbers, not concentrated. Among the farmers of Hartford district during the 1690s, only 15 percent left none at their death (N-120). Barrels of pork, at a steady price of 70 shillings per barrel, were more common and brought in more money than barrels of beef.

Taken collectively, livestock provided almost all of the people's meat, supplemented by "dunghill fowl," domesticated geese, and wild game. They added milk and cheese to the diet; helped to furnish clothing and bedding with their wool and leather; supplied overland transportation and horse- or ox-power on the farms; and became in Connect-

[14] Hartford district probate records, 2:82-85.

icut the most important surplus commodity, thus enabling the infant colony to maintain a respectable standard of living despite the rapid growth of population and a prolonged depression.

Whereas livestock furnished the major export commodity, grains and other crops were primarily consumed at home. Connecticut's land, except in a few areas, was not fertile enough to produce a surplus. The yield of wheat per acre even in the relatively rich soil of the Connecticut River Valley did not exceed fifteen bushels and seven or eight was normal, with a mean of eight (N-23). With the price at 4 shillings, the gross income would be only £1.12 pay per acre; plowing alone cost 2 shillings. Along parts of the Sound the yields averaged as low as five and a half bushels per acre. In the same area, an acre produced less than ten bushels of corn (£1 to £1.5), rye from two and a half to nine, peas from three to eleven, and oats between four and thirteen, which meant, on the average, a pound per acre regardless of crop. The more productive northern Valley soils yielded as much as thirty bushels of corn and fifteen was average, earning nearly £2 per acre. Farmers there also obtained half again as much of the other crops. Still, the villagers themselves needed a good deal of this. Inventories usually, though not always, exclude "provisions," so that the quantities we find supposedly formed a surplus for local sale or export; besides, we can generally subtract grains in the house and so distinguish provisions. Doing so, the value per inventory averaged under £8, which would mean about £5 per adult male and hardly enough to feed the average family. The colonists had tried to produce an export crop, especially in the Hartford district, where the average per inventory had held £12 until the depression, but it then declined to only £4 by the nineties. The Fairfield area alone revived grain-growing after the low point of the mid-eighties. In the colony as a whole, grains contributed 7 percent to gross personal wealth before 1690 and but 5 percent at the end of the century.[15]

Just as essential to the people's survival as the utensils in the kitchen and fireplace were the farming and handicraft tools. Obviously the artisans needed them, and many farmers supplemented their income or increased their self-sufficiency with axes, awls, stills, looms, adzes, augers, saws, and the like. Ownership of a plow or access to one was as important as the oxen; a cart was used among well-established farmers; harrows appeared by 1657 and a dung fork by 1659. A man could

---

[15] Wheat "rust" ruined that crop temporarily. As farmers learned to destroy barberry bushes they limited the disease, but wheat returned only gradually, primarily near the coast.

get by with some cheap old tools but a farmer really needed to have £4 or £5 worth. By the end of the century they formed nearly 5 percent of personal inventoried wealth, and that understates the importance of tools since mills and tanneries were usually listed as real estate.

The relationship between wealth and ownership of tools was weaker than one might expect, because the critical factor was what one did for a living. Of course, young men and poor men seldom owned any, using whatever their employers provided, but the independent man had to buy his own. Property in tools increased quickly with age until men of forty had bought enough, and so also personal wealth and tools rose together until the former reached £50 and the latter £8. A few men of wealth invested much more, which raises the mean. The possessions of the different occupational groups we postpone for later treatment, with the observation that if £5 worth did in fact suffice for a farmer and if we eliminate estates listing no tools as defective (probably a son had claimed them), then fully 80 percent of the farmers had enough.

Even less important among the components of personal wealth were the occasional servants and slaves. Out of the nearly 1,500 men who left inventoried estates before 1700 only 68 owned one (or, if we add New London, 73 out of 1,515), less than 5 percent. Of the sixty-eight owners eleven were members of one family, so that fewer than 4 percent of the colony's families were concerned. Servants and slaves contributed only 1.5 percent to the personal wealth of the men leaving inventories and but 1.2 percent to that of all adult men.

The distribution of servants varied less by age or marital status than over time, by place, and according to occupation. The first settlers brought with them some British household servants and also a few free laborers to perform menial chores. Indeed, the servant class may

TABLE 3.10
Median and Mean Value of Tools (country pay)

By age	21–29	30–39	40–49	50–59	60–69	70+	
Mean £	1	3½	7	8½	6	6	
Median £	0	3½	6	7	6	4	

By wealth	£1–49	50–99	100–149	150–199	200–499	500+	All
Mean £	1	4	6	8	10	14	6
Median £	0	4	5½	8	8½	8½	4

SOURCE: Hartford district probated estates, seventeenth century.

well have been proportionately larger than at any later period; we lack precise data. We will discuss the labor force in a later chapter and need only observe here that the immigrants quickly set out creating their own labor supply, and unlike the Chesapeake settlers never found it necessary or economically rewarding to import indentured workers. Until the nineties servitude occurred incidentally, often accidentally, and slaves for life were almost unknown for forty or fifty years after the founding. During the fifties and sixties the inventories mention thirteen or fifteen white servants (in two cases the number remains unclear), a Negro "maid" evaluated at £25, which suggests a slave, an Indian "servant," a Negro woman and child at £22, and just one Negro man worth £30. Through the seventies and eighties short-term black, white, and red servants seem to have equaled the slaves in number, though the records often fail to distinguish between them. In the last decade black slaves finally became a majority. The inventories for that period name only three white servants and mention eleven Indians, three of whom were slaves: a man worth £30, a Spanish "servant for life," also £30, and a Spanish girl at £24. Since these figures are in country pay, the war in the West Indies probably cast off these victims, the worse for wear. In all this Connecticut followed the same pattern as the Chesapeake colonies. By the 1690s, among almost fifty blacks only two or three seem to have remained servants rather than slaves.

Who owned these laborers? Fewer than half of the masters were farmers and some of these doubled as artisans or public officials. One-fourth were men in trade; one-sixth were artisans, really manufacturers such as millers, distillers, and tanners; and the rest were professionals including three ministers. Obviously they had more wealth than the average. Clearly the possesssion of a bound laborer had become com-

TABLE 3.11
Ownership of Servile Labor, Seventeenth Century

Occupation	N	% of svts.	% of group	Personal wealth	N	% of svts.	% of group
Laborers	0	0	0	£1–99	3	4.1	0.4
Farmers	33	48.5	5.2	100–199	10	13.7	2.5
Artisans	12	17.6	4.2	200–499	39	53.4	14.4
Traders	17	25.0	24.3	500–999	14	19.2	32.6
Professionals	6	4.4	16.7	1,000+	7	9.6	53.8
Total	68	99.9			73	100.0	

SOURCE: Estate inventories.

mon among men of large property, though not all of them bought
one. Probably most of the slaves performed household chores. Of those
we know about one-third were female and of the rest half were boys.
Geographically they were concentrated in the larger and more economically diversified towns: the trading centers of New Haven, Milford, Hartford, Wethersfield, Fairfield, Stratford, and New London
contained more than three-fourths. Thus they tended to be urban rather
than rural in a society predominantly rural. Until 1700, then, slavery
and servitude remained unimportant. It was familiar to the people of
a few towns and common among well-to-do men, but almost unknown to most of the people in the colony except only in the familiar,
voluntary form of apprenticeship.

The distribution of ships and trading stock resembled that of servants in that they correlated highly with wealth and, obviously, even
more with occupation. Shipping remained unimportant during the
colony's first century except in a very few towns, and even there only
a few men were shipowners. Stock, on the other hand, contributed 6
percent to gross personal wealth. Of this, a small amount belonged to
farmers and lesser artisans, both of whom produced a surplus for sale,
particularly lumber and lumber products but also such items as leather,
wool, cider, and cloth in the case of farmers, and the articles made by
tanners, weavers, tailors, smiths, distillers, and shoemakers. However,
most of the stock belonged to traders, especially the principal merchants. Two-thirds of the total was held by thirty individuals, primarily
living in New Haven and Hartford (we lack data for New London),
all possessing at least £200 and usually over £700 in personal wealth.

There remain for our consideration among the components of wealth,
cash, silver, and debts, which constituted the money supply of the
colony. Specie coin, as is well known, drained into overseas trade and
scarcely circulated outside of the commercial towns. The colony did
not issue paper money, or money of any sort during the seventeenth
century, nor did banks exist. People therefore sometimes invested in
silver articles, valued a little above silver coin for their workmanship.
These two combined to supply the owners with a source of cash in
emergencies. The inventories may convey a fairly accurate idea of the
amount per capita if we include women, whose gold and silver ornaments counteract the usual age bias. Cash and silver combined came
to only a little over 2 percent of the total personal wealth, about £3.5
per estate. Most people had none. Two dozen men, fewer than 2 percent of all the decedents, had 60 percent of the total. These were
mostly merchants, though they included an innkeeper, four large manufacturers, a couple of farmers, and two ministers—Samuel Hooker,

TABLE 3.12
Occupation, Wealth, and Cash, Seventeenth Century

Occupation	% with cash	Personal wealth	% with cash
Laborers	0	£1–99	0.4
Farmers	5.2	100–199	2.5
Artisans	4.2	200–499	14.4
Traders	24.3	500–999	32.6
Professionals	16.7	1,000+	53.8

SOURCE: Estate inventories.

son of the eminent founder, and Nicholas Street of New Haven whose father was an English justice of the peace and to whom the records refer as "Gent." One can read through inventory after inventory without a trace of a precious metal except perhaps for a silver spoon. Even among the married men of thirty and up (excluding the elderly) 72 percent owned none, if the Hartford district is typical. Five persons— 1 percent of the total—held over 40 percent. Obviously the great majority of men got along without money, and, as we discussed earlier, substituted a barter system, exchanges of service kept track of informally, or credit.

Finally, the distribution of debts receivable resembled that of money in that a few individuals held most of it. Five percent of the inventories in the extensive Hartford probate district contained 60 percent of the total debts for the whole period before 1700. The biggest creditors were merchants, although we find also, among the larger ones, five farmers, two millers, a tanner, an innkeeper, a public official, and a minister. Two-thirds of the people had none, the distribution of course correlating with economic class (see Appendix 3E).

During the years before 1680 in the Hartford district about half of the men's estates included debts receivable and the same proportion owned money. The balance, however, favored the asset side, because although most estates ended in debt the large ones more than made up the difference. Presumably this reflects the fact that some fortunate immigrants had assets in England or brought over a surplus for investment decidedly in excess of their liabilities, an advantage that they retained, whereas some of the smaller property-holders had to borrow. That these liabilities originated during the early years is suggested by the situation in New Haven, where our data on this point are much better. Before 1660 debts payable were four times more than debts receivable, but by the 1670s the two had become equal. In both areas debts of all sorts dropped dramatically after 1680 but liabilities declined even more than assets. In New Haven the mean of debts receivable per inventory decreased to only £7 and of payable to £11.

This downward trend ceased during the 1690s, no doubt with better economic conditions. In the end the poorest men (judging still from probate records) ended in debt, those of medium properties pulled even, and the wealthiest became almost debt-free, with assets greatly exceeding liabilities. The colony as a whole, then, may well have ended with a surplus with respect to the outside world, whereas it began in debt. However, by 1700 the sums involved were quite small.

The decline in debts as a proportion of assets and of liabilities may strike the reader as a good thing. It probably was not. The most likely explanation for the change is that the colony lost a good deal of money in the process of settlement, the quantity shown in the heavy debt burden during the first years, followed by a withdrawal from the foreign market in the later period of depression. Combined with the scarcity of coin, the decrease in debts of all sorts suggests a descent to a near-subsistence economy paralleling the decline in the value of inventoried personal wealth. The final recovery reversed this unfavorable trend but did not provide the people with an adequate supply of money or credit.

We have seen that occupation affected the various forms and quantities of property left by men at their death. Later chapters will discuss the occupational groups in Connecticut's society, so we need here only to sketch their relationship to the distribution of wealth during the seventeenth century. We want to know how much property each occupational group possessed and to what extent the differences in occupation affected differences in wealth.

Appendix 3F contains the data on personal wealth. Laborers, including soldiers and sailors, almost always belonged to the poorest category and during the early years the two were nearly synonymous. Their large numbers at that time accounts to a considerable extent for the inequality of wealth. During the following years they became proportionately fewer either through emigration or their ability quickly to enter farming or crafts not requiring much capital. Almost by definition they did not own real estate as long as they remained simply laborers, so their decrease in relative numbers helped to reduce the inequality in real property. Their small possessions included, above all, consumption goods, especially in the form of clothing since they seldom kept house, living as we would say in furnished rooms.

Farmers formed over 40 percent of the men leaving inventories or, if we excluded the categories "unknowns" and "retired," nearly half. Since few were really poor and few were well-to-do, their property was quite evenly distributed, the top 10 percent owning only about 30 percent of the wealth. They particularly benefited from the rise in the value of land, reflected in their probated estates, though that pleased their children more than the parents. The distinctive feature of their property-holding obviously lay in capital, not in money but in land and livestock. Therefore the proportion of their wealth in the form of consumer goods was comparatively small, though not low in absolute value. The farmers' property even in personal estate was relatively stable over time, so they contributed to the general tendency toward both equality and continuity.

Artisans included a larger array of subspecies than did farmers. Many were quite young and poor while some were very well-off. During the 1690s in particular, one out of every four men with personal estates of above £500 was an artisan. Probably without as much land to fall back on they lacked the farmers' security, yet could take full advantage of an economic upturn. This property was almost as equally distributed as that of the farmers' and in most respects they resembled them rather than the nonagricultural elements of the colony's society. Indeed, the two groups overlapped, exchanged personnel, and intermarried so much as almost to form a single whole, except perhaps in the larger trading towns.

Connecticut during the seventeenth century contained relatively few professional men other than ministers. While a few left quite small estates the majority were prosperous, although the depression eliminated them from the richest group. As we have seen, only they habitually owned large libraries and their household goods exceeded in value those of any other set of men. As a rule their incomes, or the arrangements made for ministers, enabled them to own farms that helped to dispel financial worries. Probably few actually operated the farms themselves, and instead either their neighbors did so in exchange for services or they hired local help supplemented by servants or slaves.

Finally the traders, though few in number, contributed disproportionately to the colony's wealth and economic inequality, owning, in fact, a fourth of the personal property. During the half-century before the depression they supplied half of the colony's richest men in terms of personal wealth and during the depression they almost alone perpetuated an economic upper class. That decade did hit them hard, however, and in fact they almost disappear from the probate records, probably withdrawing temporarily from trade in favor of agriculture. Indeed, many of them had always invested in real estate. Even in the nineties their share of total wealth did not return to the level of the years before 1680.

The traders' property is interesting not only for its quantity but also for its composition. Traders held most of the specie and debts, almost all of the ships, a great proportion of the stock in trade, and the largest number of servants. They generally left book-buying to the professional men but purchased unusual amounts of other consumer goods. Since they clustered in the principal towns they constituted an economic upper class few in number but great in influence, especially when one adds the professionals.

To sum up: these last two occupational groups much exceeded any of the others in total per capita wealth whether measured by the means, medians, or proportion holding large estates, despite the farmers' land. Because of that land the farmers ranked a respectable third, with the craftsmen considerably behind and the rest of the people still farther down the ladder. Laborers at the bottom owned scarcely one-tenth as much property as did the traders. Within each group the distribution was quite equal, the top 10 percent owning a third or a fourth of the total, except for the traders, among whom a comparatively few men stood out. The high level of inequality in Connecticut's society considered as a whole therefore owed a good deal, though far from everything, to occupational diversity.

The presence in Connecticut of traders, professional men, and craftsmen reveals the existence of towns other than agricultural villages. Moreover, the latter included several species, from the newly established settlements and poor upland communities to older, prosperous centers. These differed in the kinds of inhabitants, their functions, and economic characteristics.

No Boston developed in the colony, but even in the seventeenth century it contained commercial towns that we can call urban. Unlike modern cities they did not exist independently of the country but served primarily as market towns for the farmers. Almost half of their population consisted of farmers and many of the other residents owned a lot large enough for an orchard, a garden, and pasture for some livestock. These urban communities consumed some of the area's surplus food and other commodities, exported the rest, and produced or imported what the farmers could not provide. In addition to these and other functions they became the seats of county courts and political activity, thus attracting public officials and lawyers; they were the centers of culture; and because of all these advantages they contained most of the social upper class. Thus their small populations—not much over a thousand—disguise their true significance: functionally they acted as true cities.

Because they contained so many farmers and remained so small they did not differ from the prosperous agricultural towns as much as one might suppose. The latter contained just as many laborers, the same proportion of artisans, and almost as much property because of the land; indeed, on the tax records they appear wealthier. Differences did exist, however. The rural labor force consisted almost entirely of local boys, whereas the trading towns attracted more migrants and bought more slaves. The craftsmen included a greater variety and skilled specialists such as shipwrights, masons, joiners, and silversmiths. The villages had their shopkeepers but only these towns contained large-scale merchants. Naturally, almost all of the trading stock, ships, coins, and debts receivable (but not books) were concentrated there, and here lived the colony's richest men who built the most elegant and well-furnished houses. Finally, because of these relatively wealthy men, economic inequality was a distinctive characteristic: the top 10 percent, according to the inventories, had nearly half of the personal wealth and over two-fifths of the total property. By comparison with true cities that is practically an equality of fortunes, but in Connecticut it visibly identified an upper class.

Before 1700 we can assign only a few towns to this urban category: Hartford, New Haven, Fairfield, Milford, and presumably New London. A second species consisted of other towns established by the first settlers, located on good soil, and favorably situated for growth, in particular Stamford, Stratford, Branford, and Guilford along the coast, the river towns of Wethersfield and Windsor, and Farmington. All of these developed considerable nonfarm activities especially in the crafts, and served as secondary market centers. Their wealth came principally from the land, which produced some highly prosperous farmers but not the richest traders. The median value of their property as reported to the legislature actually exceeded that of the trading towns, but estate inventories give the latter an edge because of their great personal wealth. The absence of all but a few rich merchants made the difference and shows most clearly in the comparatively equal distribution of property in these farm towns: the top 10 percent owned only about a third of the wealth, well under the concentration in the urban centers.

The third and last type consisted of new settlements and of those located on somewhat inferior land.[16] Their newness resulted in a somewhat younger population, at least for a time, that limited their wealth and tended toward an equality of property; those with inferior land, of course, did not attract men with capital or produce great wealth. The frontier towns included, for example, Middletown, Green-

[16] Daniels in *Connecticut Town* provides a full description of types of soil and the effects on the towns. His conclusions correspond with the data from inventories except in the case of Stonington, which seems to have prospered despite rather indifferent soil.

wich, Wallingford, Derby, Glastonbury, and Woodbury, while communities such as Haddam, Preston, Killingsworth, and Simsbury lacked natural resourses. They were therefore poor, with the fewest professional men, and large propertyowners, many more small estates, and low levels of wealth. Naturally that meant a relative equality, the top 10 percent owning less than 30 percent of the personal wealth, which could not have reconciled the people to their poverty. Some of these towns would change with time, but meanwhile they offered few opportunities for the ambitious men.

These variations by town type had cultural and political implications for the residents and affected the kinds of lives that they led. Nevertheless, on the whole the towns belonged to the same broad family: not very flourishing, predominantly agricultural and middle class, with few large property holders. Only in Hartford did the wealthiest 10 percent own half of the wealth. Whereas in a colony such as Massachusetts or Virginia the existence of a major city or a staple-crop agriculture could greatly increase the level of inequality for the whole society, in Connecticut their absence worked toward a comparative uniformity.

We now proceed to examine the most important influences affecting men's circumstances with respect to property, status, and general condition: age and marital status. Chapter Two outlined stages in the life cycle and suggested their significance, so we need only to recapitulate briefly. The first stage, as the colonists viewed it, began when the young male reached age sixteen, when he became subject to military service and capable of a man's work, as evidenced by the £18 assessment on his "poll." A further phase of the same stage followed when he turned twenty-one, legally of age. He might then still remain a dependent poll but he could become an independent householder, paying his own tax and achieving somewhat higher status. This stage ended with marriage. For some men, therefore, it never ceased. Usually the older bachelor continued to depend on others, with little property or income. Exceptions do exist of men fully independent, even of high position, remaining single all their lives so that the overall average wealth of bachelors did increase with age, but these cases are rare.

The second stage then, began with marriage. One's property jumped because of the joint inheritance and because the couple, as full, respectable members of the community, had access to credit and shared in any division of land. Young parents gained ground financially despite the fact that their children cost them money, for we find that childless couples did not acquire any more wealth than those with children.

Men entered the third stage when the family contained teen-agers.

The greater expense was more than balanced by the financial benefits. The estimated contribution of £18 minus costs would seem so advantageous to the parents that one wonders why anyone ever spent money on servants or slaves, until we remember that the children would presently be claiming that profit when they received their share of the estate. Until that time, however, net income per child clearly exceeded expenditures and the value of the family's property continued to rise. The family with adult children (age twenty-one for boys, eighteen for girls) improved its financial position still further as the father, now nearing fifty, reached his maximum earning power and the children added their share as long as they remained single.

The next to the last stage began when the children married and the father and mother became grandparents—virtually the same event, unlike the sequence today. At that point the inheritances given might begin to exceed the profits earned, varying greatly from one family to another. The aging man sometimes remained active all his life both economically and in his services to the community, or he might gradually withdraw. The final stage, of retirement, came when he had divested himself of all or much of his capital, such as land, livestock, tools, and ships, retaining only consumers goods and perhaps some money, especially debts receivable. The old couples generally paid their way but sometimes ended as they began, depending on others for their necessities.

We now describe the personal and real wealth of each of these groups, examine their consumption goods as a key indication of their standards of living, and finally combine all of this information in a definitive description of economic classes. As we have observed, most young adults owned very little property. In Fairfield, among the men in the twenties, one-third did not appear on the evaluation list at all and two-thirds owned estates of under £100, including land. Almost half of that group on the Middletown rate list paid no tax and only one person out of twenty-four was rated at over £100. In Windsor, all but one was assessed for under £50 and about half owned no taxable property whatever. These propertyless adults included recent immigrants, servants, and unmarried sons not yet independent. The inventories reveal that such men left substantial estates only when appraisers estimated their share of the parental property that they would have received had they lived. A typical estate of a local son was that of Nathaniel Pond, Junior, of Windsor, who died in King Philip's War at twenty-five, leaving eleven acres of land worth £30, a horse with saddle and bridle, a cow, heifer, and steer, some hay and corn, a Bible, clothes, and six augers. Jobana Smith of Farmington, another casuality, left only £49 of which £17 consisted of land and £10 of debts including £6 coming to him from the "country" for his service. The immigrants who were not yet members of the community usually had no land. John Scott of Hartford owned £29 worth of property of which £10 consisted of debts, half due him for clearing land. He also had a mare and colt, the ubiquitous Bible, some corn, a few farming tools, and £5 in clothing. He owed £21, reducing his net worth almost to zero.[17] The median personal wealth of young single men hovered around £30 pay throughout the century. Of that sum very nearly half consisted of consumption articles and another sizable chunk of debts receivable. Thus the forty-eight such men who died during the seventies (excluding one anomaly) averaged £31 in personal estate of which £5 consisted of debts, and they owed £8 apiece. Moreover, their median real estate was not much above zero. Of course, some did own land and a house and they often had prospects. Meanwhile, as a group, they contributed little to the wealth of the colony except their labor, the fruits of which often benefited men other than themselves.

The low value of this property did not mean that they lived in hovels, lacked food, or led lives that were nasty, brutish, and short. In the first place over half of them resided with their families and fared as well as they, which meant comfort as often as not. Others served as hired men to the farmers or apprentices to craftsmen, typically living in the houses of the masters at a level only a little below that of the sons; they had clothes, a bed of sorts, ample food, and wages. The crucial question for them was their future fate, which we will examine in Chaper Five. As for those who were trying to support themselves as independent laborers, we should observe that the going wage of 2 shillings per day even in country pay was probably twice the minimum for survival, permitting a margin against sporadic unemployment. Finally, the consumer goods essential for a single man were limited, not over £10 or £12 for sufficiency, whereas the actual median for men in their twenties was £15. Taking all their property into account, it would seem that half of the single men supplied their own subsistence, the rest remaining poor and in some degree dependent as long as they remained in that status.

A dramatic change occurred when a man married, especially after the birth of the first child provided the proof of permanence. Personal wealth then tripled. We can estimate the overall average value of the newlyweds' inheritance from our knowledge that the median wealth

---

[17] Hartford district probate records, 3:151, 165, 4:21.

of men in their fifties and sixties was about £360 country pay. Subtracting the widow's third leaves £240 and if there were four children the eldest would receive nearly £100 and each of the others almost £50. Therefore our young couple (assuming the man to be a younger son) would inherit £96 at once and potentially another £48 eventually from the widows, if their shares remained intact. To this we must add in some cases a grant from the town consisting of a home lot and a division of the common land. The mean personal wealth of men with young children was £130 and real estate added an equal sum overall. By the 1690's their median, which better reflects the situation of the great majority, had reached £280.[18]

As to their standard of living as revealed by consumption goods, we must pause to consider what families needed. According to Gloria L. Main, the rock-bottom survival limit in seventeenth-century Maryland was £3 sterling, equal to £6 pay, including two beds but exclusive of clothing.[19] In Connecticut the poorest such men owned beds worth £3.10 (the median), the difference coming in the bedding. Clothing for a man at that level cost around £3. I would add a third small bed because the size of the family exceeded that in Maryland. Our requirement for a bare subsistence level in consumption goods for a family with young children thus becomes about £15. Comfort needed several times that amount. G. Main's estimate calls for £14.3 sterling or £28.6 pay, but we find beds and bedding alone worth £8 each (the median for men of average property) and at that level a man commonly owned four. Moreover, his clothing would rise to £5, totaling £50 pay. In

TABLE 3.13

Consumption Goods, Married Men with £200 Net Personal Wealth
(percentages, country pay)

	£1–69	70–99	100–139	140–199	200+	Median	N
1660–1679	7	25	34	19	5	118	68
1680–1689	5	19	28½	24	24	126	63
1690–1699	9	11	35	30½	15	136	92

NOTE: The smallest estates probably resulted from the burning of the house, a daughter's recent dowry, or a widow's claim. John Whitehead of Branford (d. 1695) apparently had owned only £9 in household goods and no clothing, but his widow had taken £56 worth. Thus, at the time of their death men possessed *at least* as much as the table shows.

[18] For the distributions, see Appendix 3H.
[19] *Tobacco Colony*, 176.

between we establish a category of subsistence plus at £30, and above the comfort level a well-to-do man required £60 or £70, the latter being the sum almost invariably invested by men with personal estates of over £200. Those with over £200 who had teen-aged and grown children, but not grandchildren, commonly owned more than £100 in consumption articles, and this becomes our standard for their well-to-do level, and so on down for these older fathers, at each level exceeding the requirement for a man with young children.

Tentatively, then, the fathers of young children and those with older children fell into the following classes according to their standard of living, insofar as consumption goods reveal the situation. The figures in Table 3.14 indicate that among parents of young children in seventeenth-century Connecticut, one-tenth lacked sufficient consumption goods for an adequate standard of living, though of course that did not mean an entire absence of necessities. Nearly half raised their children in comfort. Parents with older children had improved upon even that, no doubt with the help of the children themselves; almost none fell short of the minimum. At the top, one-eighth of the young fathers and one-third of the older men had £100 in consumption articles (perhaps $4,000 to $5,000 today). The reader will recall that these are minimums, that they omit all clothing except the father's and

TABLE 3.14
Distribution of Consumption Goods, Seventeenth Century

	Young fathers			Older fathers	
	N	%		N	%
Poor					
(under £15)	45	10.5	(under £20)	15	3.5
Subsistence					
(£15–29)	79	18.4	(£20–39)	65	16.0
Subsistence plus					
(£30–49)	105	24.4	(£40–79)	135	33.3
Comfortable					
(£50–69)	96	22.3	(£80–99)	58	14.3
Well-off					
(£70–99)	50	11.6	(£100–199)	107	26.4
Luxury					
(£100–199)	43	10.0	(£200+)	27	6.7
(£200+)	12	2.8		—	—
Total	430	100.0		407	100.2
Median		£47			£76

all personal articles from jewelry to toys unless these belonged to the father. Also, some of the poor households belonged to families in a better economic position who could help out. If we combine the bare-subsistence group with the poor, perhaps one-fourth of these families fell below a truly desirable level, requiring occasional help from family or neighbors, and the orphans would begin life at a disadvantage.

The real estate of the young fathers varied so much over time and with their occupations that generalizations are hazardous. Obviously, whereas single men frequently owned none, the married men generally had at least a small farm, the overall median being £132, which would average around sixty acres. For reasons we have seen, during the early years even these heads of families might use land without owning it and the depression prevented over a third from acquiring more than a house and a small lot, so they might still have to rely on common land. However, by 1700 almost all of them had at least a little real property. Men who made their living by some skill other than farming owned only half as much as the farmers, accounting for almost all of the landless and those with just a house and lot. By the nineties they too seldom lacked enough land to provide for their families, taken with their income, while the farmers even at this early stage in their life cycle owned £185 worth, or about eighty acres, and not more than one out of five still fell short of their needs.

The young fathers' economic progress accompanied an advance in social status. This appeared not in conspicuous offices, which came later (only 3 or 4 percent held positions such as deputies and captains), but in less important capacities such as sergeants in the militia or the numerous town posts. The newly married couple often now joined the church and baptized their babies, thus confirming their respectability. Another dozen years and the community might reward them with more honorable positions.

As the children entered their teens and the parents turned forty, a further economic advance usually occurred. The fathers of teen-aged children added somewhat to their personal property, especially to consumption goods. They needed another £10 worth to raise them to a level of living well above subsistence and they in fact doubled that. Almost none remained really poor. The principal reason for that success lay in their addition of twenty acres or so of land, craftsmen as well as farmers purchasing more throughout the century. By 1690 virtually no one in this group lacked land. This gain must have reflected the father's abilities, which by now would have peaked, but also in part if not primarily the contribution of both sons and daughters to the labor force.

They did not become leaders of the town as often as one might suppose—only one in ten. For this there were two reasons: first, Connecticut contained a sufficient number of qualified older men because of the long life expectancy. Second, most fathers of teen-aged children had their hands full. Lesser town duties they could continue to discharge but not ones that took them away from the shop or field. But as they became a little older both circumstances changed. If some children were grown but not yet married, and if the man had passed the test of minor offices, the town now needed him and he could safely leave home. More than one in five men over fifty held important positions within the town or colony.

Men at that stage continued to increase their propertyholding since they still profited from their children's labor. They now owned typically about £150 in personal wealth and very few had less than £50 worth. The value of their consumer goods rose to meet the increased expenses to such good effect that nearly half lived not only well above the subsistence level but in comfort, and fully a fourth were well-off. Their real estate also expanded, averaging almost a hundred acres by the end of the century, and very few lacked enough for their families.

As the children married and produced children of their own they needed their share of the family property. The grandparents commonly met that need, as the land owned by the young fathers testifies. Nevertheless, most of them continued to acquire additional property for another ten years or even longer, except during the depression. Indeed, men in their sixties owned more real property than did any other age group and more consumer goods, too, despite their presumably shrinking households. Thus the estates expanded as fast as young children called for help. A great many grandfathers remained active in positions of leadership as well, almost one in four holding or having held some responsible post. We know of deputies, deacons, justices, and even militia officers who clung to their offices until they died, blocking the way for the young men.

On the other hand some began to withdraw from these and other responsibilities—to retire—even in their sixties, but particularly after they reached seventy. Men beyond that age owned scarcely more personal estate than the young fathers, though they held on to most of their household effects so that they lived decently. They retained a good deal of land (a point we will discuss in Chapter Six), dividing only a third of it, on the average, among their children. Even this oldest group, at the close of their long lives, seldom fell into poverty.[20]

[20] During the 1690s we have inventories for forty-eight men who died aged seventy

TABLE 3.15
Levels of Living, Pre-1660 (percentages)

	Single	Young fathers	Older fathers	Grandfathers	Retired	N	%
Estate Inventories							
Poor	17	7	3	0	0	27	15.8
Subsistence	10	32	10	2	2	56	32.7
Subsistence plus	4	22	15	2	3	46	26.9
Comfortable	1	12	5	5	2	27	15.8
Well-off	0	5	9	1	0	15	8.8
Totals	32	78	44	10	7	171	100.0
Living Population							
Poor	19	3	1	0	0	23	23.0
Subsistence	11	14	5	1	1	32	32.0
Subsistence plus	4	10	9	1	1	25	25.0
Comfortable	1	6	4	2	0	13	13.0
Well-off	0	2	5	0	0	7	7.0
Total	35	35	24	4	2	100	100.0

Our summary of seventeenth-century Connecticut begins with a discussion of the material welfare of the people over time. We ask, how many men could support themselves and their families without relying on others, and what proportion did so more than adequately, or even comfortably? Our measures include a combination of consumption goods, personal wealth, and real estate, especially land (for details, see Appendix 3J).

We open by presenting the material for the earliest years, before 1660. Table 3.15 furnishes the actual figures from estate inventories, and the right-hand column shows the percentage of the estates in each level of wealth. Table 3.16 transforms the data to approximate that of the living population, using for the proportion of each marital group an informed guess. That table gives percentages. It shows the large proportion of poor young men dependent upon others. Married men, however, almost always achieved a subsistence level, and the fathers of

---

to seventy-nine and nine over eighty. Of the septuagenarians, thirty left estates of over £200 (pay) and forty of £100 or more. Only two were worth less than £25 and four under £50. Two out of the nine died in poverty whereas six still owned £200. Combined, then, 7 percent died impoverished, 11 percent probably and 18 percent perhaps required some help, but the rest could support themselves and over three out of five must have lived quite comfortably.

TABLE 3.16
Levels of Living, Seventeenth Century (percentages)

	Young fathers					Older fathers				
	poor	subs.	subs. +	comf.	well-off	poor	subs.	subs. +	comf.	well-off
1640–1659	9.0	41.0	28.2	15.4	6.4	6.8	22.7	34.1	15.9	20.5
1660–1669	5.3	34.2	26.3	28.9	5.3	8.7	37.0	39.1	10.9	4.3
1670–1679	16.7	31.5	33.3	9.3	9.3	17.9	19.6	32.1	16.1	14.3
1680–1689	25.5	22.4	29.6	12.2	10.2	13.0	20.7	32.6	19.6	14.1
1690–1699	9.0	29.2	32.6	20.1	9.0	7.0	22.1	37.8	18.6	14.5

SOURCE: Estate inventories.

older children ordinarily lived better than that. If one looks at the entire population one finds over half living below or a little above subsistence, but if one excludes the bachelors we see that only 6 percent were dependent and 60 percent lived safely above subsistence, half of whom achieved comfort. The young dependents, if they lived, could thus reasonably look forward to a better life: the long trip across the ocean seemed to have paid off.

The reader can trace detailed changes in Appendix 3K. Here we will simply note the bare outlines with some special attention to the fathers. The decade of the sixties brought a general improvement, the proportion of poor men shrinking to only 16 percent, with a spectacular increase in the comfortable. The next twenty years reversed that trend, the dependents again forming almost a fourth of the population, now with many older men in that category, and a heavy loss among the formerly comfortable: perhaps the long trip had not been so worthwhile! But at last the 1690s brought better times.

The two key age groups, the young and older fathers, reveal the changes over time, especially in the numbers under "poor" and "comfortable." The older men, over age forty, weathered the depression better, even increasing their wealth at the top, and grandfathers did likewise. By the end, the fathers had regained the position that they doubtless thought normal, with almost everyone above the subsistence level and nearly a third living in comfort.

The historian sees what he or she looks for. If we depict the people of Connecticut at any given moment, especially the moments during the years between King Philip's War and the accession of William III, a gloomy picture appears. One-quarter of the people seem impoverished and almost as many barely met what we would call a minimum standard of health and decency. Anyone examining a tax list, and aware of those omitted for one reason or another, would confirm that impression and note also the absence of large estates, suggestive of general poverty. The per capita wealth in personal property was only half of what the first generation had brought with them. If the index of inequality seems low, that simply confirms a situation in which few prospered. The complaints of a general declension received confirmation in the failure of the colony to hold its own; either God was punishing or Satan bewitching them.

But that portrait, if it does not quite deserve the ashcan, needs a new eye and fresh paint. We must take a longer view of the century and adopt a dynamic rather than a static approach, substituting for the snapshot a panorama such as artists once drew of an entire river on a long rolled canvas. The immigrants included the usual large proportion of unattached young men, some brought over as servants but most arriving on their own initiative in hopes of a fortune. The majority of that sort failed and died or left. The rest found wives, generally after age thirty since fewer single women than men had come over. The newlyweds settled down on farms and merged into the others of their age group who came with their parents and, being members of the community from the start, married younger and obtained land more quickly. Thus while the initial settlement included a large proportion of poor men, those who stayed in the colony did not remain poor. The rest of the newcomers consisted of married men with families, generally in their thirties and forties, who brought with them enough personal wealth and skills to assure a decent living, especially since they could obtain as much land as they could use. A few among them were quite well-to-do and generally with other advantages, especially in education, which placed them at the top of the status order. Thus the distribution of wealth and status were highly unequal, but the society was in fact basically equalitarian in that the great majority of permanent residents became respectable propertyowners. Indeed, as we shall see later, even some quite ordinary men achieved positions of leadership.

This rather euphoric period lasted only for the first generation, the duration varying from place to place. Connecticut did not produce instant fortunes and many people left, going either to other colonies or back to England. Some of the men with capital lost it and withdrew, especially after the defeat of Charles I, at which point immigration from England almost ceased. Without the stimulus of new capital and the demands of newcomers for various products (such as livestock) and services, the economy declined and per capita personal wealth dropped by at least one-third, affecting every age and wealth class. The depression was especially evident in trading goods, capital, and the value of livestock. Fortunately the land remained, and practically everybody could obtain, upon marriage, enough acreage to supply food for the family. The ability of people to feed themselves and to provide most other essentials enabled them to survive the long period of poor foreign markets and the calamity of King Philip's War; consumption goods actually increased. After that war opened much of the colony to settlement and after the Glorious Revolution assured the colony's autonomy the clouds began to lift. The West Indies provided a better market and people began cautiously to move into the new areas. The land under cultivation continued to rise, personal wealth stopped declining and, indeed, for the younger family men increased; the value of consumption goods rose. The recovery particularly benefited artisans and professionals, who had suffered much more than farmers, though not traders whose prosperity was delayed until after 1700. In terms of total wealth, the men of 1699 had recovered from the depression. The colony still had its poor, now increased by slaves and thus collectively lower in status. Its leading families remained, though they had not fully regained their earlier position, at least as measured by wealth. These two groups at either end of the social scale tended to live in the trading towns. Elsewhere slavery was still unknown, most of the poor were young local men who would soon obtain property and status, the wealthy were rare, and heads of households clustered around a level safely above subsistence, in a relative equality of circumstances. Not a bad start for a society of ordinary folk who had made it on their own.

Distribution of Real Property, Living Population
(PERCENTAGES, COUNTRY PAY)

	Pre-1660	1660–1679	1680–1689	1690–1699
None	39.5	25.5	25.5	13.0
£1–19	9.5	9.0	5.5	6.0
20–49	17.0	18.0	8.5	13.0
50–99	12.5	22.0	16.0	16.5
100–199	13.5	12.0	19.5	22.0
200–499	5.5	9.5	20.0	23.5
500+	2.5	4.0	5.0	6.0

DISTRIBUTION OF REAL PROPERTY, MEN AGED 30–60

	Pre-1660	1660–1679	1680–1689	1690–1699
None	15.3	8.5	12.6	4.8
£1–19	6.3	5.5	5.0	2.9
20–49	23.4	19.5	7.0	6.4
50–99	16.2	19.5	16.1	14.4
100–199	22.5	24.0	23.1	26.6
200–499	10.8	17.5	28.6	34.9
500+	5.4	5.5	7.5	9.9
N	111	200	199	312
Median £	68	95	140	181
Mean £	121	154	233	238
Share top 10%	44.4	41.2	42.8	33.4

Consumer Goods by Gross Personal Wealth over Time
(COUNTRY PAY)

CONSUMPTION	1–19 N	%	20–49 N	%	50–99 N	%	100–199 N	%	200–499 N	%	500+ N	%	Total N	%
Pre-1660														
1–19	14	100.0	16	66.7	17	34.0	2	6.1	0		0		49	29.2
20–34	0		7	29.2	16	32.0	8	24.2	2	5.3	0		33	19.6
35–49	0		1	4.2	13	26.0	10	30.3	1	2.6	0		25	14.9
50–99	0		0		4	8.0	11	33.3	21	55.3	3	33.3	39	23.2
100–199	0		0		0		2	6.1	12	31.6	3	33.3	17	10.1
200+	0		0		0		0		2	5.3	3	33.3	5	3.0
Total	14		24		50		33		38		9		168	100.0
1660–1679														
1–19	46	100.0	37	63.8	13	14.9	0		0		0		96	25.7
20–34	0		17	29.3	39	44.8	8	9.1	1	1.4	1	4.3	66	17.7
35–49	0		4	6.9	22	25.3	25	28.4	3	4.2	2	8.7	56	15.0
50–99	0		0		13	14.9	49	55.7	30	42.3	4	17.4	96	25.7
100–199	0		0		0		6	6.8	33	46.5	9	39.1	48	12.9
200+	0		0		0		0		4	5.6	7	30.4	11	2.9
Total	46		58		87		82		71		23		373	99.9
1680–1689														
1–19	45	100.0	53	57.0	10	10.3	0		0		0		108	24.7
20–34	0		31	33.3	34	35.1	0		0		0		65	14.9
35–49	0		9	9.7	35	36.1	19	15.2	1	1.5	0		64	14.6
50–99	0		0		18	18.6	95	76.0	20	29.4	2	22.2	135	30.9
100–199	0		0		0		11	8.8	37	54.4	2	22.2	50	11.4
200+	0		0		0		0		10	14.7	5	55.6	15	3.4
Total	45		93		97		125		68		9		437	99.9
1690–1699														
1–19	51	100.0	47	59.5	16	13.0			0		0		114	22.2
20–34	0		30	38.0	39	31.7	9	5.8	0		0		79	15.4
35–49	0		2	2.5	37	30.1	27	17.3	3	3.3	0		69	13.4
50–99	0		0		31	25.2	105	67.3	21	22.8	1	7.7	158	30.7
100–199	0		0		0		15	9.6	60	65.2	5	38.5	80	15.6
200+	0		0		0		0		7	7.6	7	53.8	14	2.7
Total	51		79		123		156		91		13		514	100.0

CONSUMER GOODS BY AGE, PROBATE INVENTORIES

	21–29	30–39	40–49	50–59	60–69	70+	Total	%
Pre-1660								
1–19	15	13	5	3	1	0	37	25.7
20–34	3	15	4	2	2	1	27	18.7
35–49	1	11	3	2	4	1	22	15.3
50–99	1	9	13	8	4	1	36	25.0
100–199	0	2	8	6	1	0	17	11.8
200+	0	0	1	2	2	0	5	3.5
Total	20	50	34	23	14	3	144	100.0
1660–1679								
1–19	47	6	8	4	1	5	71	21.0
20–34	12	12	11	11	5	10	61	18.0
35–49	1	12	15	13	7	5	53	15.7
50–99	5	8	29	31	15	6	94	27.8
100–199	0	6	4	19	15	4	48	14.2
200+	0	0	5	1	2	3	11	3.3
Total	65	44	72	79	45	33	338	100.0
1680–1689								
1–19	25	17	19	7	13	17	98	24.2
20–34	7	13	13	12	8	8	61	15.1
35–49	5	8	14	9	13	12	61	15.1
50–99	7	17	22	15	35	25	121	29.9
100–199	1	7	11	6	17	7	49	12.1
200+	0	1	1	5	5	3	15	3.7
Total	45	63	80	54	91	72	405	100.1
1690–1699								
1–19	37	17	18	7	6	13	98	20.3
20–34	7	21	17	11	6	10	72	14.9
35–49	3	10	27	13	7	6	66	13.7
50–99	13	30	37	36	21	16	153	31.7
100–199	1	10	18	26	15	9	79	16.4
200+	0	0	1	4	6	3	14	2.9
Total	61	88	118	97	61	57	482	99.9

Continued

CONSUMER GOODS BY AGE, LIVING POPULATION

	21–29	30–39	40–49	50–59	60–69	70+	Total	%
Pre-1660								
1–19	30	8	2½	1	0	0		41½
20–34	6	9	2	1	½	0		18½
35–49	2	8	1½	1	1	½		14
50–99	2	5	6	3½	1	½		18
100–199	0	0	3½	2½	0	0		6
200+	0	0	½	1	½	0		2
Total	40	30	16	10	3	1		100
1660–1679								
1–19	26	3½	2	1	0	0		32½
20–34	6½	7	2½	2	½	½		19
35–49	½	7	3	2½	1	½		14½
50–99	3	5	6½	6	2	½		23
100–199	0	3½	1	3½	1½	½		10
200+	0	0	1	0	0	0		1
Total	36	26	16	15	5	2		100
1680–1689								
1–19	20	7	4	2	1	½		34½
20–34	5½	5½	2½	3	½	½		17½
35–49	4	3	3	2	1	½		13½
50–99	5½	7	4½	3½	2	1		23½
100–199	1	3	2	1½	1	½		9
200+	0	½	0	1	½	0		2
Total	36	26	16	13	6	3		100
1690–1699								
1–19	22	5	2½	1	½	1		32
20–34	4	6	2½	1	½	½		14½
35–49	2	3	3½	2	1	0		11½
50–99	7½	9	5	5	2	1		29½
100–199	½	3	2½	3½	1½	½		11½
200+	0	0	0	½	½	0		1
Total	36	26	16	13	6	3		100

SOURCE: Estate inventories.

Distribution of Men's Clothing by Gross Personal Wealth, Seventeenth Century (COUNTRY PAY)

	N	£1	2	3	4	5	6	7	8	9	10	11	12	13	14	15	16	17	18	19	20+	Median £
£1–19	118	26	22	21	11	9	12	5	2	6	2	1	0	1	0	0	0	0	0	0	0	3
20–39	149	21	38	24	14	16	10	9	6	2	3	0	1	0	0	0	1	1	1	0	1	3
40–59	133	11	18	28	19	18	7	12	4	6	2	3	1	0	2	0	1	1	0	0	0	4
60–79	143	10	18	20	27	22	11	7	11	5	4	1	3	0	0	1	0	0	2	0	0	4½
80–99	108	7	11	18	12	10	16	7	4	7	3	3	1	1	1	3	1	0	1	0	2	5
100–119	103	3	5	11	9	19	14	8	9	5	7	2	2	4	2	0	1	1	0	0	1	6
120–139	92	0	5	7	12	14	9	8	6	8	7	2	5	0	3	1	2	0	2	0	1	6½
140–159	63	2	0	5	9	2	12	4	8	7	8	2	0	1	1	0	0	0	0	1	0	7
160–179	58	0	0	3	3	7	6	6	5	5	4	5	1	1	3	3	1	0	0	0	2	8
180–199	54	1	0	1	1	5	9	5	4	8	1	2	4	1	1	1	0	1	1	2	2	8½
200–299	163	0	0	2	7	9	9	12	11	12	14	6	6	3	12	7	6	5	7	3	19	11½
300–399	60	0	0	0	1	2	2	2	7	3	6	5	4	3	4	4	1	3	2	1	12	12½
400–499	24	0	0	0	1	1	0	0	0	1	2	1	1	1	2	2	2	1	3	0	8	16
500–999	52	0	0	0	0	3	0	0	3	1	1	0	1	1	0	1	2	0	1	3	35	22
Total	1320	81	117	140	126	137	115	85	80	76	64	34	47	22	29	23	18	13	20	10	83	6

DETAIL, CLOTHING £20 PLUS

	N	20	21	22	23	24	25	26	27	28	29	30–39	40–49	50
£1–79	1		1											
80–199	9	3	1	1								2		
200–299	19	5	1	3	2	2	2	1				3		
300–399	12		1	1	2	1	1		1			5		
400–499	8	1	2	1	1	1				1		1	1	
500–999	35	7	0	5	2	1	3	0	1	0	2	5	8	1

APPENDIX 3D

Distribution of Books by Gross Personal Wealth, Seventeenth Century
(COUNTRY PAY)

	None	Under £1	£1	£2	£3	£4	£5–9	£10+	Some	% none
Pre-1660										
£1–19	7	2	1							70
20–49	15	6	1	1					3	65
50–99	20	18	5	1					1	43
100–199	11	6	7	4					1	38
200–499	8	7	6	7	1	1		11	1	25
500+	1		2	1			2	40,300,13		11
N	62	39	22	14	1	1	2	4	6	41.1
1660–1679										
£1–19	35	6	0	0	0	0	0	0	0	85
20–49	24	31	1	0	1	0	0	0	0	42
50–99	18	32	14	5	0	1	1	0	6	23
100–199	25	24	14	7	2	0	2	10	9	30
200–499	9	10	17	7	4	1	4	49,127,18 ⎫ 82,10 ⎬ 11,12,82 ⎭	9	21
500+	1	3	2	2	1	1	1	52,61 ⎭	3	5
N	112	106	48	21	8	3	8	11	27	32.6
1680–1689										
£1–19	31	11	1	0	0	0	0			72
20–49	39	41	5	1	0	1	0			42
50–99	37	47	5	2	2	0	0			39
100–199	30	40	29	5	3	1	3			25
200–499	8	16	18	5	0	3	3	14,51,73 13,68		13
500+	0	1	0	2	0	1	2	30,17		0
N	145	156	58	15	5	6	8	7		34.5
1690–1699										
£1–19	33	16	2	1	0	0	0	0		64
20–49	39	31	4	2	0	0	0	0		51
50–99	41	43	18	2	4	1	0	0		35
100–199	44	56	30	8	0	2	4	13,30		29
200–499	15	13	27	7	3	4	7	34,31 13,15,12,54 ⎭		16
500+	1	1	2	2	0	1	3	21,120,11		8
N	173	160	83	22	7	7	14	11		34.2

DISTRIBUTION OF BOOKS, SELECTED TOWNS, 1680–1689

	None	Under £1	£1	£2	£3	£4	£5–9	£10+	Some	Total N	Total £	Mean	% with
Hartford, New Haven & Fairfield	87	113	45	16	6	4	8	4	22	303	381	£1.5	71.3
Farmington, Middletown & Guilford	51	33	17	3	6	1	6	3	13	133	313	2.7	61.7
Newly settled	40	27	3	4	1	1			5	81	31	8/	50.6

Ownership of Debts Receivable by Personal Wealth, Seventeenth Century (COUNTRY PAY, PERCENTAGES)

	None	1–9	10–19	20–49	50–99	100–199	200+	Total
£1–49	77.5	15.5	6.5	0.5	0	0	0	100.0
50–99	69.7	17.8	7.2	4.6	0.7	0	0	100.0
100–199	69.5	9.2	9.2	8.6	2.3	1.1	0	99.9
200–499	49.4	6.9	10.3	14.9	3.4	10.3	4.6	99.8
500+	11.4	0	0	0	11.4	25.7	51.4	99.9

SOURCE: Hartford district inventories.

Personal Wealth by Occupation (COUNTRY PAY, PERCENTAGES)

	Lab'rs	Farmers	Artisans	Traders	Prof.	Retired	Unknown	Total	N	%
Pre-1680										
£1–49	63.5	5.1	13.1	0	0	7.3	11.0	100.0	137	25.5
50–99	6.6	46.3	22.8	0.7	1.5	8.8	13.2	99.9	136	25.3
100–199	0.8	66.1	19.8	1.7	3.3	4.1	4.1	99.9	121	22.5
200–499	0.9	64.6	9.1	12.7	5.4	0	7.3	100.0	110	20.5
500+	0	18.2	9.1	48.5	21.2	3.0	0	100.0	33	6.1
									537	99.9
1680–1689										
£1–49	35.9	10.1	16.6	1.4	1.4	20.9	13.7	100.0	139	32.5
50–99	4.3	45.7	21.3	1.1	1.1	17.0	9.6	100.0	94	22.0
100–199	0	70.8	16.7	2.5	0	5.0	5.0	100.0	120	28.0
200–499	0	57.6	16.7	9.1	6.1	1.5	9.1	100.0	66	15.4
500+	0	11.1	11.1	77.8	0	0	0	100.0	9	2.2
									428	100.0
1690–1699										
£1–49	46.4	8.1	19.9	0	0	16.2	9.5	100.1	136	25.9
50–99	9.9	45.5	24.8	2.5	1.6	6.6	9.1	100.0	121	23.0
100–199	0.6	61.9	24.4	2.5	1.2	4.4	5.0	100.0	160	30.4
200–499	0	60.0	24.2	6.3	4.2	3.2	2.1	100.0	95	18.0
500+	0	14.3	28.6	35.7	14.3	0	7.0	99.9	14	2.7
									526	100.0

SOURCE: Estate inventories.

Economic Characteristics of Seventeenth-Century Towns

Occupational Structure (percentages)

	Inventories			Adult men		
	I	II	III	I	II	III
Laborers	20	16½	17½	40	33	35
Farmers	45	55½	60	35	45	47
Artisans	21	22	20	14	18	16
Traders & prof.	14	6	2½	11	4	2
Total	100	100	100	100	100	100

Personal Wealth (county pay, percentages)

Wealth class	Trading towns	Farm towns I	Farm towns II
£1–49	27	26	34½
50–99	21½	24½	27
100–199	27	27	31
200–499	19	19½	7
500 +	5½	3	½
Total	100	100	100
Mean £	183	140	94
Median £	108	98	79
Share top 10%	47%	34%	28½%
N	687	593	206

Continued

TOTAL WEALTH (COUNTRY PAY, PERCENTAGES)

Wealth class	Trading towns	Farm towns I	Farm towns II
£1–49	17.0	13.5	16.7
50–99	10.9	11.4	16.2
100–199	17.0	21.0	22.7
200–299	14.2	14.2	16.7
300–399	10.1	12.2	9.1
400–499	8.7	7.5	9.6
500–599	15.2	15.5	8.1
1,000+	6.9	4.6	1.0
Total	100.0	99.9	100.0
Mean £	374	327	237
Median £	236	229	175
Share top 10%	43.1	34.5	30.3
N	653	613	198

SOURCE: Estate inventories.

Personal Wealth by Age (COUNTRY PAY, PERCENTAGES)

	30–39	40–49	50–59	60–69	Over 70
1660–1679					
£1–19	2.1	1.4	0	2.1	6.2
20–49	10.6	12.7	4.8	2.1	28.1
50–99	51.1	18.3	24.1	10.6	22.9
100–199	25.5	33.8	32.5	36.2	15.6
200–499	8.5	26.8	32.5	38.3	9.4
500+	2.1	7.0	6.0	10.6	18.8
N	47	71	83	47	32
Median £	90	143	149	193	82
1680–1689					
£1–19	4.6	5.3	6.6	5.6	9.6
20–49	34.8	24.0	9.8	12.2	26.0
50–99	24.2	21.3	29.5	17.8	19.2
100–199	22.7	32.0	29.5	32.2	35.6
200–499	12.1	16.0	19.7	28.9	8.2
500+	1.5	1.3	4.9	3.3	1.4
N	66	75	61	90	73
Median £	67	77	120	133	88
1690–1699					
£1–19	7.7	7.6	4.9	4.9	10.7
20–49	24.2	10.2	4.9	4.9	16.1
50–99	22.0	20.3	24.3	21.3	23.2
100–199	29.7	44.9	35.0	29.6	23.2
200–499	14.3	14.4	29.1	31.2	23.2
500+	2.2	2.5	1.9	8.2	3.6
N	91	118	103	61	56
Median £	80	119	152	146	99

SOURCE: Estate inventories.

Real Wealth by Age (COUNTRY PAY, PERCENTAGES)

	30–39	40–49	50–59	60–69	70+
1660–1679					
None	15.2	4.2	8.4	8.5	12.5
£1–19	10.9	5.6	2.4	0	9.4
20–49	23.9	25.4	12.0	8.5	3.1
50–99	32.6	14.1	16.9	21.3	18.8
100–199	8.7	23.9	32.5	21.3	28.1
200–499	6.5	18.3	22.9	34.0	12.5
500+	2.2	8.5	4.8	6.4	15.6
N	46	71	83	47	32
Median £	50	100	130	150	115
1680–1689					
None	18.2	10.7	8.6	9.8	13.9
£1–19	9.1	4.0	1.7	1.1	1.4
20–49	15.2	1.3	5.2	5.4	1.4
50–99	10.6	22.7	13.8	6.5	12.5
100–199	21.2	28.0	19.0	20.7	25.0
200–499	21.2	30.7	34.5	45.7	30.6
500+	4.5	2.7	17.2	10.9	15.3
N	66	75	58	92	72
Median £	80	140	205	240	180
1690–1699					
None	12.1	1.7	1.9	3.3	10.7
£1–19	2.2	3.4	2.9	3.3	7.1
20–49	6.6	8.5	3.9	3.3	3.6
50–99	18.7	15.3	9.7	11.5	12.5
100–199	25.3	33.9	19.4	14.8	21.4
200–499	30.8	33.9	39.8	36.1	30.4
500+	4.4	3.4	22.3	27.9	14.3
N	91	118	103	61	56
Median £	130	162	250	260	175

SOURCE: Estate inventories.

Standards of Living

In ranking people according to their standard of living, I have first separated them according to life cycle: single men of whatever age; young married men, meaning those with children under thirteen, to whom I added the married but childless on the theoretical ground of similar needs and the practical one that their property coincided; older married men with children above thirteen but no grandchildren; grandfathers, separated because they would be divesting themselves of children, so their needs would be reduced about on a level with the young married men; and the "retired" men, who had given away the key items of production, especially land but typically tools and most livestock, thus making them in some degree dependent on others. Identification of such men came from the inventories because age, while important, did not by itself determine the division, some quite old men continuing to operate the farms or businesses.

Next, the various levels of living were determined by a combination of consumption goods, total personal wealth, real property, and the total of all these. For consumption, as explained in the text I adopted Gloria Main's scale based on Maryland data, devised primarily for a study of young fathers, which in her case meant men with children under age. This I modified for the situation in Connecticut and for my own series of wealth classes, adding clothing and bedding. In the case of beds and bedding and of clothing I assembled data from the inventories that helped to indicate the minimum of families at different levels.

For personal wealth, I added to the data on consumption the other components. Thus a farmer, to subsist, would need a cow and calf, two heifers, two steers (on the way to becoming oxen), some pigs, and tools, valued at £15 country pay. That would not include farm products since these fell under the category of provisions, usually omitted from inventories. The next level up would add a yoke of oxen, two more cattle, a mare and colt, additional pigs or sheep, more tools, and miscellaneous articles such as crops for sale and barrels. This last category would expand for the "comfortable" level, which might include, for example, a barrel of pork, some cider, a stout cart with other farm equipment, and a good saddle and bridle for the horse.

In the case of real estate I tried above all to establish the number and quality of acres. A single man, for subsistence, would need only a house and lot, where a young married couple required fifteen acres more, all improved, and the older married families, forty acres. For this and higher levels, see Chapter Six on farmers. The principal problem arose when inventories gave only the total value of the real estate. From that I subtracted the probable value of the house and barn, and divided the remainder by the average price of land for the time and place, all such information being assembled from such inventories as did furnish detail. If necessary I used simply the total value. Finally, in cases where the different scales led to widely varying conclusions, I used the total for all property combined.

The assignment of a particular individual to the appropriate category sometimes involved value judgment. Artisans did not need as much land as did farmers, compensating by their skills, so in their case I lowered the amount required. The category "well-off" I tried to make exclusive: in case of doubt, no. Otherwise I treated marginal cases in such a way as to avoid any consistent bias: if I placed one in the higher of two ranks I put the next in the lower.

A few specific examples may help. Samuel Griffin of Derby, a blacksmith, died in 1691 at the age of thirty-five, unmarried. His total property of £54 consisted of consumption articles worth £19, total personal wealth of £28, a house and a lot. The reader will see that all this places him safely above the subsistence level but just below subsistence plus. I put him in the lower category. Timothy Buckland of Windsor (1639-1689) left six children aged six to twenty-four, none yet married. His £35 worth of consumption was ample for subsistence as was the £61 total personal, but in neither case enough for subsistence plus. He owned seventy acres, an old house, and a two-and-a-half acre lot, still not quite subsistence plus, and the grand total of £89 put him right in the middle of the subsistence category. Had he been a young father or a grandfather with slightly reduced needs, he would belong to the higher level. Finally, John Andres of Farmington died in 1682, referred to as "aged" though he was not much over sixty. He was a grandfather, with five sons aged thirty or above, and had given some of his property while retaining the home farm. The consumption of £51 and personal estate of £131 would fall short of "comfort" had he been responsible for all the children, but for a grandfather, quite enough. So also ninety-two acres, a house and homestead meant comfort for him.

The reader should remember that the currency remains "country pay," twice sterling values. Houses required with acreage. Personal is net of debts payable. The two columns for real property reflect price changes.

Standards of Living

Level of living	Consumption	All personal	Acreage	All real to 1680	All real to 1700
Subsistence					
Single men	£ 12	£ 20	lot	£ 20	£ 20
Young fathers	15	30	15	40	60
Older fathers	20	40	40	80	160
Grandfathers	15	30	15	40	60
Retired	12	20	lot	20	20?
Subsistence plus					
Single men	20	30	15	40	60
Young fathers	30	60	40	80	160
Older fathers	40	90	80	160	280
Grandfathers	30	60	40	80	160
Retired	20	30	15	40	60
Comfortable					
Single men	30	60	40	80	160
Young fathers	50	100	80	160	280
Older fathers	80	150	120	240	400
Grandfathers	50	100	80	160	280
Retired	30	60	40	80	160
Well-off					
Single men	40	80	60	120	200
Young fathers	60	120	120	240	400
Older fathers	100	200	200	400	600
Grandfathers	60	120	120	240	400
Retired	40	80	60	120	200

Levels of Living, Seventeenth Century

	Single men	Young fathers	Older fathers	Grand-fathers	Retired	Total	%
1660–1669							
Poor	11	2	4	0	1	18	12.9
Subsistence	5	13	17	1	1	37	26.6
Subsistence plus	2	10	18	6	2	38	27.3
Comfortable	3	11	5	12	3	34	24.5
Well-off	1	1	1	4	0	7	5.0
Luxury	1	1	1	2	0	5	3.6
Total	23	38	46	25	7	139	99.9
1670–1679							
Poor	28	9	10	0	0	47	20.3
Subsistence	23	17	11	2	4	57	24.7
Subsistence plus	8	18	18	7	11	62	26.8
Comfortable	3	5	9	15	1	33	14.3
Well-off	0	4	8	13	2	27	11.7
Luxury	1	1	0	3	0	5	2.2
Total	63	54	56	40	18	231	100.0
1680–1689							
Poor	23	25	12	5	6	71	17.0
Subsistence	20	22	19	2	17	80	19.2
Subsistence plus	4	29	30	22	11	96	23.0
Comfortable	5	12	18	45	13	93	22.3
Well-off	5	8	11	39	4	67	16.1
Luxury	1	2	2	5	0	10	2.4
Total	58	98	92	118	51	417	100.0
1690–1699							
Poor	26	13	12	0	8	59	11.5
Subsistence	35	42	38	0	10	125	24.4
Subsistence plus	10	47	65	13	10	145	28.3
Comfortable	5	29	32	25	10	101	19.7
Well-off	4	11	23	21	2	71	11.0
Luxury	0	2	2	7	0	11	2.1
Total	80	144	172	76	40	512	99.9

SOURCE: Tax lists.

NOTE: The text contains the data for the period before 1660. These are the actual numbers. Anyone wishing to translate them into the living population can safely use this formula: single men, 25 percent, young fathers, 42 percent, older fathers, 21 percent, grandfathers, 9 percent, and retired, 3 percent.

FOUR

The Distribution of Property in the Eighteenth Century

The seventy-five years following 1700 consisted, from a socioeconomic point of view, of three or perhaps four periods. Until about 1730 the colony enjoyed steadily improving conditions, with a large amount of good land available for a small investment. Then came twenty years of economic decline, reaching bottom during the 1740s. A subsequent recovery returned the general level of wealth to the peak of the 1720s until the end of the French and Indian War. In the final ten years, however, symptoms appeared indicating another downward trend. Overall, the level of wealth on the eve of the Revolution differed very little from that in 1700, but so general a statement conceals both the fluctuations and some significant differences in detail.

Our principal source for estimating the level and distribution of wealth over time remains the estate inventories, for reasons already discussed. Tax lists do help a little. During these years the legislature continued to receive the yearly assessed valuations of the towns, but after 1708 did not preserve the number of polls. However, in 1756, 1762, and 1774 we have supposedly accurate censuses of the population. Dividing by five gives us the number of men twenty-one and over and yields an assessed value (including the £18 on each poll) of £54.14 per adult man in 1756 and £53 in 1774. In 1700 we lack such a census, so adjust the polls reported to the legislature by adding men omitted from the tax lists. This yields a mean of £52 to £54, in any case about the same as the later level. This method of estimating lacks precision but suggests an overall continuity.

Assessment lists supply data concerning the proportion of men in the several levels of taxable property and the wealth of different age groups. First, we can separate the men into wealth classes by estimating how much of this sort of property identifies a person as belonging to the poor or to more fortunate groups. The equivalent of £20 in personal and £40 in real wealth, which a young father needed for subsistence, would be around £15 on the tax list or perhaps as much as £20—the two sets of data are really incompatible. We may therefore establish two classes at the bottom: those paying no tax, most of whom would have owned little or no property, to whom we can add those with under £10 worth as clearly also poor; and secondly, men with £10 to £19 as marginal. Actually two-thirds of the men belonging to these poorest levels who died soon after the date of the tax left inventories of over £120 in total wealth, but it is probably fair to call them relatively poor within the framework of the evidence from taxes. The men with £20 to £29 in assessed value averaged £130 on their inventories and qualify as self-sufficient. That is especially true because, as we will see, most of them were under forty and many were artisans who did not require much land or livestock. From that point upward, one multiplies the assessment (still minus the polls) by seven to obtain the equivalent of median estates on probate inventories (the mean would require a higher multiplier) until the later period when land prices increased the value of inventories.[1] An assessment above £30 clearly assured an adequate standard of living. We might draw a higher line, especially for the head of a family farm, at £60 for comfort, but given the uncertain character of the data perhaps we can simply lump all those with £30 to £100 into a broad middle class, above which come the well-to-do. Arranging all the men in that way we find the class structure in Table 4.1.

As to variations over time, Table 4.2 shows a reduction of men in the middle class of £30 to £99, losing both to the top and bottom.

TABLE 4.1
Economic Classes, from Tax Lists,
Eighteenth Century

Assessment less polls	%
Almost propertyless (£0–9)	32.4
Other poor (£10–19)	14.3
Self-sufficient (£20–29)	12.4
Comfortable (£30–100)	35.6
Well-off (£100+)	5.3
Total	100.0

[1] The tax lists used here are identified in Chapter One. The difficulty of interpreting tax data for changes over time appears in the following summary. It shows the value of the inventories of men with assessed properties worth £20-29 who died within five years from the date of the tax, for lists around 1700 and 1773.

£	1-49	50-99	100-199	200-499	500+	Median	Mean
1700 set	2	1	3	4	0	146	176
Final set	2	2	4	2	6	230	447

116

TABLE 4.2
Distribution of Taxable Property

	£0–9	10–19	20–29	30–99	100+	Share top 10%
1700 set	25	15½	14	41½	4	30.0%
1730 set	29	16½	13	39	2.5	30.5
Final set	34½	12	11	35½	7	33.5

TABLE 4.3
Distribution of Taxable Property by Age over Time

	21–29	30–39	40–49	50–59	60–69	70+
£ Mean Wealth						
1700 set	13½	36	49	60	52½	38(?)
1730 set	14	32	46	67	50	57
Final set	10	37	50	63	64	40
Final less 16.7%	8½	31	41½	52	53	33
£ Median Wealth						
1700 set	8	31	44	56½	46	31(?)
1730 set	9	26	41	56½	50	48
Final set	3	30	45	58	53	30
Final less 16.7%	2½	25	37½	48	44	25

This might have been accounted for had the population become younger, but since the reverse occurred, the tax lists show a rising proportion of poor. The increase at the top probably reflects the older age structure. Obviously the level of inequality also rose, though only slightly.

We can also discover changes over time as indicated by the tax lists by looking at the age groups, asking here whether the apparent decline in the final decade affected only the old, the young, the men of middle age, or everybody. Recall here that the final figure must increase by around 20 percent to show stability because the towns involved were richer than the average; less than that signifies a drop. And a drop is what we find (see Table 4.3). Tentatively, then, on this evidence the level and distribution of wealth remained unchanged from 1700 to 1760 or later, after which, however, a decline occurred, especially among men in their twenties and in middle age, except for those at the top, notably men in their sixties; and that this created a greater inequality of wealth. However, the change may have been temporary, reflecting a shift in the types of property owned that the tax lists, with their stability, would not show; or resulting from their failure to incorporate price increases in land and livestock. We must reserve judgment on the question of a decline.

We therefore turn to see what estate inventories reveal about changes over time.[2] The best evidence comes from the data on personal property. The mean wealth in 1700-1709 was £111 "cash" or "money" values (not country pay). This increased to a peak of £130 in the late 1720s and then declined to the original level or even below in some areas, reaching bottom in the period 1745-1749.[3] The average personal wealth of the living population naturally followed the same course but about one-sixth lower. The peak at the end almost certainly results from an older population, for which I have not sufficiently accounted. The medians show the same fluctuations. The behavior of the probate medians during the periods 1755-1759 and 1760-1764 do not indicate an economic calamity at the bottom of society but a military one, which the figures for the living population correct. They indicate a recovery well under way before the war began as the West Indian market improved, and then stimulated by the military demand for the colony's products. The price of livestock, the principal surplus, in particular increased. Oxen, valued at under £7 per yoke in 1756, reached £12 three years later. The price of hogs rose 50 percent, cows by a third, and sheep doubled. Britain's reimbursement of the colony for

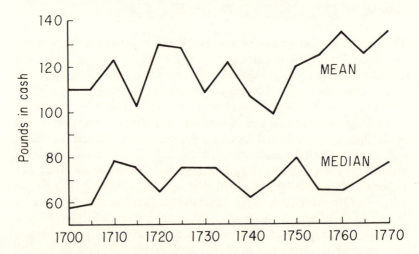

GRAPH 4.1 Personal Wealth, Estate Inventories

[2] See Appendix 4A for the probate records used for this survey.

[3] For the final two figures I have subtracted one-sixth from the top quintile of estates. The proper correction might be at most one-fifth, the difference being £1.

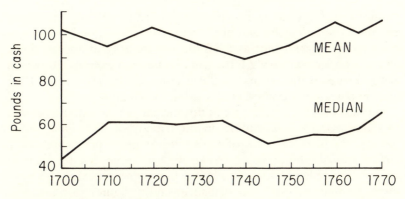

GRAPH 4.2 Personal Wealth, Adult Men

its expenses brought in several million pounds sterling and helped to cushion the postwar depression. The price increases ended temporarily after hostilities ceased, but by 1774 had returned to the highest level since the earliest years of settlement. Probate records do not furnish precise information about economic events, but the one trend they do *not* show is secular decline. At worst, personal wealth remained the same. A comparison of 1770 with 1700 indicates an increase of roughly 10 percent in both the mean and the medians. That equals scarcely 0.1 percent per year and, taken in conjunction with livestock prices, a general conclusion of no change over time, only fluctuations, seems most accurate. We must, of course, examine the distribution of this wealth, especially among age and marital groups.

We turn next to real property. Our major problem is how to deal with rising land values. Little overall change in prices occurred until nearly mid-century, because the increase in older communities was balanced by cheap unimproved tracts on the frontier. In 1723 the legislature observed that previous land values were so low that a husband could sell his wife's inheritance without injustice, but now a sale must have her consent. Actually that statement was true only for undeveloped land, which in 1700 one might still purchase for as little as 5 shillings per acre. Improved land at that point cost much more, with considerable variation. One could buy an acre of meadow for only about £2 (money) in the New London district but it took £5 in Hartford. This sort of land along the Connecticut River, scarce and relatively expensive, more than doubled in value by the end of the period, but the increase colonywide was only from £5 in 1700 to £6 about 1720, and then stabilized until after 1760, when it rose to £7.10 and finally £8. Improved land, including all types, remained stable at £2 for almost half a century, because the upward trend along the Sound and the Connecticut River Valley were counteracted by low prices in new communities. As late as 1750 the average price of improved land on the frontier was only £1.10, while values had risen by 50 percent in the Hartford district and doubled around New Haven. By 1765, the colonywide price stood at £3 and in 1770, £3.8.

In evaluating the significance of this increase we can choose between two interpretations, depending upon our point of view. First, we can consider the increased value of real estate as a rise in per capita wealth, a clear gain to the people. Second, we can argue that the gain for people owning land is cancelled by the loss to those seeking to acquire some, so that we ought to deflate inventory figures (for land, not buildings) to accord with the base price as of 1700. If we adopt the first procedure we begin with an estate inventory mean of £154 in 1700, ignoring geographical differences and other variables. This rose steadily until the end of the 1720s, accompanying the general prosperity of the period. As we know, much previously unoccupied land was now developed in response to good market conditions as well as to the increase in population. The inventory means then declined from £314 to £236 during the thirties and to only £196 in the forties. In the early fifties recovery began, so that the mean reached a peak of £360 during the early sixties, fell back after the war to £312, and ended at £374 (the last two figures adjusted for wealth bias). That represents a rise from 1700 of 140 percent or, from 1710 to 1719, of a little over 80 percent, better than 1 percent annually. For the living population the figures are lower and the increase slower—67 to 90 percent, an annual rate of about 1 percent.

If, however, we consider this rise not as a genuine improvement due (say) to transforming unimproved or ordinary pastureland into more productive farms, but solely as reflecting demand due to population pressure, we must deflate to an extent hard to judge because of local variations, but certainly 60 percent and possibly 80 percent for land, though very little for buildings: let us call it two-thirds overall. The means for the final decades become £209 and £252. This does not quite wipe out the gain in the mean since 1700 but limits it to about 50 percent for the probate and 20 percent for the living population, while the median shows no change at all. On balance this procedure seems closer to reality, because any larger rise in the productive capacity of the colony's land, taking it acre by acre, should have raised the level of personal wealth, and that did not happen. This high level of aggregation, however, does not reveal changes in the distribution and composition of wealth. For a more detailed analysis we begin by examining more closely the distribution of personal and then of real wealth by wealth classes, postponing for the moment a discussion of other variables.

Table 4.4 shows the distribution of personal property owned by adult men over time.[4] The smallest estates, in general, would not contain enough capital to support a man nor enough consumption goods to establish an independent home, and so forced one to depend upon wage labor or work for room and board. Personal property between £30 and £60 would suffice for a single man or a couple without children but not for a family. During the period as a whole, three out of ten men would be dependent and might face a struggle to avoid poverty. We will have to discover who these were and whether the poor of one decade became the independent propertyholders of the next. Two comparatively good decades, as we know, covered the years between 1710 and 1730. The population boom and the expansion onto new land stimulated economic growth, leading us to inquire whether articles of production other than land increased or whether people raised their standards of living. The decline that follows shows particularly in the proportion of poor, especially significant since the number of young men was not rising. The losses for men with larger estates is striking and suggests a trend toward a near-subsistence economy with insufficient surplus to maintain growth. A limited recovery began by the fifties and was complete by the early sixties, surely a result of the war. It is especially apparent at the top of the wealth scale and seems during the final years to have extended well down, the proportion of

TABLE 4.4
Personal Wealth, Adult Men (percentages)

	£1–29	30–59	60–119	120–199	200–499	500+	Total
1700–1709	29	25½	22½	11½	9½	2	100
1710–1719	27	24½	28	12½	6½	1½	100
1720–1729	21½	29½	27	13	7½	1½	100
1730–1739	29	22	25½	12	10	1½	100
1740–1749	35	24	23	10½	6½	1	100
1750–1759	32	22½	26	11	7½	1	100
1760–1769	30	23½	21½	13	9½	2½	100
1770–1774	29½	18	27½	14	7½	3	99½

SOURCE: Estate inventories.

[4] Appendix 4B contains the data from estate inventories. Table 4.4 incorporates the adjustment for wealth bias, 1765-1774.

121

men with under £60 having declined to an all-time low. Over seven decades had not reduced the number of people in the poorest wealth class, which seems permanently in place, but the marginal one just above had decidedly shrunk.

The absence of improvement at the bottom of society and the increasing gap at the close of the period between the mean and the median suggest a growing inequality. The data confirm this, not for the probate but for the living population, with a more equal distribution during the depression years and a rising inequality at the end, which would have been considerably greater without our adjustment for wealth bias at the top (see Table 4.5). We should not make too much of this: the increase, from start to finish, did not exceed 10 percent and changes fluctuated around the moderate level of 42 percent.[5] However, whereas the prosperity of the 1720s brought a greater degree of equality, reflecting the rising wealth of all classes, that of the Seven Years' War and after did not do so. We will investigate the reasons for that presently.[6]

TABLE 4.5
Share of Personal Wealth, Top Decile

	Estate inventories	Adult men
1700–1709	42	43½
1710–1719	39	40½
1720–1729	39	39
1730–1739	38½	38½
1740–1749	40	40½
1750–1759	43	45
1760–1769	42½	44
1770–1774	41½	47

[5] Alice Hanson Jones reviews the literature on levels of inequality in chapter eight of her *Wealth of a Nation to Be* (New York, 1980). She found that the share of the top 10 percent of free wealth-holders in the colonies as a whole, in 1774, slightly exceeded 50 percent compared with roughly 70 percent a century later. My earlier work with inventories, reported in *The Social Structure of Revolutionary America* (Princeton, 1965) did not adjust for age bias, though as it turns out that makes little difference in this particular measure. Inequality in the cities and areas with large-scale commercial farming commonly exceeded 50 percent, while in relatively self-sufficient rural societies the top 10 percent owned less than 40 percent, sometimes much less.

[6] The data for the period 1730-1750 for the living population are weak, being limited to the Hartford and Fairfield probate districts, but they would not err by more than 1 or 2 percentage points because the two together contained towns of all types and their wealth, insofar as it can be judged from returns to the legislature and from a broader sweep of inventories during other time periods, came close to the average.

As to real wealth, the pattern followed a similar course except at the end. The rapid growth of population and the opening up of the entire colony, especially after 1713, led to the occupation and improvement of most of the best accessible land. Prices of unoccupied tracts rose only slightly but intensive use meant an overall rise in values, which the inventories reflect. During the first three decades of the century almost everyone acquired at least a little land. Then for twenty years the boom collapsed. The inflation of that period prevents us from tracing exact values, but apparently the adjusted price of real estate fell back to the 1700 level. Evidently neither the colonial nor the West Indian market could absorb the colony's surplus, which consisted largely of products coming off the land, and we have seen the results for personal wealth.

The depression had several effects on the distribution of land. For one, large properties became less numerous, apparently as men disposed of undeveloped or unprofitable tracts; the former almost disappear from the inventories and if the owners had been improving them the fact should show up in rising land values. Second, the proportion of landless men, only 13 percent during the 1720s, more than doubled. This might be attributable to a shortage of land in the settled areas, but in that case the trend would have worsened throughout the colonial period, whereas it did not. We also find a reduction in the proportion of men with medium-sized holdings. Those between £80 and £300 shrank from 42 percent of the total during 1700-1719 to 28 percent in the 1740s, and this was a permanent change: either men owned less than that or more.

By mid-century returning prosperity reversed most of these trends in real estate. Values per acre began at last to rise and inventories show an all-time high by the 1770s, even after we correct for wealth bias. Only if we disregard the increase in the price of land and return to the 1700 levels do we cause a final prosperity to vanish. In that case the interpretation becomes: first the depression, then recovery until some time after 1760, and then a decline ending just a little above the level of 1700. At least a partial recovery is suggested by a reduction in the proportion of landless men from the 27 percent of the forties to 22 percent and an increase in large estates equaling those of the 1720s, unless we adjust for changes in land prices, and even then a slight rise occurred.

A final evidence for changes in the distribution of real wealth comes from the share held by the top 10 percent. Since this results above all from the fortunes of the wealthy, not the holdings of the middle class and only slightly from the number of poor, we can anticipate what

TABLE 4.6
Distribution of Real Estate by Value over Time (adult men, percentages)

£	1700–09	1710–19	1720–29	1730–39	1740–49	1750–59	1760–64	1765–69	1770–74
None	14	14	13	24	27	20½	21½	20½ (22)	21½ (23)
1–39	15½	17	12	12½	17½	13	14½	10 (11½)	14½ (16)
40–79	19½	16	12½	9	11½	14	12½	10	8½
80–119	17	15	8	9½	8	9½	6	10	8½
120–199	14	15	17	13	11½	9½	9	11½	11
200–299	10½	12	13	12	8½	10½	8½	12	11
300–499	7	5½	13	11	7	10½	11	11	10½
500–999	2	4½	8½	7	7	8	10½	10 (8)	8½ (7½)
1,000+	½	1	3	2½	2	4½	6½	8 (4)	6 (5)
Total	100	100	100	100½	100	100	100	100	100
Median £	83	99	140	99	58	88	89	118 (106)	112 (92)

NOTE: The table derives first by arranging estate inventories by age groups, and then by combining the distribution for each age group according to its proportion of the adult male population.

Probate records contain the estates of far more older men than are living at any one time. Around 35 percent of the men are in their twenties but the inventories yield only 15 percent or less. Therefore, unless we adjust for this we get an impression of rather few poor men and a lot of men fairly well-off. So we start with the land left by the young and increase their numbers, similarly decreasing the numbers of older man. That yields a reasonably accurate picture of Connecticut's landholding.

Thus out of every 100 inventories we might find this:

Age	21–29	30–50	Over 50	Total
No land	6	8	10	24
Little land	6	12	10	28
Much land	0	8	40	48

but the actual situation is:

Age	21–29	30–50	Over 50	Total
No land	18	12	3	33
Little land	18	20	3	41
Much land	0	12	14	26

No price adjustments are made. Parenthetical figures in the last two columns allow for wealth bias. Currency is cash (6 shillings to the Spanish dollar).

occurred. In 1700 the wealthiest group owned 37 percent of the total, increasing that to 46 percent during the 1720s. There it stayed through the depression until the 1750s when it rose to over half, ending at 55 percent. The new high level reflects primarily the success of older men, and we must delay a final interpretation until we have studied the various factors influencing the distribution of wealth, especially that of the life cycle.

Generalizing now about the entire period, almost all heads of households owned real estate. The proportion of men without even a house or lot was one-seventh for the first thirty years, less than one-fourth thereafter. Most of these were young laborers, half under thirty, almost all less than forty years old. Another seventh owned less than £40 worth (deflating to 1700 values), which meant a house, shop, and small lot, enough for artisans, professionals, or traders but not for farmers. Overall very close to half of the men did not possess the £80 worth that was probably the rock-bottom essential for a beginning farmer, and indeed at 1700 prices the proportion exceeded half at the end.

One may be tempted to regard this as a bad thing, but a decline in the value of men's holdings in real property does not necessarily represent any deterioration of economic conditions. Men could farm land more intensively, diversify by relying more heavily on non-agricultural income, or change occupations entirely. All of these in fact came about, and we may simply be witnessing the beginning of long-term trends so evident in the nineteenth century. The absence of significant decreases in personal wealth suggests that Connecticut was not facing an economic crisis. However, we must probe more deeply into our sources.

First we examine the principal components of personal wealth for distribution and secular changes. We have adequate data on consumption goods from estate inventories for the first quarter of a century and the final decade, correcting the latter for age bias in the records.[7] These reveal no variation whatever in the median, which started and ended at just over £35 cash. Moreover, the distribution remained stable. At both the beginning and end some 10 percent of the inventoried estates contained under the £10 minimum for subsistence, most of which belonged to single men. Those with less than £20 worth formed 25.7 of all men during the early years and 26.2 percent later, virtually the same. The proportion of the living population owning less than that, which would include those at or below the subsistence level, would be higher—about one-third—but it too showed no change. Of this lowest stratum fully half were single and the rest consisted principally of young married men. Thus the general distribution of consumer articles does not reveal any declension. At the top, as during the seventeenth century, we find very few living in luxury, though their percentage did double. Men with £100 worth, who we may consider very comfortable indeed, also doubled from 7.5 percent of the adult men to 15 percent at the end. This is primarily an effect of the older age structure, though it remained true regardless of who owned that property. We conclude, then, that except for the top 10 or 15 percent, the people of Connecticut spent no more nor less money on household goods in 1770 than in 1700 or, for that matter, the entire colonial period.

What, then, about the articles of production that created the income to maintain the same levels of consumption? The most important—land—remained stable over time. Partly as a consequence, livestock, crops, and tools changed very little: we discuss these matters in the chapter on farmers. We should repeat, however, that the price of livestock rose markedly after about 1750, a fact that affected the people unevenly but certainly benefited the colony as a whole through sales overseas.

During the seventeenth century, money in the form of gold and silver coin was a scarce commodity owned by a small fraction of the people and forming only 2 percent of total personal wealth, nor did silver articles compensate for the shortage. Nothing basic changed thereafter. Cash and silver combined accounted for only 5.5 percent of the inventoried personal property. Four out of five adult men owned

---

[7] See Appendix 4C for a table showing changes in the distribution of consumption goods over time.

none at all, and during 1700-1720 ten individuals had 40 percent of the total amount. By the close of the colonial period, despite the re-payment by Britain of wartime expenses and despite the prosperity of people who would naturally have some cash, little had altered. A few more inventories listed money or silver but the number of large hold-ers did not vary. Seventeen percent of all the hard money belonged to one individual, the president of Yale. If that gentleman be excepted, the supply of cash had actually dropped by 30 percent per inventory to £5.14, even when not adjusted for wealth bias, and only 4 percent of total personal wealth consisted of silver and gold. It is true that paper money considerably increased the supply until the British halted all such currency, and that may well have stimulated the expansion of the years after 1713. However, inflation counteracted the effect of an expanded quantity and the long depression shows that it did not stim-ulate economic growth for more than a short period.

As we have seen, debts receivable replaced cash as the principal com-ponent of total money. Before 1700 the trend had been toward the reduction of debts among the people generally except for the poor or the wealthy. The process culminated after that date when 10 percent of wealth-holders owned over 90 percent, and a dozen persons, all large-scale merchants, held half. Not over 15 percent of the farmers and laborers had any such assets (see Appendix 4D).

At some point after the 1720s the proportion of inventories con-taining debts and the significance of debts as a part of personal wealth began to increase, until by the close of the colonial period almost twice as many estates included them and they formed a fourth of personal inventoried property. Since the ownership of debts was so concen-trated, the shift accounts for the entire growth in the size share of gross personal wealth of the top 10 percent: it would have begun and ended at 33 percent instead of rising from 40 to 47 percent. Also, personal wealth minus debts receivable would have declined by 19 percent instead of by an actual 4 percent. Obviously we should try to locate the timing of this shift.

Unfortunately that is more difficult than it sounds. The two probate districts for which we have continuous data at hand between 1730 and 1765 do not agree. In Windham the process seems to have been com-plete by the 1720s, when half of the estates included debts comprising a quarter of the personal wealth, and that changed little. In Fairfield a big jump in the proportion of inventories containing debts occurred in the same decade but the sums were small, and the total quantity did not change significantly until the French and Indian War. From this it appears that money loaned out—not the same thing as money borrowed—rose first during the boom of the 1720s and retained that level throughout the depression years, though for a different reason, with local renewals during the war, and then increased as the people began to spend their wartime profits to meet a delayed demand for consumer goods.

In order to judge the significance of debts as assets we must know about debts as liabilities. Only in the probate district of New Haven did the clerks meticulously copy the information on what the estates owed.[8] There, the two amounts balanced one another during 1700-1729. The two varied around £12.10 per inventory in debts receivable and £12 in debts payable with the distribution already discussed applying to both. By 1765-1769, however, while the former had leaped to nearly £27, the latter increased by nearly fivefold. These liabilities were distributed even more widely than the assets, involving nearly 40 percent of the men, but for almost all of the people the two evened out, so we are witnessing some heavy indebtedness by no more than 1 percent of the men.

To interpret this situation requires a series of inferences. Let us suppose, to begin with, that within the colony debts receivable and payable balanced, so that any surplus in the latter equals the external debt. During 1700-1730 the colony had no such foreign debt (except for a few years after Queen Anne's War), but in 1765-1769 the liabilities were twice the assets, the difference amounting to £6,500 in the New Haven inventories. If the annual death rate for adult men was twenty per thousand (a little high) that means, in ten years, £65,000. The living men would owe only one-fourth as much because of the difference in age. According to the census, the towns in question contained a bit under 15 percent of the total population. Therefore the colony as a whole owed about £110,000, arising almost certainly from the well-known importations immediately after the war.[9] The big sums

[8] Quite often debts payable did not form part of the inventory because appraisers did not know of them. Administrators required anyone owing money to or with a claim upon the estate to produce evidence, and this information, sometimes spread over several years, formed part of the account submitted to the court. Unfortunately this account did not always form part of the clerk's copy, entered in the big bound volumes. We must search for them in their original manuscript form at the source, generally the county court house. I did this for the early Hartford district records in the Connecticut State Library but not for the rest. It would require months even in Connecticut but is worth someone's while.

[9] Of the eight biggest liabilities during 1765-1769, six were owed by men in their thirties, which surely means that they had imported extensively on credit immediately after the war. Of the nine largest debtors after 1770, five were in their forties. These obligations certainly did not precede the war and probably did not occur until its close.

involved of £2,008, £1,587, and £1,047 in New Haven suggest extensive importations on credit by wholesalers.

The same source shows a slightly smaller deficit during 1770-1774, liabilities exceeding assets by 177 percent instead of 197 percent and, applying the same assumptions, a total external debt of £95,000, reduced by over 10 percent. That seems substantial, but we should recall that the British government estimated the colony's contribution to the war at nearly a quarter of a million sterling; that Virginians complained of owing several millions; and that in 1774 the colony contained nearly 40,000 adult men whose share of the debt would come to only £2.5 apiece.[10] To repeat: most men owed no money or only the small sums arising from their normal purchases, and debts served them well, as they do us today.

Another asset consisted of trading stock by which, as a reminder, we mean most conspicuously the goods offered for sale by the traders, together with products made by craftsmen, some surplus produced by farm families as a sideline, and the medicines prescribed by doctors or apothecaries. Before 1700 only 6 percent of the inventoried personal wealth consisted of stock, belonging principally to traders. That did not change. Throughout the colonial period fewer than one in five inventories included stock. Even during the last decade, when debts were so considerable, no increase occurred unless we include some of the many slaves owned by traders. There were plenty of importers, as the ship arrivals in the *New London Gazette* attest, but they evidently disposed of their goods quickly, leaving only the debts as evidence.[11]

Finally, in this recitation of the distribution of personal property, we note the presence of slaves. Since they also formed part of the labor force we will discuss them as people in the next chapter. As a form of property they became somewhat more important over time, but much of the growth in the black population was actually attributable to free persons. By the early 1700s the white men of the colony had invested 3 or 4 percent of their personal wealth in servants and slaves, principally the latter. By 1774 12 percent of the estates mentioned slaves and they were increasing in number. As a percentage of personal wealth, however, they had scarcely grown at all, and the overwhelming majority of white men still did not own one. We need to inquire first why there were so few, since slaves became important in other colonies, and secondly why they existed at all.

[10] In New Haven 26.5 percent of the estates were in debt to the amount of £30, which might prove burdensome. But some of these held much more in debts receivable and among men generally, not over 5 percent would be in financial trouble.
[11] See Appendix 4E.

First, the plentiful supply of labor that characterized the years before 1700 did not change thereafter. Most of this labor force consisted of young whites working for their families in return for their keep or for their subsistence plus a wage, which the employer recovered from their labor. Few farms or business enterprises justified the cost of slave labor; slavery rarely paid its way; and Connecticut's citizens seldom had money to waste on non-essentials.

On the other hand some of them did buy servile labor. We must remember that no moral reason existed against it, as far as the overwhelming majority of Connecticut's people could see, until the end of the period: ministers owned slaves. So the question was pragmatic, not ethical. Occasionally an economic motive existed where a large farmer or a craftsman with a good business needed a permanent helper to perform arduous or other undesirable work for which they could not hire a white worker, or if some local labor shortage appeared. But probably half of the investment lacked an economic justification. Instead, these servants performed the dirty, heavy, dangerous, menial jobs around the household, or they acted inferior roles as valets and maids to masters and mistresses of the upper class.

The distribution of slaves illustrates these generalizations. Half of the owners were farmers, primarily those with good land along the Sound, who doubtless bought some agricultural laborers but were also investing in women and children. Indeed, these comprised a majority, not articles of production and costly to maintain. Traders, though they formed only a small part of the population, equaled the farmers in the value of their slaves during the early part of the century and continued to invest far more money proportionate to their numbers. Only the well-to-do bought slaves. Men with estates under £500, a sum well above average, seldom owned any and those with less than £1,000 were withdrawing from the market by the late colonial period. Since almost none but the wealthiest invested in this form of property it raised the level of inequality, as did the unequal distribution of stock, money, and debts. It often simply added a superfluous cost to consumption goods, performing functions that white labor could discharge almost as cheaply, and so readily discarded. It did not seem to be diminishing in importance but remained a minor element in Connecticut's economy and society.

The social and economic circumstances of Connecticut's people during the eighteenth century continued to vary with their occupation, place of residence, and life cycle as well as with their inheritance. Differences by geographical area and type of towns remained striking and significant. By 1700 the colony, as we have seen, consisted of several geographical areas, principally near Long Island Sound and north up the Connecticut River. Few settlements existed very far from either body of water. In the southwest, however, Fairfield district extended to Danbury while the valleys of the Housatonic and its tributary, the Naugatuck, enabled pioneers from Stratford and Milford easily to reach Woodbury and Waterbury. Derby and Wallingford, inland from New Haven, had also been founded, while in the east the Thames River gave Norwich access to the sea, and Preston was settled north of Stonington. The colony had therefore spread, rather unevenly, some twenty miles from the coast. Farther north an overflow from the Connecticut Valley had already reached Farmington and Simsbury to the west, while in the east Colchester, Lebanon, and Windham were just being founded. By 1730 the population and economic boom, together with the elimination of the Indians as a factor, had pushed the western frontier all the way up to Litchfield, adding two new towns along the way and forcing the creation of Woodbury as a separate probate district; while in the east no less than twelve towns came into existence, scattered over the whole area from the Rhode Island border to the older Valley communities. Thus there remained only to fill in more densely the regions already occupied with another half-dozen towns and to add a final dozen in the northwest corner.

Of these areas, the southern coast from Milford west possessed the most potential for economic development, with considerable good land, sheltered ports, a relatively mild climate, and a convenient market for its agricultural surplus in New York City. After 1700 these advantages began to stimulate growth, and by the 1720s land values exceeded those elsewhere by 50 percent. This may have been caused by the lack of room for expansion, but in any case the region from that time on led the way. The southeast also contained areas of excellent soil and the best seaport, New London, but with greater variations. In between, the coastal lands from New Haven across the Connecticut River were on average less valuable than the preceding two areas, the towns generally of a middling wealth, and those along the lower Connecticut Valley in particular lagged behind, with an above-average proportion of small, rather poor farms.

Farther north, the upper valley of the Connecticut had, of course, attracted the very earliest settlers. It contained the best meadowland and a large quantity of other good soil. The older towns on the west bank of the river from Wethersfield north remained among the colony's more prosperous although, except for Hartford, the commercial and political center, they did not rival the coastal group. Away from the Valley good agricultural land became increasingly scarce and much of it was isolated. During the first decades of the century few men of property ventured into this backcountry: the richest 10 percent there, according to inventories, owned only a third of the real estate. As time passed, some more prosperous men appeared, but semi-subsistence farming remained the primary occupation, with livestock the staple, and a rising proportion of the men owned no land—an equalitarian society perhaps, but with its lack of opportunity not a very satisfactory one.

As in the seventeenth century, Connecticut's towns, while similar in many ways, consisted of several distinct types. Every village supported some nonfarming activity with a core of craftsmen, professionals, and small traders, but each differed in the degree of diversification. A few towns we can properly call urban, which contrast with the almost exclusively agricultural communities of the uplands. In between came some prosperous and economically diversified towns, and those with equal wealth but more purely rural.

The urban centers, which we have identified primarily by their occupational mix, especially the presence of merchants, included much the same towns as described earlier. These were, in order of mercantile activity, New London, New Haven, Middletown (during the last half), Hartford, and Fairfield, collectively with 11 or 12 percent of their inventoried population engaged in trade.[12] Nearly a fourth of the men were artisans. Also, as one might expect, these towns contained a considerable proportion of laborers and only about one-third of the people were exclusively farmers. The largest number of rich men lived there as measured in personal (though not real) wealth, but the medians were just average. In both forms of property the level of inequality exceeded that of any other towns in the colony—the richest decile owning a little under 50 percent, up by 7 percent since the pre-1700 years. This does not compare with the proportion in the major colonial cities and testifies to the relative equality in colonial Connecticut. They displayed distinctive features in other ways too, notably in the value of shipping, stock, and debts receivable, which made up 30 percent of all personal wealth, increasing over time. They also contained more money than the average. The value of their consumption goods exceeded that of other towns except in the case of New Haven, and even including that city it was £53 against a general £47. However, their inhabitants did not spend any more money on clothes than

---

[12] Norwich developed its trade later, when it became a separate probate district. Its records are not followed here. A case can be made for the inclusion of several towns, such as Milford, which I place in the next category.

usual, some well-dressed men at the top being counteracted by poorly clad laborers on the bottom. They did buy slightly more books but not by much, 24 shillings' worth versus 22, New London dragging down their average. Finally, halfway between consumption goods and articles of production, slaves formed 5 percent of their population in 1754, far above the figure of 2.8 percent for the colony as a whole but nothing compared with Newport's 18.3 or New York City's 17.5 in 1755, and it was half of Boston's 9.8 percent in 1752.

A second type of town also featured an above-average amount of non-agricultural activity, equal, in fact, to those just discussed but with less trade and more manufacturing. They also contained, among the inventoried estates, fewer laborers because of the relative absence of mariners, and more farmers. In addition, they were located on some of the colony's best soil and so were among the richest both in personal and real wealth. They therefore included an above-average proportion of the wealthiest men in both forms of property, whereas the urban group led in personal wealth but was only average in real. Accordingly the concentration of property was lower than that for the urban, the top 10 percent of wealth-holders owning 42 percent versus 47 percent. Most of these towns were located along the south coast, with harbor facilities and adjacent to one of the major ports: Norwalk and Stratford on either side of Fairfield, Milford next to New Haven, and Groton just east of New London. In addition, Wethersfield lay on the Connecticut adjoining Hartford, while the exception, Windham, served as the political and economic center for the country of the same name.

The remaining towns were all primarily agricultural, meaning that over half of the inventories belonged to farmers during the first half of the century, though by the end some communities had shifted to an equal balance between agricultural and nonfarm activity. The inventories contained relatively small amounts of trading stock, ships, and debts receivable. They differed most obviously in their relative wealth as revealed by inventories and in the value of their farmland. One group that by many criteria compared with the diversified towns included a series along the coast at opposite ends of the colony. They consisted of Stamford west of Fairfield, Branford, and Guilford, with Durham just to the north, and finally, near New London, Norwich and Stonington. All contained some good soil that, with the advantage of their location, gave them some of the most valuable real estate in the colony, equal to the other two types. In personal wealth they exceeded any towns except the urban and even them in the median. They also contained an exceptionally large number of the well-to-do, especially in land, and few of the smallest estates since they did not have quite as many young laborers entering trade. In the number of slaves they greatly exceeded any other agricultural communities, and they led also in the value of consumption goods, again on the same level as the urban and diversified towns.

Next come the towns of the upper Connecticut Valley. Three of these we classed with the urban or diversified group. The others, namely Glastonbury, Farmington, Windsor, Suffield, and Enfield, were primarily agricultural, yet with land values only half of their neighbors'—£2 per acre rather than £4, and the prices rose more slowly. As a result the means and medians of the real estate were 50 percent lower than along the coast and personal estate was just average. During the early years of the century well over half of the inventories belonged to farmers and indeed, if we exclude laborers, more numerous in these towns than in most agricultural areas, the figure was two-thirds. They then began to diversify and farmers declined to 60 percent during the middle period and 54 percent at the close. For the most part people moved into the crafts full- or part-time. As this occurred the proportion of personal wealth in nonfarm articles of production and in capital rose to almost equal that of the urban. Two other characteristics deserve mention: slaves were uncommon, numbering only one-third as many as in the towns previously mentioned, and the value of consumption goods was 10 percent less.

Lagging behind the towns of the upper Valley were those of the lower, taken as a group: Killingsworth and Saybrook, which in personal and real wealth rivaled the more northern group until declining at the end, Lyme, and the two Haddams. The first two had enough good land to equal the upper Valley, though far short of the rich coastal towns, but contained a lot of indifferent soil. Taken collectively the level of agricultural activity, in farms and crops, was comparatively low. While they bought more slaves than the people of the upper Valley towns, the value of their consumption goods was less, especially in the three poorer communities. As with their northern neighbors the proportion of laborers rose over time and that of farmers fell even more, the difference going into the crafts.

Another set of towns began the century only sparsely settled but ended well-populated. These included Lebanon, Colchester, and Hebron, well inland and east of the Connecticut Valley, and to the west Derby and Wallingford. Lebanon prospered, diversified, and by the close had become quite a manufacturing center, doubling the value of its consumption goods and with high land values. Wallingford also contained some very good land, similarly increased the money invested in consumption by 50 percent, and like Lebanon added some slaves. Colchester did that too, but in general the other towns remained stable. In particular their land did not increase in value. Their residents owned very few books—Lebanon again was an exception—and their inventoried wealth lagged behind other towns of the same age.

The rest of the colony consisted of upland towns, a few such as Simsbury having been founded before 1700, but mostly later and some still frontier as late as 1750. Roughly they included the western communities of Ridgefield, Redding, Newtown, Woodbury, Waterbury, and points north, and on the east the towns from Bolton to Voluntown and beyond. A few of these benefited from an advantageous situation or prospered as a county seat, but as a group they brought up the rear in every characteristic we have been discussing. They contained the most farmers and the fewest engaged in other activities, the least sums invested in trade, debts, money, slaves, books, and consumption goods. In the last, they averaged through the years £36 worth compared with £52 in the richest towns. Their real property lagged behind whether measured in the value of land, means, medians, or the proportion of large estates, with, moreover, a sharp decrease in the median during the final decade; they ranked last except for the lower Valley in personal wealth. They also came last in the share of inventoried property owned by the top decile of wealth-holders—37 percent of real, 33 percent personal. In this case, at least, equality and poverty went hand in hand.

To some extent the characteristics of Connecticut's society and economy reflected the mixture of different town types. It is tempting to interpret colonial "development" as beginning with a frontier community distinguished by its rather low income per capita and a general equality—everyone poor together—that gradually "evolved" into commercial towns based upon staple crop agriculture, manufacturing, or trade, with consequent results, often lamented: from a Simsbury to a Hartford. But as these towns pointedly testify such an interpretation is quite wrong. Examples of such a progression, if words like progress and develop apply, do exist: Middletown remained an agricultural village for many years before becoming a trading center; but most of Connecticut's towns joined their species from birth. The likes of Hartford, New London, and New Haven originated in trade at the same time that others were being founded as frontier farming villages, so that the colony's economy and society displayed instantly its distinctive features. One can certainly note that after the 1740s "frontier" settlements ceased so that the mixture changed, but the older Connecticut almost duplicated the younger, the child being the father of the man.

To close this chapter by repeating our earlier discussion of age and the life cycle seems redundant, but it serves to integrate our separate treatment of the key forms of property and to focus our description of secular change. Merely to present data on the distribution of wealth by wealth class disguises their true meaning and distorts inferences drawn from them. To describe men who appear at the bottom of tax assessment lists or who left the smallest estates simply as "poor" is not a statement of fact but an interpretation, as is the characterization of a society as impoverished because these "poor" men are numerous. We now know that during the seventeenth century, at least, they were simply young, and we concluded that in order to judge a society we must look at the married heads of families, for these were the poor young men grown older and become responsible for the welfare of the whole community.

Historians have depended heavily upon tax lists and, indeed, where other records are absent or excessively biased one has no choice. For the eighteenth century we have already identified twenty full assessment lists containing (with some additions) over 3,700 men.[13] The relationship between age and wealth shows clearly, though crudely, in the combined means and medians (see Table 4.7). The youngest group consisted of several subspecies. One-fourth do not appear on the lists at all because they remained dependent. One-third were assessed only for their polls or a bit of land with a cow or horse, valued at under £10. Some of these were strangers to the town, others were local boys just declaring their independence but as yet with only their wages to support it. One-sixth of these youngest taxpayers owned a bit more, £10 to £19, perhaps enough for self-sufficiency if no one depended on them. Finally, one-fourth, almost always married plus a few lucky

TABLE 4.7
Taxable Wealth by Age, Eighteenth Century
(cash values as set by law)

	21–29	30–39	40–49	50–59	60–69	70+	All
Mean £	14	35	46	59	55	44	33
Median £	7	28	42	54	49	35	26

[13] These lists, though augmented by other information identifying town residents, probably miss some men in the twenties and thirties. At a guess we should add about 5 percent more in their twenties and 3 percent in their thirties, all dependent polls or servants of some sort, plus a few independent poor men freed from taxes for the particular year.

heirs, paid a tax on a larger estate. Thus among the adult men with almost no property fully two-thirds were young and single, for whom one hopes dependency was a temporary status.

Most thirty-year-olds were the fathers of young children, just beginning as farmers or artisans with small inheritances. The less capable or less fortunate remained dependent polls (one out of four) and if we require £20 in assessed value for a subsistence level, two out of five fell below it. However, the same proportion clearly earned decent incomes if the assessments are evidence. Men aged forty to seventy, the leaders of the community and its economic support, seldom were poor; if the definition of poverty is extended up to £20 to assessed value, excluding polls, it included one out of five (see Appendix 4F). Thus the large number of poor or struggling folk on the tax lists were for the most part not truly poor, certainly not permanently impoverished, but striving to reach a happier level at full maturity, and four out of five would succeed.

The estate inventories provide better evidence for the same conclusions.[14] The mean and median wealth varied with age. Men in their twenties comprised over a third of the population but possessed just a sixth of the personal wealth—about £50 apiece, the median being £30. Again, these small properties did not mean actual poverty because about two-thirds were single and often living at home. Chapter Three presented the requirements for various standards of living, and the only change we need now is to lower the boundaries to adjust for the value of "cash" or "money" instead of "pay," by subtracting about one-third. The single man could support himself with £14 worth of personal property, plus, of course, the income from his labor. Twenty pounds raised his level of living safely above subsistence. Seven out of ten owned the lower amount and two out of five the higher. The married men in their twenties needed twice as much and had it; so they divided in the same way: a majority better than subsistence plus and two-thirds above poverty. Over time, the young man's personal property varied little, following the general business cycle with peaks in the 1720s and 1760s succeeded in each case by a decline returning them to their average.

As men entered their thirties almost all would be married and the fathers of young children. To support that larger family at a minimum level of subsistence required half again as much personal property (£20) and for a higher standard of living twice as much (£40) as the single man. Most of them met that requirement; indeed, their average was

[14] See Appendix 4G.

£102 and the median £72. Only one in ten fell short of subsistence. Three-fourths had enough for subsistence plus and a third were well-off. Our "poor" young men of the tax lists, if we lump them together crudely, thus enjoyed odds of ten to one in favor of achieving enough personal wealth to support themselves at a subsistence level of living, provided that they survived into their thirties and married, and half would provide comfort for their wives and children.[15] Indeed, for some unknown reason their prosperity peaked at the end of the colonial period.

With men over forty we begin to describe the fathers of teen-aged and young adult children. Whereas the younger children cost more to maintain than they earned, the reverse became true at some point. If indeed the assessed value of £18 for a ratable poll reflects a man's net income from his labor, as we have argued, then each son of sixteen added that amount, or somewhat less depending upon cost of maintenance. Presumably the daughters performed equivalent functions without which the parents would have to hire help, but which did not develop as much cash income; if so, the property of a father with sons exceeded that of one with daughters—a hypothesis I leave for someone else to test. At any rate we probably see the effects of the sons' contribution to the estates of their fathers, just as the economic results of marriage are evident. Men in their forties owned, on the average, one-third more in personal property than the thirty-year-olds and those in the fifties added another 20 percent. The two age groups held half of all the personal wealth even though they numbered less than three-tenths of the men. The median and the mean suggest an annual surplus of £4 and £6, increasing with age, which enabled the fathers to meet the rising cost of living with something extra. This extra lifted all but 8 or 9 percent above the poverty level, by this criterion. The wealth of these older married men fluctuated wildly over time, describing a V, with the nadir during the depression, 30 percent below the two apexes, reflecting the fortunes of the large wealthy group.

These fluctuations did not much affect the oldest men. Those in their sixties began to reduce their personal estates at the annual net rate of £1 to £3 (the median versus the mean) because gifts to children exceeded their gains, but they remained wealthier than the forty-year-olds. Moreover, they were really better off than even this suggests, because most of the children had been provided for and such as remained at home were old enough to contribute. The wife of a man

---

[15] The minimums for this age group are estimated as subsistence, £20; subsistence plus, £40; comfort, £70; and well-off, £100.

aged sixty-four would herself be sixty and would have stopped bearing children twenty years or so earlier. One daughter might stay at home to help with the housework or a son to assist with the farm or shop, which he hoped to inherit soon. Only one out of ten older men had to depend upon their children or on charity, and not far from half lived comfortably, to judge from their personal estates. One change after 1700 common to men of all ages over forty was an increase in the proportion of large propertyowners. Among the living population, 18 percent of men older than that left £200.

Finally, the personal property of men over seventy followed the business cycle without any other secular change. The proportion who had given away the principal part of their estates settled down during the eighteenth century at roughly 40 percent, increasing as men aged. Overall the personal wealth of these grandfathers declined by about one-fifth and a man of eighty years would have reverted to the level of fifty years before. However, his requirements would have shrunk even more, so that fewer than one out of eight fell below the subsistence level.

We find, then, that men of various ages owned different amounts of personal property with different distributions of wealth for each age group. Men under thirty characteristically owned under £30 and relatively few exceeded £60. Those in their thirties, twice as wealthy, typically owned above £30 but less than £100, many of the men at the bottom being still single. Middle-aged men usually were worth £60 to £200 and continued to increase their property every year. The estates of those over sixty began to shrink and from seventy on they gave away their belongings as fast at they had once acquired them.

Therefore, each wealth class was associated with and in some degree explained by a particular age structure, just as in the seventeenth century. Table 4.8 shows the distribution of personal wealth in percent-

TABLE 4.8
Distribution of Personal Wealth by Wealth Class,
Eighteenth Century

£	20–29	30–39	40–49	50–59	60–69	70+	Total
1–29	64.9	20.4	6.1	3.2	3.2	0.2	100.0
30–59	41.2	27.3	13.9	9.2	5.5	2.9	100.0
60–119	21.6	29.9	21.6	15.0	8.3	3.5	99.9
120–199	12.7	27.8	23.8	20.6	11.9	3.2	100.0
200+	9.5	26.7	23.8	23.8	12.4	3.8	100.0

ages among the living population. The poorest group consisted so heavily of young men that the reader who becomes inspired by all this to study probate records can confidently attribute the small estate of an obscure owner to a young man—the odds are four or five to one in favor—and that of a single man with even greater confidence, at least in Connecticut. Very few such properties belonged to men over forty. The inventories of the next level are divided quite evenly along the age spectrum, but again belonged mostly to the young. That begins to change with medium-sized properties, held especially by the fathers of young or teen-aged children. By the time we reach the largest inventories of £200, the distribution clusters around men in the late forties and older despite their small proportion of the population.

The distribution showed little secular change. Since the proportion of marital groups in the colony did not alter until the final years, and then just slightly, continuity was the pervasive feature in the relationship of the life cycle to personal wealth.

The same generalizations apply to real wealth.[16] After 1700 everyone, young and old, began to acquire land, climaxing with the economic boom of the 1720s. Twenty years of decline reduced the value of inventoried real estate to the level of 1700. Beginning in the late forties the decline was replaced by an improvement, except for the youngest men. The growth was especially noteworthy for the rise in the price of land, but even if we discount that real property had recovered to the level of the boom during the 1720s.

Taking the period as a whole, one-seventh of the inventories contained no land. A third of these belonged to men under thirty and half to men under forty. Since they were really much more numerous than the inventories show, the young single and married men actually accounted for considerably over half of the landless element—probably three-fourths. The remainder of the landless consisted of older men, each age group contributing equally except for those over seventy, proportionately more of whom lacked real property. About one in ten of the inventories listed real estate valued under £40, the equivalent of a house and lot. These properties also belonged to the young, generally laborers who had inherited a bit of the family property or artisans just starting out. The same holds true of the slightly larger owners of £40 to £80 worth, adequate for someone not engaged in full-time agriculture or a newlywed. In short, the smallest properties belonged mostly to those who did not need much.

The more valuable estates were owned by older men. Thus the av-

[16] See Appendix 4H.

erage age of those with real properties inventoried at £120 to £199, the cost of an adequate though small farm, was just fifty. When we reach £200, men under thirty almost vanish and at £500 so do those under forty. Indeed, if we did not know the age of such a person, we could safely guess him to be over fifty, and above £1,000 sixty would come close, with heavy odds against an owner less than forty.

As men progressed through stages in the life cycle their real estate increased. One-third of those under thirty owned none at all, more than half had at best a house and lot, and over two-thirds lacked enough land to subsist even a family of young children. Once married, however, even the men in their twenties obtained enough for minimal needs. Their situation varied over time. The proportion of the landless young remained at only one-fourth during the first thirty years of the century but exceeded two-fifths during the 1740s. This high level continued for the rest of the colonial period, but without any further increase.

When a man married his real property at once leaped. The father of young children acquired at least a little land, though during the 1740s and again in the late 1760s the proportion of landless rose disturbingly—indeed, it quadrupled after the boom of the twenties. Generally, however, young fathers secured a small farm or enough to feed a craftsman's family. Not far from half owned real estate sufficient for a subsistence-plus level, but few young fathers acquired large properties.

So also, as with personal estates, the older fathers increased their real wealth. Men in their forties and fifties seldom lacked land, once again except during the depression years when as many as three in ten had less than enough for a subsistence farm (though some of these were not farmers). By the close of the period three-fourths of men in their forties and five-sixths of the older group owned a sufficiency, and indeed over a fourth of the latter had £500 worth, which meant a 200-acre farm during most of the period. The grandfathers show a different pattern: the landless began to increase but so did large properties, depending upon whether the owners kept ahead of their children's needs, and for men over seventy estates worth over £80 became fewer as more and more gave away their land. Even with these men, over one in five retained large holdings and the great majority kept enough for their necessities. All felt the effects of the depression, the oldest most of all, for during the years 1730 to 1750 a third of those over seventy were landless. Surely they had tried to cushion the effects of the depression by giving all they had to their children, and that explains why men in their forties felt the hard times less than anyone else. After the depression the elderly ceased to surrender everything and by 1770 only 10 percent had divested themselves of all real estate at their death, the same proportion as seventy years before.

We can see, then, that the high number of landless is not as evil as it might seem. The landless seldom had to support families, often lived at home or rented a room from their wages as laborers and earnings as artisans. Except during the long period of depression, men with the greatest need for real estate usually owned some. All this does not directly answer the question about the levels of living of the men in various stages of their life cycle. For further evidence we examine the consumer goods that the land helped to support.

We saw earlier that the people's household articles and personal items such as clothing constituted a large part of their property and remained stable in value over time. Men with very small estates owned nothing else. These, as we have seen, were young men, plus a few aged or very unfortunate individuals. As wealth increased people spent more on what they needed or desired—beds, clothing, kitchen utensils, books—but no longer their entire income. Thus men with personal wealth of between £20 and £49 invested three-fourths of it in this form and those with £50 to £99 spent half, but men with over £500 were satisfied with consumer goods worth only a fifth of their personal property.

The relationship to the life cycle is obvious. First, we need to repeat in eighteenth-century currency the definition of levels of living as revealed by the value of consumption articles required by men at different stages of the life cycle.[17] For two time periods we have particularly extensive probate data and the necessary biographical information: 1700-

TABLE 4.9
Requisite Consumption Goods for Levels of Living,
Eighteenth century (cash values)

	Single men	Young fathers	Older fathers	Grandfathers	Retired
Subsistence	8	10	14	10	8
Subsistence plus	14	20	30	20	14
Comfortable	20	35	55	35	20
Well-off	40	60	80	60	40
Luxury	100	150	200	150	100

[17] I raised the requirement for "well-off" by £10 throughout on the purely pragmatic ground that by the older standard more men lived at that level than the next lower one of "comfort," and this seemed unlikely.

TABLE 4.10

Percentage of Adult Men at Each Level of Living, by Marital Status, Based on Consumption Goods

(cash values, 1765–1774 adjusted)

	Poor	Subsistence	Subsistence plus	Comfortable	Well-off	Luxury	Total
1700–1724							
Single men	9½	8½	5	3½	1½	0	28
Young fathers	3	7	12	11½	8	½	42
Older fathers	1	3	5½	3½	3½	½	17
Grandfathers	0	½	2	3	3	½	9
Retired	½	½	½	1½	1	0	4
Total	14	19½	25	23	17	1½	100
1755–1764							
Single men	10½	6	6	4	1½	0	28
Young fathers	5	8½	10	7	10½	1	42
Older fathers	1	4	5	4	3	0	17
Grandfathers	0	1	1	2½	3½	0	8
Retired	½	1	½	1½	½	1	5
Total	17	20½	22½	19	19	2	100
1765–1774							
Single men	12½	6½	4	3½	3	½	30
Young fathers	3½	6	10	10½	8½	2½	41
Older fathers	½	2	6	4	3½	0	16
Grandfathers	0	½	2	2½	2½	½	8
Retired	½	1	½	1½	1½	0	5
Total	17	16	22½	22	19	3½	100

1724 and 1765-1774. As a sort of check I have added material from the Fairfield, Hartford, and Middletown districts for 1755-1764 for which data on the life cycle is less accurate. The details are in Appendix 4I, and a succinct summary is presented in Table 4.10. The reader will see that we need not attend to changes over time. The proportion of single men with insufficient consumption goods rose a bit and so did those with exceptional amounts (even after adjustments) but the situation of most age groups remained constant. The table is reasonably accurate if we remember that the conversion of probate data into material valid for the living population is imprecise, and that the values assigned to the several levels of living are based upon an informed guess.

The relationship between the life cycle and the value of consumption goods owned is strong, as we would expect. Despite the limited needs of single men, a third could not supply their own necessities (if the inventories reveal all their belongings), and these would have to rely upon others to furnish them with items such as beds and cooking utensils. One out of four or five owned just enough to get by, but the rest, not far from half of the total, could provide for themselves. The young fathers benefited because their wives' marriage portion normally consisted of just such articles. As a result very few lacked enough for their family, and many of those labeled "poor" probably had suffered some abnormal event, a fire or prolonged illness, which had led to their early death. Such disasters may also account for some among the one out of six whose inventories suggest a bare subsistence level. Three-fourths, however, possessed enough household goods to provide satisfactorily and half lived in comfort, though almost none achieved wealth. Out of every ten poor single men, seven would improve their standard of living upon marriage, and those at the subsistence level would advance into the next class as young fathers, though none would rise from rags to riches.

The fact is that luxury, in Connecticut, rarely existed regardless of age. Older men often could have lived very well indeed if they had so desired. In most societies an economic upper class of men would surely own far more than £200 in items such as fine clothing, valuable furniture, and carriages, but scarcely over one in a hundred did that in Connecticut; indeed, any sum over £300 is so unusual as to make one suspect an error, perhaps attributing to household goods what really consisted of stock in trade. The "older fathers" with children in their teens on up but not yet married seldom even qualified as well-off, on present evidence—around one out of five, the same proportion as in the case of younger men, though of course they needed more property.

On the other hand they were almost never poor. In general they bought enough for their families to live respectably, even comfortably, at a middle-class standard rather than above or below. The highest medians belonged to the grandfathers, who did not own quite as much as before they had endowed their children but whose needs diminished to the extent that two out of three lived comfortably. This includes the "retired" group whose expenditures shrank proportionately to their possessions.

Our description of the circumstances of Connecticut's people has separated their personal property, real estate, and consumption goods. These must now be reunited and reinterpreted by considering the needs of each individual with respect both to his stage in the life cycle and his occupation. Most obviously, a skilled craftsman required as much personal wealth as did the farmer but not the land, for he derived his income from his skill with the tools of his trade: for him a house and a few acres sufficed. In addition we need separate tables defining the requisite value of real estate for use when the inventories fail to state the number of acres, in order to allow for changes in the price of land (see Appendix 4J). Otherwise we can follow our tables for the seventeenth century, converting to "cash" money. This process permits a definitive description of society according to its standard of living. At the same time we can address finally and most effectively the question of whether the colony's people were declining, progressing, or just holding their own.

Again a few examples will help and replace mere percentages. Hezekiah Lewis of Wallingford died in 1713 at age twenty-seven, leaving an estate of £59 lawful money to his wife. This is £1 short of the subsistence level, and he had only a house and a home lot. On the other hand he owned £9 worth of smith tools, so that his income undoubtedly raised him above poverty, especially without children. Again, young Samuel Benham of Farmington, when he died in 1753, also left a widow but no children. His £16 worth of household goods was not much above subsistence level. However, he owned forty acres of land, at least some of which was improved, since it was worth £100, and he had bought the timber for a barn and a house. He also had two yoke of cattle and other farm animals with a personal estate of £63, safely above subsistence plus, so he belongs there. He clearly was putting his money into articles of production rather than consumption. Finally, Lt. Azur Tomlinson of Stratford (1658-1728) had enough personal wealth—£207—to rank among the well-off considering his age, but he owned only 72½ acres. Fortunately the inventory specifies that his land was just half of the family farm, shared with his only son

Zachariah, Junior, so that he clearly belongs with the more affluent. His son, by the way, left a true fortune of £11,131 when he died in 1771.[18]

The result of all this analysis is displayed in Table 4.11, which includes the entire period from the 1640s to 1775. It combines the circumstances of all the adult men as derived from the probate population, for which see Appendix 4K. The numbers reveal a long-range stability with temporary changes due to depressions and economic booms. The eighteenth century seems a little more prosperous than the seventeenth. The proportion of the poor and of those at the subsistence level never rose as high as during the depression of 1670 to 1689, and the well-to-do plus wealthy men fluctuated between 15 and 22 percent after 1700 compared with 7 to 13 percent before. The last few years show stagnation (once we have corrected for wealth bias) and a slight increase in the number of the poor. Since inventories

TABLE 4.11
Levels of Living, All Men, 1640–1774 (percentages)

	Poor	Subs.	Subs. +	Comf.	Well-off	Lux.
1640–1659	23	32	25	13	5½	1½
1660–1669	16	29	24	24	5	2
1670–1679	22	28	27	12	6	3
1680–1689	23	23	26	15	10	3
1690–1699	14	28	27	18½	9½	3
1700–1709	10	26½	27	20	15	1½
1710–1714	12½	23½	31	17½	13½	2
1715–1724	13	19½	33½	16½	14½	3
1735–1749	20	21½	20½	15	19½	3
1750–1754	13	23	27½	20	11	5½
1765–1769	16½	19½	25	19	15	4½
	(20)	(20)			(12)	(3½)
1770–1774	15	21½	26	20	13	4½
	(17½)	(22)			(11)	(3½)

NOTE: The figures in parentheses for 1765–1769 and 1770–1774 show the adjustment for wealth bias. The whole table translates the original source according to marital status. The information as to what proportion of the men were single, young fathers, and so on results from looking up the polls on tax lists. It is an approximation, so the figures are rounded. Data for 1750–1754 come only from the Hartford, Fairfield, and Windham probate districts. Those for 1735–1749 depend on Fairfield's and Hartford's, the latter based on sketchy summaries of the inventories.

[18] Lewis: New Haven district probate records, 4:153, 197; Benham: Hartford district probate records, 17:29, 69; Tomlinson: Fairfield district probate records, 8:168.

show, in part, the result of accumulations over time, this may reflect the depression of the late sixties rather than a decline during the years 1770-1774.

Applying our life-cycle approach to these generalizations we find, of course, that the poor were mostly single (see Appendix 4L). Taking the first and last decades as representative, unmarried men composed 70 percent of those living below subsistence, the rest being almost entirely young fathers. Men just getting by also belonged primarily to the same age groups, now with more fathers. The class of subsistence plus consisted principally of young fathers (who, we must remember, formed two-fifths of all men), with equal numbers single and older. They still remained the largest part of the comfortable and well-off, but older fathers appear more often and the single men diminished. Finally, the largest proportion of the wealthy were men with children in their teens on up, notably such grandfathers as remained active.

We also confirm the changes in levels of living as men moved through the usual family sequence (Appendix 4M). Single men as a rule were poor or just subsisted, roughly a third at each level, fluctuating very little over time except for an increase at the end. As we have seen the poor among them commonly either lived at home or with an employer, but the older ones, especially the married, must have gone into debt or depended in some measure upon charity, presumably forthcoming from relatives. We will discuss these "laborers" in the next chapter. Most single men could expect an improvement as they progressed through the familiar stages of life. The three out of ten who were poor shrank to only one in ten upon marriage and to only one out of twenty by the time they reached middle age. Put differently, three-fifths of the poor escaped their poverty after marriage and, if they survived until middle age, nine out of ten of those who remained in the colony succeeded in attaining economic independence. The prospect remained just as favorable at the end of the period as earlier.

Most young married men fared reasonably well despite their higher expenses. We doubled the requirements for rising out of the poor class, principally by adding land, and more than doubled the standard for a subsistence-plus level. Since by definition the young parents could not obtain much economic aid from their little children, the drain on the father's income was considerable. Despite this, fewer than 10 percent remained poor and roughly seven out of ten lived safely above subsistence; indeed, if our judgment is correct fully a third enjoyed comfort. This progress resulted from the advantages of marriage, as we explained earlier.

The further effects of these advantages appear in the standard of living enjoyed by older fathers, despite our raising the requirements 50 to 100 percent. Very few of these remained poor except during the depression and fully three-fourths lived at or above the subsistence-plus level. About half provided comfort for their families and this remains true even if at the end we subtract something for bias in the records. The success of these men surely encouraged such young fathers as remained poor or at bare subsistence level: many would eventually live well.[19] To some extent this prosperity derived from continuing gifts by parents supplementing the initial dowry or patrimony, especially upon their deaths, but as we have observed the children themselves, now in their teens or older, contributed a great deal. Thus the average young father living at the midpoint of subsistence plus ultimately reached the very edge of comfort, even though that required him almost to double his wealth.[20]

For grandfathers we lowered the definition of the levels of living to those of the young fathers, on the assumption that their needs would diminish as their children became self-sufficient. Presumably the profit from the labor of such as remained at home would at best cancel the loss from the gifts of capital and productive articles to the ones who married. This definition served to elevate the grandfathers' prosperity to a peak: almost none were poor, not more than 6 percent fell below a subsistence-plus standard, and not far from half were well-off! Yet this achievement seems genuine, even if in less degree than estimated here. If we required the same property as the fathers with growing children all at home, the group at the subsistence level would become poor, most of those at subsistence plus would drop a level, and the comfortable likewise, while the well-off would be demoted to comfort, with this effect:

	Poor	Subsistence	Subsistence +	Comfortable	Well-off +
older fathers	5½	18	26	26	24
grandfathers	7	17	30	33	14

Since this adjustment seems extreme we conclude that grandfathers continued to gain some ground, as indeed their real estate attests. Even

[19] Thus 30 percent of the young fathers at best just subsisted, but that fell to 24 percent for older men, suggesting that 20 percent improved their position. It is however possible that the poorer ones died or left.

[20] If the average young father was about thirty-three years old and the average older father forty-seven, in fifteen years he added £13 annually, not compounded, presumably at an accelerating rate. This includes all types of property.

a small improvement speaks well for their profits, since they certainly disposed of part of their wealth by gifts to the children.

Finally, retired men by definition gave even more, especially of their land, the lack of which almost defines the status along with the absence of tools and other productive items (such as oxen in the case of farmers or stock in trade for former traders). As one would expect, some of these ended in poverty, very old, crippled in some way, or having always lived near the margin, in all roughly one in twelve.[21] The proportion of poor plus those at the subsistence level, averaging a third of retired men, seems large until we remember that at any given time not over 3 percent of the men were "retired," so a town would contain only one in a hundred who might require help. The rest lived decently and a few even retained considerable property.

Connecticut's people during the eighteenth century differed in their circumstances depending upon several factors. First, the colony's towns included several types. A family residing in a newly settled area would be young, engaged in farming, and the owners of barely enough property to get by. Older communities varied with geography and to a lesser extent with the nature of the original settlement. Some, isolated or with limited natural resources, did not differ much from the new towns, remaining mostly agricultural and with low land values. The residents might own more property because of improvements on the land, and their older age would show in additional consumption goods as well as in better buildings and more livestock. However, no one could acquire real wealth and the enforced equality may have been counteracted by the inability of the people to advance beyond a certain point.

The more fortunately located communities could develop a greater degree of commercial agriculture or specialization in trade. Either brought in more profits, raising the general standard of living, enriching a few, attracting migrant laborers, and enabling some white families to purchase slaves. The larger upper and lower classes resulted in greater inequality though, except for the slaves, most of the inhabitants were better off than if they had lived in less prosperous parts of the colony.

A man's occupation also affected his economic and social situation. About a third of the men were laborers, lacking land or other income-

---

[21] These probably could depend on their children though a few relied upon charity, being taken into a home or assigned some town office like that of prisonkeeper. The same may have been true for some at the subsistence level, with properties that might be adequate for an able-bodied young man but not for the elderly and feeble. See Appendix 4M.

producing assets. For all but the slaves and a small number of whites, that was a temporary line of work, unprofitable except for skilled workers who earned a wage in addition to room and board. The great majority of laborers were local, unmarried, and young men who quickly assumed their fathers' positions, or immigrants to the community of the same sort, whose fate we trace in the next chapter. The largest occupational group, the farmers, ranged from the marginal husbandmen on poor soil on up to some of the colony's richest men. During the early decades of the eighteenth century almost half of the men were primarily farmers, but by 1770 that had dropped to 35 percent as land became more difficult to acquire and alternatives appeared. The laborers might also become craftsmen, for nearly a fourth of the men earned their living that way. Finally, some of the farmers shifted into a profession or a trade, which together doubled from 5 percent of the occupational force before 1700 to 10 percent by the close of the colonial period. These were by all odds the most profitable vocations and ordinarily meant a high standard of living together with the esteem of one's neighbors, especially in the case of the ministers, lawyers, principal town officials, and merchants.

For most men their choice of occupation and both their economic and social positions were either established or profoundly influenced by the family inheritance. However, men typically experienced major changes in both income and status, sometimes even in occupation, as they passed through the life cycle. They began with little property or prestige, gained both upon marriage, and advanced with age until, as grandfathers, they might begin to dispose of their worldly estates while still retaining their standard of living and reputations. The distribution of property in a way reflected that cycle: it remained the same, but the individuals along the scale of wealth varied. A great number of young men boarded a wide pyramidal escalator, a few of whom never ascended, but the rest rose toward the narrowing top, replaced at once by even more young men at the bottom. Fortunately the escalator expanded proportionately. The bottom, then, always consisted primarily of men just starting their careers, with some young fathers and a few older ones; and because Connecticut's population was youthful this lowest class was large. The great majority of these, however, would soon become farmers or craftsmen, supporting their families decently and, in their later years, comfortably, so that their children normally would follow the same upward course.

The preservation of this happy progression depended upon the expansion of the colony's economic base at a rate equal to the number of men involved, that is, to a per capita income that at least remained the same. As far as we can tell, that happened. During the early part of the century the economy expanded even more rapidly than the population. Then for about twenty years the colony's wealth diminished. Recovery followed, and the value of the people's property, presumably also of their income, rose to the level of 1700 without any real growth (except in land values) but with no decline.

Certain indices suggest that during the last ten years or so the welfare of some of the people diminished. Scattered tax lists contain more poor people and a lower assessed value for taxable property extending to all age groups. Estate inventories reveal a larger proportion of landless young beginning in the 1740s and remaining at that new level. Debts payable jumped far ahead of debts receivable, presumably because the importers overpurchased after the Treaty of Paris. On the other hand, taxable property as reported to the legislature showed no decrease. The value and distribution of personal wealth and of consumption goods did not change. If rising land values establish a true gain, then per capita wealth was increasing, and that certainly helped the farmers, as did higher prices for livestock and some crops. Since the circumstances of young married men, as shown by their inventoried wealth, remained stable, most of the poor enjoyed the same good opportunity. This was true in part because growth occurred in fields other than agriculture, especially trade and the professions (the proportion in crafts was constant), and because young men could and did seek land outside the colony. Even within it, the standards of living demonstrate conclusively that the great majority of Connecticut's people fared as well in 1774 as in 1700 or 1670, and that this majority included virtually all of the married men and their families. Indeed, by contrast with most pre-industrial societies, these men did not simply escape poverty but enjoyed real plenty.

APPENDIX 4A

Probate Records Used

For the years before 1730 I used all of the estate inventories with two exceptions: problems with inflation persuaded me to stop taking detailed notes on the Hartford district records between 1723 and 1750, and the few inventories that survive for the New London area prior to 1700 show a wealth bias, so I omitted them. Fairfield and Windham districts, together with the aggregate personal and real figures for Hartford, filled in from 1730 to 1750, and I also began to follow Colchester's records when they began in 1741. After surveying everything during 1750-1753, I used the Fairfield, Windham, and Hartford district inventories for 1754-1764, as well as those of Middletown, Farmington, and Simsbury as they split off from Hartford, but not the probate districts set off from Fairfield and Windham. The final ten years are covered by Fairfield, New Haven, Guilford, New London, Middletown, Colchester, Hartford, Farmington, Simsbury, Sharon, and Stafford districts, but not those of Woodbury, Stamford, Danbury, Litchfield, Norwich, Stonington, Plainfield, and Pomfret.

Distribution of Personal Property, Adult Men

£ (cash)	1700–09	1710–19	1720–29	1730–39	1740–49	1750–59	1760–69	1770–74
1–29	103	158	116	92	138	233	266	186
30–59	120	221	166	91	121	197	252	183
60–119	130	307	252	127	152	243	277	273
120–199	82	139	150	65	64	122	189	140
200–499	52	88	92	50	43	89	124	87
500+	11	20	26	8	11	22	32	29
Total	498	933	802	433	529	906	1140	898
Percentages								
1–29	20.7	16.9	14.5	21.2	26.1	25.7	23.3	20.7
30–59	24.1	23.7	20.7	21.0	22.9	21.7	22.1	20.4
60–119	26.1	32.9	31.4	29.3	28.7	26.8	24.3	30.4
120–199	16.5	14.9	18.7	15.0	12.1	13.5	16.6	15.6
200–499	10.4	9.4	11.5	11.6	8.1	9.8	10.9	9.7
500+	2.2	2.1	3.2	1.9	2.1	2.4	2.8	3.2
Total	100.0	99.9	100.0	100.0	100.0	99.9	100.0	100.0

SOURCE: Estate inventories.

The table above shows the data after an adjustment for wealth bias in the records, which required the subtraction of one-sixth of the estates in the top quintile and their addition to the lowest quintile. I subtracted a bit more from men seventy and over, taking fractions from them rather than from younger men because they seemed especially overrepresented in the records. I added to the poor men in their twenties and thirties in a ratio of two to one, which seemed again to reflect the error in the originals. The second table show the distribution of wealth before the adjustments. The adjustment lowered the mean by £8 and £14 (6 and 9 percent) and the median by £7 in both time periods (6 percent). It did not affect the share of the top 10 percent.

UNADJUSTED PERSONAL ESTATES

£ (cash)	1760–1769		1770–1774	
	N	%	N	%
1–29	234	20.5	156	17.4
30–59	252	22.1	183	20.4
60–119	277	24.3	273	30.4
120–199	197	17.3	147	16.4
200–299	76	6.7	53	5.9
300–399	44	3.9	33	3.7
400–499	22	1.9	18	2.0
500+	38	3.3	35	3.9
Total	1,140	100.0	898	100.1

Distribution of Consumption Goods

£	1700–1724		1765–1774	
	N	%	N	%
1–9	177	10.4	200 (246)	9.5 (11.7)
10–19	267	15.8	304 (327)	14.5 (15.6)
20–29	287	16.9	301	14.3
30–39	226	13.3	308	14.7
40–49	190	11.2	237	11.3
50–59	107	6.3	162	7.7
60–69	104	6.1	122	5.8
70–79	53	3.1	101 (93)	4.8 (4.4)
80–89	66	3.9	65 (54)	3.1 (2.6)
90–99	51	3.0	62 (52)	3.0 (2.5)
100–149	109	6.4	153 (125)	7.3 (5.9)
150–199	39	2.3	28 (25)	1.3 (1.2)
200 +	20	1.2	59 (50)	2.8 (2.4)
Total	1,694	99.9	2,102	100.1
Median	£35.2/6		£38 (35.11/5)	

NOTE: The 1700–1724 set includes all inventories except for some in the Hartford district. Adjustments for wealth bias in the 1765–1774 set shows in parentheses.

Distribution of Debts Receivable by Occupation and Value

	None	1–9	10–19	20–499	500–999	1,000+	Total	% none
1710–1719								
Laborers	101	18	3	3	0	0	125	80.1
Farmers	431	45	15	22	0	0	513	84.0
Artisans	167	15	5	14	0	0	201	83.1
Traders	42	5	3	20	4	5	79	53.2
Prof.	16	0	0	4	0	0	20	80.0
Retired	95	9	6	4	0	0	114	83.3
Other	12	0	0	0	0	0	12	100.0
Total	864	92	32	67	4	5	1,064	81.2
1765–1774								
Laborers	138	23	9	21	0	0	191	72.3
Farmers	317	63	41	120	2	1	544	58.3
Artisans	176	36	20	48	0	0	280	62.9
Traders	49	7	2	31	6	8	103	47.6
Prof.	35	6	1	21	0	2	65	53.8
Retired	174	26	13	22	1	0	236	73.7
Other	42	7	3	7	1	0	60	70.0
Total	931	168	89	270	10	11	1,479	62.9

SOURCE: Estate inventories, Fairfield, Hartford, and New Haven districts.

Ownership of Stock in Trade (PERCENTAGES)

	None	£1–9	£10–19	£20–99	£100+	Share of top 10%	% of total pers. wealth
1700–1719							
Fairfield	70.0	18.4	4.8	5.1	1.7	38.2	6.1
New Haven	79.2	13.3	2.3	4.5	0.7	32.2	3.7
New London	85.2	6.1	2.9	2.9	2.9	73.6	7.2
Hartford	87.0	7.5	1.5	1.9	2.1	75.4	5.4
Total	82.3	10.2	2.4	3.1	2.0	59.7	5.6
1765–1774							
Fairfield	74.6	17.5	2.0	4.0	2.0	55.4	2.8
New Haven	79.7	11.6	3.5	3.7	1.8	71.3	5.5
New London	87.4	6.7	2.2	0.7	3.0	89.8	5.2
Windham	70.7	18.8	5.5	3.3	0.6	49.1	5.1
Hartford, etc.	87.3	6.0	2.4	2.8	1.5	73.2	6.2
Total	81.9	10.3	2.9	3.1	1.7	69.8	5.0

APPENDIX 4F

Distribution of Wealth by Age

	21–29 N	21–29 %	30–39 N	30–39 %	40–49 N	40–49 %	50–59 N	50–59 %	60–69 N	60–69 %	70+ N	70+ %	Total N	Total %
Dep. poll	300	24.1	48	4.7	8	1.3	3	0.7	3	1.1	17	11.9	379	10.2
£0–9	476	38.2	182	18.0	73	11.9	35	8.0	17	6.0	27	18.9	810	21.7
10–19	214	17.2	183	18.1	67	11.0	39	8.9	29	10.3	11	7.7	543	14.6
20–29	106	8.5	180	17.8	89	14.6	44	10.1	30	10.7	14	9.8	463	12.4
30–99	139	11.2	392	38.7	328	53.7	200	59.5	160	56.9	58	40.6	1,337	35.8
100+	10	0.8	27	2.7	46	7.5	56	12.8	42	14.9	16	11.2	197	5.3
Total	1,245	100.0	1,012	100.0	611	100.0	437	100.0	281	99.9	143	100.1	3,729	100.0

COMPOSITION OF WEALTH CLASSES BY AGE GROUPS

	21–29	30–39	40–49	50–59	60–69	70+	Total
Dep. poll	79.2	12.7	2.1	0.8	0.8	4.5	100.1
£0–9	58.8	22.5	9.0	4.3	2.1	3.3	100.0
10–19	39.4	33.7	12.3	7.2	5.3	2.0	99.9
20–29	22.9	38.9	19.2	9.5	6.5	3.0	100.0
30–99	10.4	29.3	24.5	19.4	12.0	4.3	99.9
100+	5.1	13.7	23.4	28.4	21.3	8.1	100.0

SOURCE: Tax lists.

Distribution of Personal Wealth by Age (INVENTORIES, EIGHTEENTH CENTURY)

	21–29		30–39		40–49		50–59		60–69		70–79		Total %
	N	%	N	%	N	%	N	%	N	%	N	%	
£1–29	481	38.9	232	18.8	117	9.5	82	6.6	117	9.5	209	16.7	100.0
30–59	261	19.0	269	19.5	219	15.9	191	13.9	181	13.1	256	18.6	100.0
60–119	146	8.3	311	17.7	367	20.8	336	19.1	283	16.0	318	18.0	99.9
120–199	43	4.4	144	14.9	202	20.9	227	23.5	199	20.6	153	15.8	100.1
200–299	12	3.0	59	14.9	85	21.5	105	26.5	77	19.4	58	14.6	99.9
300–399	7	3.8	19	10.4	35	19.2	43	23.6	50	27.5	28	15.4	99.9
400–499	2	2.4	15	17.6	15	17.6	21	24.7	20	23.5	12	14.1	99.9
500+	4	2.3	20	11.7	36	21.0	53	31.0	27	15.8	31	18.1	99.9
Total	956		1,066		1,076		1,057		954		1,063		

Personal Wealth Owned by Age Groups (percentages)

	21–29	30–39	40–49	50–59	60–69	70–79
£1–29	50.3	21.7	10.9	7.8	12.3	19.5
30–59	27.3	25.2	20.4	18.1	19.0	24.1
60–119	15.3	29.1	34.1	31.8	29.7	30.0
120–199	4.5	13.5	18.8	21.5	20.9	14.4
200–299	1.3	5.5	7.9	9.9	8.1	5.5
300–399	0.7	1.8	3.3	4.1	5.2	2.6
400–499	0.2	1.4	1.4	2.0	2.1	1.1
500+	0.4	1.9	3.3	5.0	2.8	2.9
Total	100.0	100.1	100.0	100.2	100.1	100.1

Distribution of Personal Wealth by Age (Living Population, percentages)

	21–29	30–39	40–49	50–59	60–69	70+	All
£1–29	18.1	5.7	1.7	0.9	0.9	0.6	27.9
30–59	9.8	6.5	3.3	2.2	1.3	0.7	23.8
60–119	5.5	7.6	5.5	3.8	2.1	0.9	25.4
120–199	1.6	3.5	3.0	2.6	1.5	0.4	12.6
200–299	0.5	1.4	1.3	1.2	0.6	0.2	5.2
300–399	0.3	0.5	0.5	0.5	0.4	0.1	2.3
400–499	0.1	0.4	0.2	0.2	0.1	0.0	1.0
500+	0.1	0.5	0.5	0.6	0.2	0.1	2.0
Total	36.0	26.1	16.0	12.0	7.1	3.0	100.2

Distribution of Real Wealth by Age

The following tables consolidate the estate inventories. We remind the reader of the probate districts omitted and of the lack of age information for certain districts. I have not adjusted for price increases during the final quarter-century. Obviously that does not affect the landless nor does it influence the smaller properties except in details. The proportion of the large estates would decrease somewhat but the distribution of these among age groups, which is the subject here, would remain unchanged.

DISTRIBUTION OF REAL WEALTH BY AGE

£	21–29		30–39		40–49		50–59		60–65		70+		Total	
	N	%	N	%	N	%	N	%	N	%	N	%	N	%
None	304	33.3	165	15.8	87	8.3	73	6.8	88	9.1	169	15.6	886	14.5
1–39	198	21.7	137	13.1	86	8.2	56	5.3	64	6.6	104	9.6	645	10.5
40–79	146	16.0	164	15.7	102	9.7	72	6.8	66	6.8	93	8.6	643	10.5
80–119	93	10.2	118	11.3	127	12.1	94	8.8	72	7.4	71	6.5	575	9.4
120–199	89	9.7	139	13.3	171	16.3	147	13.8	120	12.4	132	12.2	798	13.0
200–299	52	5.7	147	14.1	215	20.5	136	12.8	120	12.4	127	11.7	797	13.0
300–399	18	2.0	59	5.6	67	6.4	110	10.3	93	9.6	83	7.7	430	7.0
400–499	4	0.4	41	3.9	46	4.4	94	8.8	75	7.7	65	6.0	325	5.3
500–999	9	1.0	58	5.5	114	10.9	183	17.2	162	16.7	142	13.1	668	10.9
1,000	0	0	17	1.6	35	3.3	100	9.4	110	11.3	98	9.0	360	5.9
Total	913	100.0	1,045	99.9	1,050	100.1	1,065	100.0	970	100.0	1,084	100.0	6,127	100.0

REAL WEALTH OWNED BY AGE GROUPS (PERCENTAGES)

£	21–29	30–39	40–49	50–59	60–69	70–79	Total
None	34.3	18.6	9.8	8.2	9.9	19.1	99.9
1–39	30.7	21.2	13.3	8.7	9.9	16.1	99.9
40–79	22.7	25.5	15.9	11.2	10.3	14.5	100.1
80–119	16.2	20.5	22.1	16.3	12.5	12.3	99.9
120–199	11.2	17.4	21.4	18.4	15.0	16.5	99.9
200–299	6.5	18.4	27.0	17.1	15.1	15.9	100.0
300–499	2.9	13.2	15.0	27.0	22.3	19.6	100.0
500–599	1.3	8.7	17.1	27.4	24.3	21.3	100.1
1,000+	0	4.7	9.7	27.8	30.6	27.2	100.0

Consumer Goods by Marital Status
(PERCENTAGES, UNADJUSTED ESTATE INVENTORIES)

		Single			Young fathers			Older fathers	
	£	1700–1724	1765–1774	£	1700–1724	1765–1774	£	1700–1724	1765–1774
Poor	1–7	33.8	36.7	1–9	6.7	6.4	1–13	4.6	3.7
Subsistence	8–13	30.1	19.8	10–19	17.0	14.2	14–29	19.3	12.0
Subsistence +	14–19	16.9	16.0	20–34	28.2	24.8	30–54	31.7	35.2
Comfortable	20–39	12.3	13.5	35–59	27.7	26.8	55–79	21.1	22.3
Well-off	40–99	5.5	12.2	60–149	19.4	21.4	80–199	20.5	24.9
Luxury	100+	1.4	1.7	150+	1.0	6.4	200+	2.8	1.9
Total		100.0	99.9		100.0	100.0		100.0	100.0
N		219	237		401	295		394	267
		Grandfathers			Retired			All men	
Poor	1–9	0.3	0.7	1–7	9.3	15.3		9.0	10.5
Subsistence	10–19	4.0	5.9	8–13	15.8	17.1		16.6	12.7
Subsistence +	20–34	19.5	20.2	14–19	17.5	15.3		24.3	22.1
Comfortable	35–59	32.8	28.6	20–39	33.9	27.9		25.5	24.8
Well-off	60–149	37.5	33.4	40–99	20.2	23.7		21.6	24.6
Luxury	150+	5.9	11.3	100+	3.3	0.7		2.8	5.3
Total		100.0	100.1		100.0	100.0		99.8	100.0
N		323	461		183	287		1,520	1,547

Eighteenth-Century Standards for Levels of Living

	Con-sumption (£)	Per-sonal (£)	Acres	1700–1749		1750–1764	
				Value Real (at £2)	Total	Value Real (at £3)	Total
Subsistence							
Single men	£ 8	£ 14	House + lot	£ 15	£ 30	£ 15	£ 30
Young fathers	10	20	H + 15a	40	60	55	75
Older fathers	14	28	H + 40a	80	110	120	150
Grandfathers	10	20	H + 15a	40	60	55	75
Retired	8	14	H + lot	15	30	15	30
Subsistence plus							
Single men	14	20	H + 15	40	60	60	80
Young fathers	20	40	H + 40	100	120	140	180
Older fathers	30	60	H + 80	180	220	240	300
Grandfathers	20	40	H + 40	100	120	140	180
Retired	14	20	H + 15	40	60	60	80
Comfortable							
Single men	20	40	H + 40	80	120	140	180
Young fathers	35	70	H + 80	160	240	240	320
Older fathers	55	100	H + 120	240	360	360	480
Grandfathers	35	70	H + 80	160	240	240	320
Retired	20	40	H + 40	80	120	140	180
Well-off							
Single men	40	70	H + 60	£120	£190	£200	£270
Young fathers	60	100	H + 120	240	340	400	500
Older fathers	80	200	H + 200	400	600	600	800
Grandfathers	60	100	H + 120	240	340	400	500
Retired	40	70	H + 60	120	190	200	270
Luxury							
Single and retired					500		800
Young fathers and grandfathers					1,000		1,600
Older fathers					2,000		3,000

163

Level of Living, Probate Population
(PERCENTAGES)

	Poor	Subsistence ·	Subsistence +	Comfortable	Well-off	Luxury	N
1640–1659	15.8	32.7	26.9	15.8	7.0	1.8	171
1660–1669	12.9	26.6	27.3	24.5	8.6	3.4	139
1670–1679	20.3	24.7	26.8	14.3	11.7	2.2	231
1680–1689	17.0	19.2	23.0	22.3	16.1	2.4	417
1690–1699	11.5	24.4	28.3	19.7	13.9	2.1	512
1700–1709	7.5	23.6	25.6	23.6	17.5	2.2	504
1710–1714	8.2	19.9	30.9	20.8	17.3	2.8	643
1715–1724	8.7	17.7	30.5	19.8	18.7	4.6	587
1735–1749	15.3	20.5	22.0	15.6	22.7	3.9	463
1750–1754	11.4	19.0	26.2	22.4	13.5	7.5	562
1765–1769	12.1	16.9	24.1	21.3	18.9	6.7	729
Adjusted	12.4	17.3	24.7	21.8	17.8	6.0	
1770–1774	11.4	17.6	22.8	20.5	18.8	8.9	771
Adjusted	11.3	18.3	23.6	21.2	17.6	8.0	

Composition of Classes, Standard of Living by Life Cycle, Living Population (PERCENTAGES)

	Single Men	Young fathers	Older fathers	Grand-fathers	Retired	Total
Poor						
1700–1709	70	23	3	0	4	100
1765–1769	58	31	7	1	2	99
1770–1774	71	17	6	0	5	99
Subsistence						
1700–1709	38	40	16	1	5	100
1765–1769	48	32	12	2	6	100
1770–1774	37	43	12	1	7	100
Subsistence plus						
1700–1709	17	56	18	6	4	101
1765–1769	22	52	14	7	5	100
1770–1774	25	51	14	5	5	100
Comfortable						
1700–1709	13	40	26	17	4	100
1765–1769	17	42	24	12	5	100
1770–1774	20	47	20	8	5	100
Well-off						
1700–1709	20	37	20	20	3	100
1765–1769	10	42	29	14	6	101
1770–1774	5	40	30	21	4	100
Luxury						
1700–1709	0	23	31	46	0	100
1765–1769	13	22	22	35	8	100
1770–1774	4	25	25	39	7	100

Levels of Living, Probate and Living Populations

The following tables rely a little too much, after 1724, on the Hartford probate district and its subdivisions, but the error would not exceed a few percentage points. The reader should remember that grandfathers did not actually own more wealth than their juniors; they presumably required less, which is the point here. For each time period we provide first the actual numbers derived from inventories and secondly the levels for the living population. The proportions for the men's marital status are derived from tax records and the big genealogies as before. They are inexact but not far off, except perhaps for my interpretation of "retired." If the reader feels that these should be considered on a par with other grandfathers then they fall in a lower category.

APPENDIX 4M

Probate and Levels of Living, Living Populations

	Single men		Young fathers		Older fathers		Grandfathers		Retired	
	N	%	N	%	N	%	N	%	N	%
1700–1709										
Poor	23	26.1	7	5.5	2	01.6	0	0	6	9.1
Subsistence	33	37.5	32	25.4	30	23.4	4	4.2	20	30.3
Subsistence plus	14	15.9	45	35.7	35	27.3	17	17.7	18	27.3
Comfortable	8	9.1	24	19.0	37	28.9	36	37.5	13	19.7
Well-off	10	11.4	17	13.5	21	16.4	32	33.3	9	13.6
Luxury	0	0	1	0.8	3	2.3	7	7.3	0	—
Total	88	100.0	126	99.9	128	99.9	96	100.0	66	100.0
									All	
Poor	7		2½		½		0		½	10½
Subsistence	10		10½		4		½		1	26
Subsistence plus	4½		15		5		1½		1	27
Comfortable	2½		8		5		3½		1	20
Well-off	3		5½		3		3		½	15
Luxury	0		½		½		½		0	1½
Total	27		42		18		9		4	100

Continued

	Single men		Young fathers		Old fathers		Grandfathers		Retired	
	N	%	N	%	N	%	N	%	N	%
1700–1714										
Poor	24	28.9	15	8.4	11	6.1	1	0.7	3	4.5
Subsistence	24	28.9	47	26.4	37	20.4	7	5.1	9	13.4
Subsistence plus	20	24.0	65	36.5	58	32.0	28	20.6	30	44.8
Comfortable	8	9.6	28	15.7	45	24.9	41	30.1	14	20.9
Well-off	5	6.0	21	11.8	26	14.4	50	36.8	10	14.9
Luxury	2	2.4	2	1.1	4	2.2	9	6.6	1	1.5
Total	83	99.8	178	99.9	181	100.0	136	99.9	67	100.0
										All
Poor	8		3½		1		0		0	12½
Subsistence	8		11		3½		½		½	23½
Subsistence plus	6½		15½		6		2		2	32
Comfortable	2½		6½		4½		2½		1	17
Well-off	1½		5		2½		3½		½	13
Luxury	½		½		½		½		0	2
Total	27		42		18		9		4	100

1715–1724

										All
Poor	29	29.0	13	9.2	3	2.0	1	0.8	8	11.4
Subsistence	24	24.0	26	18.4	31	20.4	6	4.7	16	22.8
Subsistence plus	23	23.0	64	45.4	40	26.3	33	26.0	19	27.1
Comfortable	13	13.0	21	14.9	35	23.0	30	23.6	17	24.3
Well-off	10	10.0	13	9.2	37	24.3	43	33.9	8	11.4
Luxury	1	1.0	4	2.8	6	3.9	14	11.0	2	2.8
Total	100	100.0	141	99.9	152	99.9	127	100.0	70	99.8

					All
Poor	8	4	0	0	½
Subsistence	6½	8	3½	½	1
Subsistence plus	6½	19	4½	2½	1
Comfortable	3½	6	4	2	1
Well-off	3	4	4	3	½
Luxury	½	1	1	1	0
Total	28	42	17	9	4

	All
Poor	12½
Subsistence	19½
Subsistence plus	33½
Comfortable	16½
Well-off	14½
Luxury	3½
Total	100

Continued

	Single men		Young fathers		Older fathers		Grandfathers		Retired	
	N	%	N	%	N	%	N	%	N	%
1735–1744 (inaccurate)										
Poor	20	35.1	24	17.0	12	12.0	2	2.1	13	19.4
Subsistence	11	19.3	35	24.8	18	18.0	9	9.3	21	31.3
Subsistence plus	8	14.0	32	22.7	24	24.0	20	20.6	18	26.9
Comfortable	7	12.3	23	16.3	18	18.0	16	16.5	8	11.9
Well-off	9	15.8	25	17.8	26	26.0	39	40.2	6	8.9
Luxury	2	3.5	2	1.4	2	2.0	11	11.3	1	1.5
Total	57	100.0	141	100.0	100	100.0	97	100.0	67	99.9
										All
Poor	10		7		2		0		1	20
Subsistence	5½		10½		3		1		1½	21½
Subsistence plus	4		9½		4		1½		1½	20½
Comfortable	4		7		3		1½		1	16½
Well-off	4½		7½		4		3		0	19
Luxury	1		½		0		1		0	2½
Total	29		42		16		8		5	100
1750–1754										
Poor	35	30.7	8	5.7	5	4.3	1	0.8	15	19.2
Subsistence	38	33.3	30	21.4	18	15.6	6	5.1	15	19.2
Subsistence plus	24	21.0	47	33.6	31	27.0	21	17.9	24	30.8
Comfortable	10	8.7	30	21.4	38	33.0	31	26.5	17	21.8
Well-off	5	4.4	16	11.4	21	18.3	31	26.5	4	5.1
Luxury	2	1.8	9	6.4	2	1.7	27	23.1	3	3.8
Total	114	99.9	140	99.9	115	99.9	117	99.9	78	99.9

										All
Poor	9		2		½		0		1	12½
Subsistence	10		9		2½		½		1	23
Subsistence plus	6½		14		4½		1½		1½	28
Comfortable	2½		9		5		2		1	19½
Well-off	1½		4½		3		2		½	11½
Luxury	½		2½		½		2			5½
Total	30		41		16		8		5	100
1765–1769										
Poor	44	32.4	20	12.8	10	6.7	4	2.4	10	8.3
Subsistence	43	31.6	24	15.4	22	14.7	6	3.6	28	23.3
Subsistence plus	25	18.4	50	32.1	33	22.0	36	21.5	32	26.7
Comfortable	15	11.0	30	19.2	41	27.3	48	28.7	21	17.5
Well-off	7	5.1	24	15.4	41	27.3	45	26.9	21	17.5
Luxury	2	1.5	8	5.1	3	2.0	28	16.8	8	6.7
Total	136	100.0	156	100.0	150	100.0	167	99.9	120	100.0
									All	*Adjusted*
Poor	10		5		1		0	½	16½	(19½)
Subsistence	9½		6½		2½		½	1	20	(20½)
Subsistence plus	5½		13		3½		1½	1	24½	(24½)
Comfortable	3		8		4½		2½	1	19	(19)
Well-off	1½		6½		4½		2	1	15½	(13)
Luxury	½		2		0		1½	½	4½	(3½)
Total	30		41		16		8	5	100	(100)

APPENDIX 4M

Continued

	Single men N	%	Young fathers N	%	Older fathers N	%	Grandfathers N	%	Retired N	%
1770–1774										
Poor	44	35.2	9	6.3	8	5.7	3	1.4	20	13.5
Subsistence	33	26.4	32	22.5	22	15.7	8	3.7	41	27.7
Subsistence plus	27	21.6	46	32.4	31	22.1	37	17.3	35	23.6
Comfortable	17	13.6	33	23.2	35	25.0	44	20.6	29	19.6
Well-off	3	2.4	18	12.7	34	24.3	76	35.5	15	10.1
Luxury	1	0.8	4	2.8	10	7.1	46	21.5	8	5.4
Total	125	100.0	142	99.9	140	99.9	214	100.0	148	99.9

	Single men N	%	Young fathers N	%	Older fathers N	%	Grandfathers N	%	All	Adjusted
Poor	10½		2½		1		0		15	(17)
Subsistence	8		9		2½		½		21½	(22)
Subsistence plus	6½		13½		3½		1½		26	(26)
Comfortable	4		9½		4		1½		20	(20)
Well-off	1		5½		4		3		14	(12)
Luxury	0		1		1		1½		3½	(3)
Total	30		41		16		8		100	(100)

Standards of Living of Active and Retired Grandfathers
(IN PERCENTAGES)

	Poor	Subsistence	Subsistence plus	Comfortable	Well-off	Luxury
Active						
1700–1709	0	4	18	38	33	7
1710–1714	1	5	21	30	37	7
1715–1724	1	5	26	24	34	11
1735–1744	2	9	21	17	40	11
1750–1754	1	5	18	27	26	23
1765–1769	2	4	21	29	27	17
1770–1774	1	4	17	22	35	21
Retired						
1700–1709	9	30	27	20	14	0
1710–1714	5	13	45	21	15	1
1715–1724	11	23	27	24	11	3
1735–1744	19	31	27	12	9	1
1750–1754	19	19	31	22	5	4
1765–1769	8	23	27	17	17	7
1770–1774	13	28	24	20	10	5

FIVE

The Laborers

Determining the number of laborers in colonial Connecticut depends upon how one defines the term. For this study we have called men who owned a farm, farmers, and those who had the implements of a craft, together with a shop or the like, artisans or craftsmen. Laborers were men who worked for or with the farmers, artisans, professionals, and traders. The key distinction lies in the possession of means of production—capital, or in the case of professionals, technical training.

In reality the word "men" distorts the true situation. We have seen that males under twenty-one—boys—performed an adult's work beginning at age sixteen. No doubt the younger lads contributed more than they cost for several additional years. The colony did not levy a poll tax on females but when southern colonies did so they rated women equally with men, also beginning at sixteen. Most of the labor of wives and daughters did not produce an income but, for that matter, neither did the work of house servants or many slaves. If we include as "laborers" all those who produced something needed by the family or community, then most women and their daughters above a certain age belong in this chapter, though not as complete equals since some of their work, such as cleaning, earning nothing. If we insist that the labor must yield an income (not necessarily cash) then the female share diminishes but does not disappear, because they added to the family's assets both outside and inside the house, even aside from the activities of widows and unmarried daughters. A full treatment of the colony's laborers might well require two books, one entirely on the women; instead, we furnish only a chapter principally on adult males.

The laborers, then, consisted of four groups. First, slaves included persons of both sexes and all ages. Second, servants here mean those with monetary value, of the indentured or apprentice variety, and so generally under twenty-one, of both sexes and all three races. Third, free dependent men, almost all the sons of local families, single of course, and generally young. Finally, free independent men who appear on the tax lists or other rosters (such as church records) as heads of households. The last group can be subdivided into three: local single men, migrants, and married men who had not acquired the property needed to qualify as farmers or craftsmen. All of these owned very little property and, except for the sons, can properly be called poor. All but the fourth group were dependent, lacking any cash income and relying upon a master or parent to supply their needs.

We can identify these men and estimate their numbers from both tax lists and probate records. The former show that about a third of the adult men had little or no taxable property, a proportion increasing somewhat over time but varying particularly by place. To these we must add servants and slaves and whomever the assessor omitted. The probate records suggest that one-fifth of the men were landless and poor, and another tenth lived close to the margin, with insufficient property to support their families so that they had to supplement their regular income by wage-work. Again we add servants and slaves. If we include the young polls (who, after all, were adults for military service), "laborers" become nearly half of the male population age sixteen and over. Among adults, local young sons provided more than half of the labor force, older men one-fifth, migrants one-sixth, servants and slaves one-twelfth. During most of the colonial period slightly more than a third of the adult men were laborers, rising to 40 percent by the end because of an increase in the number of slaves and (possibly) migrants.

Although at any particular time all these men acted as laborers, they did not constitute a class. The local sons normally outgrew their poverty and low status and would replicate their fathers' history in the community.[1] The immigrants and white servants did not enjoy the advantages of local birth but all could and many did reach at least a subsistence level. Some of the older men—one-fifth of the laborers but less than a tenth of all men—would eventually make the grade. Only the slaves and nonwhite servants lacked any real chance of rising. These, with the few permanently poor whites, constituted potentially a self-conscious class of discontented men, but only in a few towns were they ever numerous enough to combine effectively. The others differed too much in their circumstances and expectations to support such resistance.

We now begin a more detailed examination of the laborers with a discussion of the slaves and servants. During the first four decades of

---

[1] In some societies sons could not count on succeeding their fathers directly because fathers did not live long enough to establish their children. For example, if the parent married at twenty-four and died at forty-five, over half of the sons would not have reached twenty-one. In Connecticut a man aged thirty, who would have two or three children, lived on the average for thirty years more. Sixty percent survived for twenty years when the eldest son would normally have come of age.

the colony's existence it contained few servants, almost all of whom became free after a few years, if they lived. Some of these turn up as free men on the tax lists, usually at the bottom. Estate inventories mention only a few; indeed, until 1680 there were only 0.05 such persons per inventory. At that point whites equalled blacks in number and a few Indians appear too. Judging from the prices, only a half-dozen individuals were slaves for life, all of them black except for one Indian "servant" valued at £24 country pay. The records specify the ages of some of these, and the low prices of others suggest that only four or five out of twenty-six were adults. The medium value of the whole group was £8 (cash), the mean, £9. During the next two decades the frequency increased slightly: 0.7 per inventory during the 1680s and 1.2 in the 1690s.

Connecticut followed the other colonies in rapidly replacing white and Indian servile labor with black, the proportion of the latter rising rapidly from 2:3 before 1680 to 9:2 by the next decade and 9:1 thereafter. These figures come from probate data, which understate the number of white apprentices, "maidservants," and laborers on one-year contracts because they could not be sold. However, the trend is very clear. Considering the ample supply of free labor, the increase in black slaves seems odd. Their price increased rapidly, more than doubling between 1680 and 1700. Probably the colonists were beginning to replace West Indian castoffs with healthy young adults, so that importations as an incidental, even accidental consequence of trade or war became deliberate. Whites were clearly preferring slaves to servants despite the cheapness of the latter.

For most of the seventeenth century, however, slavery was rare and played virtually no part in Connecticut's economy. During the 1680s, when the inventories first began to record a significant number, men in trade owned ten of the twenty-two who were presumably black. Probably these formed part of the "stock in trade" obtained in the West Indies; one individual had five of them. Two ministers owned one each, a man and a boy, and a distiller had one man. Decedents who had farmed owned two boys, an old woman, two women without any adjective, a girl, and only one man, while an official-farmer had two of unspecified nature, probably men. All told, aside from the merchants' stock, only five were men who might supplement white laborers. The others we may regard as household help who raised their owners' standard of living rather than engaging in production for the market. To these data we may add by way of confirmation from the scattered New London inventories during the late seventeenth century the following four holdings, in country pay:

- a sixty-year-old Indian squaw, £6
- an Indian maidservant not valued
- a Negro servant freed and given ten acres
- an Indian servant and his black wife, freed after three years, together valued at £8, a mulatto servant with three years to serve, £5, and a deaf and dumb Negro woman, at £2

This hardly suggests a slave economy but rather, if anything, a form of poor relief in which those laborers who could, paid their keep. The colony depended almost exclusively on free workers.

During the next quarter-century white servitude almost disappeared. Negro slaves kept pace with the general population growth, reaching a peak during the war years of 1710-1714 and then dropping back to 0.1 per inventory. What occurred thereafter varied greatly from place to place. In the northeastern hill country of the Windham district no slaves appeared until 1730, except an Indian family group of a man, woman, and child, and a male of no value. Thereafter about 7 percent of the Windham estates included slaves, at first with some Indian, later only Negro. By mid-century 1 percent of the adult male population were slaves, and there were 0.13 per inventory by 1770. On the census of 1774 blacks constituted 2 percent of the total, and since the number of slaves per inventory had remained the same, free blacks must have equaled the slaves. In the Hartford district the major growth occurred before 1750 and the number per inventory was only 0.14, scarcely above Windham's despite the better soil and larger number of well-to-do men there.

Fairfield County, on the other hand, was one of Connecticut's centers for the slave system. The number of slaves per inventory began at only 0.11—one for every ten or so—during the 1690s. That doubled during the next decades, doubled again by 1750, and reached about 0.6 by the 1770s. Taking the colony as a whole, the slave population as it appears in the probate records started the century at a shade over one for every ten estate inventories and did not increase until after 1730, when it doubled, and rose very slowly to one in four just before the Revolution.

From this information we can infer the proportion of slaves in the living population.[2] In 1700 they composed 1.5 percent, reached only

---

[2] Almost all of the slaves belonged to men over age forty, who made up about 37 percent of the men, and most of them to men still older. About 25 percent of the living adult men owned slaves. Thus if there were 0.10 slaves per inventory there were 0.025 slaves for each man. The actual figure would vary according to the age structure involved. For the numbers of slaves in the probate inventories, see Appendix 4A.

2.0 percent by mid-century, then rose again during the Seven Years' War and ended at 2.6 percent. Census and other estimates run a bit higher. One guess put the Negro population at 1,500 in 1715, which would mean 3.16 percent of the total according to that source and almost 5 percent by my reckoning, in either case far above the proportion inferred from inventories. Free blacks surely would not be numerous enough to make up the difference, and probably 1715 saw an unusual number of slaves recently captured or bought during the war. The census of 1756 sets blacks at 2.4 percent of the total compared with the probate figure of 2.0 percent for slaves, and both of the later censuses give 3.3 percent versus 2.6 inferred from inventories (adjusted). This leads us to a guess that free blacks had reached one-sixth of the total black population at mid-century and one-fifth by 1774. Adult black slaves, as we will see, averaged twice as large a proportion of the slaves as white men did of the whites, rising therefore from 4 percent of all men in 1700 to 6.6 percent by the 1760s.[3]

The slave population did not duplicate the age or sex structure of white society. The latter featured an equal number of men and women and a majority of children, reflecting the growing population. But instead of an equal sex ratio, necessary to and evidence of natural growth, that of the slaves was male by a margin of five to three. Mature women, identified as "woman" or "wench," constituted a near-normal 23 percent of the population, but "boys," "girls," and other youngsters were only 37 percent against the whites' 60 percent. Either the women did not produce as many babies as the whites, or more slave children died before reaching maturity, or the importers preferred adult males, or very likely all three. These conditions did not change at all during colonial period: throughout, about 40 percent of the slaves were adult men (see Appendix 5A).

We can illustrate the point briefly. Out of over a hundred women so identified during the years 1750-1753 and 1765-1774, only fifteen were accompanied by a baby whereas, since most of these women were able to bear children (judging from their value and occasional adjectives) they ought to have been caring for three times that number.[4]

---

[3] Unless slaves aged sixteen to twenty were referred to as "men" instead of "boys," as is quite possible. If so they must be subtracted and the proportion of adult men diminished by at least 20 percent, perhaps by much more if slaves died earlier than whites. That would reduce the number of slaves in the adult male population to around 3 percent in 1700 and 5 percent later.

[4] If 113 women had babies every two years, then certainly 50 ought to be listed with a child, if that word means someone so small as not to warrant the use of "boy" or "girl." In any event, 15 is clearly far too few.

About 1750 out of nearly two hundred persons almost half were not living in a family group, dwelling either alone or with people of the same sex. Only three out of ten men lived with a woman, and after all the extra women are paired with potential husbands there remain 37 percent of the men without a mate. It is true that almost as many white men were single at any one time, but the latter surely had better prospects. As for the women, one-third were residing in households without a black male and the relative shortage of children also testifies to the absence, for many adults, of the chance to establish the usual family system.

The spatial distribution of the slaves also hindered the development of a black society. At mid-century only a dozen towns contained as many as a hundred and even in those the blacks were scattered over a considerable area in different houses. Let us take the town of Fairfield as one comparatively favorable. By 1774 not far from 10 percent of the men and 7 percent of the whole population were black, a total of 319 individuals according to the census. We do find references to family groups, to a man and woman in the same house, or to a woman and children. However, only a fifth of the men resided with women of childbearing age and no more than half of the women resided with men. Still, we may suppose that in a relatively small town attachments extended beyond the particular dwelling. Moreover, around one-fourth of the blacks were free and so do not appear in the probate inventories. They would enrich the black and probably the slave community, but not by living together.

Exceptional examples of family clusters do exist not only in Fairfield but in neighboring Stratford. Peter Burr's estate included a man, wife, "Mingo," "Moll," and a girl. Elizabeth Shelton also owned a man and wife together with a six-year-old girl and a three-year-old boy. The Reverend Hezekiah Gold's curious assemblage consisted of four men, a "wench," a young man, and two boys born in the house. Captain David Judson provided £3 worth of beds in his lower kitchen for a man, wife, and boy; while Captain Simon Couch's will freed a man and a wench, leaving still enslaved a man and two girls. The chance for family formation in towns such as Fairfield seems good, yet we find that boys and girls totaled only 35 percent of the slaves, while the ratio of women to children was about one to one-and-a-half instead of one to three, as it ought to have been. The great majority of towns in the colony offered even less opportunity than Fairfield.[5]

[5] In order: Fairfield district probate records, 6:168; 9:357, 366, 397; 14:20, 119, 349; 14:186, 197; 16:279, 299.

How did this species of laborer fare in other ways? Our sources provide only a small part of the answer. On the positive side, some slight chance for an improvement in status did exist. As we saw, the colony always contained a few free blacks, some of whom had once been slaves.[6] By 1762 they may have increased to 20 percent of the black population. The slaves slept in the house with the whites on cheap but adequate beds worth £1 or £2, with enough food and clothing. Probably they could count on being cared for when they were sick or old, sometimes at considerable cost to the owner. The estate of John Smith of Milford in 1772 was debited with "supporting and taking care of an aged and infirm Negro man, called Darby" for £34.18.[7] Other men provided for such support in their wills in language very similar to that used for their parents or wives, as did Ensign Nathaniel Lewis of Farmington in 1752, whose son was enjoined to care for a Negro woman "in sickness and health and not let her want for victuals or clothes for her comfort."[8]

On the other hand the odds against the slaves' achieving freedom were very long and seemed little better in 1775 than in 1700; they could not foretell what another ten years would bring. Their status and welfare did not improve with age. Their food, bedding, clothes, and other needs depended on the fortune and benevolence of white owners. They often, perhaps usually, performed burdensome and (to our eyes) nasty tasks in order to ease the lives of masters and mistresses, and the information that they were better off than many people in other lands would not have reconciled them to permanent and debasing servitude.

The owners' point of view we have already discussed. The purchase price of slaves had remained low during the seventeenth century, that for men averaging £25 cash and for women, £17. After 1700 the value of women according to probate records rose by 60 percent and of man by a third, perhaps because of greater demand but more likely because of better quality. By mid-century the inventory prices peaked: £45 for a man, £32 for a woman, about £35 for a boy and £28 for a girl. At that point the supply evidently exceeded the demand and by

---

[6] Evidently an increasing number were freed. Thus the *Norwich Packet* reported on December 15, 1774 that Mr. Samuel Gager had freed three slaves, and as compensation for past services had leased them a valuable farm on very moderate terms, adding that Jonathan Avery had freed an able and industrious Negro man. The *Packet* inquired, "Is not this breaking off the Yoke and letting the oppressed go free?"

[7] New Haven district probate records, 11:236.

[8] Will of Ensign Nathaniel Lewis of Farmington (d. 1752), Hartford district probate records, 16:185.

1770 these values declined slightly. Some scattered prices for children indicate that when they were less than six years old they were worth the same regardless of sex. After that the cost of boys rose more rapidly than did that of girls, but the variation suggests that estate appraisers were judging by individual worth rather than a stable annual rate, as was true for indentured servants.

The considerable initial expense plus the cost of maintenance combined with the possibility of early death or prolonged illness to keep slavery a marginal institution in Connecticut. Since their labor was not necessary to the economy and since a very large proportion did not earn any money at all for their owners, few families could afford to buy one. During the eighteenth century as a whole, one-third of the slaveowners left estates of under £500, but they bought less expensive blacks: far fewer grown men than the average, indeed, as many young boys and girls as adults, and they rarely owned more than one. Larger propertyowners who held slaves commonly had more than one and bought more adult men. The colony's richest families, with £5,000 worth of property, usually were slaveowners. Slaves, then, belonged to the colony's economic, urban upper class, especially to professionals, traders, and leaders of the community, among whom it was normal, accepted, and useful.

Our second major group of laborers, the indentured servants, included blacks, Indians, and whites. A study of them is handicapped by the colonists' use of "servant" for both temporary and permanent bound labor so we cannot always distinguish between them. The values at-

TABLE 5.1
Ownership of Slaves by Wealth Class (cash values)

Size of estate	% with slaves	Number per inv.	% men	Men per inv.
1700–1719				
£2,000 +	67	3.9	49	2.0
1,000–1,999	45	1.6	45	0.7
500–999	30	1.6	32½	0.5
under 500	3½	1.2	31	0.35
1765–1774				
£2,000 +	66	3.0	46½	1.4
1,000–1,999	41	2.1	44	0.9
500–999	13	1.9	35	0.7
under 500	3	1.7	32	0.5

SOURCE: Estate inventories.

tached to the two conditions overlapped, yet these often provide our only clues. In general, servants were worth about £2 annually. Scattered data indicate that blacks were valued more highly than the whites and Indians, who rated about equally, and slaves were worth more than all three. Thus slaves were apparently more productive or performed their services more satisfactorily or could be forced into less desirable tasks than servants of all colors, including blacks.

We know little about the circumstances of these people, especially of the nonwhites. Indians appear in our records very rarely as slaves for life, several if not all of whom came from the West Indies. One individual was freed after thirteen years and the rest, almost all young children, served for a fixed term. About half of the children and some of the adults seem to have been charity cases. Thus one woman was valued at only a shilling. No doubt these originated with or were legalized by the 1719 statute by which the selectmen could care for the poor and idle by "disposing them" into service.[9] Thus in eighteenth-century Connecticut, Indian servitude survived as a curious relic, without significance except, of course, for race relations and the history of the Native Americans themselves.[10]

The colony contained few white indentured servants, whom we can discuss together with apprentices.[11] Both served on contract either for a stated period of years or until twenty-one. Few served for longer periods. John Patchin of Fairfield, however, had remained a servant for thirty years when his master, a deacon, died, at which point Patchin was sixty-eight. John Whitehead was brought over to New Haven as a servant in 1639, freed in 1647 presumably when twenty-one, then became a servant again the next year. How long he remained in that status we do not know, but he eventually married at the age of about

[9] Trumbull and Hoadly, eds., *Pub. Rec. Conn.*, 6:112.

[10] One interesting example comes from the Danbury district probate records (1:67 [1752]), that inform us that John Glover's rather modest estate of £182 included "two Indian or mallato Servants one a Garl called Pachence the other a boy called Ceasor for the Garls service During the Term or Time of her Indentor till her time is out £100" and for the boy's time £200. We must divide those figures by ten. Mulatto here probably means Indian and Negro.

[11] White servitude continued occasionally in those parts of the colony where slavery was uncommon. I found five in the Windham district probate records among 219 inventories during 1745-1754, which would mean perhaps 1 percent of the living population. White servants in Connecticut worked equally for farmers and artisans. In three instances their time was valued at £1.10 annually. Eight others varied between £4.8 and £12, which at £1.10 per year would mean service for three to eight years, and sounds right. One individual's time was evaluated at £9 for 21 months, but master and servant shared the same last name. These later servants bore English names and I suspect were local boys, but have not investigated the point.

thirty-five, sired seven children, and lived to be nearly seventy. By that time he must have given some of his property away, especially the land, of which roughly fifty acres remained. He still owned the usual livestock of an average farmer and an estate valued at £232 (country pay).[12] Typically, however, the white servant or apprentice originated when some poor man sent off a son whom he could not care for, or left a young orphan. One example will suffice, since the situation is familiar. John Wheeler, a merchant and farmer of New London, died in 1691 with an inventory of nearly a thousand pounds but debts for half that. He had sired four boys, one of whom had died young. The eldest, Zaccheus, born about 1675, was apprenticed to a cooper, and then sent off to sea with clothing, a Bible, and psalmbook, valued at £8.13 country pay. He died in 1703, childless. His brother Joshua, born in 1680, was apprenticed in 1693 to Joshua Abel for £12 pay, and William, born in 1682 or 1683, was apprenticed to a shoemaker in 1694 and "fitted out," for £13.[13] Both of these boys, apprenticed at thirteen and twelve years respectively, vanish and probably died before their majority. The appraiser valued their services at £1 per year, probably cash.

These lads enjoyed the usual rights and disadvantages of their status, receiving a small reward when their service ended, as did Zaccheus Wheeler, but seldom enough to thrive on. There are exceptions. Samuel Cole probably lived with John Hall of Wallingford after his father died. If so, he remained for ten years, when Hall sold him forty acres for £6. This land bounded on the commons and was adjacent to Hall's own farm, so the sale was a bargain; and we find the quondam servant later buying 150 acres complete with house and barn.[14] More typical were the following. Young Jeremie Andros received only a sheep in addition to what was promised him. Thomas Holt was rewarded with £20 country pay, after which he promptly died. John Legon's master willed him a loom with tackling, a gun, and £5 when he became twenty-one. We do have instances similar to those common farther south, of servants receiving land. Thus a Plainfield boy was promised two tracts, one of which measured about forty acres, if he remained with the owner's wife until age twenty-one, a New London lad received fifty acres for eight years' service, and a Hartford apprentice

---

[12] James Shepard, *John Whitehead of New Haven and Branford, Conn.* (New Britain, 1902); New Haven district probate records, 2:165.

[13] New London district probate records, A:82, 89, 148.

[14] Wallingford deeds, 4:552.

would earn the master's best hat, £10 (pay), and a lot if he stayed until his term was up.[15]

Such shares would fall far short of what a master's son would receive, but then, the poor boy could expect even less from his father and he probably fared as well if not better living with a substitute. Society certainly expected gratitude, though what it got we do not know. Henry Hollstead of Hartford willed his entire estate—all £11 of it—to his "kind and loving master," but Richard Cosier ran away, aged about twenty, and "in his flight rid through Branford with his sword drawn & pistol cockt Threatening mischief to any that should seize him." In addition to the sword and pistol Cosier presently acquired two or three wives and sired four sons after moving to Norwalk, but he never prospered.[16]

How many of the servants did prosper after receiving their freedom? We can judge the fate of the nonwhite boys from the situation of such free Indians as belonged to white society, and the black freedmen. The Indians who turn up in probate court or on tax lists seldom achieved more than a bare subsistence. An exception was Peter Tusso of Farmington, a Spanish Indian who died in 1767. Since he had neither wife nor children, he willed all his property to the Custis family, whom he had perhaps served, and with whom he was undoubtedly living since he lacked a house and the necessary articles for independence—one of which was probably a wife! His £87 included thirteen acres, £5 worth of clothes, one book, and a note for £31.3 against one of the family, adding up to a subsistence plus level. Probably more usual were the following. Benjamin Cusshaw of Middletown (d. 1747), single, left only £9. Andrew Shelon of Windsor (d. 1755) possessed nothing but £11 due him for military service, and "Timothy" of Farmington (d. 1751) left to his young daughters only a house and one acre, with £35 in personal wealth. Materially, they might have fared better as indentured servants if, indeed, they had not so served.

The freedmen seldom progressed beyond the standard of living of slaves. "Cuff, a negro," formerly slave to John Dennison of East Haven, had accumulated by 1757 an estate of £111, over half in notes owing to him. He owned three acres (£11) but must have rented a room somewhere. He did possess a comfortable featherbed with ample coverings including sheets, dressed well in £11 worth of clothing, and had accumulated some other consumption goods, but he remained

[15] New London district probate records, B:55; *Pub. Rec. Conn.*, 5:371; Ephraim Turner, servant to Phineas Willson, Hartford probate records, 5:139.

[16] Hartford district probate records, 5:144; Donald Lines Jacobus, *Families of Ancient New Haven*, 9 vols., 1922-1932, reprinted in 3 vols. (Baltimore, 1974), 1:160.

single. So did Frank of Farmington worth £3, Primus of Wethersfield (a migrant from Hatfield) who left £21, and Edward Willobe of the same town, who had four acres and a house worth £28 but no clothing, probably the victim of an infectious disease. One Captain Hollister of Glastonbury allowed "August" to build a house and fence on his land and probably to raise a crop while he served as a laborer. August died in 1760 leaving £51 in property including £1 worth of clothes. One freedman, Joseph Negroes, had attained the dignity of a sergeant, perhaps during the French and Indian War. However, when he died in Simsbury in 1758 he left only £7, some of which consisted of joiner and turner tools, but again no clothing. "Sampson" illustrates the exception: a married slave who became free. Unfortunately, he also indicates a common end. We encounter him first, with his wife, as part of Capt. William Lewis's estate in Farmington, in 1690. Valued at £50 country pay, they had no children. Eight years later one of Lewis's sons, Ezekiel (Harvard '94), freed them, now with children, but Sampson lived only until 1704. His inventory in country pay totaled just £40.174, less than £30 cash. The records do not mention children. He and his wife did not own a house. On four acres of upland, fenced, they kept a cow, heifer, calf, four pigs, and (says the inventory) two-and-a-half sheep, no doubt his share of five. He owned less than a minimum of clothing and 5/7 in cash, perhaps from wage-labor. The consumption goods were just at the subsistence level. Unhappily for the widow the debts ate up practically all of the property and she ended with only a few pounds.[17] A final example is that of Jacob Way, whom the town of Wethersfield taxed in 1730 for his poll and a horse. Called "Negro" in deeds, he sold 1¼ acres in 1751 and died in 1760 leaving us neither a will nor an inventory but clearly a failure, in material terms. He at least left some traces. Most men of his color were like Richard Negro of Glastonbury whom we meet only once, assessed for £27 in 1756. In short, nonwhites gained little by freedom except liberty itself.

The white servants also began at the bottom, inheriting very little, without parents to help them. Tracing such obscure people often proves impossible, but fortunately the sources in Connecticut are exceptionally good. We ask of them what proportion of these youngsters, with less opportunity for advancement than any of their peers, did succeed, judging success by their acquisition of enough property for an adequate standard of living or by evidence of respectability, of status, such as holding a responsible office.

[17] Hartford district probate records, 5:65, 7:62-63, 112.

We begin with forty-five servants almost all born before 1700 (for the excellent reason that few existed later). Of these, three died before their majority, one after impressment into the crew of a British ship. That leaves forty-two. Two vanish from the records, and since their brothers remained in the colony and succeeded they probably had died. That leaves forty. For three others information does not permit a decision either way. One moved to Westfield, Massachusetts, and disappears. Another married, had four children, obtained a little land one year, and lived at least until age fifty-seven but left no will or inventory. As to the third, two James Williamses confuse matters. Both married, one moved and the other probably did so, too, for he disappears without trace (the death of a married man ought at least have been noted by the court in some way). The name is too common to track with confidence. So we subtract these three without prejudice, leaving thirty-seven. Ten succeeded, twenty failed, and seven vanish, either dying or leaving the colony. Of those known, one-third succeeded, and, if all the seven unknowns failed, 27 percent did so. The most likely statement is that 30 percent achieved respectability and a decent livelihood.

A few examples show the range. None of the thirty-seven became a leader of his community. The best estate belonged to Francis Bradley of New Haven and Fairfield (ca. 1630-1689), who had the advantage of an apprenticeship with Governor Eaton. He left his wife and seven children £446 (cash) including a nice farm and an old Negro woman.[18] Thomas Buck of Wethersfield (1665 to after 1727), a husbandman, acquired eighty acres and the town trusted him as a guardian. His son Thomas, curiously, served with the son of his father's master. In 1739, aged twenty-seven, Thomas Junior was able to buy 50 acres and between then and 1752 he sold 173.[19] Finally, Henry Stiles of Windsor (1629 to after 1724) became a sergeant and was assessed for over £100 on the assessment list of 1702.

At the other end comes John Ayres, a poor lad whom we meet in 1662 as the apprentice of James Ensign, who in his will of 1670 gave him 90 shillings to buy tools when his time expired. In 1675, able to write and having received the money due him, he was freed, and disappeared from Hartford, apparently spending some time in Canada. In 1685 he turned up in the Boston probate records, a mariner, leaving a small property to a brother in Hartford.[20] David Carpenter of

---

[18] Fairfield district probate records, 3:267.

[19] Charles William Manwaring, *A Digest of Early Connecticut Probate Records*, 3 vols. (Hartford, 1904-1906), 2:214, 329, 3:113, 114, 146.

[20] Ibid., 1:112, 196; Suffolk County (Mass.) probate records, 1685.

Farmington died in 1652 at the age of thirty-one, married with three children. He lived in a cellar and left £53. Of Steven Becket we know only that he was born in 1623, served as an apprentice, and in 1687 had property worth £54 on Norwalk's tax list, which, unlike the later one, recorded the total value of the estate, so that he died at the subsistence level. Conceivably this was a different man, but we have trouble enough finding just one: he never married, nor did he buy or sell land. Peter Simpson of New Haven almost made the grade. After serving his term he moved to Milford, had a family, acquired about twenty acres, a house, and a barn, leaving upon his death, age about forty, £163 and debts of £54 that would net £76 cash. That would suffice for a father with young children, but not for his older ones. Finally, ex-servant John Cook died aged twenty-nine, worth only £8 despite receiving land given both by his master and by the town.[21]

The last example focuses our attention on the general character of the servants' careers. First, one-third of those we know about died before reaching forty years of age. The median age at death, for such of them as reached maturity, was about fifty-three, or even less if the unknown group died young. That is well below normal for Connecticut in the colonial period. All of those who died at less than forty years of age failed. Those who lived longer scored 50 percent, and of those who reached sixty or more, 67 percent succeeded. Among the ex-servants who married, the median age was twenty-six, but over one-fourth and probably one-third remained single. The single men failed with only one exception, whereas the married men had an even chance of leading a normal life in status and property. Thus the typical success story involved as essentials marriage and living until fifty. Those who remained at the bottom of society had died young and usually single.

The next group of laborers is just as interesting: the young men who show up at the bottom of tax lists, assessed only for their polls or a few pounds more, almost always (90 percent) without relatives in the town except for a few whose fathers were poor—clearly outsiders. They allow us to study the category of migrants, most elusive of the poor.[22]

[21] Hartford district probate records, 2:33; New Haven district probate records, 1, part 2:128.

[22] The series of lists around 1670 shows 4.9 percent coming from outside; this may be a bit high since my genealogical data is incomplete and I erred on that side (N = 781). A selection of lists 1701 to 1738 (N = 1,454) yielded 5.9 percent. To the names on the lists I added a few derived from probate records. More than these must have been on the move during the colony's early years and since migrants may have increased again at the end (judging from New Haven records and historical opinion) the overall

For the most part we do not know where they came from, even though their age can be inferred from known facts, or learned from positive evidence such as a gravestone, a vital statistic, or a church record. Because so many of them had moved into the towns we are not surprised that many moved out and cannot always be traced. Out of 102 such men, between 40 and 50 percent died elsewhere than in the town where, for a moment, they paused and paid a tax, as follows:

moved within Connecticut	25
moved out of the Colony	11
probably moved	3
disappeared	<u>12</u>
	51

Whereas among the servants about one-third remained single (excluding those who probably died young), few of the outsiders we know about failed to marry. Thus they multiplied their chance for status and property. Indeed, we know of only eleven out of eighty-one who did not find a wife. Concerning thirteen who disappear we know nothing and remain uncertain about another six. A majority of these very likely remained single, for we generally know of marriages, so that among the whole number 24 percent died unwed. The median age at marriage

TABLE 5.2
Age of Migrant Workers on Tax List and at Death

Age on list	Age at Death							Median
	25–29	30–39	40–49	50–59	60–69	70–79	80+	
Under 20	—	—	—	1	—	—	—	—
20–24	1	3	4	4	2	3	1	51.5
25–29	1	5	5	1	8	5	1	62.5
30–34	—	—	1	1	3	2	2	63.0
35–39	—	1	—	1	2	2	1	67.0
40–44	—	—	1	1	—	—	1	—
45–49	—	—	—	1	—	—	—	—
50–59	—	—	—	—	—	1	—	—

average surely exceeded 6 percent and may have come close to 10, though I think not. Tax collectors had a vested interest in including at least the names of potential payers even though they might not catch up with them. The tax lists also show the local variations one would expect. Leaving aside the newly settled towns, where everybody came from outside, the more purely agricultural communities attracted few from any distance, the diversified ones far more.

was the same as that for the servants—twenty-six. The median age at death was naturally higher than that for the servants since our taxpayers had already reached at least twenty-one. We know of only two who certainly died in their twenties, though others must have done so simply to equal a minimum expectancy. The average age at death was only sixty-one of those known, and including best guesses it drops to fifty-nine ($N = 65$), probably six or seven years more than the servants but low for Connecticut. The life expectancy for men in their mid-twenties was around thirty-one years.

Inadequate data again limits accuracy in our study of their degree of success. We know with reasonable assurance the fate of seventy-seven, among whom thirty-eight had risen out of poverty, or virtually half. Ten certainly or probably moved away beyond our ability to follow them. Thus Moses Trim of Bolton, originally from Lyme, bought thirty-seven acres of land and obtained a division and a house, but sold out in favor of New York, a move either made possible by success or forced by failure.[23] In the same way George Black of Derby turns up on the 1718 list, sold out for £76 eight years later, went to Stratford, and vanished.[24] John Crampton occupied a lowly position on the Norwalk list of 1671. It was probably he who had married in 1662 and who took a second wife in 1676. In 1687 he was assessed for £53, still low for that particular list, suggesting a subsistence level at best, and then emigrated to Rye, New York. For three more men the evidence does not justify a decision. John Prior of the 1686 Windsor list married an Enfield girl and sold out his land in Windsor gradually between 1688 and 1713, eventually moving to Enfield, where he was still alive in 1738. The odds are very good that he achieved a subsistence level, knowing what we do about married men of his age, but the selling makes one a little suspicious and I could not look at the Enfield records. There remain twelve men about whom we know nothing for practical purposes. Either they died in the town, in which case the absence of deeds or other traces indicates almost certain poverty, or more likely, given their youth, they left.

Thus the lower and upper estimates for the proportion of success of the total number are 42.7 and 49.4, with a midpoint of 46 percent, half again as high as the figure for the white servants. As in their case, age played an important role. Those who died before reaching forty years almost never (1:9) attained independence, while those who reached

[23] Bolton deeds, 3:68, 271, 540.
[24] Derby deeds, 3:403, 408, 412, 416, 569.

sixty had a better than even chance (19:12). Also, the single men failed, or the failures remained single, whereas married men succeeded by a ratio of three to two, of those known (if all the unknowns failed, half).

The most successful of these men in terms of rank was Capt. Henry Craine of Killingworth (1635-1717), who appeared at the bottom of a Guilford list in 1672. Philip Smith (1633-1685) did not stay in Wethersfield but moved to Hadley, Massachusetts, where he became a deacon, lieutenant, and legislator. As a rule, however, the upwardly mobile group became at best small propertyowners. Samuel Church of Hartford (1667-1718) is a borderline case, leaving a small farm and five young children. Joseph Dewey of Windsor (1677-1731) never married, but he became a miller with a farm in Hebron, while Francis Bushnell moved from Norwalk to Danbury, where he died in 1697 at the age of forty-eight. He left an estate of only £182, but as a cooper, with a sawmill, he presumably received a decent income; also his land was worth £105, which in Danbury at that date probably meant sixty acres or so. Seven young unmarried daughters could not have helped much.[25]

Typical of those at the bottom were James Browne of Norwalk (d. 1702), Thomas Stanton of Groton (1708-1746), and William Goring of Simsbury (1679-1715). Browne married about 1676 and had five children, but left only £73. He did have a house, barn, home lot, and well, but these together were worth just £28. He also owned about thirty acres, which, however, remained mostly unimproved, and he apparently earned his living as a shoemaker. Stanton never married and left only £103 when he died, still a laborer, at the age of thirty-eight. Goring married twice, remained childless, and died at thirty-six with £35 worth of property. We close with the case of Matthew Bellamy of Guilford, a schoolmaster, who at thirty-seven ran off, deserting his wife, their two children, and his pupils; he made good his escape from them and us.[26]

The final category of laborers consisted of the residents' own sons. We will focus here on the sons of poor men, dividing them into three groups according to age when their fathers died: five through nine, ten through nineteen, and twenty or more. "Poor men" were those who died insolvent or leaving estates worth less than £100, or some-

---

[25] For Church, Hartford district probate records, 9:307, 10:145. For Dewey, ibid., 11:81, 157. For Bushnell, Fairfield district probate records, 4:172.

[26] For Browne, Fairfield district probate records, file no. 1107. For Stanton, New London district probate records, E:407. For Goring, Hartford district probate records, 9:44, 119. For Bellamy, Jacobus, *New Haven*, 1:184.

what larger properties but with several children. The distribution for fathers of our youngest group was as follows:

insolvent or under £50	45	42.1%
£50-99	44	41.1%
£100-149	13	12.1%
£150-199	5	4.7%

These five- to nine-year-old orphans numbered 121. Eight moved without our being able to follow, and we also dropped 5 more because of uncertain evidence. Six died before reaching maturity. Twenty-four remain obscure, of whom 6 married and the others simply vanish. Some doubtless died young—at least 8, if life expectancy tables can be applied. From 121, then, we subtract the 8 who moved, 5 uncertain, and 14 probably dying young, leaving 94. Fifty orphans succeeded, 28 failed, and 16 remain unknown. Thus the parameters for success rate varied between 53 and 64 percent. Given the steady movement out of the colony during these years, and the probability that a few additional orphans died during their early twenties if not before, we should probably split the difference, and estimate the proportion of the successful at about 58 percent, certainly within 2 percentage points one way or the other.

A few other facts about the lives of these children are interesting. One-third are known to have moved from their place of birth. This group succeeded more often than those who stayed put. The median age at marriage of twenty-five was identical to that of the white men generally. The age at death of those we are certain about was sixty-one, but this contains an upward bias for two reasons: first, for some of those whose precise dates of death we do not know, we have terminal dates when they disappear, as follows: in their twenties, one; thirties, five; forties, five; fifties, two; sixties, two. They probably did not live more than a decade or so, on the average, beyond the date noted. Thus William Barton of Wethersfield, born in 1740, bought and sold a small amount of land, but not as late as 1790 and the census does not list him, so he presumably died in his forties. Benajah Barlow of Fairfield had four daughters and then we lose track of him, so he very likely died at that point. David Dibble of Stamford bought over sixty acres between 1733 and 1735, then disappeared, aged thirty-two. If we assume that men in their thirties lived for twenty more years, those in their forties for fifteen, and those older for ten, a little under the usual life expectancy, the median age at death drops to sixty. In addition, we have postulated that a few more orphans died in their

twenties, without leaving any trace, unmarried and probably dependent laborers. They would lower the median by another half-year. The
best guess is 59.5.

The young orphans who survived into their teens entered the labor
force: What happened to them? Apparently, like the other laborers
already discussed, some years passed before they became economically
independent and capable of achieving full status in the community.
Either that, or the same deficiencies that prevented success contributed
to an early death. Men who died before reaching age forty failed 90
percent of the time, whereas those who lived longer succeeded almost
80 percent of the time! None of the single men became self-sufficient.
The age at death of those who failed contrasts sharply with that of the
successful: median age 38 versus 69.5. Only one person out of twenty-
six among those known who lived to be seventy failed to rise into the
middle group of propertyowners. How much we should attribute to
childhood poverty rather than physical, mental, or psychological disability we cannot know; they may have inherited traits that had helped
to impoverish their parents. We can state only that of every hundred
poor orphans who lived to maturity, twenty would die young, usually
single, and still poor, another twenty lived longer but remained poor,
and the other sixty ceased to be laborers, becoming instead propertyowners—and ancestors.

Among the last, a few joined the leaders. Only one went from rags
to riches, but the group included a lieutenant, a Yale graduate, and a
deacon, along with some assorted farmers, prosperous artisans, and
lesser officials. Most, however, simply earned enough to support their
families decently. Under the circumstances, that was enough of an
accomplishment.

The largest group discussed here consisted of poor orphans between
the ages of ten and twenty. There is no reason to suppose that they
would enjoy any advantage over the younger children; ten more years
of poverty would not improve matters, and indeed, the younger ones
might actually have benefited from their mother's remarriage or some
form of town aid. But in fact these older lads did fare a little better,
at least in their economic careers.

We again confront uncertainties. To start with the known: out of a
total pool of 158, 82 succeeded and 25 failed, for a success rate of 76
percent. Among the remaining 51, 10 emigrated, 5 we drop for in-
conclusive evidence, 6 died young, and 30 we know nothing about
except, in 6 cases, that the age at death exceeded thirty years. Applying
again an estimated proportion of young deaths, we subtract 2 more
presumably dying before age twenty and another 2 within a few years

thereafter, before the median age of marriage. Twenty-six remain in the pool. The lower estimate for percentage of success becomes 62 and the midpoint, 70. In this case we have no reason to suspect an abnormal emigration because we know of 38 percent who did move. Thus the success rate for orphans aged ten to twenty was fully 10 percent higher than for the younger group. Life expectancy, however, was the same—they lived to be sixty years old or, after the same adjustments, perhaps a year less. The correspondence of the two figures adds to our confidence. The median age of marriage was one year older, at twenty-six.

The difference between the two with respect to the rate of success resulted, curiously enough, from a better record among those dying in their thirties, more than half of whom had succeeded. Twenty-year-olds remained at the bottom, and men over age forty outshone the younger orphans, 84 percent successful to 78 percent. Once again the failures were young, just about half under forty, and again the average age of the achievers was much higher, at sixty-one years. This suggests that the children who remained longer with their own parents were indeed better prepared to face the world, and made the grade more often and at a younger age, than those deprived at an earlier age.

A few more illustrations will remind us that the numbers describe real people. Samuel Crow of Windsor never improved on his father. He married in 1689 and after his wife died he married again, whereupon the two ran off, deserting their children. I set him down, perhaps with some bias, as a failure. When Henry Humerston of New Haven died in 1664 he left £73 to his widow and four sons, none of whom succeeded, including the eldest, Samuel, who at the age of thirty-eight died with even less property than his father. A nephew, also in this pool, lived until age eighty, had seven children, and did buy land, but he sold as much as he bought.[27] Peter Abbot of Branford (ca. 1642-1667) killed his wife, moved from farm to farm, and finally died insane in Fairfield.[28] Lastly, the probate judge intervened on behalf of a widow who had been appointed a guardian of a neighbor's children, but who married one of our group, William Chitester, "a poor shiftless man, and the children are in a suffering condition, not likely to be provided for."[29] When he died we do not know, but his chances seem poor.

At the other extreme we have two deputies, a justice, a sheriff, two deacons, the namesake for a section of a town, two captains, and sev-

[27] New Haven district probate records, 1:132, 2:87.
[28] *New Havn Colony Records*, 2:308.
[29] Hartford district probate records, 12:116.

eral men of substantial property, the general level of success clearly above that of the preceding group. None became famous, but Greenfield Laraby, a Norwich farmer who lived for ninety years, did have the honor of being Joshua Hempstead's uncle.

Finally, our oldest set were in their twenties when their fathers died. Three of the original thirty-one left. Of one we know only that he married at age twenty-seven and either died or emigrated at forty-six. In the absence of other data we omit him, leaving twenty-seven. This group married when a little older—at twenty-seven. Since they had already lived longer than the last set of orphans we expect them to survive still longer, but in fact they did not, the median age at death being only fifty-seven; however, the N is low. As usual, success correlates very highly with age: only 27 percent for those dying before they became forty, but 86 percent for the rest. We know or can infer the situation of all except the one mentioned, which yields a success rate of 67 to 69 percent, just above the same as the next younger group. At least one-fourth moved, all of whom as far as we know did well. As before, the men included all types, from poor John Lucas who could provide only £60 for his widow and five children, to a Simsbury selectman and deputy who became a founder and benefactor of Fairfield's Trinity Church. The great majority, however, simply became average small farmers like Joseph Garnsey of Stamford, assessed for £47 on the 1701 tax list, whose estate in 1709 was worth £173 including his seventy-acre farm.

In this survey of Connecticut's laboring class we have distinguished several groups: slaves, servants, and free whites. We summarize first by noting their circumstances as laborers, second by their prospects as measured by frequency and age at marriage and by life expectancy, and third through an analysis of their opportunity to rise out of the status of dependent laborers.

The situation of slaves, servants, and free whites varied with their relative status and rights, in the order given, and less predictably with the circumstances of the family with which they lived. Only the well-to-do whites could afford to buy or hire a laborer, so that slaves, servants, and white hired help potentially enjoyed a decent standard of living, and surely at least subsisted. Children of the poor white families may have fared less well, especially when their fathers left them with little property.

Marriage among slaves was uncommon and among freedmen also rare: the occasional Negro or mulatto who turns up in the tax lists or probate court generally left neither wives nor property. What little we know of their demography indicates too few families to maintain their numbers. The situation of white servants and apprentices was considerably better in that two-thirds did marry, a proportion far short of the norm but even farther above that of the slaves. The median age for those who took this step, an important upward movement, averaged only one year more than the normal; and the median age at death of fifty-five, while a few years younger than usual for the colony, is not bad, even if we subtract a few years for unknowns. These servants, like the freed blacks and Indians, rarely became financially independent, our best guess indicating that only 30 percent improved on their origin as laborers. However, those fortunate enough to reach age forty had a fifty-fifty chance.

Among the free whites, who formed the great majority of the laborers, we recall and then dismiss, first, the sons whose fathers provided a decent living and who in most cases would retain that level. A survey of sons of older, well-established fathers during the years 1660-1689 and 1700-1714 showed that among those reaching age thirty, and for whom we have enough evidence, one in ten became leaders, two out of ten failed to equal their fathers' position, and the other seven did so, for a success rate of 80 percent (N = 153).[30] The second group we omit here consists of the men over age forty who died poor, remaining laborers. Some of these as we have just seen were born into families with property but retrogressed, through some disability. The others, probably a majority, began as the migrants or poor local boys whom we have been considering.

Migrants enter our field of vision as servants, on tax lists, or in the probate records. Where they came from we usually do not know; such evidence as we possess indicates an equal division among other Connecticut towns, another colony, and Europe. In any case, at least one-third died elsewhere than the place where we first meet them. Most of them (probably 80 percent) married and they lived to be nearly sixty. Fewer than half succeeded, but that means 50 percent more than was true of the servants. As to the poor orphans, they moved around as often, generally married at the median age of twenty-six, and lived for the same number of years. Two-thirds of them improved their position, ceasing to be laborers, their degree of success varying with age: almost never if they died in their twenties, two out of five if they lasted another ten years, five out of six if they lived longer. The final figure

[30] Of those who died in their twenties some certainly, and many probably left small properties, but that raises the proportion of failures only from 19.0 to 20.2. The same may be true of the ten individuals who departed without a trace. Incidentally, we have inventories for 70 percent of the children whose fathers died during 1660-1689 and 61 percent of the later group. In both cases three sons per father reached age thirty.

is the most striking, and we have found that even the servants and outsiders, those with the least prospects, had a better than even chance to advance if they reached age forty. Thus, of the whole laboring class taken collectively, excluding the two we dismissed, three-fourths of the whites could look forward to a decent living and respectability unless death intervened too soon.[31] This fits with our conclusion stated in the previous chapter, differently derived, that poverty among the middle-aged was rare in Connecticut. Indeed, the small number of our poor orphans testifies to the infrequency of economic failures among the fathers, just as the infrequency of servants and slaves proves the preponderance of laborers who would soon become small propertyowners—the native sons of the propertyowners themselves.

[31] The reader may incline to argue that all of the men who disappear from the records had failed. If someone lived long enough in a particular town we almost certainly discover the fact from deeds, church records, gravestones, vital or marriage records, or the probate court. Men who disappear are of two types: those who died before marrying or joining a church, and those who moved. The first would ordinarily be under twenty-one or a few years older (the probate caught most of the men of age) so we would exclude them from our pool as not enjoying a decent chance. I tried to trace those who moved by looking through the deeds of nearby communities and the card indexes to the other sources covering the entire colony. I also consulted published primary sources for other colonies (such as the *New Jersey Archives*) and genealogies, catching some, but the net was too coarse for the fish. There is no reason to suppose that all of the emigrants failed any more than my migrants did, and a test run using men who left New Haven showed the opposite. That is probably biased, but we certainly cannot set down all our missing persons as failures, and a midpoint between that and the proportion for the knowns seems to err, if at all, in exaggerating the rate of failures.

Number and Sex of Slaves, Eighteenth Century

Time period	No. inv.	No. with slaves	% with slaves	No. slaves	Per inv.
1700–1724	1,788	128	7	204	0.11
1725–1729	730	46	6	72	0.10
1730–1739	597	66	11	136	0.23
1740–1749	743	91	12	130	0.175
1750–1753	1,144	97	8½	204	0.18
1753–1759	1,053	96	9	196	0.19
1760–1764	978	98	10	242	0.25
1765–1769	916	96	10	202	0.22 (0.18)
1770–1774	1,012	128	12½	285	0.27 (0.22)

	Adult men			Adult women		Young males		Young females		
	No.	Per inv.	%	No.	%	No.	%	No.	%	Children
1700–1724	81	0.04	40	43	23	27	17	31	20	10
1725–1729	36	0.05	50	16	22	10	14	10	14	0
1730–1739	43	0.07	32	26	19	41	30	23	19	3
1740–1749	59	0.08	45	33	25	19	16	15	13	4
1750–1753	89	0.08	44	46	25	31	19	20	12	8
1753–1759	68	0.07	37½	36	20	41	24	29	18	7
1760–1764	83	0.085	34	58	24	52	22	44	20	5
1765–1769	71	0.08	35	51	25	40	21	35	19	5
1770–1774	112	0.11	40	67	24	57	21	42	15	4

SOURCE: Estate inventories.

NOTE: Fifty-eight unknowns allocated according to value. Some "men" and "women" may be under age twenty-one; contemporary definitions uncertain.

APPENDIX 5 B

Summary Table, White Laborers (N = 397)

	Successful	Failed	% success	Med. age at death	Med. age married	% single successful	% who moved			Total
							colony	outside	?	
Servants and apprentices	10	20–27	27–33.3	53	26	33	30	6	0	36
Outsiders, tax lists	38	39–51	43–49	56?	26	30	25	11	3	39
Orphans										
age 5–9	50	28–52	53–64	59½	25	0	29	4	0	33
age 10–19	82	25–54	62–76	59?	26	20	28	8	2	38
age 20+	22	10–11	67–69	57	27	0	22	8	8	38
Total	202	121–195	51–62	56	26	12	28	7	2	37

Property of Free Laborers, Estate Inventories

The probate records contain inventories of men whom I denominated "laborers." These are free whites, and include the people this chapter considers: ex-servants, former orphans, immigrants, and local failures. A few of them owned above-average properties of one sort or another, but such assets would be cancelled by liabilities, especially debts, and the lack of income-producing assets. The following table records their economic situation for comparison with other economic groups and to round out our presentation. Values in cash.

	Single men		Married men		Total	
	No.	%	No.	%	No.	%
Personal wealth						
£1–19	231	62.6	58	34.9	289	54.0
20–49	110	29.8	84	50.6	194	36.2
50–99	24	6.5	20	12.0	44	8.2
100+	4	1.1	4	2.4	8	1.5
Total	369	100.0	166	99.9	535	99.9
Median £	16		29		18	
Land, in acres						
None	198	53.7	76	45.8	274	51.2
1–9	75	20.3	44	26.5	119	22.2
10–19	46	12.5	22	13.3	68	12.7
20–39	29	7.9	17	10.2	46	8.6
40–99	18	4.9	6	3.6	24	4.5
100+	3	0.8	1	0.6	4	0.7
Consumer goods						
£1–19	319	86.4	120	72.3	439	82.1
20–39	38	10.3	34	20.5	72	13.5
40–79	11	3.0	11	6.6	22	4.1
80+	1	0.3	1	0.6	2	0.4
With books	149	40.7	79	47.6	228	42.6
Silver, cash, livestock, ships, trading stock, and debts receivable						
None	128	35.0	34	20.5	162	30.5
£1–19	198	54.1	107	64.5	305	57.3
20–49	29	7.9	21	12.6	50	9.4
50–99	11	3.0	4	2.4	15	2.8
Median £	6		12		7	

SOURCE: All inventories 1650–1699 and those as previously identified, 1765–1774. Consolidated because no differences by time or place appeared.

SIX

The Farmers

Next to laborers, farmers were the most numerous occupational group in colonial Connecticut, and among the married men, exclusive of the elderly, they formed over half. We may distinguish three subspecies: the young married men just starting their careers; those well established, characteristically in their forties and fifties with teen-aged or grown children; and the grandfathers over sixty, who often continued to work with full vigor, but sometimes withdrew from an active life and turned the farm over to their children.

We can follow the process of advancing from the farm laborer to the owner by beginning with the young married group. As we have seen, the bachelors seldom owned land and usually worked for wages. Marriage changed that status abruptly. Of those aged twenty-five to twenty-nine, three out of ten remained wage-workers. The same number, however, had acquired some non-agricultural skill, normally a craft but occasionally in trade or even a profession (as a doctor or minister). The rest—40 percent—became farmers at once. The slightly older men, aged thirty or more, now with additional young children, succeeded in shifting out of the labor force into farming, a move that brought a major economic gain. The proportion of artisans, traders, and professionals remained nearly the same, with a steady shift into agriculture. Among men aged thirty-five to forty, nearly three out of five were farmers, only one in seven worked for wages, and one out of five was an artisan. Finally, the still older group had almost ceased to rely upon wages (remember that these are heads of families); over 60 percent had become primarily farmers, and more than that owned farms. This situation did not alter fundamentally over time, though in the late colonial period there was a reverse movement out of agriculture into another occupation, a shift involving all age groups but especially those over forty, among whom the proportion of farmers declined by about 20 percent. Thus, in general, the proportion of farmers among married men increased with age from 40 percent to over 60 percent.

Of the beginners, a few got off to a fast start thanks to their fathers. Twenty-five-year-old Lemuel Richardson of East Haddam left property worth some £300 including 140 acres when he died, and John

Morehouse of Fairfield was worth twice as much, with upwards of eighty acres at his death in 1754 at the age of twenty-seven.[1] Youngsters in their twenties, however, seldom inherited estates of such dimensions, normally leaving only a little over £100 worth, sufficient to support a family on a subsistence level but not more, though their consumption goods (at £31) raised them safely into the subsistence-plus standard of living, no doubt thanks to the wives. A majority owned fewer than the forty acres they probably needed and some had none at all. The distributions for all of the farmers in their twenties, for those over thirty, and for all these beginners, is shown in Table 6.1.[2] Sixty percent of the husbands under thirty left their widows with less than the desirable forty acres, and over one-third received fewer than twenty. One hopes that they prospered upon the usual remarriage.

Before we leave the youngest group, a few examples will add some detail. As a rule, they owned not only too little land but also insufficient capital goods for comfort. Abraham Colt of Glastonbury (1692-1717), with a wife and two sons aged three and one, apparently was living with his father who had given him half of the house. He had cleared three-and-a-half acres and owned also one-and-a-half acres of orchard, but thirty remained uncleared. He would have to borrow his

TABLE 6.1
Acres Owned by Young Farmers

Acres	21–29		30–39		Total	
	N	%	N	%	N	%
None	8	16.0	3	3.4	11	8.0
1–19	10	20.0	9	10.2	19	13.8
20–39	12	24.0	23	26.1	35	25.4
40–59	7	14.0	22	25.0	29	21.0
60–79	10	20.0	11	12.5	21	15.2
80–99	1	2.0	4	4.5	5	3.6
100+	2	4.0	16	18.2	18	13.0
Total	50	100.0	88	99.9	138	100.0

SOURCE: Estate inventories.

[1] Hartford district probate records, 8:247 (1713); Fairfield district probate records, 10:502.

[2] The data here and throughout the chapter come from inventories during 1670-1714, 1730-1754, and 1760-1774, with the limits described previously. In the case of the Hartford region I did not follow, for the farmers, the records for Middletown and Colchester districts. Pound values cash except as stated.

parents' oxen and farm tools. The livestock consisted of a cow and calf, a horse, and some pigs. He and his wife did have enough household goods, so were fairly under way.[3] Samuel Benham of Farmington had just married when he died in 1753. Potentially he owned the essentials for a decent life. He had improved much of his forty acres and had bought the timber for a barn, for £4.16, and the house, for £8. He also owned a few tools, though not a plow, and a yoke of steers that would soon become oxen. His household furnishings remained just above the subsistence level but he did have twenty-four bushels of wheat and twenty-three of corn, so was well launched.[4] Finally, we instance young Samuel Filer (Fyler) of Hebron. Filer had a house and sixty-two acres, the whole valued at £50, which means that most of the land was unimproved. He owned only one ox but six other cattle, two horses, and a couple of pigs, £3 worth of farm tools, and more than a necessary £31 in consumer items. The total estate of £116 makes him one of the poorer young fathers for the time, but he, like the others, verged on success. Another £4 would elevate him into our subsistence-plus level.[5]

Farmers in their early thirties improved their position in various ways. Most importantly, they had obtained more land: the median was nearly sixty acres, half again as much as for the younger men. If we set forty acres as minimally sufficient for full-time farming, 60 percent owned enough. The fact that they were still just starting shows up in various ways other than the size of the farm. The median value of their landholdings hovered around £1 per acre during the years 1670-1714, a low price that reflected the proportion of their land remaining unimproved. The only important change over time was the rise in value to £2 by mid-century and to £3.10 by 1770 (all in cash). This increase resulted in part from a general trend but in particular because a much larger proportion of the land was improved, so that even the beginners inherited better-developed farms.

The young married couple often depended upon renting additional land to support the family. A few—about 8 percent—had no land at all, and another 14 percent held less than twenty acres, far too small for survival when one considers the need for firewood. Some did not even own a house, but either lived with a parent or, presumably, rented. This situation became more common over time, probably as higher land prices delayed their becoming entirely independent. On the other

---

[3] Hartford district probate records, 9:280.
[4] Ibid., 17:26, 69.
[5] Hartford district probate records, file no. 1952.

TABLE 6.2
Houses and Tools Owned by Young Farmers
(percentages)

	1670–1714	1750–1774
Without a house	20	36
With part of a house	8	10
With a house	72	53
With no tools	24	18
With under £5 worth	59	54
With over £5 worth	17	28

hand, they had more tools, though generally not as many as the fully developed farm required, namely £5 worth. During the early period only one out of six of the beginners had that much, which improved to one in four later; but an equal proportion owned none at all. Presumably one could borrow the use of the more expensive implements such as the plow and harrow and a cart in exchange for labor at critical periods. Just as important was the possession of oxen. Fewer than half owned the necessary yoke, and while some men could use steers and a few had one of the required two, there remained about 40 percent entirely lacking. Here again they must either borrow or rent, and one major handicap of outsiders was surely the difficulty in obtaining draft animals and essential implements. Thus nearly half of these young farmers lacked enough land, tools, and oxen; but the men over thirty improved upon that.

The generally marginal circumstances of the group show up in other ways, too. Their median total wealth was £120, barely at the subsistence-plus level. These beginning farmers did rather better in the way of households goods, half actually living in comfort, since their families needed only £35 for that and the wife brought much of the necessary articles to the marriage. Only 4 percent owned less than the £10 that meant real poverty, with another 4 percent close to the margin. Their problem lay with capital and production goods.

A farmer needed not only a yoke of oxen but at least six more cattle to provide milk, meat, and a surplus for sale. But of our young fathers, 60 percent had fewer, the median being six. Similarly, two horses would seem the minimum—a mare and colt most commonly, or one of each sex; but during the years before 1715 half had fewer and during the later period, the median was only one. No doubt the "average" man could not pasture much more on his limited acres and with the chil-

TABLE 6.3
Value of Consumer Goods, Young Farmers
(cash values)

	N	%
£1–9 (poor)	5	3.5
10–19 (subsistence)	24	16.7
20–34 (subsistence plus)	55	38.7
35–49 (comfortable)	26	18.3
50–99 (well-off)	31	21.8
100+ (luxury)	1	0.7
Total	142	99.9

SOURCE: Estate inventories.

dren too young to help. The combination set the land he could work, his income, and therefore his other property. In addition, the young fathers had little cash money. One out of five included debts among their assets, a proportion that rose to 30 percent later, but these were only small sums, usually owed by a relative, and they were balanced by debts owed to others. To summarize, at least half of the starting farmers had to depend on others for draft animals, husbandry and other tools, and the use of additional land, while some lacked a house or a barn and might have to borrow household articles or money. However, the degree of dependence lessened as men moved through the thirties and in the end most had freed themselves from having to borrow or rent anything to make a living.

Again illustrations are better than aggregate statistics. Ephraim Beach of Stratford, who died in 1717 at the age of thirty leaving two young children, did not own any land as yet, but he had fourteen cattle, three horses, eighteen sheep, and twenty-nine pigs, with £58 in consumer goods, all sufficient for a good living; and besides, he was a shoemaker as well as a farmer.[6] Similarly, Joseph Bishop of Guilford (1682-1710) left only four cows, one horse, and ten sheep, £25 in household articles and apparel, £3 in tools, and nothing but the frames for his house and barn, but he owned sixty-four acres.[7] Both men, therefore, could expect to achieve full independence within a few years. Probably they would have added rather little in the way of household utensils since they already had a sufficiency, but would invest their money in livestock and improving the land. The next step up is represented by Na-

[6] Fairfield district probate records, file no. 413.
[7] New Haven district probate records, 3:191.

thaniel Hitchcock of Wallingford (d. 1710), who in his early thirties furnished his home sparsely, but he owned all the necessary livestock, £5 worth of tools, a house, barn, and fifty-three acres, plus ten acres of meadow and a fifty-acre division. Much of this must have remained unimproved, for the whole 113 acres with buildings were valued at only £157; yet he had harvested £9 worth of corn and flax and was pasturing fifty-seven animals. At the moment he owed £12, but was clearly on the way to success.[8]

Those with less favorable prospects had an alternative: they could sell out and buy land elsewhere. Until after 1700 unimproved land in the colony sold for 5 shillings an acre on the average. Therefore a starting farmer with twenty improved acres, who sold that for £20 plus another £10 if he had a small house, could buy eighty unimproved acres, and the extra £10 would purchase the lumber for his first little house, or help in erecting it. Actually, this route seems to have been taken most often by the single men who sold off their shares of the paternal estates to brothers and moved. During the eighteenth century the price of new land in the colony rose gradually to 15 shillings, and the value of improved land also increased. Less expensive tracts were opening up outside in the colony. When Congress eventually established the famous dollar per acre for government land it was competing with alternative sellers such as the states of New York and Pennsylvania. By that time the going rate for a farm, taking the acres and buildings collectively, had risen to at least £4 per acre in Connecticut, so that the young head of household could sell a twenty-acre inheritance and buy a quarter-section, joining with three other families in the minimum 640 acres, with a hundred dollars left over, thus obtaining two eighty-acre farms for the average two sons. This prospect, of course, goes far toward explaining the economic and social stability and, quite likely, the political placidity and "steady habits" of the colony. The sedentary and conformist stayed at home and bore adversity quietly; the ambitious left.

The first thing we notice as we look at the older, established farmers is their much larger estates. Whereas those just starting owned, on the average, barely the minimum forty acres, so that half fell below that level, men with teen-age or adult children had acquired over a hundred even without considering the unimproved tracts. Taking the colonial period as a whole, and studying 440 estates of such men from all over the colony, we find them all containing the magic forty acres just of improved land clearly identified as such, plus more than fifty of mis-

[8] Ibid., 212, 282, 329.

cellaneous but mostly improved land such as fenced pasture, and another thirty-five of unimproved acres, all told three times as much as the younger men. Of this amount, perhaps half was inherited, but the rest was purchased out of profits, as the voluminous deeds clearly show. That prospect obviously kept many men at home, content, unimpressed by the opportunities elsewhere. Also, the value per acre of this land as a whole equaled that held by the younger men, even though much of it remained unimproved, because of the greater worth of their improved part due to the labor on it over the years. By the end of the colonial period the average established farmer could sell out for £400, including buildings, enough to buy two full sections in the Northwest Territory after the war.[9]

This broad generalization conceals the actual variety, partly over time, but especially among individuals. The value of land, as we have seen, rose during the eighteenth century. This holds true for all varieties. Before 1700, home lots, meadow, orchard, and plowland (taking the colony as a whole) were worth £3 per acre. By 1730 this reached £4 and ended there, for these men, probably because the larger holdings were less intensively cultivated than the smaller, and so did not reveal the increase that we find among land generally. Their land of all sorts other than unimproved tracts began at a little over £2, which stayed the same until after 1730, then advancing by 50 percent as they brought a larger proportion of their land under careful cultivation. Unimproved land rose even more sharply, starting at 3 shillings per acre (some being listed without any price attached), reaching 10 shillings shortly after 1700, 12 shillings by mid-century, and a pound or so in 1770. Overall, including all sorts of land, these men held farms valued at £1.5 per acre before 1700, £2 by the 1720s, and £3 by the 1750s. The value of farm buildings also nearly doubled during the eighteenth century due to somewhat better houses and additional outbuildings. My data here come from too few cases for precision, but the generalization is solid, of a high point reached by 1750-1754, remaining unchanged thereafter.[10]

[9] The unadjusted data yields medians of £375 for the land plus £65 for buildings, totaling £440 ($1,667), but adjustments for wealth bias lowers the sum by about £20.

[10] These are medians of the estates, but the means are close to the medians because the estates with the largest acreages have the lowest value per acre, small farms being more highly cultivated, with less idle land. Evaluators sometimes simply lumped all real property: 100 acres and buildings, £200. The larger the farm the lower the value per acre, so that 200 acres might be valued at £2 and a 50-acre farm at £4, where the overall median was £3. However, the variation from the norm prevents precision. Four estates of above 200 acres, during 1720-1729, ranged in value (including the buildings) from only 3 shillings to over £2 per acre, while several under a hundred acres varied

TABLE 6.4
Composition and Value of Established Farms
(estate inventories, cash values)

	Buildings		Improved land			All but unimproved			Total		
	N	Median	N	Acres	£/acre	N	Acres	£/acre	N	Acres	£/acre
1670–1699	58	34	143	35	3	180	70	2.5	182	100	1.10
1720–1729	50	45	97	34	4	116	102	2.5	123	170	2
1750–1754	31	60	48	41	4.10	62	105	2.10	62	137	3
1765–1769	57	62	73	59	4.10	73	106	2.10	73	119	3

NOTE: Acreages for 1765–1769 are adjusted for age bias by subtracting 4 percent of the total from the largest estates. Columns headed "acres" give medians. "Acres" include inferences drawn from prices to obtain the maximum N, the result closely paralleling the values derived from inventories furnishing prices. The number of cases for the "All but unimproved" category exceeds that for "Improved land" because some inventories furnish only the total acreage.

The rise in value per acre accompanied and was partly caused by an increase in the quantity of improved land per farm. This proceeded unevenly. The median of total acreage per estate rose steeply between 1700 and 1730 from 100 to 170, mostly due to purchases of unimproved land. After that it dropped back to 125 acres as men divested themselves of speculative holdings, but stayed well above the old levels. The percentage of improved land did not increase until after 1750, presumably because the formation of new farms, with their lower proportion of such land, lasted until that time; but by 1770 half of these estates consisted of land that the inventories clearly identify as improved, and probably a rising proportion of the acres not so described also belonged to the more valuable category. Since improved land was consistently three times as valuable as the unidentified or miscellaneous type, the rising price of farms registered the gradual clearing, plowing, and fencing of new land, so that even though the total acreage of farms declined during the final decades their value remained unchanged. Put differently, the colony supported a growing population on smaller farms without an economic decline by more intensive use of the land.

This satisfactory median of improved and improved-plus-miscellaneous land suggests a general prosperity among the farmers in their forties and fifties, an age that most of them lived to enjoy. But the single figures hide a great diversity, for some families owned far less

from £2.8 to £6. The medians of all "farms" increased from £2 prior to 1700, to £2.10 during the 1720s, and to £4 by 1750 where it remained. This knowledge permits generalizations when we know only the total value of the real property, as long as we have a sufficient number.

TABLE 6.5
Acres Owned by Established Farmers

Acres	1670–1699		1720–1729		1750s set		1769–1774		Total	
	N	%	N	%	N	%	N	%	N	%
(None)	(2)		(2)		(2)				(6)	
Under 40	44	24.4	17	14.5	4	6.4	6	8.4	71	16.5
40–79	63	35.0	21	18.0	17	27.4	13	18.3	114	26.5
80–119	48	26.6	23	19.7	14	22.6	20	28.2	105	24.4
120–199	20	11.1	24	20.5	20	32.3	20	28.2	84	19.5
200+	5	2.8	32	27.3	7	11.3	12	16.9	56	13.0
Total	180	99.9	117	100.0	62	100.0	71	100.0	430	99.9

SOURCE: Estate inventories.

property and a few far more. We can divide these older fathers into five groups. First, those with less than the necessary forty. Before 1700 a quarter of the farmers belonged there but thereafter the proportion declined to less than 10 percent. Next, the group with between forty and eighty, which we suppose to permit a standard of living above bare subsistence. Again, during the seventeenth century this category included a large number, over one-third, and again that declined later to one-fifth. One in four farmers of this species owned a respectable 80 to 120. Those with 120-199 (here and throughout excluding un-improved tracts), which would provide comfort, at first formed only 11 percent of the total, but after 1700, one-fourth. Finally come the well-off, fewer than 3 percent during the 1600s, one-fifth later.[11] Our total sample size of 430 enables us to study each of these wealth classes in turn, separating the seventeenth and eighteenth centuries when differences appear.

We begin with the group poorest in terms of improved land, which included, before 1700, one-fourth of our farmers. About a third were truly poor, owning less than twenty acres of improved land, but nearly half had thirty or more, which would suffice depending on its quality (which varied from £1 to £8) and access to vacant land where livestock could run. Indeed, if we consider all the land listed in the estate, including unimproved tracts, their situation brightens considerably. In that case, only one in ten had less than twenty acres and three out of four owned above thirty. Since so many of these men had access to

[11] Two men in each period had no land. These either had access to family property or, less likely, rented. The small number and the lack of any change over time makes them insignificant—2 percent overall.

undivided or common land of the towns, we probably must almost discard acreage as a definition of economic status for them and depend rather on personal wealth such as livestock. We can, however, observe that during this early period far fewer than one-fourth of the mature farmers fell into the below-subsistence level. The actual situation is best judged by *all* of their land, which would reduce that proportion to one-eighth.

As the decades passed, vacant land adjacent to the homesteads became rare. Men with a claim or who could buy a right then incorporated such property into their farms, so that fewer farms fell short of the magic forty. By the 1720s one out of seven still belonged to this lowest group but half of these, as earlier, owned undeveloped tracts, now rising in value as they became less extensive. Therefore only 7 percent of our group were truly poor in terms of acreage. This now remained unchanged until 1774. Taking the colonial period as a whole, fewer than one-tenth of the mature farmers owned less than forty acres and some of these certainly enjoyed free access to more. To this we might add, by way of substantiation, that nine out of ten of those with fewer than forty acres owned houses equivalent in value to their more affluent neighbors'.

We turn now to a more detailed description of the property owned by these mature men, beginning with those holding under forty acres exclusive of unimproved tracts. Our sample numbers eighty cases, 60 percent of whom lived during the seventeenth century. Half of these owned unimproved land, a fact that made little difference to their economic situation because almost everyone had ready access to such woodlands. We can therefore discuss them collectively. Though by definition all owned small farms by colonial standards, they were not identical. A few individuals—only 2 percent—had none. This did not matter as much as one might suppose. Most dramatically, landless Capt. Samuel Newton of Milford (1677-1728) owned thirty-seven cattle, three horses, and twenty-six sheep on his zero acres and had £291 in personal wealth at the time of his death. As one might suspect he had belonged to a prominent family. His younger and only other brother, Colonel Roger, still owned over 150 acres at the age of eighty-six, plus around 200 more in Salisbury. The captain was therefore not poor but, for whatever reason, had given or sold his land. If so, he really does not belong among this set.[12] Indeed, of all the other landless men in our sample only one seems genuinely to have been poor. The rest had household and personal articles, cattle, farm tools, and

[12] New Haven district probate records, 3:143, 2:37.

even grain equal to the landowners', and we suppose that for some reason the inventories were incomplete or that they were using land owned by other members of the family. This means that when we find a certain proportion of men without land we are stating a maximum figure, the true percentage being less.

Most of the other men with under forty acres had at least twenty, commonly more than thirty which, depending on the quality and access to woodland, enabled many to live quite decently. They did not, in short, constitute any sort of homogeneous class or distinctive species. Since changes over time were minor, other than the virtual disappearance of unimproved land late in the era, we may describe their property collectively.

In glancing at the value of their real wealth as opposed to acreage, we do, of course, encounter a rise in prices for which we must adjust. We then find the following distribution (see Table 6.6). The two with exceptional properties were Capt. Steven Burrett of Stratford and Josiah Tibbals of Milford, both of whom owned some unimproved land but above all had soil of excellent quality—Burrett's had produced a crop of grain worth £42.[13] Almost by definition, however, these men's real property clustered around £100 in value, over half falling between £50 and £150.

In personal wealth, a farm family at its most numerous probably needed £30 for minimum subsistence and £60 for subsistence plus. The latter would include £30 in household goods and the same in livestock and tools. The livestock would consist of two oxen, four other cattle, a mare, and a few pigs, especially a brood sow; some inventories would show calves, a colt, piglets, and provisions for the family such as cereals and cider. According to that standard, about one-fourth of these smallest farms provided no better than a subsist-

TABLE 6.6
Value of Realty, Farmers with under Forty Acres

£	N	%	£	N	%
1–49	14	17.5	300–499	1	1.2
50–99	24	30.0	500+	2	2.5
100–199	31	38.8	Total	80	100.0
200–299	8	10.0	Mean £120	Median £104	

NOTE: Date for 1750–1774 multiplied by 0.67 to adjust for the price increase.

[13] Fairfield district probate records, 9:471; New Haven district probate records, 16:475, 650.

ence level, but only one in ten of the owners lived in poverty. Nearly half owned less than enough real estate, but some certainly had access to additional land. Others would have inherited or married, so to speak, some of their personal property, which would therefore not depend immediately upon the land, and could borrow certain items in time of need, such as a yoke of oxen or a plow. The two sets of data thus probably harmonize. The great majority of these families fell into the next higher bracket, the subsistence-plus level, between £60 and £100 in personal wealth. A fourth achieved comfort, and three individuals owned £200 worth. The median was £80 and the mean £84, both well up on the scale of subsistence plus, and impressive when we recall that certain articles never appeared in inventories, notably the clothing of wives and children, and that other items were sometimes missing, such as provisions, the father's clothes, or household articles claimed by the widow, not to mention those borrowed.

Articles of consumption made up nearly half of the total personal wealth of these men, a proportion characteristic of poor people. Even that may fall short of reality since so many of the missing items would belong to that category. Taking the inventories at face value, we find that one out of ten contained too little for subsistence and no more than one in five achieved comfort. However, the median of £34 and the mean of £40 permitted a satisfactory life, given the size of the family, 60 percent reaching subsistence plus (the reader will remember that we are here discussing fewer than one-fifth of the mature farm households). The relationship between acreage and personal wealth is especially strong. The men did not splurge on clothing, £3.5 worth being the median, even when one subtracts men who had none. Two exceptions are John Honeywell or Hennewell of Wethersfield (d. 1683) who had £17 worth and Nathaniel Fowler of Guilford; but Fowler (1721-1764) belonged to a prominent family and simply owned more than he ought. Hennewell apparently had immigrated, perhaps after the Restoration, bringing a good property: his inventory included £6 in silver plate (at 5/6 per ounce) and no less than twenty-eight cattle.

Of books, important in their own way, three-quarters owned at least one, but nobody had a library, and the median value was just 6 shillings. Only a few men kept silver articles or money. Four inventories contained servants. One of them belonged to a Mather—Timothy of Windsor (1710-1752), the second son of Captain Samuel, Esquire, son of Reverend Samuel and the daughter of Governor Treat. Joseph Couch of Fairfield (1726-1769) had a Negro boy worth £12. Samuel Collins of Middletown (d. 1696) owned an apprentice boy, Samuel Lucas, who eventually acquired more land than his master. Collins was the third son of Deacon Edward, a Massachusetts deputy, whose other children did very well. Finally, Nathaniel Porter of Stratford (1640-1680) held thirty-nine acres of good land and thirty-four unimproved, so only barely fits within this category, but his personal property was valued at £241 and his farm produced £50 in grain. He owned a Negro worth £25 and, incidentally, chamber pots, a sign of gentility.[14] All these men were atypical of this set. More characteristically, only half-a-dozen had any stock for sale and few left debts receivable. Two men did have money coming to them, one of whom was also a carpenter, and the other possessed the largest personal estate, which together with 354 acres of unimproved land really should raise him to a higher class along with Hennewell, Mather, and Porter. For most farms at this level, debts owed much exceeded credits and several insolvencies resulted. Disregarding exceptions we can say that these smallest of the middle-aged farmers possessed adequate personal estates, with consumer goods safety above the poverty level, but minimal clothing, only a couple of books, no servants, no goods for sale, no money, and no debts owing to them—about what one would expect, with all of the criteria converging on a picture of enough but just enough.

Perhaps more important for these men was the income or produce derived from the land, but the inventories do not tell us as much as we need to know. One-third of them do not list grains, as is true of the inventories for large farms. Discarding those with none, we find that the median was £8, and if we throw out the two extraordinary estates of Porter and Burrett, the mean was only a bit more, just under £10. Judging from this, a man of this class could feed his family but with little surplus. As one might expect, farm produce included the whole spectrum of grains and other crops such as cider, hay, and flax. Wheat was prominent even in these small farms along the southern coast, appearing primarily among estates belonging to men with exceptional quantities of grain, almost certainly raising it for sale. The only individual worth noting was Israel Dean of Salisbury, in which (then) remote town, and almost without land, he nevertheless raised, or at any rate came into possession of, seventy-three bushels of wheat and fifty-seven more of oats, corn, and rye, along with some flax and hay, presumably, the product of twenty or more improved acres, not just the three mentioned in the inventory.[15]

In livestock our small farmers fared rather better. If one needed a yoke of oxen, a cow and a calf, and two heifers coming along—half a

[14] Fairfield district probate records, file no. 5034.
[15] Sharon district probate records, file no. 980.

dozen animals—then most of them had that, plus indeed another cow and a pair of steers, all valued at £21.20 per inventory. Most of them owned two horses, either a mare and her colt or a horse and mare, though a few had none and several five or more. The "usual" number actually declined after 1750, because their price more than doubled while the farmers' wealth did not increase at all, so they apparently got along with only one. As to sheep, a third had none. The flocks, for such as kept any, averaged around ten, with the usual exceptions, their value being less than £3 because they cost only 5/6 per head including lambs (6/6 during the seventeenth century, 4/6 later). Finally, the farmers generally had seven or eight pigs worth £4, the number and total value declining over time. To some extent these farmers raised livestock for cash, but not much; pigs did not appear as barrels of pork nor did the sheep as wool for sale; rather, the family consumed most of both. All this livestock amounted to almost as much money as did consumption goods—£27 as a median, £33 as the mean, meeting the requirements for a subsistence-plus level.

A few illustrations of men close to the average will help to describe this group. John Sperry of New Haven (1650-1692) was the first of eight surviving children, whose father outlived him. He himself left five. Sperry had a house and orchard but no barn, which was probably attached to the house, as its value, £70, suggests. He also had twenty-eight acres of plow- and meadowland at £38 and thirty-seven of out-land valued at £11 cash. His personal estate of £80 was right at the median, his consumption goods, worth £38, just above it. He himself and his wife had a nice featherbed, but the five kids evidently shared two, and he owned only four pairs of sheets. Sperry had the normal complement of farming tools worth £6, four sheep, and nine swine, but no horses. His inventory mentioned no grains, but came in strong on cattle, with oxen, three cows, four heifers with calves (the meaning of the word "heifer" has changed), five two-year-olds, and three year-lings, so that his investment in capital other than land equaled the value of his consumer goods.[16]

Samuel Causon or Slason of Stamford died in 1723, having been married for thirty years. The 1701/2 assessment list showed him as an average farmer. His real estate included seventeen acres at £3.10 cash per acre and a homestead. A daughter received some of his "movables" valued at £39, a large part of his £82 worth of personal wealth. Wool and a loom suggest some additional income. Seven pounds' worth of wheat, corn, oats and barley provided food, not items for sale. He

---

[16] New Haven district probate records, 2:137.

owned the normal ten cattle, two horses, twenty sheep, and fourteen swine, collectively worth £32, right on the mean.[17] This is not poverty but far from comfort. Men with fewer than forty acres seldom achieved more.

One might suppose that the next groups of farmers, with twice as much land—forty to eighty acres exclusive of unimproved—would own twice as much wealth, but in fact that did not always follow; indeed, of some sorts of property they owned no more at all. As we have seen, the ownership of land was only one variable affecting wealth, and not always the most important, a situation that we will try to evaluate more closely later on.

Once again we discover in what seems a homogeneous class considerable variation, without any really wealthy people and of course no propertyless, but everything in between. Even in land, once unimproved tracts are added, the range stretches from barely forty acres to nearly two thousand (John Wilcox of Middletown, otherwise undistinguished in property). Differences in the value of this land result in a spread in real estate from £48 for Joseph Gates's forty acres in Colchester to David Osborn's fifty of improved land valued at over £7 each in Fairfield. However, half of these men were worth between £100 and £200 in real property, and most of the others did not diverge much farther from the median of £170, well over twice that of the group just discussed. The mean of £195 was also 50 percent higher. The small difference in these two figures reveals an equality in this respect.

The same narrow range exists for personal wealth, where the median was £110 and the mean £129, once more about half again as much as for men with fewer than forty acres. Now we find no men with less than the needed £30 and the proportion of those simply subsisting is reduced from one-fourth to one in seven. As a rule, then, these farms provided a sufficient living. A majority, indeed, had enough property for a surplus, while as many men lived very comfortably on £200 in personal estates as fell below £50. Consumption levels confirm this. Almost nobody had less than the requisite £15 and all but one-fifth enjoyed the subsistence-plus level of £30, even without the occasional missing articles. Over half owned the £55 that meant comfort and a few had upwards of £100. These include the usual anomalies. Mr. William Leete of Guilford, besides owning 198 acres of unimproved land, had inherited a considerable property from his father, Governor William (an older brother left £1,000 a few years later). John Thomp-

---

[17] Fairfield district probate records, 6:152.

son of Stratford had two slaves and valuable land; while both Ebenezer Mix and Ephraim Willard of Hartford and Wethersfield were coopers as well as farmers and the former had nearly three hundred acres of all sorts. In general, doubling the land had doubled the prospect for a subsistence-plus level of living.[18]

Other changes in personal wealth were less significant. Three-fourths lacked silver or money. Only seven men had a slave. Stock for sale was held by more, because a few additional men practiced a craft, but only 13 percent diversified in that way. Ownership of books had been usual among the smaller farmers and even more of these men had at least one—82 percent. But again no one owned a "library." Clothing did increase sharply, from what must have been a marginal £3.10 to an adequate £5. Also, debts receivable became more frequent, appearing in 30 percent of the inventories, and now perhaps exceeding in value debts payable.[19] This group of men also had slightly more tools, a median of £5 against £4. The half who owned less probably needed more.

In livestock, farmers of this class added only a few of each type, but these added up to a substantial increase. Of cattle most owned at least six and over half had ten, enough to be called a herd and to produce a surplus. The median and mean numbers were both eleven, worth £24.12 per estate and valued at £2.4 per head. The great majority kept two horses and almost half held three, probably the desired minimum. Presumably these were of superior quality as well, since they were valued at £3 each, higher than the £2.10 for lesser farmers. The average price of sheep was not higher, but again these men had more of them, indeed, nearly twice as many, and only one-fourth owned none. The greater availability of wool might explain the better clothing of these men. The number of their pigs, however, scarcely differed; every farmer kept some. Combined, these men on their forty to eighty acres (and vacant land) kept thirty-two farm animals, almost entirely in small groups, not big herds or flocks. The mean value of this livestock was about one-third higher than that of the smaller farmers. Equally important was the value of other farm products. The proportion of inventories listing grains and other like crops did not increase, because that depended upon the time of year when the farmer died. However, the inventories show larger quantities, the median rising from £8 to £13.10, and seven men had crops worth over £30. These

[18] New Haven district probate records, 1 part 1:163, part 2:15; Fairfield district probate records, 15:145; Hartford district probate records, 20:121, 126, 202, 331-332.
[19] The mean for debts receivable was £14, that for debts payable was £10, but the latter are incomplete.

lived in the Connecticut Valley or along the southwestern coast—Milford, Stratford, and Fairfield.

Again, a few fairly typical examples will turn numbers into people. John Drake of Simsbury died in 1689 leaving three children, of whom the oldest was thirteen (his baby, John, Junior, moved to Danbury). His father, John of Windsor, died in the same year leaving an ordinary property. Our John's inventory specifies fifty-nine acres that seem to have been improved, notably forty acres of meadow valued at £70 cash. A home lot and a meadow, judging from the price, probably added seventeen acres more. In addition he owned a bit over 200 acres worth less than £20. He had raised a crop of wheat and corn and owned four oxen, two steers, three cows, three yearlings, and a calf, one or more swine, and three horses plus a yearling colt, collectively valued at £40. Some wheelwright tools helped out. A supplementary inventory after his wife's death four years later added five stocks of bees and a bit of flax, valued his clothes at £8 instead of £5, and notes a Bible. His clothes with other articles of consumption amounted to a subsistence-plus £38.[20]

Samuel Adams of Fairfield (ca. 1652-1694) also died in his forties, leaving a personal estate of £108 and forty-four acres of improved land plus some lots, the land and a house being valued at £145. He was almost certainly the son of Edward who in 1671, with a comparable estate of £154, received 715 acres in the great division of the town. Samuel's "lots" probably had been part of that division. His inventory was distinguished by the presence of a Negro woman worth £1 current money. The land had produced twenty bushels of wheat plus another crop of the same amounting, to judge from its value, to thirty bushels more, thirty bushels of corn, ten of meslin, the same amount of barley, some flax, and tobacco. He had stored away, or had available for sale, three-and-a-half barrels of pork, some hides, and yarn, collectively worth £16. Miscellaneous farming and carpentry tools came to £5 or £6. He also owned oxen, a cow, eight other cattle, eighteen pigs, thirty-one sheep, and horses valued at £15 currency, which means around five of them, all in all a fairly prosperous man though the value of his consumer goods was only an average £35.[21]

Finally, John Hodgkin of Guilford (1671-1727) owned seventy-six acres of improved and ninety of unimproved land, but the appraisers thought his real estate worth only £214 including a house, barn, and Sabbath Day house, so its quality could not have been high. He had

[20] Hartford district probate records, 5:25.
[21] Fairfield district probate records, 4:114, 173.

produced a mixed crop of wheat, corn, oats, and flax, with a modest number of livestock—oxen of course, a cow, a cow with calf, eight other cattle, four horses, eight sheep, and two pigs, the others having gone into a barrel of pork. These animals, valued at £50, helped to sustain enough household goods to make him well-off, worth £73 including £11 worth of clothing.[22]

We now come to the "average" mature farmers, with 80 to 120 acres, and whose median, adding unimproved tracts, was 115. One would suppose that a man with nearly two-thirds more land would increase in wealth by the same proportion, but, as we have already seen, the relationship was not proportional: more acres brought only a little more personal property. The various other factors that affected the accumulation of wealth tended to limit inequalities, and besides, men in Connecticut generally could not efficiently use large amounts of land, which they acquired primarily to hold for their children. Since around eighty acres produced an adequate standard of living, the men used the overplus for some additional comforts, but above all as a form of family investment. As with the previous group, over 40 percent inherited or acquired tracts that they left idle—sometimes a good deal of it, led by Deacon Stephen Hosmer of Hartford with 3,300 acres, but the proportion declined toward the end of the colonial period. The value of their real estate rose by more than half, after adjusting for price changes, to a mean of nearly £300 and a median of £267. In each, the value of the farms rose less than the increase in acreage over that owned by the men with forty to eighty acres, probably due to less intensive use. The top 10 percent of this group owned only 22.6 percent of their total real estate.

Personal wealth and its components also increased proportionately much less than that of the smaller farmers, considering the quantity of land. However, the improvement elevated almost everyone above the poverty level, and two-thirds owned over £100, which probably permitted comfort. Of the 104 estates, 16 recorded values of £200 or more. So also the median of consumption articles rose only from £47 to £53, but that was enough for nearly half to live comfortably, and again almost everyone escaped poverty. The exceptions included two insolvent debtors. A few more men at this level owned silver articles or money, the mean doubling to £2, and during the last quarter-century they bought another pound's worth of clothing. Eighty-three percent owned at least one book, the median value rising a bit to 11 shillings, but no large collections appeared as yet. Only eight individ-

[22] Guilford district probate records, 2:158, 183, 190.

uals had a servant when they died. Few owned goods for sale; instead, these assets, together with debts receivable, declined—but so did debts owed. The median value of tools increased from £5 to £6.10, especially toward the end of the period. £5 was ample for a variety of implements but it would not include a cart, a highly desirable addition. Four owned £20 worth and fifteen, £10 or more, often including items used in carpentry or cooperage.

Of livestock, these farmers owned a little more of everything. They added three cattle, £6 worth, clearly a surplus for sale. Most did not increase their horses but the value per inventory rose due to a few relatively larger herds. They kept another half-dozen sheep, which helps to explain the better clothing. The flocks now numbered around twenty on the average, and probably included proportionately more ewes than lambs since the average value increased slightly. The price of their pigs did not vary from those on smaller farms, but they had a couple more. These increases, of course, translated directly into a higher standard of living, not of food (for they already had enough to eat) but of additional household goods, and they converted the rest into land. Altogether the median value of livestock had risen from £39 among farmers with forty to eighty acres, to £47. If the minimum needed for subsistence plus was £32 worth, then 80 percent exceeded that, and 40 percent owned the £51 that would contribute to comfort. Finally, these farmers produced a little more grain and other crops, the median being £14 (of those with some) and the mean up from £15.10 to £17. Again this does not include grains clearly part of the "provisions" but we cannot always distinguish what the family needed from what they expected to sell. Most of the farms did not yield over £20 worth, but 30 percent did so and the men with larger returns must have benefited considerably, since (unlike livestock) most of the crop was available for immediate consumption.

Let us look at a few of these average farms, in different parts of the colony and at various times. Ezekiel Loomis of Lebanon (1716-1766) owned a 102-acre farm valued at £5 per acre, and ten acres of woods worth £15. The inventory lists no grain, but he did have fifteen loads of hay for his livestock. These included the yoke of oxen, three cows, and eleven others, mostly young, two horses, eleven pigs, and twenty-four sheep, together evaluated at £60. He had £10 worth of tools including a plow, harrow, and cart. The only real symptom of prosperity, aside from the land and animals, was his possession of a few gold and silver articles, at £12.10. His £7 in clothes, and six books at 6/9, were about normal, as was £132 in personal wealth. The £54 in consumer goods lay directly on the median, just a pound short of our estimated requirement for comfort.[23]

At the opposite end of the colony, Josiah Whitlock (1727-1769) of Redding also owned a 102-acre farm, worth somewhat less at £3.10 per acre, but with a house (£70) and barn (£15) specified whereas Loomis's buildings were incorporated into the price of his land. Whitlock had twelve bushels of wheat and if the wheat on the ground was worth the same amount, forty-two and a half bushels more. Six bushels of oats, a barrel of cider, and two barrels of pork complete the list of farm produce still on hand. Like Loomis, he contented himself with two horses and sixteen cattle. He owned just seven pigs—we have seen why—twenty-one sheep and six lambs, collectively worth exactly the same as Loomis's. He owned a pound more in tools but no silver articles, a sermon and prayer book but no Bible (probably his wife claimed it), and only £2 in clothing. His personal wealth of £137 was identical to Loomis's, as were his consumer goods, or a shade less depending upon the classification of the pork.[24]

Over eighty years before, in 1683, Thomas Wright of Wethersfield died in his early fifties, leaving four children aged eleven to twenty-three, and property valued at £673, or £475 at the later values. His best land, thirty acres on an island, was worth £180 in country pay (£126), as was his homestead—the home lot and buildings. In addition he had seven acres of swamp, forty-nine of upland, and another fifty of little value. We now encounter an Indian boy servant, and some debts receivable. The barn contained hay and corn, and he also had some cider along with the expected farm animals—fifteen cattle, two horses, sixteen sheep, and fourteen swine. Farm and carpentry tools came to £8 cash. "Purse and apparell" were listed at £13 cash and books at 10 shillings, on target. In cash money, consumer articles totaled £62, safety above what he needed for a comfortable home.[25]

Daniel Thomas of New Haven (ca. 1643-1694), a son of John, had six children when he died, but a daughter had just married so the seven members of his household could fit, a mite uneasily, onto four beds. Thomas owned the usual "homestead," which probably included upwards of half-a-dozen acres, fifty-eight more adjoining it, three of meadow, and forty to fifty miscellaneous, totaling some 110. Of grains we know only of some corn growing. He had seventeen cattle, a mare and her colt, seven sheep, three lambs, and "swine," probably sixteen

23 Windham district probate records, 7:238.
24 Fairfield district probate records, 17:295.
25 Hartford district probate records, 4:151-152.

or twenty, so that he made up in livestock what he lacked in grain. His personal property came to £122, consumer goods to only £46, with a Bible. He may have given some furniture and linen to his daughter. Of what remained, nearly half consisted of bedding, and the rest sufficed for a subsistence-plus level.[26]

David Loomis, Junior (1694-1752) supplemented his Windsor farm with weaving in a shop, and he also had a separate cider house. His home lot of sixteen-and-a-half acres at about £3.10 per acre, and sixty-five more at £3, provided a good estate, which produced cider of course, and the inventory lists barley, oats, corn, and beans in small amounts, for this was February. The inventory for the same reason lacked piglets, lambs, and calves, but his horse and mare did have a colt. Otherwise the livestock consisted of twelve cattle, thirty-one sheep, and six pigs. Debts receivable came to £13, his money to a few shillings. Consumer goods of £55, on target for comfort, included £5 in clothing and nine books along with his Bible, worth about 8 shillings.[27]

Our final class of farmers with teen-aged or young adult children consists of men owning at least 120 acres exclusive of unimproved tracts. This largest group numbered 144 out of the total of 432, or exactly one-third. They owned nearly twice as much land as did those with 80 to 120 acres, the median without unimproved being 179 and with it, 222. Twenty-six had upwards of 500 acres and four held 1,000 or more. Since their buildings and land values lagged behind acreages, their real estate was not worth twice as much, but around 60 percent more depending on what one measures. The median stood at £466

TABLE 6.7
Consumption Goods, Farmers with 120 Acres

	1670–1729		1750–1769		Total	
	N	%	N	%	N	%
£1–14	0	0	1	1.7	1	0.7
15–29	6	7.1	5	8.5	11	7.6
30–54	25	29.4	10	16.9	35	24.3
55–69	15	17.6	11	18.6	26	18.1
70–99	21	24.7	13	22.0	34	23.6
100 +	18	21.2	19	32.2	37	25.6
Total	85	100.0	59	99.9	144	100.0

[26] New Haven district probate records, 2:149.
[27] Hartford district probate records, 16:192.

and the mean, £482, both impressive figures for the colony, and two-and-a-half times the value of their personal estate.

Personal wealth rose by half, with none under £50 and all but 10 percent achieving comfort. Nearly half owned the £200 needed to qualify as "well-off" and four estates exceed £500. At the other end a dozen men lacked enough consumption goods for more than bare subsistence, though one suspects some flaw in the records or error in mine. However, two-thirds enjoyed comfort, as they ought, given their land, and one out of four was, for a farmer, wealthy in household goods. The increase in consumption lagged behind that in personal estate, rising by one-third where personal property was one-half above that of the slightly smaller farmers. More strikingly, although this most prosperous class had nearly eight times as much real property as the smallest group and two-and-a-half times as much personal wealth, the value of their consumption goods only doubled. If this reflected a choice on their part, as it surely did, they preferred to invest in capital goods—production—rather than in comfort, at least relatively.[28] Clothing illustrates the point perfectly: these men, many of whom had plenty of spare money, only added one pound's worth and almost none of them spent lavishly. Four individuals spent more than £20, but that is just 3 percent of this group, and the mean value was only £9 against the median of £7.

Perhaps less happily, they didn't splurge on books either. The proportion owning some did not change—a little over 80 percent—and the median rose only a little, to 14 shillings or, of those with some, 17/6. However, a few individuals now possessed real libraries. Capt. Samuel Talcott of Wethersfield owned £8 worth: he was one of the larger landowners, with 316 acres plus 250 unimproved. Talcott (1635-1691) was a Harvard man, as was Maj. Peter Burr of Fairfield (1668-1725) who had a library valued at £9. The books of Capt. Asahel Strong, Esq., of Farmington (1702-1751) equaled Talcott's. All of these men belonged to prominent families and may have inherited some of their books. Strong's are partly itemized. They included a Bible, fifty-one pamphlets, three lawbooks, ten of history, a clerk's guide, a military book, one on arithmetic, and a dictionary, plus two dozen not identified; moreover he had subscribed to the local lending library for 7/6. These three seem different from the ordinary farmers

---

[28] The mean for consumption doubled, that for personal wealth rose by 250 percent, and realty quadrupled (deflated). The median value for holdings in land increased 500 or 600 percent.

we have been discussing and, indeed, we might as easily classify them as professionals rather than farmers.[29]

Farmers of this class collectively owned far more servants. All of the others combined owned only twenty-four, one servant for every twelve masters; these men had twice that number, one for each three owners, and their value added £9 to each estate. Three men owned five each (Maj. Peter Burr again, Matthew Bellamy of Wallingford, and Lt. Joseph Platt of Milford), but a single person was usual, and 80 percent had none at all. They left a little more in debts receivable, less than they owed, somewhat more stock but still only £2.5 worth, and invested another 10 shillings in tools, bringing their median to £7, which, however, was still less than double that of their neighbors with under forty acres.

While the livestock of these farmers did not double in proportion to their land, it did increase, showing that clear surplus over need, which enabled them to buy more comforts and more land. We are dealing now with some of the most prosperous farmers in colonial Connecticut. What, then, did the well-to-do farmers pasture on their land? Seventeen cattle, four horses, twenty-four sheep, and eight pigs, and the land was also yielding a crop worth £20 in very mixed products, the combined total value, taking one month with the next, amounting to over £80, with the mean not far from £100. Indeed, nearly one-fifth owned more than that, whereas the smaller landowners rarely (one in forty) had so much.

A few individuals held much more than this. Herds of over fifty cattle occur; five men owned flocks of a hundred sheep, and Maj. Peter Burr had thirty horses. However, the majority of men did not deviate far from the median. Nearly half owned between ten and twenty cattle, at least at the date of the inventory; half had three to five horses, flocks of sheep ran generally from ten to forty, and pigs, from five to twenty. All of these figures are considerably in excess of family needs. Roughly, the typical farmer of this size owned, above the number needed for subsistence plus and so available for sale, eight cattle, three pigs, a couple of colts, and the wool from a dozen sheep. But of course they actually sold much more, since the inventories would always lack some of the surplus animals, disposed of continuously throughout the year, in the same way that barrels of pork at a given moment did not reflect the pigs killed and sold.

So also, finally, these men produced a much larger crop from their

---

[29] Talcott: Hartford district probate records, 5:122-124. Burr: Fairfield district probate records, 6:168, 7:11-12. Strong: Hartford district probate records, 16:45.

fields than they needed, worth £18.10, excluding the inventories with none, and we find nearly a third with more than £30 worth. They, with a few smaller farmers, clearly engaged in large-scale sale of specialties such as wheat, flax, or cider, a concentration uncommon in most of New England.

Surnames prominent in Connecticut history jump out from the list even of average farmers within this group. Samuel Wolcott of Wethersfield died in 1695, leaving to his wife and eight children, of whom the oldest was sixteen, an estate of £793. He was the third son of Henry, a prosperous merchant and assistant; his brother Henry, Esquire, and John both actively engaged in politics. Samuel owned a six-acre home lot, eleven of meadow, ten of "grass," eighteen in "dry swamp," the same amount in ordinary swamp, and eighty of pasture and woodland, the last two valued at £2 per acre, the rest at around £7 cash. In addition he held 108 acres worth £5 (about 8 pence each, in cash). His personal wealth came to £210, of which half consisted of household goods including £7 in clothing, about the same in cash and silver, and £3.10 in books. For livestock he owned sixteen cattle including three calves—this was June—five grown horses and two colts, nineteen sheep, and five swine. Luckily the appraisers specified ten acres in rye, five in "young corn," and one of oats, but no wheat. Presumably left over from the previous year were corn, rye, barley, cider, and some apples totaling £21, giving him in all nearly £40 worth of crops from the field. He kept four "stocks" of bees, but owed £200 in debts.[30]

Half-a-century later Ebenezer Gregory of Stratford (1696-1750) left to his heirs 131 acres valued at £2.10 per acre. He had just replaced two old, dilapidated houses that the appraisers thought together worth only £6 with a new building—they noted its glass and boards—six times as valuable. On the ground he had planted wheat and rye, together worth twice his corn, oats, and flaxseed. Livestock followed the familiar pattern except that he owned fifty-eight sheep. Consumption goods, at £93, included a modest £4 in clothing and not quite 10 shillings in books, mostly a single Bible.[31]

Finally, in the northeast we introduce Henry Ladd (1717-1769), farmer and cooper. The assessors followed an annoying habit in that region of simply noting £734 in real estate, leaving us to infer from the oc-

---

[30] The land was producing ten bushels of rye, twenty of corn, and probably fifteen bushels of oats per acre, unless the appraisers included the cost of tending and harvesting, which would reduce the yield; but these figures are all right. Hartford district probate records, 5:214-215.

[31] Fairfield district probate records, 10:130.

casional prices they did supply that his farm consisted of around 186 acres, of which no doubt much remained in woods. He raised, or had bought a small quantity of wheat and more of rye, but his grain was composed primarily of forty-one-and-a-half bushels of corn. He was really a livestock grower with thirty head of cattle, five horses, thirty sheep, and four pigs, more of the latter converted into almost a barrel of meat. His £2.8 in money and £28 in debts receivable perhaps resulted from cooperage activities, though we know only of his tools; he left no stock of goods for sale.[32]

Before moving on, we should notice a couple of the exceptional men who farmed in colonial Connecticut. Capt. Ebenezer Steele of Farmington (1671-1722), the son of Lieutenant Samuel, left only two daughters. His land, except for 581 acres of outland, is not specified, but from its value it certainly contained several hundred acres, the total worth about £770. In addition he had £287 in personal estate, including consumption goods of £136. The inventory, taken in November, gives us his minimum crop for the year, less what he might have sold: 16 bushels of wheat, 50 of rye, 50 of oats, 5 of barley, 110 of corn, and 10 barrels of cider, with a little flax. The value of the hay was included in that for the livestock. This seems to have been a common, though not invariable practice, which when adopted ought to have raised the price of the animals but did not. The appraisers also noted seed and labor on the ground, at £4 cash. Steele owned an unusual three yoke of oxen with a yoke of steers, five cows, two calves, but no heifers or young steers, no doubt disposed of, twenty-one sheep but no lambs, three large swine at £2 but no smaller ones, five horses (one old), two mares and a colt. He did not have a servant to help with the farm.[33]

Lastly, Capt. John Woodruff of Milford died in 1726 at age fifty-one worth about £2,600. His father John had died when only thirty-three, leaving a small estate, but the family, including the wives, possessed ability as well as property. Woodruff, like Gregory, had built a new house on twelve acres, together worth £270. He also owned a house and barn, much inferior, on four acres, half of a barn and a little house on thirteen acres, and 206 other acres averaging £10 per acre, an exceptional price for so large a tract. He had also invested £87 in one and a fourth rights in New Milford. Woodruff owned a Negro man and fifty-three cattle, including a yoke of old oxen, one of fat oxen, and two called working oxen. His grain consisted mostly of

[32] Windham district probate records, 7:427, 516.
[33] Hartford district probate records, 9:126-127.

wheat and corn, with small amounts of oats and barley. The rather small £75 in consumption featured books written in Latin and Greek, the whole totaling £4.10. He also had paper money worth £18 but had spent only £10 on clothing. His slave's bed and bedding cost 14 shillings. The captain's estate thus consisted principally of articles of production, so we are not surprised that his eldest son also became a captain and left a similar property with even more land—597 acres.[34]

These mature farmers, in Connecticut, not only provided for themselves and their wives and children until the latter married, but also represent the climax of the life cycle, to which all the rural laborers, the newlyweds, and the men with young children looked forward. The success of a colony's society depended in large degree on the ability of these fathers to care for the poor, and to produce the wealth that sustained the material standard of living, without considering their political and cultural contributions. We therefore aggregate their property, without further distinctions among them.

Tables in Appendix 6A display most of the generalizations. "Improved land" includes some rather slightly improved, and the large holdings in particular err on that side; but the data up to one hundred acres or so is reliable if we remember that improving did not always mean cultivating, but sometimes only fencing (that is, "using"). As we have argued, the rise in land values reflect more the degree of improvement than scarcity. Most of the farms were small enough for a family to care for, and, as we have seen, the larger ones correlate with larger families. Any owner who lacked enough sons to operate a given acreage would normally call upon neighbors with more than they needed. Fewer than 14 percent resorted to servants or slaves; indeed, if among the servants only males over sixteen helped in the fields, perhaps 6 percent. However, they could hire the migrants and their poor neighbors. Notice the moderate concentration of acreage owned by the top 10 percent. Since the smaller farms were more highly cultivated, the proportion with adequate holdings actually exceeded that suggested by Appendix 6A. Anything over eighty acres provided for the next generation, the figures for total land being especially significant in that respect. Both real and personal wealth were also equally distributed. The former incorporates changes in price, so that the values reflect those before 1750.

Men of this family status needed £55 in consumption goods for comfort, and we find close to half succeeding, while almost all avoided poverty even if we raise that boundary line to £20. They did not

[34] New Haven district probate records, 5:312, 322.

splurge on clothing; indeed, relatively few could have worn anything other than the essentials for warmth and work. Most had not so much as a sixpence in their purses: remember that this category combines silver articles with coins and notes of the colony. Incidentally, even fewer held debts receivable: as late as the final decade, when these had increased, 60 percent died without any. Almost all did own a book, especially when we remember that the inventories understate the true number, but farmers obviously were not great readers. Only those with relatively large libraries, say over £3 worth, would own anything other than religious works.

Finally, we include data on livestock and crops for comparative purposes with the reminder that both fluctuated during the year and that "none," in the case of grains, almost always meant merely that the inventory was taken during the winter or early spring before the man had planted his yearly crop. Connecticut's farmers, by the way, never stopped growing wheat. The inland towns produced rather little during the years 1680 to 1714, but by 1770 it had returned to about a fourth of the crop. In the south, the towns of New Haven district reached a nadir in wheat-growing just before 1700 but it ended at one-third of the grains, while to the west, Fairfield's farmers increased the proportion from one-fourth before 1680 to 40 percent by the turn of the century and as much as half during the next twenty years. During 1765-1774 in that district, wheat comprised over a third of the crop, including flax, hay, and cider.

Our last set of farmers, in this survey of their progress through the life cycle, consisted of grandfathers. We divide them into two age groups—the sixties and those over seventy—in each of which we further distinguish those who had "retired" from those who remained active. In both cases, but particularly for the latter, we want to know whether they had distributed part or all of their land to the married sons or whether they clung to their estates until death pried them loose. Finally, in order to trace changes over time, we start with men dying 1670-1699, totaling 142 in the Fairfield and Hartford districts, and close with the inventories of 1760-1774, of which there were 277.

We begin with the question of inheritances. In the seventeenth century, among men in their sixties, two-thirds remained active, while the others seem to have ceased farming, as revealed by their lack of land, of livestock, or of agricultural implements. Of the inactive, nearly all had given part or all of their land to the children. They did sometimes retain property destined for the younger children, such as the last son who remained at home, helping his folks, until he would inherit the home farm. The sixty-year-olds who continued to work obviously kept

enough acres to support themselves and their families. Some of these
lacked grown sons. Of those whose sons had grown and married, only
about one in four had failed to grant their inheritance (estimates range
from 72 percent to 81 percent).[35]

Men over seventy were much more often retired—over half—and
were even more willing to relinquish control of the farms. Eighty-six
percent had provided for their sons as these married, though as before
they sometimes kept a part of the home farm. If we combine all of
these seventeenth-century grandfathers, we find that 43 percent had
retired and that between 78 and 85 percent had surrendered part or
all of their land to their sons.

At the end of the colonial period, all this remained unchanged, a
rather remarkable stability. Among men in their sixties, once again
two-thirds continued to support themselves, while again slightly over
half of the older men had retired, the last figure having increased
somewhat, but not enough to raise any eyebrows.[36] "Retirement" here
does not imply a total withdrawal into poverty-stricken dependence
on an offspring, any more than it does today, but rather that the active
support of the household devolved on someone else, as our more detailed analysis will show.

The key to the farmers' wealth and in part status lay in their land.
The men who had not yet become grandfathers held, on the average,
around one hundred acres, almost always at least forty. The present,
older group, taken as a whole, owned about a fourth less, the median
being seventy-five, and one out of five did not even have twenty. But
these last had retired, and the aggregate numbers do not reveal the
true situation. In the first place, we find that men in their sixties who
remained active continued to accumulate property, their median acreage
increasing from the 100 acres owned by the under-sixty group before
1700 to 124 acres, and for the later period, from 125 to 140. That
may be misleading, since some of our retired set had always been poor.

---

[35] Ninety-four clearly had done so. I have eliminated nineteen who had no sons, or
none of age, and two men who lacked any land to give up. Sixteen clearly retained
control and I am uncertain about ten, whence the estimates. In most cases the inventory
by itself makes the situation clear, but the wills are a better source. I did not consult the
land deeds, but I did look at tax lists and the inventories of sons who died before their
fathers, as well as at accounts of administration and the distributions of estates.

[36] Exact percentages of "retirement" are:

	1670-1699	1760-1774	N
Men aged 60-69	34.0	34.5	141
Men aged 70 +	53.0	61.0	133
Combined	43.0	49.0	274

Including all those in their sixties, active and not, the medians are 90 and 102. These figures make clear that the farmers continued to buy land even while giving it away. Thus one with a hundred acres and three sons did not pass on fifty to the eldest and twenty-five, a scarcely adequate amount, to the others, but at least sixty-thirty-thirty and probably more than that, while permitting our "retired" grandfather to retain for his own use, as we said, twenty or thirty acres of the home farm. Of course, some of this land had never been improved, especially during the first century of settlement. The median farm in actual use, among the still active sexagenarians, included 69 acres before 1700 and 126 acres after 1760, the earlier group also owning another 55 acres of unimproved while the later had improved all but 14.

Even men over seventy continued to add land, provided they still farmed. Such oldsters owned almost as much as their younger equivalents: in the seventeenth century, exactly the same amount of improved land (68 acres versus 69) and only a little less total acres (112 to 124). In the late colonial period, they increased their median from 68 to 105, not far below the sixty-year-olds, and their total from 112 to 152, the last figure actually exceeding the quantity of men in their sixties. This striking accretion did not come at the expense of their own children, as we have seen, though it may have hindered the landless.[37]

The inclusion of all the grandfathers reduces the acreages. Our retired men in their sixties owned about twenty acres of improved land and a few acres more of all types, during both time periods. Men over seventy had the same quantity before 1700 but at the close of our period they considerably increased that amount, their mean improved land rising to thirty-three acres and for all land, forty-six (however, adjusting for wealth bias reduces the figures to twenty-four and thirty-eight respectively). If we combine all farmers in their sixties, the median acreage of land of all sorts increased over time from 90 to 102, and of the older men, from 60 to 72. Allowing for wealth bias, the medians change from 90 to 96 and 60 to 63, which means essentially no change.

Since the differences between the two time periods were small and the two age groups resembled one another, we can combine them into one unified set of grandfather farmers, omitting for later consideration all those who had ceased to farm. Table 6.8 shows the basic distribu-

---

[37] The data for both Hartford and Fairfield districts agree on this point: 152 acres was the median in both, the number of cases being thirty-seven and thirty respectively.

TABLE 6.8
Acres Owned by Grandfather Farmers

	Improved acres		Total acres	
	N	%	N	%
None	1	0.5	1	0.5
1–19	5	2.2	3	1.4
20–39	25	11.2	11	4.9
40–79	65	29.2	46	20.6
80–119	43	19.3	35	15.7
120–199	44	19.8	50	22.4
200–499	33	14.8	54	24.2
500+	7	3.1	23	10.3
Total	223	100.1	223	100.0

tion for land. The overwhelming majority did own the minimum forty acres to support their families, especially since less than that would suffice if all were improved. The eighty acres that we suppose to have raised the standard of living well above subsistence was enjoyed by close to three-fourths. The largest farms of "improved" land doubtless included some unimproved, not always clear in the inventories. Certainly in New England, 200 acres may be considered a large farm, identifying one as well-to-do. Most of these date from after 1700 and belonged to men under seventy. Excluding undeveloped tracts, fewer than one in five grandfathers owned such estates.

The total value of real property of course included buildings, which averaged £40 or £50. The rise in land prices makes comparisons of the two time periods difficult. The median for 1670-1699 was about £215, that for 1760-1774 rose to £670, a threefold increase as against the doubling that we found for most farms, probably due to improvements. The distribution by value, omitting the "retired" men, is shown in Table 6.9. The person with none actually owned considerable property, which the inventory omitted with the notation that he had willed it to his heirs. Most of the farmers enjoyed substantial estates, but of course they had reached the very peak of wealth accumulation.

Personal property furnishes a better indication of economic status over time. For both age groups we find a considerable gain, the median for men in their sixties rising from £110 to £160 and for the older group, from £110 to £177. Once more we must subtract, off the top, 4 percent of the totals, but that makes a difference of only £10 or so. These men clearly increased both in real and personal wealth.

TABLE 6.9
Value of Realty, Grandfather Farmers

£	1670–1699	1760–1774
None	0	1
1–49	3	0
50–99	5	0
100–199	28	10
200–299	21	10
300–399	8	16
400–499	4	13
500–599	12	50
1,000+	10	42
Total	91	142

TABLE 6.10
Personal Wealth, Grandfather Farmers

£	N	%
1–49	6	2.7
50–99	67	30.2
100–199	87	39.2
200–299	26	11.7
300–399	19	8.6
400–499	11	5.0
500+	6	2.7
Total	222	100.1

Since age, in this case, did not affect wealth, we can lump them, combining also the two time periods. The important feature of the distribution is the small proportion of men with less than £50, below which those still supporting households would live only at a subsistence level. We see also the clustering in the middle range around the mean of just under £150. The top 10 percent owned only about 27 percent of the total. Possession of £400 would not have cut much of a figure in Boston (to use their expression) but in Connecticut anything over £200 meant well-off and £500 equaled riches.

So also in consumption goods our oldest farmers had no less property than men in their sixties, or of even younger men. The median hovered around £55, which was just about that needed for comfort in

TABLE 6.11
Consumption Goods,
Grandfather Farmers

£	N	%
1–19	12	5.4
20–39	55	24.8
40–59	53	23.8
60–99	64	28.8
100–199	37	16.7
200+	1	0.5
Total	222	100.0

the case of men with all the children still at home, and makes the grandfathers well-to-do. Bare subsistence, at £10, almost everybody reached. Grandfathers, with grown children to help, actually required not more than £40 to sustain a household comfortably. If so, 70 percent exceeded that level and probably more, given the occasional missing items. We note that almost no one strove for the luxury level of £200: the farmers continued to invest in production rather than in comfort. The value of consumption goods did not change over time. Perhaps the most curious feature in all this is the ability of men over seventy to sustain the same standard of living even when many must have been giving portions to their daughters. Even if we concede that the "retired" group absorbed some poor farmers, the general level remains higher than one might expect. The median for the entire set of elderly and aged men was a respectable £35, only some £8 less than that for men in their sixties.

Since the identification of these men as farmers depended partly upon their possession of livestock, especially oxen, we need only to note the quantity and any changes. The number, though not the value of cattle diminished marginally for men over seventy, who until the late period owned as many as those in the sixties. Virtually no differences appear in the distribution of horses. Younger men had slightly more sheep and the same number of pigs. In brief, practically everyone had a horse, with two the median and three or four common; only one-fourth of the younger men but two out of five of the older lacked sheep, the usual number being ten to twenty; and almost everyone kept a few pigs, with seven the median. The total value of livestock did increase, following the movement of prices, especially for horses, at the end. The medians for the two age groups were £37 and £34 before 1700, £55 and £44 after 1760.

Crops, as we know, do not appear at their true value in the inventories. No change developed over time, and men in their sixties produced no more than their elders. The general median remained at about £11, with values of over £20 limited to only 18 percent of the estates, or 24 percent subtracting those with none. Finally, the value of farm tools increased from £5.5 to over £7, both age groups participating, probably because of a greater use of carts. Older men also added craft tools to help out the family.

The life cycle among farmers began its decline with grandfathers, but only among a particular segment of them. Two-thirds of the sixty-year-old group remained active in their occupations, continuing to acquire property as fast as they gave it away, and two-fifths of those over seventy kept pace. The rest, about half of the total, withdrew gradually from labor and finally became dependent—they retired. The proportion did not change significantly over time and their circumstances did not vary in any important way. Collectively they declined in wealth, sometimes because they had always been poor, otherwise as they gave their property to their children while losing the earning capacity to replace the gifts.

Curiously, the difference between men over and under seventy scarcely warrants the distinction: what mattered was the retired status, and within that some men retained a good deal of property while others died "poor." The distribution of land illustrates the situation: the median number of improved acres among the retired farmer under seventy was nineteen (N = 60), for men over seventy, twenty-seven, nor did the younger ones overtake them through undeveloped land. As a group, then, the distribution of land was as shown in Table 6.12.

TABLE 6.12
Acres Owned by Retired Farmers

Acres	Improved acres		Total acres	
	N	%	N	%
None	43	22.0	38	19.5
1–19	46	23.6	38	19.5
20–39	40	20.5	35	18.0
40–79	42	21.5	37	19.0
80–119	13	6.7	22	11.3
120–199	5	2.6	10	5.1
200+	6	3.1	15	7.7
Total	195	100.0	195	100.0

Presumably the landless one-fifth depended entirely upon their children or in a few instances on the town. Another one-fifth probably enjoyed at least a little independence. Men with twenty acres could take care of themselves and their wives, while those with forty, about one-third of the total, may even have turned a profit, with their diminished needs; that was certainly true of those owning eighty. A few individuals, five to be exact, even retained 500 acres or more including at least some of value, despite their legacies.

Appendix 6C displays the principal properties owned by these oldest farmers. The only difference between the two age groups appears in the case of the real estate held by men under seventy during the later period: the median ought to have doubled to allow for the price change, but did not, reflecting a decline in acreage held and probably the fact that buildings did not rise substantially. Men over seventy, on the other hand, nearly doubled their acreage. Wealth bias does not seem to account for it, so we may see a tendency on the part of some elderly to hang on to their real estate as security. If so, it affected about one out of six, that being the proportion who must surrender most of their land in order to reduce the median to that of the men aged sixty to sixty-nine, or one in ten for the median to equal the seventeenth-century level.

In personal wealth the "retired" aspect of these men appears clearly, around half supporting their families only at a subsistence level. Lacking a family, however, most would be comfortable. The median rose over time. Nearly half owned less than £20 in consumption goods (the comfort level); that rose a little but not significantly. Almost none depended upon their children for subsistence if we accept £8 as adequate, following the requirement for a single man, and only one-fourth lacked £14, which would serve an elderly couple very well. So also most retained a few farm animals. Almost all kept at least one cow. Half owned a horse, and the same proportion had sheep, pigs, and farm tools of some sort. As a broad generalization we might say that among retired farmers over sixty, half remained as active as ever, and at least three-fourths continued to support themselves without assistance.

We conclude this survey of the farmers' property over their life span by a general statement about the picture at a given moment. The median farm increased steadily from the forty acres owned by the beginner to the sixty-odd held by the young father and over a hundred for the middle-aged man, dropping then to ninety and finally to sixty as the grandfathers provided for their children. At any particular year, however, the visitor would have perceived the average at a little over sixty because of the numerical preponderance of men in their twenties and thirties.[38] He would have met one out of ten who either owned no land or fewer than twenty acres. Almost all of these would have been young, probably having access to some family land, or renting. Two in ten would own between twenty and forty acres, a marginal amount depending on quality and degree of cultivation. Again, these would be primarily young men. Three in ten owned adequate farms of forty to eighty acres, enough to support a family though without much margin. Two-thirds of these were still young, but now some older fathers appear—the less successful among the mature citizens. Finally, four out of ten held at least eighty acres. What the observer would fail to perceive was the process by which the newlywed steadily increased his property, another ten acres every four years, continuing for thirty years on the average, forty or even more for the long-lived, so that the "average" farmer would have added, to his original thirty-eight acres, another seventy-five or even a hundred acres. That would obviously provide for his sons—still referring to our "average"—and this capability remained undiminished at the end of the colonial period. The description is perhaps too flattering. Those added acres came hard, little surplus would remain for luxury, and too many farmers fell below the norm for us to use a glowing palette. Yet they did own their farms and most of them lived above mere subsistence, not ideal, but worth defending.

---

[38] Men in the twenties and thirties as we know comprised over 60 percent of the total, but of these only 20 and 40 percent, respectively, were farmers, the rest being laborers or artisans, with a few scattered. Thirty percent of all the men were aged forty to fifty-nine, about 60 percent of whom were farmers, a proportion that continued to rise with age, but since so few men lived beyond sixty, they contributed few farmers to the total. Thus if we add up all the farms above 200 acres as they appear in our survey, they make nearly 16 percent of the total, but they actually formed only 11 percent.

Property of Farmers, Older Fathers
(ESTATE INVENTORIES)

Acres	Improved land N	%	Total land N	%	Real wealth (adjusted) £	N	%	Personal wealth £	N	%
None	8	1.8	6	1.4	0–49	15	3.4	1–49	28	6.5
Under 20	15	3.5	7	1.6	50–99	43	9.8	50–99	129	29.7
20–39	50	11.5	27	6.2	100–199	99	22.6	100–199	184	42.4
40–59	63	14.5	85	19.6	200–299	72	16.4	200–299	59	13.6
60–79	48	11.1			300–399	61	13.9	300–399	24	5.5
80–119	106	24.4	90	20.7	400–499	46	10.5	400–499	5	1.2
120–199	83	19.1	89	20.5	500+	80	18.2	500+	5	1.2
200–499	48	11.1	97	22.4	1,000+	23	5.2			
500+	13	3.0	33	7.6						
Total	434	100.0	434	100.0	Total	439	100.0	Total	434	100.1
Median £	103		122			286			133	
Mean £	127		191			352			153	
Share top 10%		32.4		37.2			32.5			25.7

APPENDIX 6A

Continued

Consumption*

£	N	%
1–19	29	6.8
20–39	118	29.8
40–59	99	23.1
60–79	76	17.7
80–99	40	9.3
100+	57	13.3
Total	429	100.0

Median £ 46
Mean £ 58
Top 10% 27.8

Money, silver

£	N	%
None	257	60.9
Under 1	41	9.7
1–4	57	13.5
5–9	26	6.2
10+	41	9.7
Total	422	100.0

Mean £3.7

Clothing

£	N	%
None	18	4.3
1–4	162	38.5
5–9	161	38.2
10–19	75	17.8
20+	5	1.2
Total	421	100.0

Median £5

Books

£	N	%
None	82	19.7
Under 10/	137	32.9
10/–19/	101	24.2
£1	52	12.5
£2	21	5.0
£3+	24	5.8
Some	14	
Total	431	100.1

Median 10/
% with: 81.0
(including "some")

| | Cattle | |
Number	N	% of known
?	38	
0	1	0.3
1–4	26	6.5
5–9	100	25.2
10–19	192	48.4
20+	78	19.6
Total	435	100.0

Total No. 5,741 Median 13
Total £13,295 Mean £30.12
Mean of known £28.14
Val. per head £2.3.5

| | Horses | |
Number	N	%
?	44	
0	18	4.5
1	64	16.1
2	88	22.1
3	71	17.8
4	47	11.8
5–9	89	22.4
10+	21	5.3
Total	442	100.0

Total No. 1,405
Median 3
Total £4,694
Mean £10.12
Mean of known £11.2
Val. per head £3.3

| | Sheep | |
Number	N	%
?	47	
0	85	21.9
1–9	58	14.9
10–19	90	23.1
20–29	60	15.4
30–39	42	10.8
40–49	26	6.7
50–99	22	5.7
100+	6	1.5
Total	436	100.0

Total No. 7,975
Median of all 16
Median of owners 21
Total £2,150 Mean £5.10
Mean of known £5.3
Val. per head 5/

APPENDIX 6A

Continued

Pigs

Number	N	%
?	93	
None	36	10.5
1-4	76	22.2
5-9	110	32.2
10-19	86	25.1
20+	34	9.9
Total	435	99.9

Total No. 3,079
Median known 7
Total £1,835   Mean £4.4
Mean known £4.5
Val. per head 9/

All livestock

£	N	%
None	0	0
£1-9	6	1.4
10-19	29	6.7
20-29	70	16.1
30-39	69	15.9
40-49	69	15.9
50-99	159	36.5
100+	33	7.6
Total	435	100.1

Total £22,620
Median £46
Mean £52.0

Grains

£	N	%
None	129	29.7
£1-9	107	29.6
10-19	99	22.8
20-29	48	11.0
30-39	18	4.1
40-49	21	4.8
50+	13	3.0
Total	435	100.0

Total £5,510
Median of owners £14½
Mean of all £12.13
Mean of owners £18.0

*Consumption includes clothing and books but not silver articles.

Crop Yield per Acre

The estate inventories occasionally evaluate the anticipated return from a given number of acres planted in some crop, which, if we know the current price of the crop, enables us to estimate the yield per acre and the shillings returned per acre. These data are especially numerous for the Fairfield and Hartford areas, and permit some generalizations.

The colony as a whole produced about six bushels of wheat per acre during its first century and seven during 1750-1774 (N = 143 and 149) but the great variation deprives this of significance. Returns ranged from less than four to over twelve. That works out to 24/ per acre during the seventeenth century and 28/ toward the close. No change occurred in corn per acre, about ten bushels with a range of from less than six to over twenty. The general seventeenth-century value of 2/6 pay equals 2/ cash and means of course 20/ per acre, with a slightly higher price after 1760 raising the return to 22/ (total N = 120). The yield for rye (N = 135) increased fractionally from 4 1/2 to 5 bushels, with a profit of about 14/. The farmer got more bushels out of an acre of oats, around twelve, averaging 18/ worth (N = 37). These are all medians with a great spread, which invalidates the information for other crops about which we have fewer facts. Thus twenty-nine instances of flax per acre ranges from ten to over one hundred "hundredweight" so that a return of 20/ per acre is little more than a guess. Scattered figures for meslin also suggest 20/, but 18/ for peas and barley. In general, then, a farmer would make the most money bringing in a wheat crop, with corn, meslin and flax next, while peas, oats, and barley brought up the rear, the overall gain averaging one pound cash money per acre.

Property of Retired Grandfather Farmers

Real Property

£	17th century			18th century		
	60–69	70–79	Total	60–69	70–79	Total
None	6	7	13	8	15	23
1–49	5	5	10	5	16	21
50–99	3	13	16	9	9	18
100–199	8	7	15	6	18	24
200–299	2	4	6	4	12	16
300–399	0	1	1	1	5	6
400–499	0	0	0	1	6	7
500+	0	0	0	2	17	19
Total	24	37	61	36	98	134
Median £	70	75	72	80	150	131

Personal property

£	60–69	70–79	Total
1–49	34	74	108
50–99	16	46	62
100–199	7	9	16
200–299	2	2	4
300–399	0	2	2
400–499	1	0	1
500+	0	2	2
Total	60	135	195
Median £	43	46	45

Consumption

£	60–69	70–79	Total
1–19	25	60	85
20–29	22	44	66
40–59	10	21	31
60–99	3	7	10
100–199	0	3	3
Total	60	135	195
Median £	25	23	24

Livestock

£	60–69	70–79	Total
None	10	22	32
1–4	33	71	104
5–9	16	34	50
10–19	1	6	7
20–29	0	1	1
?	0	1	1
Total	60	135	195
Median £	12	11	12

Tools

£	60–69	70–79	Total
None	26	62	88
1–19	21	50	71
20–39	7	17	24
40–59	2	4	6
60–79	0	2	2
80+	4	0	4
Total	60	135	195
Median £	1	1	1

SEVEN

The Craftsmen and Professionals

Next to the farmers and laborers, the craftsmen were the largest occupational group in colonial Connecticut. From the very beginning, when immigrants brought their skills and tools to support their convictions, fully one out of five adult men were artisans, a proportion that remained unchanged. Most of these, to be sure, acquired land for food or raw materials, and some presently supported themselves from their farms more than by their crafts; but, on the other hand, farmers about as frequently became part-time artisans. Thus the contribution of the craftsmen to the economy in all probability was proportionate to their numbers until the relative decline of agriculture at the close of the colonial period, when manufacturing became almost as important as farming.

These skilled workers raised the general level of living in two ways. They produced some articles for export, notably ships, barrels, and other wood products for the West Indian trade, and processed other items by milling and distilling, thus earning badly needed foreign exchange. Of even greater importance, they performed essential services for their neighbors as did the tanners and millers; made what the other people could not, from houses to carts; repaired what otherwise must be replaced, the task of blacksmiths; and manufactured items that would have been imported, from barrels and furniture to cloth and saddles. In this way Connecticut's people kept their profits at home and maintained throughout the colonial period a standard of living safely above subsistence. Indeed, the colony became very nearly self-supporting as far as necessities were concerned. Tools such as plows, harrows, axes, and augers they did have to import, along with pewter, most of their iron, and miscellaneous metal articles such as guns and cooking utensils. What their exports enabled them to buy were for the most part really non-essentials: the better grades of cloth for clothes and bedding, chinaware, wine, sugar, tea, drugs, servants, and slaves; and even these the local craftsmen helped to pay for.

Each agricultural village, then, needed a sizable number of these specialists, especially since many enterprises involved several people, usually though not invariably families. Mills and tanneries especially required a good deal of capital and might support several adult men. The coopers, smiths, joiners, and housewrights sometimes employed a second full-time hand, and many communities supported more than one such shop. There would be a shoemaker and a weaver, and, depending upon local circumstances, someone for the quarry, mine, or lumbermill. In the larger, diversified towns both the larger manufacturers and the specialists multiplied. Thus the shipbuilder needed ropewalks and sailmakers, the well-to-do men patronized a barber, tailor, maltster, turner, silversmith, and printer; the house-carpenter hired a mason and a glazier.

We might increase the proportion of artisans considerably by adding their helpers. Some craftsmen got along by themselves but most of them, like the farmers, were aided by boys or other men. A few bought slaves or servants but that was rare. A large number obtained the help of apprentices, generally local boys whose families, for reasons of poverty, the father's early death, or a superfluity of sons, could not provide for them. The master craftsmen took over the functions of a parent and, like a father, received the benefit of the lad's work until the boy reached his majority, when the relationship (if it continued) shifted to that of a wage laborer. Most often, of course, the artisan's own sons filled the need. He might hire a capable "journeyman," but the colony lacked a sufficient population of adult, skilled workers who would work for someone else, and besides only some of the specialized crafts required the additional hands or could justify the expense. Such men do appear in the larger towns, but as we saw in Chapter Five they were uncommon in Connecticut. For the most part the master craftsmen and their helpers did not interact as employer-employee or capitalist-laborer but as father and son. That did not prevent conflict of course, but the conflicts occurred within a family, between men equally interested in the profits of the business and belonging to a society that stressed cooperation; besides, in most cases the worker presently became a master. One could easily define both men as members of the same occupational group with high internal mobility and so eliminate any differences at all, class or otherwise, from our discussion; but since the laborers did include men other than sons in positions quite unfilial, a distinction seems justified as long as we do not project back the modern assumption about labor relations.

The artisans, then, were independent men of some property, their tools and usually a shop in which they worked, on a level with farmers with respect to status and prospects. They did not, however, constitute a single unified group. As we will see shortly, they ranged from poor to well-to-do. Some became leaders while others remained obscure.

Those who resided in the port towns shared little with their contemporaries in the country villages. We cannot even separate them totally from the farmers, for they often owned farms, the farmers sometimes doubled as craftsmen, while their children worked for both and often intermarried.[1]

We can divide these men into several groups possessing distinctive characteristics. First, the men making or repairing clothes were young—either single or with small children—and poor. They formed about a fourth of the total and almost never hired a helper. Second, over two-fifths were the familiar owners of craftshops in every town—coopers, smiths, carpenters, and joiners. Third, a less numerous but equally important group conducted sizable enterprises, notably millers and tanners, but in the larger towns or locally there were shipwrights, distillers, printers, the owners of ropewalks, iron manufacturers, and others. They composed one in seven of the craftsmen. Finally, the urban centers supported a miscellany of small artisans. These seldom appeared in the small towns except as migrants (tinkers) and even the more populous community would support only one or two of each, so they derive their importance only from total numbers (about a sixth), not from any unity or even similarity other than their all being skilled workers. They were older and possessed of more property than the first group, younger and less well-off than the third, and more varied than the second whom, however, they resembled most closely. We will discuss the first three separately and then include the last in a general summary of the craftsmen as a whole.

Shoemakers, tailors, and weavers ranked at the bottom of the artisans' social structure in property, age, and presumably status. Shoemakers and tailors in particular needed only a small capital investment and even a weaver's loom did not compare in cost with the implements in, say, a smithy. Moreover, one did not need a shop of any size, only part of a room, nor land or raw materials, for the customers commonly provided the leather, cloth, or yarn, in contrast to the situation of a cooper who needed a woodlot containing particular sorts of trees and a proper shop. Also, none required a long apprenticeship except perhaps for a tailor catering to a wealthy clientele. Therefore, young men could begin business quickly and cheaply. Two out of five were single and most of the rest were young fathers. Their median age was only thirty-one, and older men were few indeed. Estate inventories show their median age at death as under forty and only one in six dying when past fifty although, as we know, at least half of the men lived

[1] See Appendix 7A.

243

longer than that. Since we have no reason to suppose that the tailors et al. died at an early age, we conclude that a large proportion shifted occupations beginning in their forties, perhaps as soon as they could.[2]

Two reasons seem obvious. First, farmers and their wives or other artisans could readily buy small looms, lasts and awls, needles and thread, and pick up enough skill if they weren't too particular, at least for repairs. Elderly men contributed in this way too. In fact tailors, instead of increasing, declined in relative numbers over time except for those obviously serving the upper class. Thus neither the degree of skill nor the demand encouraged a lifelong vocation.

Second, these circumstances together with their youth kept their incomes low, as far as property reveals income. In consumption goods they did not fare so badly. Being young, they needed little and their work directly contributed. Still, one out of six lacked enough for independence and more than a quarter just subsisted. They owned far less land than most men. A fourth had none at all and even in the boom years of the early 1700s their median acres did not exceed seventeen. In the later decades nearly a third owned no land, two-thirds held under twenty acres, and one in three did not have a house, so that they must have lived with relatives or rented a room. Furthermore, they often possessed no livestock and little other property. As a consequence their standard of living, according to our definition, while better than that of common laborers, fell below that of all other occupational groups, three out of ten living in poverty and another fourth just at the subsistence level. It is fair to add that the value of their consumption goods and their level of living rose over time; but contrary to the usual life cycle, advancing age did not improve their situation and they turned elsewhere for their support.

Two examples will suffice. Samuel Forward of Devonshire immigrated to Windsor about 1666, married in 1670, and died in 1684 leaving two sons and only £38 (pay), minus £7 in debts outstanding. He had a house and lot, a cow, two swine, and his "weavers loom" with its tackles, worth £5.18. After subtracting his clothes we find just £12 in consumption goods. The boys thus became two of our poor orphans. The younger either died or left for parts unknown, but the elder moved to Simsbury and prospered as a cooper—a good choice as we will see—leaving an estate of almost £600 when he died at age sixty-seven.[3]

John North of Wethersfield (d. 1682), the eldest of four sons, also

---

[2] Information on the ages of craftsmen, with other data, is in Appendix 7B.
[3] Hartford district probate records, 4:220-21.

TABLE 7.1
Standard of Living, Shoemakers, Weavers, and Tailors
(probate and living populations)

	Single men		Young fathers		Older fathers		Grandfathers		Total	
	Probate	Living	Probate	Living	Probate	Living	Probate	Living		
Poor	14	14	17	13	7	3	1	0+	39	30
Subsistence	11	11	11	9	15	6	4	½	41	26½
Subsistence plus	6	6	25	19	8	3½	4	½	43	29
Comfortable	9	9	4	3	1	0	1	0+	15	12
Well-off	0	0	2	1½	0	0	3	½	5	2
Total	40	40	59	45½	31	12½	13	1½	143	99½

became a weaver and also died fairly young, at forty-one. He owned more property, with sixteen acres, half improved, and a small home lot. From that he had raised thirty-five bushels of corn and twenty of rye, and on it he pastured a mare and some cattle and pigs. The family of five slept on two beds. His personal estate came to £35 cash, but he owed £14 and could not have lived much above bare subsistence.[4]

The second and largest major group consisted of a ubiquitous middle class, virtually all of whom owned some property and resembled the farmers in their life course, status, and value to the community. They included those skilled in woodworking, especially the coopers, the joiners, the carpenters or "housewrights," and the blacksmiths. No town could get along without these men, who ordinarily performed a variety of functions related to their skill: a carpenter could make all manner of things. Larger urban centers contained the specialists such as a wheelwright, turner, and gunsmith, who belonged to this same category but with narrower functions.

Whereas the shoemakers and their like were younger, poorer, and less apt to rise than most men, the present craftsmen were typical, laborers aside. During the seventeenth century fewer of them were young and single than one might expect but thereafter their age structure became normal. All of them could make some of their own household articles or repair them, which must have helped in improving the quality of their consumer goods. Only one out of ten lacked what they needed, most of these being young and single. One out of four did not much exceed the subsistence level, but on the other hand one-third owned enough household articles for comfort. As usual the older men lived especially well—I found only two poor grandfathers out of eighty-four.

An important reason for the economic success of this group, or an evidence of it, was their ownership of land. Indeed, half of the smiths and almost a third of the others had the forty acres that sustained a family. Actually, the picture is not quite that rosy. They all needed an abnormal amount of wood, the smiths to help stoke their fires and the others for their crafts. All but the smiths began to hold much smaller lots after 1730 or so and they, too, were losing ground by the 1760s. At the end, two-thirds owned less than forty acres and one out of five had none. On the other hand almost all of them owned houses, and in many cases the customers could supply wood (though not coal for the smiths).

In any case the partial loss of land does not seem to have lowered

4 Ibid., 4:103.

their economic position as measured by their household goods, personal wealth generally, or standard of living. Their personal property as recorded by the inventories did drop after the usual boom during the early 1700s but not to the level of the previous century. Taking the colonial period as a whole, one in seven lived in poverty (half of them single) and one in three did not reach a subsistence-plus standard (almost half single). At the close even more were poor, but the number eventually achieving the subsistence-plus standard did not change, the increase of the dependent group being due entirely to the decline in the position of single men. Interpretation is a risky business, but apparently the young members of this group encountered difficulty in getting land, as did others in the colony, and this delayed their successful entry into the class of master craftsmen; but once they had overcome that handicap they fared as well as their predecessors. This is supported by the fact that the crafts included fewer twenty-year-olds during 1760-1774 but that loss was exactly balanced by more men in their thirties.

Of all these men, blacksmiths were most likely to acquire large properties, possessing skills which their neighbors could not dispense with. Farmers could erect and repair houses of a simple sort, as well as other buildings; they might construct rude chests and tables and even to some extent containers; but they could not deal with anvils and hammers or repair their guns. The smiths did indeed shoe horses, but they also repaired the universal iron articles of the day such as plows and kitchen and fireplace utensils, and they manufactured many simple ones. Smiths were, of all this group of craftsmen, the most apt to own servants, buy sizable farms, and keep relatively large numbers of livestock. Their personal wealth was in fact almost half again as much as that of the coopers and house-carpenters and nearly one out of six left estates of £200. However, the great majority were middling propertyowners, seldom landless or poor, but never wealthy.

Three men of the seventeenth century illustrate the careers of colonial blacksmiths. All died near the age of fifty, so they show these artisans in their prime. The first of such "typical" men we come to in the records is Sgt. Joseph Nash of Hartford.[5] Nash was born about 1620 and immigrated to New Haven in his late teens with his father Thomas, a skilled gun- and locksmith. We have chanced upon an unusual family here, for Joseph's older brother John became a major whom we will meet again. Joseph received only 20 shillings of his

[5] Ibid., 4:340-41; Donald Lines Jacobus, *Families of Ancient New Haven*, 9 vols. 1922-1932; reprinted in 3 vols. (Baltimore, 1974).

father's estate, half what two married sisters inherited. John already had a house and land and would now inherit £40 more, while the youngest son, Timothy, took over the rest of the property: he had been "very helpful" to his father. So Joseph left for Hartford to make his own way. This he did, marrying and living until 1678. Besides his house and home lot he had acquired twenty-five acres of land. The shop contained an anvil, bellows, and other tools, which with the usual farming implements came to £25. His consumption goods were worth £65, almost luxurious since he left only his wife and a daughter. He did not bear any resentment toward his older, more favored brother, by the way, who would inherit Joseph's real estate if his daughter died and who served as executor.

The next smith we encounter in the Hartford area was Nash's contemporary and neighbor Robert Reeve, who died in 1680 at about forty-five.[6] We know nothing of his origin but his record in the probate court lists nine children ranging from three to nineteen. The father expressed some concern over them but also gave forty shillings toward building a house for the minister. Reeve owned about fifty acres, judging from the price, two houses, one old and of little value, with a barn nearby. He kept the usual livestock (oxen, eight other cattle, a horse, and eight pigs) and he had the typical tools in a shop. He not only repaired but made iron implements, for he owned 3,197 pounds of iron and 225 of steel, twenty-four horseshoes, and seven new spades, all worth £42, cash. The room-by-room inventory names a parlor and a kitchen, each with "chambers" overhead, garrets, and a cellar. Incidentally, the nine children and two adults somehow crowded into two regular beds, two trundle beds (which fitted under the other), and a cradle. However, the estate included consumption goods valued at nearly £70 and the total came to a solid £484, cash.

Thomas Hurlbut of Wethersfield, by contrast, owned no land and only £41 in personal wealth upon his death in 1689. He was the first of five sons of Thomas, who died between 1682 and 1689. A brother, John, became a smith in Middletown and another brother moved to Woodbury. The wife and three young sons inherited an insolvent estate, and the boys form part of my group of poor orphans. The eldest died young, the second moved to Simsbury and remained poor, and the third lived in Windsor, married, and died in old age without an inventory. Hurlbut owned one cow, a horse, only £4 worth of tools, and £25 in consumption goods, an adequate amount except for the

---

[6] Hartford district probate records, 4:57-58; Charles William Manwaring, comp., *A Digest of Early Connecticut Probate Records*, 3 vols. (Hartford, 1904-1906), 1:354.

insolvency. Nash's widow had fared pretty well, since he left her not only the customary widow's third but an additional £4 annually for life, which would buy some amenities. Hurlbut's, however, must have remained poor, and was still a widow nine years later when she approved the final settlement of the estate with her mark.[7]

The coopers fashioned barrels and wooden containers of all sizes— their name comes from the Latin *cupa*, a tub or cask. Everyone needed these for storing grain and other foods such as apples, pork and beef, cider or beer; and people also used them when products were sent long distances as in the case of flour and meat. In the larger towns coopers worked full time at their craft. In the smaller ones they diversified by doubling as general handymen in woodwork or by farming. More farmers learned this skill than any other—either that, or an abnormal number of coopers changed their primary occupations. The median land held by 151 of them was twenty-six acres and a third owned forty, which with their craft earnings would guarantee security and comfort. The one out of four who did not live at a subsistence level were mostly young bachelors.

Very few coopers accumulated estates of any size. An exception, James Raymond of Norwalk, left £218 worth of personal property in 1763. In addition to producing barrels in his shop he farmed fifty-three acres and furnished his house, which was valued at £100, with £138 in household goods including his clothing. Raymond came from one of the town's wealthier families and he probably owed his position to that, not entirely to the craft.[8]

One average example will serve. Ephraim Phelps of Windsor died in 1697 at thirty-four leaving a wife and a five-year-old son. Ephraim was the fifth of six sons of Samuel, who had died in 1669 with a perfectly respectable property including around two hundred acres, which, however, had to be divided among nine children. He also owed debts of £50. Ephraim's share was £51. At his death he owned ten or twelve acres plus the home lot, his house, and part of a barn, and another small building, probably for the cooperage. The land had produced the usual rye, oats, flax, corn, and hay for the cow and calf and a horse; he also had kept five pigs. His personal property totaled £78, perhaps plus some in Stamford that was not itemized. The consumer goods were worth a comfortable £50. His widow married a Stamford man but his son, another Ephraim, eventually chose an uncle back in

---

[7] Hartford district probate records, 5:53; Manwaring, *Early Connecticut Probate Records*, 1:473.

[8] Fairfield district probate records, 13:124.

Windsor as guardian, moved to Simsbury, married, and at the age of forty-eight was "called" into the expedition against the Spanish West Indies, where he died. A weaver, he had acquired only a small estate, insufficient for the family, and had probably hoped to gain by his fatal decision.[9]

The word "carpenter" is generic for anyone making or repairing things of wood, but since coopers make barrels, joiners and turners take charge of the furniture and other interior articles, and we also have words like wheelwright, cartwright, and shipwright, carpenters specialize in what is left, trespassing on the territory of housewrights. In colonial days they constructed buildings of all sorts, not only houses but also barns, churches, and schools. The joiners, who commonly added the skill of the turners, created a variety of household furniture from cabinets to chairs. Since ordinary folk could erect simple houses and barns and make serviceable stools, tables, and boxes, the craftsmen produced the finer, more elaborate products, such as the beautiful Georgian houses, the lovely churches, and the treasured furniture. One finds, therefore, a considerable variety within this group of men. During the seventeenth century and for many people long after, the common type of house and the usual furnishings did not require advanced training, and one finds a considerable number of young men, probably not very skilled, engaged in these activities. Their age structure averaged six years below that of the population generally: thus probate records show smiths dying at fifty while carpenters, joiners, and coopers lived only until age forty-four. As in the case of our first group of artisans, we cannot suppose that they actually suffered from a shorter life span, but that the less successful shifted vocations, probably into farming, where we may see them among those numerous farmers who owned the characteristic tools.

Table 7.2 comes straight from estate inventories without adjusting for age, but it shows clearly the sizable number without any land, especially during the later periods, and the considerable group with only a few acres. On the other hand three out of ten had true farms of forty acres and, as we have seen, once they married they achieved on the average a decent standard of living that became, for grandfathers, comfortable. Thus they earned in the end a sufficient reward and their numbers testify to the steady attraction of the crafts.

Our one example, William Hough of New London, represents them well. He was the son of Deacon William who died in 1683, leaving a probate record now lost. Hough (1657-1705) left seven children, none

[9] Hartford district probate records, 6:81-83, 14:130:-31.

TABLE 7.2
Acres Owned, Carpenters and Joiners

Acres	pre-1700	1700–1729	1745–1759	1760–1774	Total	%
None	6	9	22	23	60	20.8
1–19	15	22	16	30	83	28.9
20–39	7	18	10	21	56	19.4
40–79	8	10	3	15	36	12.5
80–119	3	8	3	10	24	8.3
120–199	1	14	2	7	24	8.3
200+	0	5	0	0	5	1.7
Total	40	86	56	106	288	99.9
Median	33	34	10	19½	20	

SOURCE: Estate inventories.

of age, and his widow was pregnant with another. For nine people, including himself, he had four beds, two pillows, plenty of sheets, and ten coverlids. He owned a house, barn, shop, and twenty acres, together worth £90. The land supported nine cattle, a horse, mare, and colt, twenty sheep with ten lambs, and six swine. His carpentry, joiner's, and turner's tools were valued at £6, which was average, and he also owned some farming implements. The personal estate came to £83 and consumer goods to £53 including £7.13 in clothing—above the norm—and a parcel of books. All this was enough for a decent standard of living and the gain of only another year or two would have brought comfort. Hough's brother John (1655-1715), a farmer and carpenter, probably a shipwright, served as militia captain and accumulated a much larger estate; an additional twelve years of life might well account for it.[10]

We turn now to the most prosperous of the artisans, men whom we would now call manufacturers, headed in point of numbers by millers. Civilizations have survived without mills, but only at great physical cost to many of their people who had to pound away with something (a pestle) upon something (the mortar). The inhabitants of a village could reduce their own grains to flour for local consumption by putting the teen-agers to work, but any community raising grain for export required a much faster, more efficient operation. The grist-mill was so important even to the earliest settlers that towns granted concessions in the form of land, a monopoly of the site, and relief for taxation to whoever would construct one. The same water power that

[10] New London district probate records, A:300; B:161.

revolved the grindstone could in the months after harvest be used for sawing lumber as well, though separate lumbermills also existed.

Building a large gristmill involved the construction of a dam, the purchase and placement of a water wheel, the installation of other wheels to carry the power to the mechanism turning the stones, and the making or buying, transportation, and mounting of the big quern stones themselves, not to mention the saws if these were to be used. All that required capital, which often came from several persons, but the profit was very attractive. People had no choice but to use the mill and to pay its owner (or the miller, if the two differed) promptly because he retained a share of whatever he ground or sawed.

This steady income persuaded some of the colony's wealthy men to erect mills on their streams, from which point we can assign them to whatever occupational group we choose. Thus Leonard Chester, self-styled "Gentleman" (1610-1648), whose mother was the sister of Reverend Thomas Hooker, built a mill in Wethersfield that he left to thirteen-year old John, along with a share of Leonard's considerable other property. Thus John, at nineteen, could marry the daughter of Governor Thomas Welles, become a captain and justice of the peace, and pass on an estate of £793 cash including several hundred acres of land. The mill, with some pasture around it, the appraisers valued at £70. His eldest son continued the milling and branched out into trade; we will meet him in the next chapter. The second son also became a merchant and the youngest was a prosperous farmer.[11]

TABLE 7.3
Millers' Land and Consumer Goods (percentages)

Land		Consumer goods	
Acres	%	£ cash	%
None	1.65	1–19	3.2
1–19	8.3	20–39	30.3
20–39	14.05	40–59	20.2
40–79	19.8	60–79	16.9
80–119	13.2	80–119	12.4
120–199	17.4	120–199	12.4
200+	25.6	200+	4.5
Total	100.0	Total	99.9

SOURCE: Estate inventories. N = 121.

[11] Hartford district probate records, 2:8-11, 6:64; Henry R. Stiles *The History of Ancient Wethersfield*, 2 vols. (New York, 1903), 2:210-15.

This account, like most biographical sketches introduced as examples, exaggerates the prosperity of most millers. A few were actually poor. About one in ten supported their families minimally and the same proportion owned less than twenty acres. But although Chesters were rare, the millers as a group fared very well indeed. This is perhaps suggested by their age at death, which rose from a median of forty-eight in the seventeenth century to fifty-four early in the 1700s and ended at sixty-nine, older even than the ministers. One out of four left over two hundred acres and their median was almost a hundred; they rivaled farmers in livestock; half owned enough consumer goods for their families to live comfortably; and three out of ten personal estates exceeded £200.

To counteract the impression of wealth conveyed by the Chesters we offer one much poorer and two nearly average. Ephraim Hayward of Windsor died insolvent in 1690, leaving a son of four and a two-year-old daughter. His father, Robert, had died six years earlier at the age of seventy-one. He had perhaps practiced medicine, owning three "physick" books and some "physical things." Ephraim's mother was then about seventy, which means that she had her first child at thirty and Ephraim at forty-two. Robert's entire estate consisted of £67 in personal property. He had already given Ephraim the land, then being rented by another man. Ephraim appears on the 1686 tax list with the moderate property of £47 and married that year, age thirty. On his death four years later the inventory listed fourteen acres, part of a sawmill and some land, part of another mill, one acre with an old house, and "the frame" presumably of a better home for the family. All this was worth only £91 in pay, or £64 cash. He also had a horse, one great Bible, two smaller ones plus some other books, and £34 in cosumption goods, sufficient except for the debts; he had died too young.[12]

Henry Whitman did not appear on Norwalk's assessment list of 1672, presumably excused or exempt from taxes, for he died there the next year leaving an estate of about £180 and no family. He had owned a house and lot, the mill with some land, and a bit of meadow totaling around twenty acres to judge by the estimated value and the presence of two oxen, five cows, three younger cattle, an old horse, and quite a few pigs. That he intended to farm is suggested by his owning more in husbandry tools than in those of his trade and some timber for a barn. In all, his personal property came to £100 of which £37 was in consumption goods. He would have married well had he lived.[13]

[12] Hartford district probate records, 4:186-87, 5:461.
[13] Fairfield district probate records, 2:70.

Richard Ogden, our last example of a miller, died in Fairfield in 1687, worth about £300 in real estate and £123 in personal property. He probably had between forty and seventy acres, with fifteen cattle, three horses, seventeen pigs, and twenty-one sheep, but no oxen. He had planted five-and-a-half acres of wheat valued at £15 pay per acre, an expected yield of thirteen bushels per acre. His consumption goods came to £36, little different from Whitman or Hayward. His son Richard kept the mill and left a slightly smaller property, but he died at a considerably younger age. The mill at that time was worth £42 cash and he had owned £45 work of consumption articles, probably thanks to his wife. For that period both men were nearly average, far below some other millers but with an adequate standard of living and able to provide decently for their children.[14]

Tanners took the hides of the livestock and turned them into leather by using tannic acid from the bark of trees, especially oak. They usually added the function of a currier, further processing the leather, and sometimes completed the logical progression by acting as saddlers or shoemakers. One occasionally finds them fulling cloth as well. Like the millers they were essential to a community wishing to sell or use their hides; they too required capital for the tanyard and bark; and they sometimes bought and processed hides on their own account in addition to tanning their neighbors'. It is not surprising that they always owned land and livestock for bark and leather, but they went far beyond the requirements of their business, usually operating a forty-acre farm with at least £20 worth of livestock (seven or eight head of cattle and a horse). Their families lived comfortably, even better than the millers, for the combination of an essential, profitable skill and a farm virtually guaranteed a decent livelihood.

To some extent their property reflects a delayed entry into the field, few of them being younger than forty. On the other hand, somewhat fewer than the millers survived into old age, at least on the evidence of the probate records. Perhaps the older men had passed along their property so that the distinguishing features of their craft were absent from the inventories. The tanning vats produced an evil smell and may have been bad for the health, shortening their life expectancy or persuading them to shift into a pleasanter and more prestigious occupation. They already had the property for the change.

Benjamin Farrington of Branford (1672-1713) illustrates the profits possible for a tanner. He owned a seventy-acre farm, of which, however, sixty were of inferior quality, and he had only a small number of

[14] Ibid., 3:222; 4:156.

farm animals. His personal property came to £460. He owned a Negro man and woman—tanners often had servants or slaves—a mill and tan vats, leather, lime, bark, oil, and tools for shoemaking and currying, collectively valued at nearly £100. He could display a nice silver tankard and thirty-eight ounces of silver besides. He owed £27 but was a creditor for £74.[15]

Caleb Chidsey of New Haven comes closer to the average and derives additional interest as a deacon. His father John was also a deacon and tanner who died in 1688 at the age of sixty-seven, having probably given away his land. Caleb, the third of four sons, married that same year and at his death in 1713 left three teen-age boys and a younger daughter. By that time he owned sixty-five acres and the homestead, the normal complement of livestock, leather, and bark, the tools for shoemaking, and the tanyard. His personal property totaled £118, below normal for the craft particularly for a man of his age, but his £66 in consumer goods meant comfort. We should also note that the two deacons demonstrate that tanners could achieve high status in their community, smell or no smell.[16]

Indeed, a variety of artisans acquired wealth and sometimes became leaders of the community. Many of these we might easily call manufacturers, running large business enterprises with numerous laborers and a large capital investment, such as those in charge of ironworks, the owners of ropewalks and of shipyards, and distillers. These commonly owned large farms of over a hundred acres—the median was 150 acres—with considerable livestock, and they accumulated more than £200 in personal wealth including £100 in household goods. One of the large landowners was Samuel Beers of Newton (1679-1728) who acquired 343½ itemized acres plus a division, some rights, and a small bog lot, probably 400 in all, valued with the buildings at about £747. His fulling equipment (iron screwbox, mill, and dam) came to £30 and he owned a yoke of oxen, fourteen other cattle, an unusual six horses, eighteen sheep, and eleven swine. He had once owned more of the last, as attested by 236 pounds and one barrel of pork.[17] An example of an artisan leader was the glazier Capt. Samuel Bryan of Milford (d. 1698), whose grandfather had served as assistant in the legislature (like our senators) and whose father was a well-to-do merchant. The mason and deacon Thomas Johnson of Middletown was the son of a J.P. and the father of the clothier Edward Barker,

[15] New Haven district probate records, 4:220.
[16] Ibid., 4:165.
[17] Fairfield district probate records, 8:144.

Esq., of Branford who was like Bryan a prominent merchant. At the least connection with these crafts did not preclude high status.

This survey shows the great variety among the men we lump as artisans and mechanics, or craftsmen. Appendix 7B provides the detail about their ages and wealth. It shows that we can to some extent differentiate among them. Some, like the shoemakers, worked with limited capital, almost always alone, and earned small incomes that limited their opportunity. Their youthful age structure suggests that they advanced either by becoming small farmers or shifting to another craft. Others, like the tanners and millers, seldom began as young men but waited until they obtained capital or their inheritance. They often owned large and profitable business enterprises and employed laborers, sometimes achieving high status. So too we can distinguish between those artisans, often specialists, who lived in the larger towns and those who resided among farmers in the village centers.

We cannot easily think of the craftsmen as a uniform whole. They certainly did not form an economic or a distinct social class. In the smaller communities especially, but in some degree everywhere, they married outside their occupational group, often into farm families, owned farms themselves, attended the same churches and shared the same values as the rest of the people. Thus they contributed both to the diversity and cohesion that characterized Connecticut's society.

We turn now to a less numerous but more varied and interesting assortment of men—the professionals. To start from the bottom: among nearly eight thousand inventories only eight clearly belonged to men who were teaching at the time of the inventory: one college professor and seven of the primary school variety. Of the seven, five were single and only one was more than forty; four owned consumer goods valued at under £20; three had no land, two others just an acre, and one of the landowners was insolvent; five had no livestock; and five left personal property worth less than £60.

The colony contained far more teachers than our eight, and drawing upon more varied records, especially for Windsor and Guilford, we can distinguish two types. During the seventeenth century only about a fourth were young men of the poor and single variety shown in the probated estates. Connecticut contained no college and had to enlist whatever men it could find who could and would teach. The salary for the year averaged £31 pay, not enough to attract a full-time man with other capabilities, so the towns persuaded various men to teach briefly. Thus the sixty-year-old deacon William Johnson, Guilford's town clerk, agreed to take over the school in 1681 "for as much as he can attend it,"[18] and in Windsor the lawyer Capt. Daniel Clarke similarly pinch-hit at age fifty-six. As a rule such occasional teachers were not especially prosperous, to judge from their later inventories. They rarely remained teachers until they died, so their inventories show them with another occupation—ministers, farmers, doctors, a justice. The only real professional on my seventeenth-century list was Eleazer Kimberly, Esq. (1639-1709) who taught in Wethersfield for a least twenty-five years, his salary rising from £25 to £42 pay. Kimberly, however, served as secretary of the colony and became a substantial farmer by marrying the daughter of "Gentleman" John Robbins.[19]

During the eighteenth century the towns could enlist Yale graduates, and the occupation became almost exclusively limited to men under age thirty who quickly left it for a more profitable career. An occasional individual received enough to keep him in the field, as did Henry Bates of Wallingford who received £50 annually, about £35 cash, plus fifty acres and a millpond.[20] But even this fell far below the earnings of most educated men, and teachers as a group were not only young but poor. The inventories of those few who died in harness probably show the situation of the teacher at the time that he so served the town, rather than the man of property that he might have become. We find, for instance, Daniel Russell, Junior, of Wethersfield (1732-1759), newly married, a creditor of the town for £7.12.7 as his salary, about one-third of what he needed to live on. The rest presumably came from his father, Reverend Daniel (1701-1764) who did not himself possess an extensive estate but who belonged to the colony's upper social stratum through his own father, Reverend Noadiah, his mother Mary (Captain Giles) Hamlin, and his wife, the daughter of the prominent merchant George Stillman. Daniel, Junior, as yet owned no house, and we must suppose that he would soon have found a better job.[21] So, too, Samuel Seward of Durham (1739-1773) was being paid £11 for keeping school during the winter, also far from enough. He was sharing a house and at the age of thirty-four was perhaps stuck. His little collection of books included a *Complete Letter Writer, The Fair*

[18] Bernard Christian Steiner, *History of Guilford, Conn. . . . , and Madison* (Baltimore, 1897), 396.

[19] Stiles, *Wethersfield*, 1:358-61; Hartford district probate records, 7:211.

[20] Bates continued from 1711, the year before his marriage, at least until 1721, when the congregation allowed him to sit in the first pew in the front gallery of the new meetinghouse. Charles Henry Stanley Davis, *History of Wallingford, Conn. . . .* (Meriden, 1870), 312-13.

[21] Stiles, *Wethersfield*, 2:600, 603; Hartford district probate records, 18:123.

Greek, an *Essay on Elocution*, and a dictionary.[22] Joseph Thacher of Lebanon (d. 1751) was perhaps the son of Reverend Ralph. Thacher had earned about 6 shillings cash for keeping school, probably less than he made from his shoe bench and leather. He had just erected the frame of a house over his cellar and had bought shingles and six window frames.[23]

Thacher possessed only a Bible, and Josiah Willard of Wethersfield (1635-1674) had just four old books valued at 2 shillings. Like Thacher he could borrow from a father, Major Simon, a prosperous merchant.[24] As a rule the teachers had more books though not more property than these two young men. Austin Punderson (1744-1773) owned £18 worth including fifty-three pamphlets and a map of the world, while Samuel Mansfield (1671-1701) left a "library" of seventy-six volumes in addition to twenty-one old schoolbooks worth £9, a Bible, and some mathematical instruments.[25] Both of these were college men and Punderson, in fact, had preached. Indeed, the possession of books combined with relative prosperity differentiate these men from most of their neighbors. Both Mansfield and Willard, incidentally, tried their hand at trade, at which the latter failed, leaving an insolvent estate, while the former succeeded. Mansfield led the way among this otherwise penurious group, owning one-third of a sloop, £67 in stock, and £57 in debts receivable. Like Russell, Thacher, and Willard he had family backing and, moreover, he was a Harvard man.

Taken as a whole, then, this group shows teaching as a poorly paid, part-time, temporary occupation from which men escaped as soon as possible. Our little collection includes one rarity: Reverend Thomas Clap, president of Yale. Clap left £4,505 in personal wealth and at least 600 acres of land, the total value being £6,656. Some readers will not be surprised to learn that the fortune derived from marriage rather than from teaching. Clap owned tracts not only in the older towns of New Haven and Farmington but in nine newer ones, and his acres may have totaled as much as 2,000, suggestive of a Yankee rather than a Puritan. The impression is strengthened by an extraordinary £2,082 in specie money and £1,993 in notes and bonds. He also had £81 worth of books, unfortunately not itemized, instruments for astronomy and mathematics (£15), and thirteen maps. He did not own a farm but lived richly in the town with £336 in consumption

[22] Middletown district probate records, 3:161, 243.
[23] Windham district probate records, 4:210.
[24] Hartford district probate records, 3:132.
[25] New Haven district probate records, 2:266, 11:400, 501.

goods including a chaise at £18 plus £71 in silver articles.[26] Let us classify Clap as a college president who married money, and we then see the teachers as young, poor, and ephemeral.

No such general statement applies to doctors, who ranged from poor to rich, some without training and others with excellent preparation, from men without the books or implements needed for their calling to owners of fine libraries and the drugs of their day. The doctors' age at death, averaging forty-three, compares favorably with that of such teachers as turn up in the probate court but is otherwise quite low. The state of the art enabled men under thirty with little training to identify themselves as "doctors" (the title almost always appears) even when their inventories contain no hint of such a capability; so we find over one-fifth of the sixty-two for whom we have data in their twenties and one-fifth in the thirties. This suggests that some of the young men, probably the most poorly prepared and in country towns, shifted into more profitable occupations; indeed, we know of some who went into trade. On the other hand the practice remained an important source of income for men on up into their old age.

Some of the young doctors were poor, as one might expect, but as usual living longer brought wealth, and those in their forties and fifties acquired decent properties. One out of four became well-to-do with £200 in personal wealth and averaging £70 in consumption goods. Both of these sums increased over time, the median value of personal estates in the last quarter of a century exceeding by more than half that of the years before 1730. Only six or eight men fell into the class of truly poor. On the other hand, four men died possessed of over £750 in personal property, all after 1750.

These four men, like Clap, deserve attention because they represent one extreme. The estate of Dr. Thomas Langrell of Hartford, an immigrant, consisted principally of debts and a boy slave. He had a wife but little else—no children, no land, very little in the way of consumption goods, and none of the appropriate books or equipment; if it were not for the "Doctor," the debts, and the slave we would set him down as a poor young laborer.[27] The title also identifies Dr. Norman Morison of the same town, whom we would otherwise call an extremely successful merchant. Morison (d. 1762) had graduated from Edinburgh, where he presumably studied medicine. His library in-

[26] Ibid. 20:478.
[27] Hartford district probate records, 18:14, 111; *Connecticut Courant*, January 12, 1767.

cluded Dutch, Latin, and French dictionaries, twenty-four books in French, mostly on physick, and seventy-four pamphlets. He also owned £5 worth of medicines. However, his estate featured 793 gallons of rum and no less than thirty-one slaves valued at £867, including eleven girls and nine boys described as "sundry new negroes being 7/16 part Schooner Cargo from Africa." Listed separately, probably at least in part for sale, were three more Negro boys, four girls, and an old man, his wife, and child; another Negro girl appears in a different section of the inventory. The doctor owned half of a sloop, cash and silver worth £98, £631 in debts dating from 1731, and roughly 1,500 acres in Hartford, Bolton (where he had a farm), Waterbury, Windsor, Ellington, and Hartland. Morison had immigrated by 1741, apparently in his thirties, having married a widow in or shortly after 1732. He was probably the brother of Rhoderick Morison, another doctor who died in 1755 aged about forty-two, leaving a wife and son. Rhoderick's will refers to brothers Alexander and Reverend Murdoch. Norman, at least, certainly made good in the new world, though apparently in the slave trade rather than in medicine.[28]

The other two prosperous doctors were Samuel Shipman of Hebron (1702-1765) and John Herpin of Milford (1722-1767). Herpin, like Morison, was a creditor for a considerable sum. His other personal wealth totaled £311, and adding the difference between debts receivable and owed raises that to £642. Herpin clearly was a doctor, with £19 in medicines and £3 worth of instruments. He owned a Bible, fifty books in English, and forty-three in French, collectively valued at £4.16. His consumption goods included pictures and maps, a watch, and a fine clock (£5.10), and he also had a male slave. He owned, finally, thirty-one acres of good improved land, seventeen more probably in woods, and a right; but he seems not to have utilized this except for a few animals, unless he rented some of it.[29] Shipman also owned considerable debts but even more personal wealth and a true farm of seventy-three acres with twenty-five more in wood, two acres as a home lot for a second house, and another tract of somewhere between ten and forty acres. He, too, had a Negro "servant" valued at £38, whom he freed in his will. Also like Herpin, he possessed medicines and surgical instruments but in lesser amounts, nor did he have such a library, very likely depending on the farm as much as on the practice.[30]

[28] Hartford district probate records, 17:119, 165; 18:240.
[29] New Haven district probate records, 11:380.
[30] Colchester district probate records, 3:209.

A few other doctors must have brought knowledge and skill to their jobs. The Reverend Gershom Bulkeley, son of Dr. Charles of New London, owned a very large library valued at £84, and other men also had books on medicine. Samuel Whitman of Farmington (1681-1750) enjoyed a "study" and a "library" that he left to one son, while another was to receive a liberal education. John Osborn of Middletown (d. 1753) owned books by Ovid, Virgil, and Spencer; Elijah Adams of Stratford (1631-1771) also read Ovid as well as Pope and his medical books; Timothy Kimball of Coventry (1721-1765) likewise had medical books along with Ovid and *Pamela*.[31] Some owned many pounds' worth of drugs, Kimball's being valued at £60. John Copp grew herbs in his Norwalk garden. Thomas Mather had £55 invested in medicine, £13 in rum, and £4 in doctor's implements. Virtually every doctor owned at least a few books, the median being over £2, they often had farms with livestock, and by the last quarter of a century one-third held slaves. Some of them learned a supplementary skill other than farming. Naturally there were several apothecaries who sold other goods as well, and we find a miller, two joiners, a cooper, and a turner. Hardly typical but worth noting was Hon. Jonathan Huntington, Esq., of Windham (1695-1773), a lawyer and large farmer.

Near the average, with a comfortable £120 in personal wealth and £50 worth of consumption goods, were Jasper Gunn and his grandson Abel, Joseph Andrews and his son John, and John Welles. Jasper Gunn of Milford (1606-1670), an early settler, left his physic chest and £6 in books to one of four sons, Abel. Jasper had acquired about sixty acres of land, with the usual tools and livestock, which another son inherited, and also artisanal tools for a joiner or carpenter. The estate totaled £205. Abel moved to Derby, married about 1670, and passed on the name and some of the knowledge to his son, Sergeant Abel. To what extent the sergeant actually practiced medicine is hard to tell. He owned about £3 in the technical books, a good sum. He also had upwards of 200 acres of which at least 100 was improved, and the fact that the eldest of his three sons inherited 100 suggests 200 all told. He had, in fact, doubled the estate of his grandfather.[32] Joseph Andrews of Wethersfield (1651-1706) possessed a "physick" book and a chest with medicines, as well as a sawmill, turner's and carpenter's tools, and a seventy-acre farm with a hundred more in reserve. The farm probably provided the main income. He left an estate of £413.

[31] Hartford district probate records, 8:279, 16:166; Middletown district probate records, 1:152-154; Fairfield district probate records, 16:366; Windham district probate records, 7:84.

[32] New Haven district probate records, B:39-40; 5:54-58, 359, 524.

His eldest son, who died at the age of seventy-eight, referred to himself as a doctor. By that time he had given away most of his property, keeping more value in books than in clothing, half of the house, and twenty acres or so.[33] Finally, the inventory of John Welles, also of Wethersfield (1710-1771), refers to him as a doctor without any supporting evidence, though he did own more than the usual amount of cash (£5) and books (£3.2). Otherwise, he had an estate adequate for a family: personal property of £83, consumption articles valued at £54, and a farm of thirty-five acres with two houses and two wells.[34]

The doctors thus included men of education and wealth mixed with those possessed of neither. However, excluding the young they acquired more than enough property, in particular books far above the average, suggesting a status on a level with reputable farmers and probably above them.

Lawyers differed from doctors in their greater age, wealth, and status, if selection to high office proves the last. Identification of a lawyer does not come easily, since the colony contained few who earned their living solely in this way, and the list here being discussed includes a large number who simply owned lawbooks. Since justices of the peace commonly did so, we may often mistake one for a lawyer, besides which lawyers frequently were chosen as J.P.s, having at least one of the qualifications. Among our whole group of twenty-two individuals, only three lacked a title, commonly esquire (thirteen) or a military one (ten). Of the three, one was too young—Ebenezer Wakeman of Fairfield (1699-1727), a Yale graduate of distinguished family whose intended career is shown in his £22 worth of lawbooks.[35] Francis Hall of Stratford died at the age of ninety, so we cannot tell much from his inventory. The third was Henry Crane of Durham (ca. 1710-1768). Crane may well have supported his wife and seven children from his large farm, perhaps as much as 300 acres, or his "corn mill," but he also did own lawbooks and more cash than farmers or even millers commonly possessed.[36] The ownership of a farm really proves nothing, since almost all of these men had considerable land, the exceptions being ancient. The median, in fact, exceeded 300 acres even if we exclude undeveloped tracts. They kept £60 worth of livestock and indeed, if we consider only the men under seventy, thereby eliminating one-third, and young Wakeman, the median livestock rises to £90 and

---

[33] Hartford district probate records, 7:154.

[34] Ibid, 21:59, 62.

[35] Fairfield district probate records, 8:97. The inventory itemizes many others including "Cato's" *English Liberties*.

[36] Middletown district probate records, 2:416.

the land, of all types, comes to 400 acres. The group did not enter trade, so their considerable debts receivable arose from legal practice or government service.

The unusual age structure of these men suggests some kind of bias arising from our use of probate records, probably the difficulty of judging occupations correctly. Only Wakeman was under forty, half a dozen died in their fifties, and the median age at death was in the high sixties. That in itself would almost guarantee personal property well above the norm, but our assumed-to-be lawyers left even more than that—above £200, especially during the last fifteen years of the period, from which most come. Their mean personal wealth was close to £300, not because of any large estate but because only two left less than £200. Their consumption goods corresponded: very comfortable but not luxurious. The only men with less than £50 were all over eighty and if we exclude the elderly, their median was nearly £90. They almost always owned silver articles and cash, and six held slaves. The most notable feature of their estate, however, was books. Everyone owned some, often many, with the average value £5, meaning anywhere from two dozen to fifty. These of course included lawbooks as well as the obligatory Bible, but we find a considerable assortment including Locke and the English Cato.

Another common characteristic was membership in a prominent Connecticut family. The list includes the Pitkins from Hartford, an Allyn and a Wolcott from Windsor, a Burr and a Dimon from Fairfield, two Wests from Windham County, a Mason from Stonington, and a Belding from Wethersfield. William Pitkins, Esq. (1626-1698), who served the colony as attorney, himself founded a dynasty. He did not become rich; probably the economic depression of his mature years prevented that; and two of his five sons had married before his death. He kept the home farm of sixty or eighty acres and also a 480-acre undeveloped tract. He owned only a few animals but in December the inventory still listed over £20 worth of grains and two barrels of pork. His books were valued at £5.10 cash and consumption goods totaled £85.[37] Capt. John Fitch of Windham (1705-1760) was the only son of another Captain John (1675-1743), the grandson of Reverend James of Norwich. The elder John's will mentions over 2,000 acres and he had more than that, all of which his son inherited as the will shows— £5,667 worth of real estate. Otherwise his property was near the average for his profession: £180 in personal wealth, £75 in consumption, with a good but not exceptional operating farm. Included was

---

[37] Hartford district probate records, 5:200.

£3.14 worth of lawbooks. The account of administration notes that he had paid his son James's college expenses of £132.[38]

The occupation of a lawyer overlaps with that of the public officials, both sharing vague boundaries and uncertain definition. Clearly some citizens derived their principal income from full or part-time service, such as the colony's treasurers, the governors, clerks of major courts, the judges of probate, the combination of assistant with judge, and the top military ranks. Many of these offices brought grants of land, especially in the early years when the colony could pay its servants in nothing else. Later, the salaries in cash permitted such purchases. However, large estates tended to precede officeholding. We will delay a discussion of the social origins of these men until Chapter Nine and focus here on the property held by thirty-nine persons whom I set down impulsively as officials rather than assigning them to some other, perhaps equally defensible occupation. Two, for example, were lawyers, two engaged in trade, two doubled as millers, and three others as artisans or manufacturers (a distiller, a maltster, and a cooper); while at least twenty-two were active farmers and most of the rest had formerly been such. One served both as town clerk and schoolmaster. What follows, then, includes only a fraction of the colony's officials, to say nothing of the towns', most of whom served for no recompense, or even at a loss, and concerns with few exceptions the principal, not the minor personages.

Since higher rank came with age, most of these men died after reaching age sixty, the median being sixty-seven. The only youngster was Caleb Stanly, Junior (1684-1712), clerk of the county court and of probate for the extensive Hartford district. Caleb's father was a captain of large property. Our clerk had a seventy-acre farm and his books nearly equaled the livestock in value. The personal wealth of £268 was outshone by the £167 in consumption. He also had £68 worth of cash and silver.[39]

In many ways Stanly reflects the characteristics of this group. Most of them bore names familiar to the student of Connecticut history, such as Fitz-John Winthrop and Gurdon Saltonstall. Their median personal wealth exceeded £310, 40 percent leaving over £1,000 despite the fact that thirteen men were at least seventy and four over eighty. Almost all, like Stanly, lived comfortably, with over £100 in consumption goods. Typically they owned at least 120 acres of land, the median being 250, and five men held upwards of 1,000. Their £2 worth of books was less than that of lawyers, but good for the colony,

---

[38] Windham district probate records, 6:221, 498.
[39] Hartford district probate records, 8:201, 10:19, 12:93.

and five collected real libraries of £40 or more. Half had money owed to them totaling £4,665 among twenty persons. Finally, half owned servants, sometimes several. Lt. Col. John Talbot's 1688 estate included two Negroes and two Indians, a boy and a girl; all these seem to have been servants, not slaves. Governor Fitz-John Winthrop's household benefited from two Negro girls, a black boy, and an Indian woman, apparently all slaves. Col. John Whiting, secretary of the colony, held six slaves, two men, two women, a girl and a boy. Hon. Robert Walker owned a Negro man, two women, and three boys, while Hon. Col. Roger Newton had a man, a woman, a boy, and a girl. We are obviously dealing with an elite group, who therefore belong in a later chapter, so we pause only to notice two men who seem to vary from that description and offer particular points of interest. William Andrews of Hartford had immigrated to Cambridge, and when his wife died there in 1640 he moved on, remarrying. He became first the schoolmaster in his new home, then town clerk—a step up, as we have seen. He was probably just over sixty when he died in 1659, leaving his wife Abigail and three sons, two of whom died poor. Andrews's inventory offers no clue to his vocation, not even books, and he left little more than a house, barn, and eighteen acres of improved land plus forty-nine of upland.[40] John Winston of New Haven (1657-1712) also served as clerk, his books including works on geometry, arithmetic, and the law, but he fared better. His father (1621-1697) had become a sergeant and John, as the only son among five children, inherited some land. He sired six, and had over fifty acres of improved land, probably another hundred, and a cooper's shop, the whole estate valued at about £450. His books came to a respectable £3 and he owned one small symbol of status—a silver spoon.[41] These two men, of course, operated on the local level, and we simply observe, without discussion, the distance that separated them from, say, Joseph Buckingham, the judge of probate, with £542 in personal estate and 250 acres, or Col. John Allyn (1631-1696), secretary and assistant, with his £574 in personal property and 772 acres of land.

Neither the officials, lawyers, or teachers constituted a profession as they do today. The doctors perhaps did so, though many resorted to other sources of income. Ministers, however, from the first formed a distinct group of men who devoted full time to their specialty and derived from it an income making them independent. As we know, the people accorded them the greatest respect, and tried to make them

---

[40] Ibid., 2:129-30.
[41] New Haven district probate records, 4:43.

comfortable so that they need not worry about money. They received at the outset a "settlement," as though they and the community had married, which might come to £100, roughly a year's salary, and they also obtained a farm. Since many inherited property, coming from families who could support them through college and then endow them, they immediately became economic as well as intellectual, social, and spiritual leaders of the community. For those who died before 1700 we have inventories of all except the group around New London, and these records reveal characteristics that varied only in details. From the start they lived longer than did most men—sixty-one, primarily because of their late entrance into the field (none died during the twenties). Accordingly, most had children when they died and a majority, grandchildren. During this first period none left personal property worth under £100 cash and the median was £230, even higher than that of lawyers. They maintained that level throughout the colonial period. The mean of £266 indicates an equal distribution of property within the group, and, indeed, only two estates exceeded £400, both of Hookers, the famous Thomas and his son Samuel of Farmington. The latter's inventory included a debt of £100 (pay) owed by the town for his annual rate, the same sum due to two other ministers.

The salary by itself would have supported a family decently; the comfort came from the addition of land. Seventeenth-century ministers in fact owned as much as did farmers—100 acres. Only one person had none, and two others held around twenty acres. Everyone else had at least the minimum forty, the median for improved land being above sixty. Some acquired large tracts from the colony or towns as a reward for long service, as did John Bishop of Fairfield who received 200 acres. The median value of consumption goods including their books and clothing was £135. Only one person fell short of the figure we set as the minimum for a subsistence-plus living (aside from two very old men). On the other hand they did not flaunt their wealth. Except for Thomas Hooker none left over £220 in personal property. Almost all possessed silver or money and they commonly kept enough livestock for the family needs, £28 worth. Finally, their books exceeded livestock in value and made up more than one-fourth of their household goods, one-sixth of their whole personal wealth. Not one minister went without and only one owned less than £10 worth. Indeed, libraries valued at over £40 equaled those in the £20 and £30 range. The median of £37 represents at a very crude guess 150 volumes and the same number of pamphlets.

The appraisers of Nathaniel Collins's Middletown estate have favored us with a room-by-room inventory[42] Collins, who died in 1684 at age forty-one, left a property near the average for ministers, with 48 acres of good land and 163 remaining undeveloped. The house (£70 cash) was more valuable than usual because it included a study containing his "library" worth £72.12.9 pay, about £50, and for some reason, 1,700 nails. In the garret above it were twelve pairs of sheets and twelve pillowcases. Beds for the six children, his wife, and himself were scattered about the house. In the parlor was a nice featherbed with a straw bed under it (for the Negro boy Peter?). Another featherbed was in the parlor chamber, and there were two more plus a trundle bed in another room. Samuel Stone's Hartford home also included a study and a garret, this one with a bed, a parlor with its chamber and a bed, a hall with two beds, its chamber and bed, the kitchen and kitchen chamber with bed, and a closet. He therefore owned one bed per person. Joseph Rowlandson's house in Wethersfield, however, conforms to the usual very modest structure, with no study, two main rooms here called parlor and kitchen, a parlor chamber, garret, and cellar, with three beds, adequate for the couple and their two teen-aged children.[43] Finally, Joseph Haynes represents the top of Hartford's order. Haynes, a son of the governor, died at thirty-eight leaving to his wife and three children over 500 acres of land and a personal estate of £238 cash, with a library valued at £36. His house consisted of a parlor, hall, and kitchen, the first two with chambers, a porch chamber, cheese chamber, little chamber, garret, inward cellar, outward cellar, and buttery. Scattered in five rooms, but not in the kitchen, were four large good beds, four ordinary beds, and a "settle" bed (doubling as a seat), collectively with the furnishings worth even more than the books—£44 cash.[44]

We close this sketch of the seventeenth-century ministers with an "average" one, Roger Newton of Milford (1615-1683). Newton, a Cambridge man, married a daughter of Thomas Hooker by whom he had four sons and four daughters, all alive when he died, but four had married and gone. He left £210 in personal and £301 in real estate, the latter probably over 100 acres. His £136 worth of books were mostly theological, but he did own an Ovid. The household goods minus the books were worth £109, including five full-sized beds plus a bedstead and a trundle bed, supplied with eleven pairs of sheets. He had £21 worth of livestock but neither tools nor oxen. These, with

[42] Hartford district probate records, 4:221-23; Manwaring, *Early Connecticut Probate Records*, 1:292-93.

[43] Hartford district probate records, 3:4-6, 4:17-18.

[44] Ibid., 4:22-25.

some of his land, may have been given to two of the sons, for his parishioners would surely care for his farm. However, the town still owed him £35 for his salary. The inventory contains no signs of ostentation. Newton dressed well but had no silverware and passed on a moderate property, considering his high social rank.[45]

After 1700 the reporting rate for ministers in probate court dropped abruptly to 60 percent, recovered to 72 percent by 1750 and 85 percent at the close. The final figure perhaps reflects a bias in overreporting large estates, but the main puzzle is the 60 percent earlier rate below the general average; I have no idea of the reason for it unless the judges began to excuse ministerial families from the usual procedures except when the estate presented some problems, as seems to have been the case with a good many. We therefore indicate changes over time with some misgivings. The age at death steadily declined, reaching fifty-four at the end, by which period more young men appear (not due to the Great Awakening), and no men over seventy, a fact that runs counter to the possibility of bias. The overall age at death for the century was fifty-seven. Despite the change in age, the median personal wealth reached a high of £260 during the final decade, double the low of 1750-1764. This low, rather than the high, needs explanation, since it fell far short of the ministerial norm. It may result from the well-known erosion of salaries during the inflationary period, or from the long depression. Also, a few men who joined the ranks lacked the usual background. The value of consumption goods slipped but still remained above £100, and the ministers continued to own adequate farms. These, with silver, money, and livestock, all reached a high during 1700-1729, dropped to a low and recovered in the way now familiar.

The value of the ministers' books never equaled the seventeenth-century median of £37, declining first to £23, then to the quite modest £8.10 at mid-century, after which it doubled. A few men continued to own fine libraries, and relative to the population as a whole they must have seemed well-read; moreover, the local subscription libraries, to which they contributed, would have met some of their own needs. Thus Sterling Graves, rather isolated at Hartland and with only £7 in books of his own, had a 12-shilling right. Even rather small collections testified to an education. Nathaniel Hunn of Fairfield (1708-1750) had Locke and several Latin classics with the usual Latin and Greek grammars among his £5 worth. A few libraries were quite extensive. Benjamin Holton of Hartford (1670-1759) owned fifty books and the same number of pamphlets while Ebenezer Devotion of Windham

---

[45] New Haven district probate records, B:69, 104-107.

TABLE 7.4
Value of Books Owned, Ministers

£ cash	Pre-1700	1700–1729	1750–1774
None	0	0	0
1–4	1	0	5
5–9	0	1	12
10–19	1	4	10
20–29	3	5	6
30–39	4	2	3
40–49	2	1	4
50+	5	1	0
Total	16	14	40
Median £	37	23	12

(1714-1771) had 113 books, 230 pamphlets, and 10 volumes of the *London Magazine*. Devotion also displayed five maps, two large pictures (£12), and twenty-five other pictures.[46] The decline, if such it was, perhaps represents rather a return from an abnormally high beginning to a still respectable level.

The financial resources of the ministers we may estimate from their silver, money, and debts receivable. By colonial standards they had a great deal of money, the mean value averaging about £40, dropping below that only after 1750. Moreover, they could afford to buy slaves. Before 1700 only three men out of sixteen owned any. By 1750 the proportion doubled, one-third having at least one, and at the end over half did so, the average for the whole colonial period being one-third.

Granted that other professionals and members of the economic upper class also acquired slaves, one still wonders whether ministers had some particular reason. As we know, the congregation furnished the minister with a farm. He himself would not labor upon it, so the parishioners commonly did so to help pay for their "rates." Conceivably the church members became more reluctant to work as time went on, perhaps preferring to pay in the gradually depreciating paper bills. The most likely explanation is that ministers of the eighteenth century often did not marry or if they did so, produced no sons.[47] Since half of the slaves were male, and obviously could not have been assisting the ministers professionally, they might have filled a near vacuum in the labor supply and so freed the ministers as their church members

[46] Simsbury district probate records, file 1241; Fairfield district probate records, 10:112; Windham district probate records, 8:230.

[47] Twenty-four out of sixty-one ministers born between 1700 and 1720 failed to sire a son who reached adulthood, a percentage twice that before 1700.

had before. Possibly too the slaves, by working the glebe farm for income, helped to prevent any reduction of the ministers' standard of living insofar as that was threatened. If that was the purpose it succeeded.

The ministers, teachers, lawyers, public officials, and doctors contributed to the colony out of all proportion to their numbers, most obviously through intellectual leadership but also in critical functions that we might call social welfare. The rewards in both income and prestige attracted some of the most capable men in the colony including most of the college graduates. Teachers, aside from those at Yale, form the only exceptions, because their low salaries eliminated almost everyone except young men who taught until they found something better. Even in their case we find a man such as Eleazer Kimberly who taught the children all his life, though he did not need the small income and was a busy man. Teachers aside, the professional men acquired properties far above the average, even doctors leaving respectable estates. Lawyers, officials, and ministers usually owned large farms. They also had cash at their disposal, often debts receivable, sometimes slaves. Their general standard of living was high; indeed, more became wealthy than remained poor or at the subsistence level. They furnished the colony with its cultural upper class as their possession of books shows, to which the ministers added moral leadership. They lived ten years longer than other folk. We can hardly deem this a reward for virtue, and perhaps it was only because they lived more safely than farmers and artisans, certainly than laborers; but one is inclined to think that they deserved it.

The Artisans in Connecticut's Society

The data for craftsmen come primarily from over a thousand estate inventories and biographical sources. For the numbers see Appendix 7B.

The separation of artisans and farmers into two chapters distorts the actual situation. Instead, as the text points out, they lived together in a society in which occupation did not matter except as some other consideration intervened, as in the case of ministers. Whether the artisans constituted a separate class needs research rather than mere statement, but the evidence suggests a community of interest maintained by men and their children changing occupations and by marriage across occupational lines.

One evidence for this is that during the years 1700-1729, among the adult male population exclusive of laborers, 60 percent were farmers, 30 percent were artisans, and the rest were professionals and traders. If this proportion were to hold constant, either all the sons must follow in their fathers' footsteps, as we know they did not even aside from the frequency of men without sons of a superfluity; or twice as many artisans' sons must become farmers as farmers' sons did artisans. That had certainly been the case, for the availability of good land enabled men to acquire farms cheaply and on the very general average farming was more profitable than most crafts. But by 1770 the ratio changed to 50-35-15, which means that fewer artisans' sons became farmers, more farmers' sons shifted, or both, reflecting the high land prices and perhaps improving prospects in the crafts.

A glance at the evidence for a half-dozen towns with the best genealogical evidence shows that among artisans dying before 1700, two-thirds of their sons moved over into farming, some of whom, however, remained part-time craftsmen. A few entered another occupation, leaving only one out of four who continued as artisans. The N is only forty-six partly because many artisans left no sons, but mostly for lack of data ready to hand. I doubt that pursuing the matter would change the result significantly. On the other hand, about half of the fathers of these craftsmen had been farmers and only one-fourth had been full-time artisans (N = 36). These data indicate what we already suppose: the people of Connecticut moved from one occupation to another, both out of and into farming, but with farming retaining its superior appeal during most of the colonial period. In this case artisans drew twenty of thirty-six men away from farming but gave back thirty of forty-six.

271

APPENDIX 7B

Characteristics and Property of Artisans

Age	Millers		Tanners etc.		Smiths		Coopers		Carpenters & joiners		Shoemakers, tailors etc.		Large manuf.		Misc. small	
	prob.	livg.	prob.	livg.	prob.	livg.	prob.	livg.	prob.	livg.	prob.	livg.	prob.	livg.	prob.	livg.
21–29	4	12	3	13	18	30	19	36	47	42	54	49	0	0	30	35½
30–39	9	18	10	29	21	22½	20	24	43	24½	48	28	6	36½	40	30
40–49	21	28	17	32	30	21	27	21	47	17½	44	17	4	13½	29	14
50–59	20	22	8	11	31	17	15	9	35	10½	15	4	9	27	30	11½
60+	35	20	17	15	31	9½	27	9	35	5½	12	2	13	23	40	8½
Total	89	100	55	100	131	100	108	99	207	100	173	100	32	100	169	99½
Median	55.5	47	48.8	43	49.0	39	45.7	36	43.0	33½	36.8	30½	57.2	49½	45.0	35

Personal Wealth

£ cash	Millers	Tanners etc.	Smiths	Coopers	Carpenters & joiners	Shoemakers, tailors etc.	Large manuf.	Misc. small	Total	%
1–19	2	0	6	8	21	33	0	18	88	8.6
20–49	9	7	25	34	62	71	0	41	249	24.2
50–99	30	11	41	40	92	53	0	76	343	33.3
100–199	23	20	44	29	41	22	8	52	239	23.2
200–499	23	15	24	3	8	1	21	2	97	9.4
500+	4	4	0	0	0	0	5	0	13	1.3
Total	91	57	140	114	224	180	34	189	1,029	100.0
Median £	122	150	96	69	66	44	271	74	76	

CONSUMER GOODS

1–19	3	4	23	25	61	76	0	40	232	22.9
20–39	27	11	29	46	83	46	1	71	314	31.0
40–59	18	9	22	23	50	30	3	40	195	19.2
60–79	15	7	25	15	17	11	3	28	121	11.9
80–119	11	14	18	4	15	8	13	11	94	9.3
120–199	11	9	13	1	3	0	10	3	50	4.9
200+	4	0	0	0	0	0	3	0	7	0.7
Total	89	54	130	114	229	171	33	193	1,013	99.9
Median £	57	70	52	34	33	24	111	36	38	

LIVESTOCK

None	2	0	14	14	31	34	2	42	139	13.6
1–19	20	14	55	55	110	118	3	100	475	46.4
20–39	26	18	30	25	63	20	5	39	226	22.1
40–59	20	13	20	14	13	8	12	8	108	10.5
60–99	15	6	15	3	8	1	12	4	64	6.2
100+	8	3	0	1	0	0	0	0	12	1.2
Total	91	54	134	112	225	181	34	193	1,024	100.0
Median £	38	35	26	16	15	10	52	11	16	

APPENDIX 7B

Continued

ACRES

£ cash	Millers	Tanners etc.	Smiths	Coopers	Carpenters & joiners	Shoemakers, tailors etc.	Large manuf.	Misc. small	Total	%
None, no house	1	9	23	18	53	61	0	49	205	15.7
None, house	1	0	3	3	7	10	0	8	32	2.4
1–19	10	10	41	49	86	97	2	57	352	26.9
20–39	17	9	21	26	56	47	6	42	224	17.1
40–59	15	12	24	15	26	8	2	16	118	9.0
60–79	9	3	15	5	10	7	10	9	68	5.2
80–119	16	11	18	14	26	7	6	10	108	8.3
120–199	21	13	21	12	24	5	17	5	118	9.0
200+	31	13	9	12	5	1	13	0	84	6.4
Total	121	71	175	154	293	243	56	196	1,039	100.0
Median acres	100	87	39	26	20	10	132	15	26	

NOTE: Most of this material and the data in the text come from the following probate records: all districts through 1729; for 1745–1764 from Hartford, Middletown, Colchester, Windham, and Fairfield districts; and 1765 and 1774 as described earlier. For personal wealth, however, the years 1745–1760 are omitted.

APPENDIX 7C

Characteristics and Property of Professional Men

Years	Age at death					£ cash	Personal wealth				
	Teachers	Doctors	Lawyers	Officials	Ministers		Teachers	Doctors	Lawyers	Officials	Ministers
20s	2	13	1	0	11	1–49	3	12	0	0	3
30s	3	13	0	1	21	50–99	3	20	4	2	6
40s	1	12	0	3	30	100–199	1	24	5	9	21
50s	0	6	6	7	60	200–299		8	5	7	25
60s	1	10	8	15	79	300–399		2	4	5	11
70s	0	8	3	9	85	400–499		3	3	1	6
80+	0	2	4	4	57	500–999		3	1	11	5
Unknown	1	9	0	0	3	£1,000+	1	1	0	4	0
Median	34	45	66	67	63	Median £	56	120	233	310	230

	Level of living					£ cash	Silver & cash				
	Teachers	Doctors	Lawyers	Officials	Ministers		Teachers	Doctors	Lawyers	Officials	Ministers
Poor	0	6	0	0	0	None	4	30	3	8	14
Subsist.	1	4	0	0	3	1–4	2	19	8	7	13
Subsist.+	6	22	1	1	3	5–9	0	8	3	2	11
Comfort.	0	19	1	3	11	10–19	0	5	1	4	10
Well-off	0	21	14	22	56	20–49	1	2	5	7	18
Wealthy	1	1	5	13	5	50+	1	9	2	11	7
Median	Subs.+	Comfort.	Well-off	Well-off	Well-off	Median £	0	1	5	12	9
						Mean £	—	12	16	40	18

£ cash	Consumption					Acres	Acres of land				
	Teachers	Doctors	Lawyers	Officials	Ministers		Teachers	Doctors	Lawyers	Officials	Ministers
1–19	4	10	0	2	0	None	3	17	2	0	4
20–39	2	20	2	2	7	1–19	2	15	0	5	7
40–59	0	11	5	6	5	20–39	1	9	0	1	4
60–99	1	21	8	9	26	40–79	0	9	1	4	15
100–199	0	7	5	15	26	80–119	1	7	2	0	8
200+	1	3	1	5	5	120–199	0	8	1	6	8
Unknown	0	2	1	0	0	200–499	0	6	10	11	15
Median £	21	50	84	102	105	500+	1	0	6	11	13
						Median	1	28	307	250	112

Debts receivable

	Teachers	Doctors	Lawyers	Officials	Ministers
With	5	36	10	20	30
Without	3	37	12	19	74
% with	62.5	49	45	52	41

Value of books — £ cash

	Teachers	Doctors	Lawyers	Officials	Ministers
None	0	3	0	4	0
Under 1	3	7	1	8	0
1–4	2	46	8	15	6
5–9	1	12	6	5	13
10–19	1	3	4	3	15
20–49	0	0	2	0	27
50+	1	1	1	1	6
Median £	2/	2.10	5.10	2	21

Servants

	Teachers	Doctors	Lawyers	Officials	Ministers
With	0	12	6	19	26
Without	8	61	16	20	76
% with	0	17	27	48	34

Value of livestock

	Teachers	Doctors	Lawyers	Officials	Ministers
None	5	7	1	0	4
1–9	0	19	1	1	6
10–19	2	18	2	6	11
20–29	1	7	3	1	15
30–39	0	9	2	5	8
40–49	0	4	1	6	9
50–99	0	9	7	12	16
100+	0	0	5	8	5
Median £	1	16	57	50	31

EIGHT

On Traders, and a Summary

The last occupational group in our survey of Connecticut's men at work includes those who my best friend, only wife, and severest critic unkindly terms residuals and I call traders. Lumping quite disparate genera into a family requires only some critical attribute in common, and if we can discuss schoolteachers with doctors and shoemakers with millers we can reasonably combine peddlers and ships' captain.

All of these men had something to do with commerce, the transportation, buying, and selling of goods. They consisted of two general groups. To one belonged the men engaged in overseas trade, ranging from the common sailors in the economic and social cellar—or bilge— to the great merchants, with ships' captains, shipowners, and "mariners" in between. The second set of traders transported or sold goods within the colony. They included the peddlers, a variety of shopkeepers, and men who operated over considerable distances, generally between the import-export centers and the interior towns, commonly called "traders" as distinguished from the overseas "merchants."

In general, commerce had not yet become as specialized as it did during the nineteenth century, though the process had begun. Thus until after 1700 ships' captains were rare; at least, the title almost never appears, apparently because it had not become a distinct occupation. The owners of ships usually engaged in trade and sometimes commanded their vessels at sea. Wholesalers acted as retailers, importers, and exporters. The same men purchased livestock from the farmers as sold farm implements back to them, and they also offered for sale everything else, running a true "general store." As late as 1766 the schooner *Squirrel* anchored far upriver at Hartford, offering fish and blubber, suggesting the returns from a fishing and whaling voyage, but also a variety of ironware, powder and shot, and tea, in exchange for which the master advertised that he would accept pork, butter, cheese, hogs' fat, tallow, or small furs.[1] By that time larger towns contained stores that concentrated on certain types of articles such as books and drugs. The undifferentiated shops remained characteristic

---

[1] *The Connecticut Courant* (Hartford), December 22, 1766.

primarily of the country villages where the owner might sell almost everything in exchange for practically anything.

If an increase in the number of traders signifies prosperity and economic expansion, Connecticut was progressing during the decades before independence. Before 1700 only 4 or 5 percent of the men over age forty engaged in trade, but that reached 7 percent after 1760. The colony had never been isolated from the outside world, but we may hypothesize a change over time starting with the depression of the later 1600s, when the lack of a major cash crop, poor foreign markets, and impediments to territorial expansion forced the people toward self-sufficiency. A reduced population growth was either a symptom or another cause. Shortly after 1700, and especially after 1710 or so, we begin to see considerably more merchants, ships' captains, and the property associated with foreign trade. The number then diminished or stabilized until it revived during the 1750s and especially the early 1760s. As we know, the colony did not grow in wealth over time, but it does seem to have become increasingly a part of the Atlantic economic world. The volume of trade at least kept up with the population explosion and may very well have risen faster during the last quarter-century, though, if so, the balance sheet remained the same. From all this the speculation follows that although the value of the people's household and personal goods did not change, the quality improved as superior imported goods replaced local products (nice English cloth for homespun) so that the people lived better, after all. But that hypothesis remains to be tested.

Even if none of this be true, the traders performed essential functions. The farmers and artisans could not quite survive in isolation, and the sale of a surplus meant, at the minimum, subsistence instead of poverty and, beyond that, the prospect of comfort. The village shopkeepers accepted the community's surplus of pork and beef, corn, rye, and wheat, and a miscellany such as flaxseed and butter, at the current price, forwarding these to the merchants. They offered for sale, as we pointed out, what the community could not produce but needed (iron houseware, gunpowder, steel, tools, salt, writing paper) or could make good use of (cloverseed, paint, empty bottles, buttons, looking glasses) or just wanted (cloth of all sorts, ribbons, tea, rice, rum). The apothecaries and booksellers served people in their particular ways much as did the local craftsmen. Moreover, when the customer could not pay either in money or acceptable surplus from the farm or craft, the shopkeepers extended credit, thus in effect replacing specie.

The overseas traders, our "merchants," contributed in the same way, with the shopkeepers as customers and foreign markets the destination. To the former they sold imported goods at wholesale and to the latter they sent the accumulated surplus from the country towns plus the products of their own skilled workers—ships, house-timber, barrels, gravestones. They obtained overseas credit and employed or created jobs for the sailors and, indirectly, many others in the shipyards, wharves, and shops. During the revolutionary years the merchants, and men in commerce generally, came under attack as nonproductive consumers, but in fact their activities enabled the rest of the people to survive and some to live comfortably. Indeed, if our speculations prove correct they not only protected but elevated the colonists' standard of living, especially since in their absence the profits derived from buying, transporting, and selling would have remained in the pockets of overseas merchants instead of enriching Connecticut. As we will see, the traders as a whole did acquire more property than other men, but the difference came not from profits extracted from their neighbors but the money earned by services rendered within and without the colony. As a final point, traders were only a little more separate from the rest of the people than any other occupational group. Some, indeed, arrived as representatives of British companies or the captains of visiting ships, but most were natives, and the newcomers commonly married local women and became full members—a process that after all was hardly new in Connecticut and not limited to any segment of the population. Traders were unusually mobile almost by definition, and among 137 of them dying during 1700-1729 were 27, about a fifth, who had immigrated. This includes the most migratory types such as peddlers, ships' captains, and mariners, yet of these newcomers half had married and settled down. On the whole, then, they belonged and contributed to the colony's society as much as anyone else.

The smallest and least important segment of the trading population consisted of peddlers. These were less common in Connecticut than in some other parts of the colonies because most of the people lived near enough to towns for trips to the store. At a later period Yankee peddlers became well-known and by traveling with a horse and cart could carry a considerable quantity of merchandise, making a career of it. The few that turn up in our records were with one exception young, poor, and on foot, leaving properties that consisted of little more than their clothing, miscellaneous lightweight goods, and debts.

The exception was Thomas Selden of Hartford, who died in 1665 at the age of thirty-eight. Selden, whose occupation we have surmised, was born in 1617 and immigrated by 1639, marrying the daughter of

John Wakeman, a man of substance.[2] He served as constable and left an estate of £205 cash at his death. Of that sum, however, nearly half was in the form of debts "certain and uncertain." Of real property he had only a house lot and some upland, on which he kept a cow and two hogs, so he certainly was not a farmer. His consumption goods of £38 barely sufficed to provide some comforts for a wife and four children. Most significantly, he owned "one pack of goods" worth £28 cash. Since Wakeman was a New Haven man (though he died in Hartford) and since the widow took her family to Hadley, Massachusetts, we may infer a peripatetic quality in her husband. A settled trader, moreover, would own a store. Of the two sons, John stayed with his mother in Hadley where he lived to be eighty-nine. Joseph apparently moved to Lyme, dying at seventy-three, leaving three sons, one of whom enters our field of vision as a captain whose son, in turn, became a colonel and prominent lawyer.

Samuel Adjett is more typical. He and his brother John both died during the winter epidemic of 1712-1713. John had acquired forty acres and had started to farm it with a yoke of oxen, producing a small crop of grains and hay, but Samuel's little estate consisted almost entirely of small items for sale, his clothing, a Bible, and a couple of pounds in cash. His father, John, who came up from Block Island to claim the estate (unsuccessfully), is called in the records a "transient person," though perhaps anyone "formerly of Hartford" who had so little sense as to emigrate to Rhode Island had lost all status.[3]

If young Adjett had lived past thirty he probably would have married and settled down, most likely as a shopkeeper. These were sedentary, limiting their activities to one community. They bought on wholesale on credit, usually from a merchant in a port town, though some did order directly from overseas. Thus in 1765 Caleb Bull of Hartford advertised that he had just received a variety of articles from London, and Benjamin Henshaw claimed to have imported an even more extensive assortment that must have come from both Britain and the West Indies. Such men would have hoped to sell their entire stock quickly enough to turn over their capital three times each year, reinvesting part of their markup so as to preserve their reputations, and steadily increasing their investment. From their customers they collected money when possible, otherwise the local surplus, and advanc-

[2] Hartford district probate records, 2:74-75.

[3] Lucius B. Barbour, *Familes of Early Hartford* (Baltimore, 1977), 325; Hartford district probate records, 8:138; Charles William Manwaring, comp., *A Digest of Early Connecticut Probate Records*, 3 vols. (Hartford, 1904-1906), 1:147.

ing credit when necessary. Their command over money, including the possession of above-average amounts of specie, enabled them to serve as bankers to the community, charging interest on loans where they generally did not on the ordinary transactions.

The shopkeepers collected debts whenever they could but especially when someone died. Then the probate court performed one of its primary functions. The administrators called upon anyone owing money to the estate to pay, and all creditors put in their claims. If necessary the court authorized the sale of enough property to satisfy the debts or if worst came to worst declared the estate insolvent. Then the widow was taken care of first and the rest of the property divided among the claimants. Fortunately for the shopkeepers, Connecticut's farmers and artisans very rarely became insolvent, and their debts could generally be paid by the sale of some land. Nobody has investigated all this systematically, but probate records show that the shopkeepers lost money only to young men or to other would-be traders, also mostly young, who overextended. This occurred most often at exceptional times during one of the sporadic downturns. Out of 211 traders dying before 1730 not more than a dozen were bankrupt, most of them young or single. A group of 56 inventories between 1745 and 1759 included only 2 such estates and for the years 1760 to 1774 there were 13 such out of 136, 10 of these occurring between 1764 and 1771. This averages just 6.7 percent, and remember that estates with problems such as heavy debts were *most* likely to enter probate. Conceivably obligations outside of the colony were ignored so that one should look at other court records; but on this evidence the people of Connecticut rarely borrowed more than they could handle.

The shopkeepers were especially exposed to local calamities and overall nine out of ninety-one of them left insolvent estates. Of these four were single, one a newlywed, and the rest young fathers in their thirties. Thomas Bidwell (1682-1717), a member of a good Hartford mercantile family, gambled after Queen Anne's war and lost everything, his liabilities exceeding assets by a thousand pounds;[4] while the druggist Daniel Hubbard of Wallingford tried to expand when the end of the Seven Years' War allowed such imports, and ran up a spectacular £2,008 in debts with an estate of only £377.[5] In his case he would probably have gone under even if he had lived past thirty-six. The estate included both a Negro woman and a riding chair, suggestive of a lack of caution uncharacteristic of a Connecticut man.

[4] Hartford district probate records, 9:109-110.
[5] New Haven district probate records, 20:310.

A majority of retail shopkeepers were under forty like those just discussed, but successful; and some went on to become wholesale merchants as did Governor Jonathan Trumbull.[6] Their personal wealth was more than double the general average with a median of £235 and a mean of nearly £300. Nearly half consisted of debts receivable, however, a more insecure form of property than others. Few poor men appear on the records, only three owning under £50 and 13 percent less than £100, but nobody exceeded £1,000 in personal wealth, the shopkeepers thus being concentrated around the median: generally comfortable, but seldom more than that unless they enlarged their scope. Almost all lived well above the poverty level. Among the fathers of children over twelve who had not yet retired we find only two individuals with under £40 in household articles and four out of five owned over £60 worth, enough for a decent life; the median was a quite comfortable £110. Even including single men the overall median was £80. Only four individuals owned the relatively luxurious £200.

In addition, the shopkeepers as a class acquired enough land to supply their minimum needs in food and fuel. One out of five had none, but these were generally single men. The median was thirty acres and nearly a third had a full-sized eighty-acre farm. Two became really large landowners with over five hundred. This land enabled most of them to pasture sufficient livestock, and helped to elevate the shopkeepers into what we might call an upper-middle class, even if they remained retailers.

The inventories of shopkeepers included by definition trading stock ranging from only a few pounds' worth to a median of £70 on up to our maximum of £449. No clustering appears because of the diverse ages and general economic circumstances, though the commonest holdings were around £100. If the normal markup was one-third above the wholesale cost and if a man turned over his stock three times yearly, as they attempted, then he would earn £100 annually on that investment, which would permit savings unless he spent it all on a higher standard of living, which as we have seen he generally did not. Curiously, half of the inventories did not list debts, perhaps because customers periodically paid what they owed. The other half had advanced credit all the way from a few pounds to five hundred, with a median of £145. They commonly owned cash or silver, seldom in large sums, but the holders averaged £10 worth.

Eighteen percent held slaves or servants, not a great proportion considering their property; but many of these men lived in country towns

---

[6] Glenn Weaver, *Jonathan Trumbull, Connecticut's Merchant Magistrate* (Hartford, 1956).

where slaves rarely existed. They seldom bought adult males but usually women or girls as household help, averaging just £25 per servant and £7 per shopkeeper. Finally, like most citizens they owned books, but generally few and of small value. Only one in ten had a library worth £5 or more. In this respect they resembled the average among all traders.

Fairly representative was Samuel Robinson of Fairfield, who left a wife and small children when he died in 1698. He owned a personal estate of £272 of which over half consisted of goods for sale. An invoice listed items that he had just imported and he previously had stocked rum, sugar, and nails. In addition he had collected the produce of the country: pork, beef, and 240 bushels of wheat. He supplemented the inevitable house and lot with £122 worth of other land, which at the average price meant forty to sixty acres. Consumption goods of £88 took care of his family even without the £13 in clothing. Cash and plate came to £3, and he owned £1 in books, variety unspecified.[7]

Similar in occupation, value of property, and place of death but otherwise strangely different was Andris Trubee, who died in 1759 leaving teen-aged children. Trubee's £372 in personal wealth consisted primarily of £177 in cash and £130 in hardware and dry goods. His books, at £2.4, included eight volumes of the *Turkish Spy*, which ought *not* to have been in a Connecticut library, but then he was surely foreign. In Fairfield he owned nothing but a shop but he had bought 420 acres in Cornwall valued at £263.[8]

Representing the druggists is Peletiah Bliss of Windsor, who was not yet forty when he died in 1758. Bliss had the desired small farm, twenty acres with house and barn (£125), a few farm animals, but no grains except provisions. At the time of his death the apothecary drugs were valued at only £10, yet he possessed £11 in cash and £89 in notes. Probably he had been converting his trading stock into liquid assets. His £4.13 in books made him relatively well-read, and £77 in consumption goods supported his family more than adequately.[9]

Finally, Dudley Kent of Suffield died in 1766 at seventy-two. He had turned over his house to a son but retained eighteen acres of pasture, fifty-six of other less valuable but improved land, and forty-seven unimproved, totaling £248. The personal estate came to only £149 but as an elderly grandfather that and £60 worth of consump-

---

[7] Fairfield district probate records, 4:155.

[8] Ibid., 14:406. We have neither a birth nor a marriage record, and the name suggests an immigrant.

[9] Hartford district probate records, 18:125-126.

tion goods made him well-off. The item that concerns us is dry goods "come by Paul," at £32, and £8 in cash also suggests some business dealings. Very likely Kent, late in the colonial period and well along in life, had diversified his economic activities.[10]

Innkeepers perhaps do belong to a residuum, but they did sell meals, the use of a bed, and usually drink. The towns regulated these men carefully as they did the owners of "ordinaries," who provided food but not lodging, so only respectable men or women could own them. Since reputable generally implied propertied, innkeepers earned a better-than-average income almost by definition. Out of fourteen inventories that certainly belonged to innkeepers just two listed less than £50 in personal goods and the median was a hefty £250. Of consumption articles only two fell below the comfort level for a family man, one belonging to a retired person and the other to a bachelor in his thirties. Indeed, the median was £130. The owners were generally middle-aged fathers, clustering around the median of fifty-two years at death. The majority belonged to good families. Thus Jonathan Gilbert served as marshal of the colony and married the daughter of Elder John White. Gilbert (1618-1682) left £1,740 at his death including four farms and probably over 200 acres. His own house consisted downstairs of the usual hall and parlor plus a "great" kitchen, an ordinary kitchen, porch, and shop. Upstairs were four "chambers" plus a "closet chamber" over one of the three closets, and a garret. Two cellars and a warehouse added storage space. His guests could use sixty-five pairs of sheets and 115 pounds of pewter. He offered an assortment of articles for sale and his estate included £61 worth of debts in cash and £69 in pay, much of it due in Boston, plus another £564, probably in pay, some labeled "desperate." He also had a quarter-share of a vessel on the stocks, 140 ounces of plate at 7 shillings per ounce, and the usual Bible, with other books, but only a few farm animals. His second wife, Mary (Hugh) Wells, took over the inn and lived for another eighteen years, leaving an estate of over £500.[11]

Our small group of fourteen may not yield accurate data, but a few other points are worth noting. Only two men were landless and one of those owned more livestock than any of the others. The majority operated true farms, over half more than 100 acres, and many had been buying vacant tracts. Most kept cash on hand for this business and the occupation is revealed by their goods for sale and debts. Only

[10] Ibid., 20:152, 189.
[11] Ibid., 4:311, 6:144.

one lacked books. Three had purchased slaves, two buying maidservants while the third had a woman and two men.

We close this survey of the innkeepers with a final example of a fairly representative man. John Lay the First of Lyme died in 1657, aged, leaving a good farm. He named his first son, born in 1633, after himself, married a second time, and again called a son John, whom the records refer to as "Junior" and who kept an inn, dying testate but without an inventory in 1712. John, Junior's, son John—another "Junior," to confuse matters—inherited the inn, referred to as a tavern upon his death in 1723. The family lacked distinction but married well. The third John's estate consisted of a house, barn, stable, shop, cider mill, home lot, meadow, and orchard collectively valued at £450, so the land must have covered fifty or sixty acres, and he also owned half of a 650-acre purchase. The farm pastured considerable livestock. His personal estate of £156 included £56 in consumer goods, more than adequate for the wife and four small children, about £2 in cash and £24 in bills of credit. For a man of only thirty-one years he left a good estate, derived both from the farm and the profits of the tavern despite the absence of liquor. Innkeepers, then, were respectable, propertied men who occasionally became leaders of the community.[12]

Sailors were the laborers of the maritime trade and form part of Chapter Five. The word might include everybody involved with sailing a ship, and as here used it should be thought of as preceded by "common." People involved in probate proceedings did not use it, but the noun "mariner" does appear. Mariners, however, almost always owned more property, were older, and sometimes family men. The identification of a sailor comes from statements in wills or in other records and by inference from their estate inventories. Table 8.1 displays their basic characteristics as shown by the probate records. Their actual age structure might have been even younger. Many must have lived longer than the age at death indicated, but if so they had graduated to the status of a "mariner" or settled ashore in some other occupation. As long as they remained ordinary sailors they seldom acquired enough property to make them fully independent. Roughly a third would have needed economic assistance when on shore, another third would have been self-sufficient but not by much, and the rest lived decently with a house and small lot. The way to wealth for them as seamen would be through investing some of their wages in trading stock, but as we see only a few did this, nor did they possess the necessary cash or credit. On the other hand three out of five did own at least one book.

[12] New London district probate records, 14:195.

TABLE 8.1
Inventoried Property of Sailors (cash)

Age at death		Marital status		£ Personal wealth		£ Real wealth	
Unknown	7	Unknown	2	Under 10	10	None	29
21–29	33	Single	44	10–19	9	1–19	8
30–39	13	Married, childless	4	20–29	13	20–39	2
40–49	3	Young fathers	4	30–39	9	40–59	4
50+	2	Older fathers	4	40–49	4	60–99	8
Total	58			50–59	2	100–199	7
				60–99	10		
				100+	1		

Books		Cash		Trading stock		Consumer goods £	Single men	Married men
Unknown	3	None	31	None	51	1–9	15	0
None	22	Under £1	8	1–4	0	10–19	15	4
Under £1	28	£1–9	11	5–9	1	20–39	11	3
£1	4	£10–19	4	10–19	5	40–49	1	2
£2	1	Over £20	4	20–29	1	50–59	2	0
% with	60					Median £	14	26

Just what "mariner" signified is obscure but it clearly brought more prestige. The first definition in the OED calls him a person who helped with the navigation of the ship, and our records show them as men of some property. However, since in this account a person of substance winds up with mariners rather than sailors the distinction rests more on idiosyncrasy than evidence, the mariner becoming simply a slightly glorified sailor. Thus Jabez Gray of Fairfield (1728-1760) died in Maryland of smallpox leaving an estate of £64 in personal property. What distinguished him (aside from 2 shillings' worth of snuff) is this entry: "1/4 sloop and 1/4 long boat as she came in from the voyage in which Gray died £22.10." Therefore he becomes a mariner, not a sailor.[13]

Mariners differ from sailors in that they showed signs of upward mobility, often belonged to a settled, even prominent family, and were seldom poor. The people who used the designation clearly intended to distinguish their man, or themselves, from a captain on the one hand and on the other from those not qualified. Out of twenty-one mariners two-thirds had married and they averaged ten years older

[13] Fairfield district probate records, 14:195.

than mere sailors. One indeed had reached ninety years and another was sixty, while two had turned farmers, all still referring to themselves as mariners though none any longer went to sea. Most of them owned sufficient personal property of between £50 and £100 and their household goods supported their families adequately. Six died landless but five left over forty acres and the rest had lived in a house with a small lot. Many invested in some trading stock, the expected foundation for economic success.

A typical mariner was Elisha Paine of Middletown, who married in 1747 and died seven years later. Paine owned a small lot in the town but not a house; he must have been renting. His estate came to £110 of which £47 was in the form of consumption goods. He had one Spanish dollar and some silver articles of the same value. His occupation shows up notably in a quadrant and compass and—what distinguishes him from the common seamen—166 gallons of rum and 100 pounds of sugar.[14]

Gamaliel Prince of Milford (d. 1717) is less typical but interesting. I do not know anything about the family other than that three died within a few years, all evidently single. Gamaliel left only £11 worth of consumption goods and no record of a marriage exists. He probably died at sea or shortly after his return, with the considerable sum in cash of £23 due him in wages. So far he seems just a sailor, but in addition he owned small shares of two sloops and a share in the cargo of one of them. He also had a bit of the ships' store consisting of beef, pork, and flour, and an interest in some slaves, probably being imported for sale: one-eighth of an Indian boy, one-eighth of an Indian woman, and all of a Negro boy. Finally, he had bought a "small" house and lot in town—a *very* small house, it would seem, for it and the lot came to £14. All this was however encumbered by a debt of about £80, reducing the net estate to £88. Not a bad start though, and Prince was on the verge of becoming either a land-based importer or the captain of that sloop.[15]

Ships' captains surely included some one-time ordinary mariners in addition to many other sorts of people. They were indeed a diverse lot. Some appear out of nowhere, dying by some mischance in Connecticut, even their marital status unknown. Thus we encounter a Capt. Daniel Goldsmith, designated a transient when he died in Milford in 1684, or Peter Demill, whose small vessel got as far as Stamford in 1722 and who owned some books in Dutch as well as English. On

[14] Middletown district probate records, 1:75.
[15] New Haven district probate records, 4:457.

the other hand, John Sellick of the same town belonged to an established family and left a large estate at his death in 1700.

During the first century of the colony's existence few ship's captains enter our view in probate court even though the records are quite complete. Connecticut was simply not a maritime colony then. Many men owned shares of ships, but when one adds up the shares they total just six full vessels before 1700 and only twenty more by 1730. Quite possibly other men sailed in command of vessels without calling themselves "captains," as in the case of Richard Whiddon, "mariner," who owned part of a sloop. Nathan Whelpley of New Haven, who died in Barbados in 1687, was called a ship master, and conceivably men only adopted the title when it became their full-time occupation. But that emphasizes the rarity of the occupation until well after Queen Anne's War. From that time on they appear in growing numbers even during peacetime, though obviously wars brought an increase both of opportunity and of inventories.

Some of these men seem only to have sailed a vessel from one port to another without investing anything in it or the voyage. Such captains were generally single and young. However, to depend entirely for one's livelihood upon wages received, while defensible for a bachelor, would not do for a family man or anyone seeking comfort and high status. The older captains bequeathed property that included investment capital in the form of trading stock, money, or debts receivable. These acted as agents for the merchants, seeking out the best markets and the cheapest products for the return voyages, buying and selling, collecting debts from previous ventures, obtaining bills of exchange, even arranging for the sale of the vessel itself. Such responsibilities brought higher pay, sometimes commissions, and the opportunity for trading on their own. The profits might lead presently to a full-time commercial business and to marrying into the best families back home, if they did not already belong to them.[16] Such captains were just as important to the economy as the merchants who provided most of the capital and ships, and the former might become the latter. Thus Norwalk's John Raymond (1693-1774) retired from the sea and settled down as a larger farmer to live in some luxury with the help of six slaves.[17]

As one might expect, the vocation required a physical vigor most

---

[16] I made a trial run through captains dying 1760-1774 based on a fair though far from expert knowledge of local families and found this division: no relations twelve (but four had married local women), ordinary families twenty-one, good ones fifteen, leading seven.

[17] Fairfield district probate records, 18:272, 370.

TABLE 8.2
Age at Death of Ships' Captains

	Pre-1730	1745–1774
Unknown	3	8
21–29	0	7
30–39	3	13
40–49	3	15
50–59	4	15
60–69	2	6
70+	2	5
Total	17	69

SOURCE: Estate inventories.

often possessed by youthful men. The median age at death of the captains, exclusive of those who had ceased active seafaring, was in the middle forties, which must mean that a majority of those living were in their twenties and thirties. This age structure is much lower than that of farmers, professionals, and most artisans; but one is impressed by the ability of the captains to survive as well as they did so hazardous an occupation.[18] Almost all of them had married by the time they assumed command of a vessel.

The opportunities for income beyond their wages were good enough so that the captains lived well. Four out of five owned some land, which might consist only of the house lot but usually enabled them to raise most of their own food, the median for the landowners being almost forty acres. Many had genuine farms to which they could retire when age or injury unfitted them for life at sea; four held large country estates of 200 acres. They had much more cash and silver than the norm, the mean being £21 and the median £5. Some owned part or even all of their ships. Half of the inventories list trading stock and nearly one-third include over £50 worth of articles for sale. Nearly half were creditors when they died, twice as many as left debts payable. One out of eight estates were insolvent, which seems a good record in view of the speculative nature of their careers. In general the captains who acquired above-average properties seldom succeeded while they remained commanders of ships but built upon that to become traders ashore.

[18] The unknown group of the early set were all young. The later ones, guessing from their property, were divided evenly among the age groups. If we assort them in this way the medians become 47 and 46 1/2, and if we eliminate those over 70, all of whom seem to have ceased active seafaring, both figures become 45.

The captains owned more books than one might expect, 84 percent having at least a Bible. One-fourth of the estates included more than £2 worth, which means a number, and a few had real libraries. Capt. Joseph Prince of Stratford (d. 1748) left £5 of books including law, history, and divinity, as well as some pictures and maps, while Richard Caldwell (d. 1755), also of Stratford, read Dryden and history. Nearly one-third owned slaves, a high percentage but average for our traders. Probably most of the slaves were house or personal servants.

A slaveowner who failed was Capt. Joshua Ray of New Haven (ca. 1720-1773). Ray left a personal estate of £249 including half of a sloop, a Negro girl, and £82 worth of sugar and molasses, but he also was indebted for £626, exceeding the total assets by £217, so that his wife and three children were left poor.[19] In contrast, 120 years earlier, Capt. John Peintre or Pantry died in Hartford. His father William, a joiner, had immigrated in 1634 and moved to Hartford two years later. He left the good estate of £708 cash including a solid farm, so that his only son John began with advantages. Of him we know that he became a freeman in 1650 and left a son, a daughter, and a pregnant wife, so that he must have been around age thirty at death. John inherited the farm and tools, tripled the livestock, and added "servants." We would not know that he had been a captain if the probate court had not obliged.[20]

Ebenzer Riley of New Haven (1748-1773) did not enjoy such advantages but was on the way up when he died at twenty-five. He owned a sloop and presumably had imported in it his £70 worth of rum, sugar, and brandy. He also owned a quadrant, a silver watch, two pictures, £9 worth of clothing and 3 shillings in books, and no land, but £57 in consumer goods for a wife to appreciate, had he lived to wed.[21]

The Sellick family furnish a different record. David immigrated in 1633, became a trader out of Boston, and died in Virginia in 1654 leaving an inventory barely above his debts and two sons, Major Jonathan (1641-1713) and Captain John (ca. 1646-1689), both of Stamford. The latter died a French prisoner. We have his inventory from 1700 valued at £2,367 probably in pay (the appraisers did not make this clear). Of this, half consisted of real estate, a considerable property. He also owned a half-share in two servants and three slaves, a

<hr />

[19] See the list of Ray's creditors in New Haven district probate records, 12:28.

[20] Hartford district probate records 4:311, 6:144. The alternate spelling of Peintre, together with the immigrant's considerable estate and his skill as a joiner, suggest a French Huguenot origin.

[21] New Haven district probate records, 11:426.

trading stock of dry goods, enough money in cash for an ordinary man's entire personal estate, £3 worth of books, and a flourishing farm. His nephew Jonathan also became a ship's captain, dying in 1711 at forty-six. He too owned an excellent farm, probably well over 100 acres, and a personal estate of £218. The property included a Negro woman, a silver-headed staff and a silver-hilted sword, a silver tankard and spoons, and as evidence of his occupation a sea quadrant. Since he had served as a justice of the peace and deputy in the legislature, the almost insolvent immigrant had produced some winners, with the help of two capable women, the daughters of Richard Law.[22]

As these illustrations suggest, captains acquired large properties in one of two ways: some inherited it and the others became traders as well as mariners. Of those who left personal estates under £100, only one in five owned stock in trade, but of the prosperous men with £500 or more all but one out of seventeen did so. Put differently, the trader-captains left nearly £400 in personal estates while those who remained only captains were worth just over £100. In business lay the path to wealth.

That fact places the merchants at the top of the economic order. These men consisted primarily of the importers and exporters but also included the extensive inland traders, who sometimes doubled as moneylenders in addition to their wholesale business. As we have seen, their activities covered a wide geographical area and required both a substantial investment of their own capital and credit obtained from their suppliers. For most of them the rewards exceeded the risk. Failure came usually when young men obtained credit without enough of their own capital and were caught with large inventories at a time of declining purchasing power. The older merchants commonly avoided these calamities or perhaps had just lucked out; in any case they became large propertyowners and eminent men.

The eminence, curiously, did not extend to positions of leadership. During the seventeenth century only one-sixth achieved the offices of status discussed in the next chapter, and thereafter one out of four. Those that did so commonly came from prominent local families, which they themselves sometimes had helped to found. They often owned land and almost always held large estates even for merchants. Yet mere possession of substantial property did not predict such high rank, for out of fifty-seven wealthy men thirty-seven—nearly two-thirds—never received such a recognition. It is tempting to conclude that the people held merchants or wealth in low esteem, but in fact they did select

[22] Fairfield district probate records, 5:15, 181.

both types; one out of three isn't bad. Without eliminating this factor we suggest that businessmen, like craftsmen, could not readily leave someone else in charge while they attended to other duties: trade required their full-time personal attention. In other colonies as well they tended to leave noncommercial affairs to others. Also, while some of them may have preferred private matters to public interest they did not necessarily sacrifice their influence, which might be exerted in private ways. For what it is worth the newspapers, at least, treated them with great respect and, we repeat, some did hold important positions and most did belong to prestigious families.

The merchants started business when young as did the ships' captains, but whereas the latter tended to leave their jobs as they grew older, the merchants (excepting the bankrupts) continued until they retired. It was highly profitable. The median personal wealth was £490, the mean £875, very high for the colony. Only two young single men left personal estates of under £50 and only a dozen less than £100; we have almost twice that number with over £2,000. So many of them owned large personal properties that the top 10 percent held only 38 percent of the total value.

Most merchants lived well. The median for consumption goods was £108, and very few failed to achieve an adequate level, the dependents being, as usual, young: indeed, four-fifths were well-off. Among those with teen-age or older children, a third owned over £200 in consumption goods and even more had £100-199. Grandfathers, exclusive of a few retired men, enjoyed an equal amount, enabling most of them to live as close to luxury as Connecticut circumstances and attitudes allowed.[23]

All but 12 percent of the merchants owned at least a little land, three out of five held forty acres, two out of five had eighty, and 30 percent at least two hundred: they were, in short, large landowners both by inheritance and investment. This land, of course, supported livestock, £22 worth on the average. Twenty-four of them had upwards of £100 worth, by Connecticut standards a sizable number of at least fifty animals, so that two out of five could legitimately be called merchant-farmers.

The merchants also left to the heirs substantial sums of money in cash and debts, or assets in the form of ships, stock in trade, and servants, which collectively accounted for most of their personal property. As in the case of shopkeepers, debts receivable totaled nearly half of all personal estates. Only a minority of the inventories listed none,

[23] See Appendix 8A.

and over £200 worth was usual. Indeed, twenty-four persons left £1,000 or more. This included several individuals living in the interior of the colony who acted really as bankers to a wide area. Again most of them had silver or cash, commonly both, with a mean value of £75; and while none rivaled President Stiles, they probably made better use of this capital. Their stock in trade, by definition, formed a crucial element not only in their own wealth but also in that of the colony, each having for sale £145 worth or, excluding the 25 percent who at their death owned none, £184. This is surprisingly little, considering that these men included the leading importers, and we may speculate first that some of those with none had felt death at hand and tried to leave their families with the maximum ready cash, while others were at one extreme of the cycle in which they had disposed of their commodities without yet replenishing their shelves. Nevertheless, the large number of rather small importers, spread over diverse towns, emphasize both the degree of the colony's independence and the absence of economic concentration. The same consideration applies to ships, for only two of these men left over £500 in vessels, three out of five owned none, and the mean was just £35. In this case, properties clustered between £20 and £100.

These assets may convey some notion of the income merchants earned. The sale of stock, on our assumption stated earlier, would bring in £145. Let us assume that debts payable equaled debts receivable, so that these cancel out. Thirty acres of land would bring in a pound per acre, less whatever the owner had to pay hired workers, which probably means that he obtained food and firewood, but no cash. If ships earned as much as stock, £35 would come from that. All this may total £200, which would put the average merchant rather below the level of a respectable Bostonian (as reflected in a famous newspaper debate), comfortable but certainly not luxurious.[24]

Perhaps because their sons and daughters would not normally help with the farm or other tasks, and as men of a cosmopolitan upper class, they bought more slaves than any other occupational group, nearly half owning at least one, even including the pre-1700 merchants. By the final decade two-thirds had become slaveowners. Just one-third of the slaves were grown men who would return a profit from their labor, if they were so used. One-fifth were adult women, doubtless house-servants, one-fourth were boys, one-sixth girls, and a few were children. In all, males outnumbered females by a little more than three to two. Clearly these servants did not pay their way, since

[24] See my *Social Structure of Revolutionary America* (Princeton, 1965), 118-20.

few could have been used for productive purposes and any appreciation in value or accretions by birth would be almost equaled by maintenance or deaths. And indeed, the less prosperous merchants seldom bought them, the dividing line being a personal estate of £500, above which 70 percent of the inventories included slaves, below which only 13 percent did so.

Since the merchants possessed a surplus income, did they buy books? Yes, though not as many as one might expect, nothing to compare with ministers. All but 11 percent owned at least one, but the median was only a pound's worth, which a good Bible and a psalmbook might account for. If £5 denotes a respectable library—almost all ministers had that—then one out of six possessed one, but no more than six individuals, 4 percent of the total, equaled even the median of the ministers and just two individuals owned truly notable collections: John Eliot of Windsor (1667-1719), a minister's son, and John Richards of New London (1687-1765), a justice of the peace, who had built his own library.[25]

We should, however, add that after 1700 some of these men began to buy pictures. The merchant Alexander Allin of Windsor (d. 1708) probably brought along one of the royal couple, William and Mary, when he immigrated in 1689; it was worth nearly a pound. Four years later Jonathan Bidwell's Hartford inventory listed two dozen at 12 shillings and "more" for another 24, both in "money." In the same year, Thomas Trowbridge of New Haven left four valued at 10 shillings. John Gardner's New London estate of 1725 included fourteen for a pound in cash and one worth all the rest combined. The wealthy merchant James Dennie owned or was offering for sale sixteen large pictures in gilt frames at 4 shillings each, plus four smaller ones for half that price, in 1759. The retired ship's captain John Easton of Middletown owned, in 1774, twenty-six glass-framed pictures valued between 3 and 6 shillings each, one of Boston, another of the St. Lawrence River, and two family pictures worth £12, thus claiming the record. However, the estate of Nicholas Hallam of New London had contained more—thirty-four—a few years earlier. The ten "glass pictures" in frames owned by Crafts Wright of Wethersfield (d. 1766) totaled only 16 shillings 8 pence.

Since the wealthiest merchants belong among the colony's leaders to be considered in our next chapter, we here illustrate their characteristics by men close to the average, rather than the most successful.

---

[25] His father Lieutenant John, another merchant, left a sizable estate but only about a pound's worth of books. New London district probate records, B:388.

We begin with Mr. William Gibbons who died in Hartford in 1655 leaving a widow, two young daughters, and a teen-aged boy, who all moved to Boston. Gibbons, presumably born at least by 1613 and probably by 1610, began life in the colony as the agent of Governor Wyllys, immigrating in 1636 to prepare for his employer's arrival. His estate of £900 net included extensive tracts of undeveloped land and what must have been a large farm in Hartford, probably over eighty acres, with livestock in proportion. He also had two male servants, debts receivable exceeding debts payable by £20, a small quantity of English goods on hand and, most interestingly, the value of "an Adventure to Ginny at present uncertain but conceived to be" £100 in his money, or £70 in cash. Incidentally he left land to a Latin school. Consumption articles totaled a very comfortable £139.[26]

Death took Daniel Hall (ca. 1645-1675) in Barbados before he could realize his potential, but he left his young New Haven wife £350. In his home town he had built a house and a warehouse on two acres of meadow, on which he pastured one cow. The personal estate of £275 included £119 in consumption goods, among which were three beds and fourteen-and-a-half pairs of sheets. In addition, the wreck of his ketch was worth £5, he had 3,500 pounds of sugar due him in Barbados, a parcel of goods imported from England was still at Boston, another parcel was in New Haven, and he had a considerable amount of cloth, probably for sale, the stock totaling £97. He owed £24 but was a creditor for £50.[27]

Jonathan Bidwell of Hartford was about Hall's age but more advanced economically, having inherited some property from his father John and again when his mother died. He and his twenty-one-year-old wife had only a baby girl, and she therefore inherited the £1,400 estate in 1712.[28] Bidwell owned a farm of probably sixty acres, a share in a cider mill and sawmill, a shop containing over £500 in goods including 200 brooms, a vessel with its rigging, and considerable book debts. His £127 in consumption goods was more than ample, but some of that may have been for sale, including perhaps the three or four dozen pictures mentioned above.

Like many men near the median, Richard Rosewell of Branford died comparatively young, at about thirty-seven, leaving £973 to his wife and children. Rosewell (ca. 1665-1702) also owned a farm of which about 40 acres were improved and 186 remained wild. Perhaps as the

26 Hartford district probate records, 2:115.
27 New Haven district probate records, 1:172.
28 See his will in Manwaring, II, 156.

only surviving son of William, Esquire (1634-1694) and his wife, the daughter of Hon. Richard Russell of Boston, Rosewell had an exceptional amount of plate, probably eighty-seven ounces, and cash identified as Boston, Spanish, and Old England money, plus some gold. Along with a half-share in a brigantine he owned sailcloth, a quadrant, and a large map, and had imported tar, salt, rum, and molasses. His consumption goods of £163 included four beds, fifteen-and-a-half pairs of sheets, fifteen pillowbiers, and £5 worth of books. He also owned a Negro man and £105 in debts receivable, owing none.[29]

The inventory of Nicholas Hallam is notable partly for the pictures but also for children's toys. Hallam was the second of two sons of John of Barbados, whose widow married the well-to-do merchant John Livien, inheriting one-third of his property in 1689. Nicholas probably started as a hatter, for his inventory still contained £8 worth of the tools for that craft, which he willed to his second son. In 1686, at twenty-one, he married young Sarah Pygan, whose father Alexander died in 1701 leaving nearly £2,000 and no sons. Nicholas therefore became a merchant with a warehouse and wharf, built a fine house valued at £275 with its barn, well, and one-and-a-half-acre lot, and was worth about £1,200 net in 1714 when he died, aged forty-nine. By that time Sarah had died and he had married Elizabeth, whose last name we do not know. He still had some of his first wife's clothes and £36 worth of his own, supplementing that evidence of prosperity with a £9 clock, the pictures, 126 ounces of silver, and a Negro woman. He and his wife and five children had five beds among them and there were also two cheap ones at 7 shillings each, one probably for the slave. The shop goods included rum and molasses. The inventory also listed £154 worth of the colony's bills of credit and he had invested in 500 acres of land, not evaluated. Of the children, incidentally, the first, a sailor, died young and poor, but the destined hatter, Edward, had two sons who in turn became prosperous merchants. Nicholas's elder brother John also married young, left a good estate that his son Amos increased, acquiring over £5,000 by the time of his death at age forty. He had become a farmer.[30]

We conclude with an older man whose personal property fell close to the median but whose real estate and diversified activities reflects a subspecies of the merchants, or perhaps of which they formed a subspecies—the entrepreneur. James Smedley's father Samuel was obscure, but had the good sense to marry a daughter of Capt. Moses

[29] New Haven district probate records, 2:284.
[30] New London district probate records, B:88, 106.

297

Dimon, all of whose four sons became leaders of Fairfield. James himself (1705-1771) married at twenty-six Jane Sturgis, of good family, and later married the widow of his maternal grandfather, a daughter of Col. John Burr. He also became a colonel and—what with one thing and another—left £2,741 in property even after endowing his three children.[31]

Smedley's mercantile side was limited by this time—he was sixty-six—to shares of a wharf and sloop, and either he owned £422 worth of consumption goods, which is exceedingly unlikely, or he had some of that for sale. He also owned a mill in New Milford, a blacksmith's shop, and a mortgage for £48. The inventory itemizes for us 377 acres of land, of which half remained undeveloped and 83 was quite valuable, the remainder consisting of woodland but even that worth £5 per acre. He kept no more than the normal livestock but had raised a considerable crop, notably sixty-five bushels of wheat. The value of the real property totaled nearly £1,900. He owned only a few books, including, however, Virgil and Ovid, and he also had bought three Negro men, a woman, a boy, and a riding chair—by now a familiar article in the larger towns among men of Smedley's class. When the reader recalls that these sketches describe average merchants, with properties near the median for their occupation, their economic importance becomes obvious.

The picture of Connecticut traders that emerges from this survey shows the great variety of what we today would call the businessmen. We can, however, generalize about them with reference to men of other occupations. By comparison with farmers and professionals they died young, at an average age of forty-seven, and three out of five were under forty compared with the farmers' two out of five. Three reasons account for this difference. Many of the traders could enter the field with small amounts of capital, as was true of peddlers, mariners, and ships' captains, or could borrow readily. The hazards of seafaring must have lowered their life expectancy. Finally, they confronted the danger of business failure: the loss of a ship, a glutted market, a depression, the bankruptcy of a debtor, which must have made retirement seem attractive. Among farmers we found that one out of eight were over sixty, but only half as many traders belonged to that age group. Early death can account for only a part of this, and clearly many merchants, shopkeepers, and ships' captains invested their capital in a secure form, usually land, and lived peacefully.

They could afford this partial withdrawal because of the considera-

[31] Fairfield district probate records, 23:128.

ble property they accumulated. We do not know their income but can examine its results. Their mean personal wealth of around £500 cash during the early 1700s reached £615 for the years 1760-1774 while the median overall was £250. Seventy-percent of this property consisted of debts receivable, money, trading stock, and ships. If one reduced their personal estates by that amount they did not own any more than other people, but after all most of that sum earned money for them, thus placing the successful traders at the very apex of the economic pyramid.

The traders, like other men, increased their wealth with age, the difference lying in the heights at the top. Large personal estates appear even before 1700 when ten individuals owned half of the traders' total, five men being worth over £2,000 each. Such opportunities continued through the colonial period and must have lured many farm lads and artisans' sons to the trading towns. While they could not reasonably aspire to James Dennie's £6,656, the chance of reaching a comfortable £200, exclusive of realty, were very good indeed: three to two for men in their forties, three to one for the fifty-year-olds, and even better than that for still older men. If the ownership of £500 in personal wealth qualified a man as well-to-do, 30 percent of the traders belong to that economic class.

Since so large a proportion of this wealth was in capital and money, we need to ask about consumption goods as evidence of the traders' standard of living. Appendix 8B presents the data from inventories. Table 8.4 shows the high level reached during the seventeenth century, which remained unchanged thereafter. Yet the wealthy did not indulge

TABLE 8.3
Personal Wealth, Traders, 1745–1774 (cash)

Age	20–29	30–39	40–49	50–59	60–69	70+	Total	%
1–49	4	2	2	0	0	0	8	4.2
50–99	7	13	5	4	3	1	33	17.2
100–199	8	12	8	5	2	2	37	19.3
200–299	4	6	6	5	3	2	26	13.5
300–399	2	4	5	1	3	3	18	9.4
400–499	2	4	2	4	0	1	13	6.8
500–999	1	7	6	8	7	3	32	16.7
1000+	1	2	5	10	4	3	25	13.0
Total	29	50	39	37	22	15	192	100.1
Median £	140	180	267	475	450	367	270	

SOURCE: Estate inventories.

TABLE 8.4
Standard of Living, Traders, Seventeenth Century

	Single & Retired	Young fathers	Older fathers	Total	%
Poor	3	0	0	3	4.0
Subsistence	1	0	0	1	1.4
Subsistence plus	0	2	2	4	5.4
Comfortable	3	5	3	11	14.9
Well-off	11	11	8	30	40.5
Luxury £100	0	8	10	18	24.3
Luxury £200	0	0	7	7	9.5
Total	18	26	30	74	100.0

in conspicuous display. The number of really elegantly furnished homes in Connecticut, as we noticed in discussing professional men, was quite small. In the last fifteen years among 136 traders' estates entering probate only 8 contained more than £300 in consumer goods and none with over £500, except perhaps that of Nicholas Hallam—it is hard in his case to distinguish what he was selling from what he used. Probably none envied the comfort of Capt. Nathaniel Hooker of so admirable a family, though the Scottish and perhaps part-French immigrant and slave-trader Dr. Normand Morison may have caused some resentment by his home's rich furnishings. Within this occupational group we may guess that most of the poor regarded their positions as temporary, quite reasonably, since they did not expect to die and few who reached middle age failed to attain financial security.

The possession of books is the best evidence we have of the education and intellectual level of Connecticut's people. While mariners and peddlers might be excused from possessing more than the almost obligatory Bible, most traders could well afford to buy some. Public officials averaged £2 worth, doctors £2.10, lawyers £5, but the traders invested scarcely £1. While a steady 85 percent owned at least one, the great majority had only a few, a decent library of £5 belonged only to one out of ten, and a really respectable collection to a handful. It is true that one did not need a formal education to succeed in business, but the colony needed educated and literate businessmen to support a culture. Before 1700 twenty-one traders left estates exceeding £500 in personal wealth, just two of whom had £10 in books—James Wadsworth and Governor Theophilus Eaton. Between 1700 and 1730, forty-four men owning that £500, of whom nineteen exceeded £1,000, included only five individuals with books valued at £10, one of them a Scottish immigrant and another a French newcomer, René Grignon, called "Gentleman" apparently in this case with some excuse for it. Even the final fifteen years, when colonial culture presumably reached its height, offer little evidence for educational aspirations among Connecticut's businessmen. Of twenty-one persons with over £1,000 in personal wealth, a third owned less than £2 worth of books and only three had over £10. Even if some of the heirs liberated a few that is not a distinguished showing, especially when we remember that it included men from the principal towns. One of the three largest again belonged to an immigrant, Capt. Samuel Lancelot of Wethersfield. The best we can say is that a few men did own evidences, or remembrances of education, as in the case of young William Gardiner of Hartford with Homer, Ovid, and Pope; Capt. John Coleman of the same city with Chambers's *Dictionary* and the *Independent Whig*; James Smedley's Virgil and Ovid; and George Mumford's books on history and geography, Swift, and Milton. But Mumford belonged to a Rhode Island family, and Capt. Richard Nicholas may have picked up his *Independent Whig, Spectator, Gulliver's Travels*, and Ovid on his voyages to New York City. That is the best we can do!

The traders differed from the rest of the colonists in the quantity of money that they had available, consisting of silver, cash, debts receivable, and also in the capital peculiar to their business: stock in trade. Money formed half of their total personal wealth, slightly less before 1750, slightly more thereafter. Silver and cash, the more readily convertible form, averaged £43, but during periods when paper money did not circulate, only £24. That is still a considerable sum, far more than other men possessed. How representative our decedents are of traders in general we cannot know because, in addition to the inherent age bias, we may be dealing with men who, feeling themselves ailing, chose to retain an abnormal part of their assets in fluid form rather than reinvesting it. In any case the sum is impressive. The median fell much lower—about £7, but possessing even that amount of ready money put traders in a class almost by themselves, rivaled only by professional men.[32] The ownership of cash and silver was widespread, with four out of five leaving at least a little to their heirs. The true proportion was surely higher since a widow or a child could easily secrete a few coins and perhaps claim the silver spoon. One cannot believe that Governors Thomas Welles and Stephen Goodyear, both dying in their primes with substantial estates, were (so to speak) penniless. We may also surmise outright robbery in the case of mariners dying at sea, though most of these were indeed credited with some

[32] See Appendix 8C.

cash. Otherwise, men without any money included principally the young and retired. Another 20 percent owned less than £5 and a nearly equal group £5 to £10, which may represent a desirable sum for current expenses such as cash purchases or payments to employees, doctors, lawyers, innkeepers, or tax collectors.

The larger amounts reflect the peaks and valleys of the business year. More than one out of four inventories listed £50 worth and one in ten, £100. Very few men would save so much in silver or retain so much idle cash. Rather, as we know, traders would invest their capital and draw upon their credit for as many ventures as possible, diversifying their activities in order to limit risk in the days before insurance. The profit from such an enterprise as a voyage to the West Indies or the sale of trading stock would create a temporary surge in financial assets followed by a gradual reduction as men paid their debts and spent or reinvested their earnings. Thus the estate inventories catch traders at various stages of their private business activities. We might eliminate the age effect and omit peddlers, mariners, innkeepers, and ships' captains, retaining only the mature active wholesalers and retailers in order to study their cash holdings during the first and last periods when no paper money circulated. Table 8.5 shows their silver and cash extending from zero to £231. Both median and mean were twice that of all the traders. While the very largest holdings belonged exclusively to men with exceptional estates of £500, sometimes these died with quite small sums. A rather unfair example is that of John Hazzard, whose Fairfield estate in 1771 included £3,505 in personal property and who had accumulated upwards of 300 acres of land, but only £4.5 in silver articles and no cash at all!—doubtless a momentary situation, for he was a large creditor, with stock, a slave, and a sloop.[33]

Debts receivable particularly distinguish the most extensive traders,

TABLE 8.5
Cash of Active Traders Aged Forty to Sixty-nine,
1660–1699 and 1760–1774

£	N	%	£	N	%
None	5	8.6	50–99	8	13.8
1–9	19	32.8	100–199	8	13.8
10–19	7	12.1	Total	58	100.1
20–49	11	19.0			

[33] Fairfield district probate records, file no. 2817.

running as they sometimes did well over a thousand pounds.[34] Among
the traders generally, half had none at all, and in this case we cannot
suspect any theft, though there may be something wrong with the
recordkeeping. A small group left only a few pounds' worth of property in this form, but the sums then rise rapidly. Over one man in four
held £100 and 6 percent more than £1,000. As we have seen, where
the clerks of the court recorded debts payable the balance sheet showed
an equality between assets and liabilities, so that full information would
reduce their economic advantage over other colonists.

The value of stock in trade and of ships totaled half of debts receivable, and, indeed, traders owned as much stock as the generality of
citizens did of total personal wealth.[35] Almost by definition most of
them sold something—the little articles of a peddler, food and drink
of the innkeepers, drugs of the apothecary on up to the costly and
varied contents of the wholesaler's warehouse. In 1690 Roger Hooker,
grandson of the founder, offered in his Farmington store a typical
variety, especially rum, sugar, and powder, and his inventory also listed
furs, flax, and pork, presumably paid to him by local customers and
intended for export.[36] During the seventeenth century when, as we
know, we have inventories of the estates left by most men, only ten
out of seventy-four traders owned no stock; the mean value was £103
cash and 30 percent were selling goods worth over £100. These seem
large sums compared with the personal wealth commanded by ordinary folk in the colony, but the profits from such an investment, even
if turned over three times a year, would permit no more than a decent
living. Basically Connecticut's traders were small operators with limited amounts of risk capital. Among nearly 400 men only 2 owned
stock worth over £1,000, both in the seventeenth century—Richard
Bryan of Milford and John Livien of New London. Eleven others had
£500 or more, namely Jonathan Bidwell of Hartford in 1712, James
Ward of Middleton in 1757, and after that date four Hartford merchants plus one each from New Haven, Durham, Milford, New London, and Windham. As much as any other piece of evidence this illustrates the limited scope of the traders' business activity and their wide
geographical distribution, in sharp contrast to the concentration in
most other northern colonies.[37]

[34] See Appendix 8C.

[35] Ibid.

[36] Hartford district probate records, 6:35-36.

[37] However, half of the stock belonged to the top 10 percent of the owners. There is
no reason to believe that an unusual proportion of large businessmen escaped the probate courts; indeed, if anything the reverse was true during the final period because of

Ships contributed less than any other form of income-producing property, but the colony's ownership of these, such as they were, helped to avoid or limit an unfavorable balance of trade. During the seventeenth century only one-fifth of the traders owned some part of a vessel but by the end one-fourth did so, and the average value of the investment had tripled. However, one would not expect peddlers and shopkeepers to invest in that way. If we consider only the more extensive merchants and their like, two out of five possessed some part of a ship at the time of their death.

The size of the vessels rose substantially though they seldom exceeded £200 in value. Before 1700 the only reference to a large ship appears in the inventory of Hartford's Richard Lord, who in addition to an eighth interest in a ship valued at £168 had invested £86 in a one-sixteenth share (type unspecified), which would mean a total value of £1,376 cash. Otherwise the cost of sloops averaged £100, higher than two ketches but below two pinks. Fourteen traders owned, adding all their shares, sixteen parts of seven vessels plus two being built and a ketch wrecked at Barbados, the owner dying with it.

Between 1700 and 1729, forty-five individuals had shares in thirty-seven vessels, the value of which ranged from three scows at £5 apiece through the sloops with a median value of £118, on up to three brigs worth £140, £260, and £264. Once again the shipowners did not or could not invest all their capital in a single venture but bought as little as one-sixteenth. Thus the most considerable fleet, that belonging to Capt. Joseph Sexton of Stonington (1656-1715), consisted of one-sixteenth of a brig (£6.10), one-fourth of a brig (perhaps the same one), one-fourth of a sloop, and one-half of a sloop. However, Jonathan Bull of Hartford (1649-1702) himself owned a sloop worth nearly £100 and Stonington's John Hallam had one almost twice as valuable. Data for the years 1745-1775 simply confirm the general situation. The value and presumably the size of the ships continued to increase. The median cost of thirty-seven sloops rose to almost £200, one reaching £448, exceeded only by a 180-ton brig worth £517 and another valued at £600. Despite the larger tonnage, Connecticut-owned vessels remained small, clearly intended for the coastal trade or at most that with the West Indies.

New London newspapers during 1760 and 1761 convey some idea of the colony's shipping. These show more clearances for the Caribbean than for any other area—36 percent. New York City ranked sec-

their debts, owing and owed. Our coverage here omits some commercial centers but in no greater degree than other towns.

ond with 30 percent and Boston a poor third with 12 percent. More-over, since the Caribbean was much farther it must have involved far larger and perhaps more numerous ships. From that point of view the trade with northern ports, notably Halifax but including Falmouth and Newfoundland, collectively 13 percent, may have exceeded that with Boston. Another significant group sailed for the Chesapeake area and a scattering intended for diverse ports in Guinea, the Canaries, Quebec, New Jersey, and Honduras. Only 4 out of 359 went to New-port and 2 to New Haven, which perhaps means only that the boats used locally did not attract notice in the press. Of course, not all of these ships involved New Londoners. The names of their captains and such cargoes as the inventories mention indicate that New Yorkers controlled the trade with their city, but the commerce with the West Indies was a Connecticut affair. In this trade, as we know, the mer-chants exported the colony's surplus in exchange for commodities either consumed locally or processed and reexported, all crucial to the econ-omy.

Slaves were also important to the traders, who owned relatively more than any other occupational group except for the principal officials and perhaps ministers. We cannot always distinguish with certainty blacks imported as part of the trading stock from personal servants, but ap-parently about a third of the traders bought one for their own use. The number per inventory rose over time until at the end of the colo-nial period slaves equaled decedents and the mean value per inventory had reached £30, the same as the investment in livestock. As remarked earlier, only about one-third of these were adult men so that most of the traders were buying not profitable laborers, but household help.

During the seventeenth century fifteen persons out of seventy-four had purchased one or more. All the owners, with a single exception, were substantial men and slavery obviously had not become a common affair. Major investments began with the new century. During the first thirty years one-third of the estates listed some variety of servant and display of a slave became almost obligatory for men with personal wealth over £1,000. Half of those with £400 to £999 also owned at least one but the proportion then drops abruptly. Not until mid-cen-tury do we find a few genuine slave-traders. Thomas Goodwin of Mid-dletown had owned a one-sixteenth share of a sloop's cargo consisting of a woman, boy, child, and half of a boy and girl, totaling £125. This was in 1752, ten years before Dr. Norman Morison died in Hartford with an entire cargo of new Negroes from Africa. It seems certain that some slaves arrived on ships returning from the West Indies but cas-ually rather than systematically. Throughout the colonial period a majority of these people became household or personal servants. However, the adult men commonly belonged to traders who owned mills, warehouses, or large farms, and so ended as laborers performing heavy lifting and hauling or as field hands.

The traders invested no more in farm animals than in slaves, but the former were surely of greater economic importance. Three-fourths of our men had at least some livestock, the exceptions being young, retired, immigrants, peddlers, or ships' captains. The last were most apt to get along without so much as a horse or a cow, especially if they had no family to care for while they were off at sea. The absence of such animals will seem normal to present-day readers, who will be surprised rather by the number of traders with considerable herds of cattle, especially since they were townspeople. Some indeed could easily turn into country squires and very likely many so considered themselves. Those with over £200 worth included the second Richard Lord, Jonathan Sturgis of Fairfield, John Hallam of Stonington, Jonathan Prentiss of New London, Nathan Bennet of Stratford, and Theophilus Morgan of Killingworth, all except perhaps Sturgis primarily merchants. For such men raising livestock may have acted as a hedge against business reverses, enabled them to supply their ships with meat for consumption, and was a profitable investment considered by itself. The increasing population density in the commercial towns did not affect the habit at all; indeed, the distribution of livestock just before the Revolution was almost identical to that of the seventeenth century.[38]

Raising livestock and the purchase of land go together, and in colonial Connecticut practically anyone who could, did both. Indeed, prosperous traders bought a great deal. Several motives account for this. They may have been searching for status, seeing as did many Americans some peculiar virtue in owning a farm, though that admiration for the yeoman may have been stronger among farmers than others. They may have supposed that such a purchase would compensate for a lack of prestige associated with business, as was true in England. In the colonies, however, traders probably did not suffer such prejudice, and besides, mere possession of a farm did not automatically lead to positions of leadership: traders held offices of honor as often as did farmers. Other considerations probably were more influential. Since trade was so risky, the purchase of a farm secured a family's economic future, a sensible diversification of capital. Aside from the food and profits, it helped to counteract inflation because the value of farm products rose in unison with other prices and that of land appreciated

[38] See Appendix 8C.

more rapidly. In addition one could, during most of the colonial period, buy unimproved land for a low price. Since no tax was levied on this, the owner could retain it at no cost other than the loss of return on capital. Also he might rent it, benfiting from the improvements, and pass it on to a son who displayed no talent in business, or retire to a working farm, incidentally sheltered from the diseases of trading towns. If land conferred added prestige, so much the better, but he had reason enough without that.

During the seventeenth century we need not ask why a man owned land but why he did not. Usually such a person was young and single, or old and retired, or an outsider who did not yet merit a division from the town or did not intend to settle down. Of our traders, only 18 percent owned none, almost all of whom are accounted for by one of these reasons. Another 30 percent had just the few acres of a house lot, enough for a garden and orchard, a cow or horse. The rest—half—owned at least twenty acres and often the forty needed for a farm. Twelve persons, or one out of six, had upwards of 200 acres, some of which consisted of unoccupied tracts.

The ensuing boom after 1715 enabled the traders to continue their purchases and if we look only at the heads of families we would suppose ourselves dealing with well-to-do farmers. The median acreage during this period was around 150 and 40 percent held upwards of 200, much, to be sure, unimproved. Two-thirds owned the adequate farm of forty acres and half of the rest had at least twenty. They thus supplied their own food and earned at least some profit. Some had invested in really large tracts for Connecticut, nine men owning upwards of a thousand acres.

Even when the great age of speculation subsided the traders retained large improved estates. During the final twenty years the distribution of land among traders of all sorts is shown in Table 8.6. The median was nearly twenty acres and of those with some land, forty. Once again

TABLE 8.6
Acres Owned, Traders, 1750–1774

Acres	N	%	Acres	N	%
None	38	20.2	80–119	15	8.0
1–19	44	23.4	120–199	18	9.6
20–39	30	16.0	200–499	19	10.1
40–79	16	8.5	500+	8	4.3
			Total	188	100.1

the transient mariners, peddlers, and ships' captains account for half of the landless and a fourth of those with the smallest properties. The settled members of the community invested in or inherited quite nice farms, four out of ten owning eighty acres or more. By this time fewer had bought speculative tracts, the price of which was less attractive. The Scottish doctor Norman Morison, however, owned 1,100 such acres along with 265 of improved land. Maj. Josiah Griswold had 1,268 all told, John Morton of Wethersfield 1,265 of which 985 remained undeveloped, and Elisha Hurlbut of Windham probably 500, most of which was presumably wild land. If we suppose that twenty acres would suffice for a nonfarm family, three-fourths of the mature residents were buying land as an investment over and above their own needs. We can interpret the consequences of this in various ways, among them an integration of traders into the community of farmers, as opposed to their forming a separate class of capitalists, especially since many of them originated from farm families.

The last four chapters have described certain attributes of the five major occupational groups: laborers, farmers, artisans, professionals, and traders. Each of these included subspecies that differed from one another, sometimes greatly, yet each also possessed a certain unity not only in type of work but also in the process by which the members moved within the group, as the starting farmer grew into the fully established one. Having supplied much detail, we now aggregate to focus on a few outstanding characteristics of the five.

First we note the two types of income-producing assets in land and personal estate. The great majority of Connecticut's families owned land. Servants and slaves, of course, did not. However, even among the free laborers, some of whom were heads of households, about half had at least a few acres. More than four out of five artisans and traders owned some, as did nearly nine out of ten professionals and, obviously, almost all farmers. The possession of a few acres, which continued nearly universal until the end of the colonial period, relieved most families of any danger from lack of food, and surely also provided enough for the laborers who worked for landowners. Even many who held little property, including townspeople, could raise food crops and keep a few farm animals on their three-acre "home lots." This self-sufficiency enabled the colony to export considerable quantities of food, even some grains from favored areas, but mostly pork and beef. With the local population thus fed, farmers could turn their attention to other needed or desirable crops such as flax, wool, and tobacco; while agricultural byproducts included leather, tallow, and cider.

In addition, aside from the laborers, not far from two-fifths of the

men other than farmers and nearly three-quarters of the farmers themselves had a genuine farm of at least forty acres, or, put another way,
exclusive of the laborers not far from three out of five men owned
farms adequate to support their families, and even a few laborers did
so. However, large landed properties, say 200 acres, were less common, being owned more often by professional men and traders than
by farmers themselves. This resulted from the obstacles limiting "plantation" style agriculture, so that properties in excess of 200 acres almost always included extensive undeveloped tracts, sometimes a form
of investment, but also to provide for children and security in one's
old age, capable of improvement or sale as needed. To be exact, 15
percent of the farmers, 6 percent of the artisans, 21 percent of traders,
and an impressive 34 percent of professionals owned such large farms.
Indeed, the median land of the professionals equaled that of farmers—
sixty-seven acres, with the traders and artisans trailing.[39]

To study productive personal property we add up cash, livestock,
tools, stock, ships, and debts receivable. Once again laborers owned
little. Servants and slaves by definition held virtually none, nor did
seven out of ten free workers, though the rest averaged some £30
each. The mean for farmers was £71. Again by definition all of them
had at least either livestock or tools; 90 percent owned more than £10
worth, and the great majority between £20 and £100. Just how this
translated into income I don't know. Livestock, stock, ships and tools
may well have returned not far from pound for pound. Thus a calf
became a cow in three years, worth £2.10 cash, and a five-year-old
yoke of oxen brought £7.10, which means 15 to 17 shillings annually.
Tools surely paid for their cost every year, and we guessed that the
hoped-for profit (perhaps not the actuality) from trading stock was
100 percent annually.

This rough estimate draws some support from what we know about
men of nonfarm occupations. The mean of these articles of production
for artisans was £60, a little less than the farmers'. Skilled craftsmen
earned £75 annually, and if to the £60 we add some income from the
land, the figures coincide. The fact that many artisans had much less
property meant that collectively they lived at a level below that of
farmers, avoiding poverty because they could earn wages. Professionals
had twice as much income-producing assets as farmers and traders six
times as much. Be all that as it may, we perceive that the economic

[39] This is for the living population with its large proportion of young men. The
inventory figures are, in order, 100, 93, 30 and 25, which in this case convey a more
accurate idea of the acres owned by the typical heads of households.

position of artisans taken collectively did not equal that of the farmers, and both would envy the professionals, but the road to wealth lay along the trade routes.

Total personal wealth confirms this. Nine out of ten of even free laborers owned less than £50. One-third of the artisans did likewise against one out of seven farmers, but almost none of the professionals and traders. Again, we need to remember that the farm workers, sailors, servants, and apprentices belong with the laborers. The median for such of these as owned property was only £18 against £74 for artisans, £110 for farmers, £200 for professionals, and £260 for traders. Older fathers would live, in order, at these levels: laborers, poor; artisans, subsistence plus; farmers, comfortable; and the others, well-off. The means marched up in order, starting with laborers: £26, £102, £130, £279, and an impressive £520. Obviously the level of inequality in Connecticut arose less from differences within the ranks of artisans, farmers, and professionals than from the poverty of laborers opposed to the wealth of the traders. The proportion of personal estates worth more than £500, only 1 percent for farmers and artisans, rose to 17 percent in the case of professionals and 32 percent among traders.

To some extent the differences in wealth were affected by the age structure of the men in the several occupations. We can study this by examining the composition of each age group and by analyzing the distribution of ages in each occupation (see Table 8.7). Men in their twenties ordinarily remained laborers. About one-third succeeded in

TABLE 8.7
Proportion of Age Groups in Each Occupation, Living Population, 1660–1730 and 1760–1774

	21–29	30–39	40–49	50–59	60–69	70+
Laborers	59.2	20.9	11.6	6.1	2.4	1.0
Farmers	14.3	44.1	55.9	64.6	53.2	35.0
Artisans	21.7	24.4	24.4	17.8	14.6	8.0
Traders	3.6	8.6	6.1	7.1	4.4	2.0
Professionals	1.2	2.1	2.1	3.2	4.9	4.0
Retired	—	—	—	1.2	20.5	50.0
Total	100.0	100.1	100.1	100.0	100.0	100.0

NOTE: The proportion of laborers should be a little higher because the years 1730 to 1750 do not enter into the table. Statements in the text take that into account. The retired group seems large, but actually only a few men belong there. In their active careers fully two-thirds had been farmers and most of the rest, artisans. The general age structure shown on the bottom line of Table 8.8 relates to the time period of this data.

rising above that dependent, unrewarding condition, most often by becoming artisans, who required little capital, or petty traders, and a few inherited enough land to start farming at once. Only during the years between 1700 and 1730 did the proportion change. Then only two out of five remained laborers due to the general expansion that allowed more of them to buy land or become craftsmen.

The men in their thirties, typically fathers of young children, quickly moved out of the laboring class, a process that began with marriage. By that time only one out of five still remained at the bottom. Death had removed some from the pool but the rest had shifted occupations.[40] The other men of that age entered farming and a few more became or remained artisans than their proportion of the whole population would predict. Trade also attracted some for reasons just described. Connecticut's forty- and fifty-year-olds seldom remained laborers and had settled into their permanent work. Three out of five were farmers, over one in five chose a craft, and the rest usually selected trade; the professions were more difficult to enter. The oldest men began, as we know, to retire, especially from the most physically demanding occupations.

From the second point of view we see the obvious, that the laborers were young and ordinarily elevated themselves to some more rewarding vocation by their thirties, certainly thereafter (see Table 8.8). If the "retired" men were considered laborers the 0.1 under the seventies would read 5.5, the transfer affecting 2.4 percent of the men. Obviously, this does not change the interpretation that Connecticut's laborers were in a temporary, not a permanent, position. Farmers were older than the general population because they needed land, livestock, and tools, and they remained farmers until old age compelled or persuaded some to cease active work and let the youngest son take over. This age structure raised the value of their estates, especially in real wealth. Artisans became skilled workers comparatively young and were numerous relative to the population until their fifties. This reflected two contrary tendencies: many young men began in poorly paying

---

[40] Since overall 35 percent of the men were age 21-29 and 26 percent were 30-39, something like one-fourth of the former would die, of whom two-thirds would be laborers. Death, then, would take 6 percent of the 24 percent who were laborers, leaving 18 percent who, if they did not improve their situation, would still be laborers in their thirties. But since of the 26 percent of the men in their thirties only five or a little more (5.4) remained laborers, nearly 13 of that 18 had entered another occupation, a success rate of 70 percent. This is a little high because slaves do not enter into the calculations. Their inclusion would lower it to 60 percent. These figures are for the entire period, disregarding secular changes.

TABLE 8.8

Age Structure of Each Occupational Group, Living Population,
1660–1730 and 1760–1774

	21–29	30–39	40–49	50–59	60–69	70+	Total
Laborers	71.2	18.8	6.4	2.9	0.6	0.1	100.0
Farmers	12.7	29.4	22.8	22.7	9.4	3.0	100.0
Artisans	35.1	29.5	18.1	11.4	4.7	1.2	100.0
Traders	21.4	38.7	16.8	16.8	5.2	1.2	100.1
Professionals	18.5	24.6	15.4	20.0	15.4	6.1	100.0
All men	34.5	25.9	15.9	13.7	6.9	3.3	100.2

crafts and left, while others replaced them in more profitable vocations as they acquired skill and capital. However, some older men tended to leave in favor of farming, except in the late colonial period, or perhaps trade. The professionals included men of all ages because, like the craftsmen and traders, very different men belong among them, from the relatively young teachers and doctors to the older lawyers and professionals. These last two varieties, together with ministers, contributed an unusual proportion of elderly men. Finally, the traders also were so varied as to span the whole spectrum, with more younger men and fewer old ones than the professionals. Like the artisans, some were retiring or becoming farmers in their sixties. The median ages of these groups were, in order of youth, laborers, 27; artisans, 35; traders, 37 1/2; farmers, 43 1/2; and professionals, 44.

The occupations of Connecticut's men also influenced the kinds and value of property they owned—the composition of their wealth. Laborers never owned slaves, which hardly seems worth mentioning except that the phenomenon did occur in the South. Only 11 percent of the farmers did so, and if we adjusted for age bias the number might be halved. Even fewer artisans—4 percent—found use for a servant. In contrast 30 percent of the professionals and a third of the traders owned one or more at the time of their death. As we have observed before, since these people were so little needed on the farms or in shops we cannot suppose that the professionals and traders were investing habitually in a form of production, but rather of consumption. In that case the failure, or refusal, of the farmers and artisans to spend money in that way must be due either to their inability to afford it or a preference, namely, that they preferred to invest their surplus in land rather than to display it in consumption.

That in turn leads us to ask about levels of consumption. First, at the bottom end, almost all of the laborers left less than £20 worth of consumption goods. Fewer than one in ten of the traders died so poor, and only one out of fourteen professionals. Fifteen percent of the farmers did so, not a bad showing considering the proportion of "retired" men, and one out of four artisans, reflecting to some extent the age structure but also low incomes among certain groups. At the top, £200 worth of consumption goods clearly indicates luxury, a way of life far above the utilitarian, so that anyone spending that amount surely preferred a style of living, if not elegant, then civilized, urbane. Only 1 percent of the artisans lived like that and even fewer farmers, but 14 percent of the professionals and 13 percent of the traders did so. The differences in income cannot account for the contrast, certainly in the case of professionals, whose mean personal wealth was only twice that of the farmers; the latter simply did not choose to live in such style. The medians suggest the same distinction in standards and styles of living: £35 for craftsmen, £46 for farmers, £74 for traders, and an impressive £100 for the professionals. These figures do not include servants, though, as we have argued they might well do so; that would increase the gap.[41]

A final item among the consumption goods also informs us about the people's attitudes: books. We do not know whether slaves or indentured servants owned any. Among free laborers, 43 percent had at least one, probably not a bad showing, though of course they may have received it by inheritance or as a gift, and never read it. Three out of four farmers and artisans had one or more and a few (7 or 8 percent) owned £2 worth, which might mean a couple of dozen or a valued Bible with a few sermons. They clearly read. Traders, however, reached a different level. Fewer lacked books—14 percent against the farmers' 25 percent—but more importantly 30 percent owned at least £2 worth. Above all, practically every professional had some and 70 percent owned more than £2. We might repeat the word urbane here since so many of these men lived in relatively large towns or had acquired an education. It may have rubbed off on the artisans, whom one would not expect to equal the farmers, owning as they did less personal and real property; but they did. The question needs extensive investigation, and we can here only hypothesize that not only the quantity of property but the style of living and the values of the people varied with their occupations and from country to town.

[41] Among the mature men with teen-aged or grown children, £40 worth of consumption goods might be considered a desirable objective, not really comfortable but adequate, in the middle of the subsistence-plus level. Forty percent of the artisans died without attaining that goal but only one of eight farmers and traders failed. Professionals did less well—one in five falling short—because of the teachers and doctors. However, most teachers and some artisans shifted into another field, so their record is better than indicated.

APPENDIX 8A

Merchants' Consumer Goods and Levels of Living

The first table presents the basic data, in cash values, from which the interpretative table derives. SOURCE: Estate inventories 1660 to 1774 as previously identified, not converted into the living population.

CONSUMER GOODS

£	Single men	Young fathers	Older fathers	Grand-fathers	Retired	Unknown	N	%
Under 10	3	0	0	0	0	0	3	2.1
10–19	1	2	1	0	0	0	4	2.8
20–29	0	3	0	1	0	1	5	3.5
30–49	2	2	3	1	3	1	12	8.3
50–69	0	7	1	5	1	2	16	11.1
70–99	1	11	9	2	0	1	24	16.7
100–199	0	13	20	8	0	0	41	28.5
200+	1	2	18	15	1	2	39	27.1
Total	8	40	52	32	5	7	144	100.1

LEVELS OF LIVING BASED ON CONSUMER GOODS

	Single men	Young fathers	Older fathers	Grand-fathers	Retired	Unknown	N	%
Poor	3	0	1	0	0	0	4	2.8
Subsistence	1	2	0	0	0	0	3	2.1
Subs. +	0	3	3	0	0	1	7	4.9
Comfortable	0	2	1	2	0	1	6	4.2
Well-off	2	7	9	7	3	3	31	21.5
Well-off+	1	24	20	8	1	0	54	37.5
Luxury	1	2	18	15	1	2	39	27.1
Total	8	40	52	32	5	7	144	100.1

Distribution of Traders' Consumer Goods

	1650–1699		1700–1729		1745–1759		1760–1774	
	N	%	N	%	N	%	N	%
£1–19	4	5.4	16	12.4	7	13.5	17	12.6
20–39	14	18.9	20	15.5	8	15.4	19	14.1
40–59	11	14.9	15	11.6	8	15.4	19	14.1
60–99	20	27.0	24	18.6	16	30.7	26	19.3
100–199	18	24.3	35	27.1	8	15.4	34	25.2
200+	7	9.5	19	14.7	5	9.6	20	14.8
Total	74	100.0	129	99.9	52	100.0	135	100.1

SOURCE: Estate inventories.

Components of Personal Wealth Owned by Traders over Time

	CASH (PERCENTAGE)			
£	pre-1700	1700–1729	1745–1759	1760–1774
None	18	18	20	21
1–4	16	17	20	26
5–9	24	7	13	15
10–19	14	11	16	13
20–49	10	16	9	14
50–99	14	15	9	5
100+	4	15	14	7
Total	100	101	101	101

Continued

DEBTS RECEIVABLE

£	pre-1700		1700–1729		1749–1759		1760–1774		Total	
	N	%	N	%	N	%	N	%	N	%
None	32	43.2	63	48.8	24	42.9	69	50.7	188	47.6
1–9	4	5.4	8	6.2	2	3.6	4	2.9	18	4.6
10–19	3	4.1	5	3.9	3	5.4	3	2.2	14	3.5
20–49	9	12.2	8	6.2	4	7.1	4	4.4	27	6.8
50–99	6	8.1	8	6.2	9	16.1	8	5.9	31	7.8
100–499	9	12.2	24	18.6	8	14.3	26	19.1	67	17.0
500–999	5	6.8	8	6.2	3	5.4	10	7.4	26	6.6
1,000+	6	8.1	5	3.9	3	5.4	10	7.4	24	6.1
Total	74	100.1	129	100.0	56	100.2	136	100.0	395	100.0

TRADING STOCK (£ CASH, IN NUMBERS)

£	pre-1700	1700–1729	1745–1759	1760–1774
None	10	30	15	44
1–9	7	4	6	14
10–19	3	13	6	15
20–49	20	18	8	12
50–99	13	28	4	15
100–199	12	13	9	19
200–499	7	22	7	8
500–999	0	1	1	9
1,000+	2	0	0	0
Total	74	129	56	136

VALUE OF LIVESTOCK

£	pre-1700		1700–1729		1745–1774	
None	15	20.3	28	21.7	47	24.5
1–9	17	23.0	17	13.2	44	22.9
10–19	12	16.2	24	18.6	26	13.5
20–49	14	18.9	29	22.5	40	20.8
50–99	19	13.5	16	12.4	24	12.5
100+	6	8.1	15	11.6	11	5.7
Total	74	100.0	129	100.0	192	99.9

NINE

The Leaders

During the entire colonial period (except for a few years in the 1680s) the men of Connecticut selected their own leaders. This does not mean that every person exercising an important function was chosen by universal manhood suffrage, but that some portion of the adult men, or their elected representatives, did choose those who governed or guided them in religion, politics, and the military. Moreover, the social "elite" presided with general consent and the economic upper class originated within Connecticut's society rather than imposing itself from the outside. Since that society was relatively homogeneous, no native elite could be or would be oppressive. In this chapter we will first discuss the general nature of each type of leader and the method by which they attained high positions. Next, we will examine the degree to which these men constituted a closed class, an aristocracy, an integrated establishment; and finally, we will comment on their economic and social characteristics.

While religion was not all-important to everyone, the church performed enough functions and attracted sufficient respect to justify discussing its leaders first. Almost all of Connecticut's churches, often called "societies," established a representative government headed by "deacons," the term "elder" appearing only in the very early years. Deacons ran the secular affairs of the congregation, which included not only internal government but matters now left to the state, such as the settlement of disputes between church members and the punishment of certain "crimes." They also carried out philanthropic functions of the church, helping the poor and tending the sick. The deacons were instrumental in choosing ministers and served as a sort of executive council, symbolized by their sitting in preferred pews of the meetinghouse. The title therefore conferred considerable prestige and occurs on most written documents, except when replaced by some other even more significant title, such as that of captain. Few such duplicates occurred, the personal qualifications for the two probably differing, so that military officers rarely seemed sufficiently holy and deacons could not pass muster.

Above the deacons in the church hierarchy came the ministers. They attained this highest position not by ascending a ladder, although sons of deacons did occasionally enter the ministry, but by a route open to anyone heeding its call and able to graduate from college or achieve recognition without it. Larger churches often hired two men, one to serve as a "teacher," delivering the sermons that informed the congregation, the other to care for the members in other ways, ministering to them as a shepherd. Both were addressed as "mister" and, over time, as that title lost status, "the Reverend." Whether their prestige declined during the eighteenth century remains debatable. They complained of it, but then in the seventeenth century as well they had accused their flocks of backsliding and failing to equal their forebears in piety. Possibly church attendance fell here and there, but that is not a sure indication of declining seriousness since other factors might account for it such as too few ministers, more mediocre ones, a closed complacency among members that repelled newcomers, or the rise of competing doctrines. Students of the Great Awakening, which counteracted some of these tendencies, assert that the ministers as a whole suffered from that movement because the people were challenging their authority and because men were entering the profession who lacked the usual qualifications, notably formal education. Indeed, some ministers suffered, but others benefited from increased attendance, and on balance the celebrations of the latter outweigh the wails of the former. As another evidence of decline the ministers cited lower salaries. Undoubtedly some congregations fell behind the rate of inflation in setting their dues, hardly surprising during the 1730s and 1740s. But these decades saw not just inflation but economic depression. People unquestionably could not pay as much, and salaries agreed upon during the boom years might well seem excessive, all the more when the recipients demanded frequent raises. Finally, we have seen that the property owned by the ministers did not in fact decline over time except for a few who entered the field during the Great Awakening without the usual background. On the whole we perceive no deterioration in the situation or status of ministers during our period.

Even in the seventeenth century they had not always come first on the assessment lists. Lyme, in 1688, opened with the deputy and perennial moderator Matthew Griswold, and Mr. Moses Noyes came second. Guilford in 1672 placed Governor William Leete first and Mr. Joseph Eliot far down the list. Mr. Hanford of Norwalk ranked sixth, first place going to a deputy. In Stonington, the 1668 list began with the political leader Thomas Stanton, next to whom came Capt. George Denison and, after four more, the minister. The significance of such a ranking may be exaggerated since the clergy won exemption from certain taxes. Derby in 1718 placed their pastor at the end as paying no tax, though that may not imply disrespect. The minister did not even appear on Groton's "Grand List" of 1734. At any rate we certainly should not visualize the townspeople lining up in order of rank with the minister at their head. We know that he was important, but others may have equaled and sometimes exceeded him in status.

The ministers, like the deacons, obtained their position from the church members. The former, however, came usually from outside the town. Naturally a few local boys obtained the master's degree and then won the acceptance of their former neighbors, but obviously the newly settled villages lacked any candidate and many older towns apparently preferred to hire an outsider. A cursory survey of forty-two men in nine towns scattered around the colony turned up only three who came from the same town and a dozen from adjacent communities, but even more originated in England or another colony, and the rest, born in Connecticut, were brought up in a distant community. At most only a third could be called local boys. The church members reviewed candidates for vacancies very carefully, tried them out, tested their doctrine and personal qualities, and bargained over the settlement. Moreover, once selected the incumbent sometimes faced serious divisions that might even lead to dismissal. One might say that he was chosen for life by a popular majority but subject to recall. The people accordingly respected and rewarded but did not worship their spiritual leaders.

Military leaders ranked high from the first, as symbolized for us by Capt. Miles Standish. When the English entered Connecticut, the Dutch already had a fort at what became Hartford and claimed the whole area west of the Connecticut River. For the first decade or so the two groups remained equal in number, and the western towns continued to be nervous until the conquest. Meanwhile they had fought the Pequot War (1637). King Philip's War came in 1676 and the Indians, with their French allies, threatened the frontier until after Queen Anne's War. A period of peace followed, but then came in quick succession the War of Jenkins's Ear, King George's War with its attack on Louisbourg, and the French and Indian War. The law requiring every town to maintain one or more militia units ready for combat continued in force, with enough actual fighting to confirm its importance. Thus while the ministers attended to the people's souls the officers saved their bodies.

Probably the officers of these local companies did not quite retain their seventeenth-century status for a whole series of reasons. At first, each town had but one captain and the colony's size did not warrant many men of higher rank. Later, larger towns supported two or even more companies and the increase of majors and colonels in a way demoted the lesser officers. Also, the militia declined in importance as the danger receded and the British regulars took over much of the burden. The condition of guns, which every soldier supposedly kept in good order, deteriorated and many inventories lacked them. Some of the captains refused to resign long after they had passed the age for active combat. The colony could no longer reward its heroes with land, so the office became less desirable economically. Finally, one gets the subjective impression that the offices of lieutenant, ensign, and sergeant no longer brought the prestige of the early decades; sometimes the titles do not appear before their names in the records. Conceivably the general use of "captain" by the ships' captains, rare during the seventeenth century but common thereafter, diminished the impact of the word. Nonetheless, the rank retained much local importance, and of course the appellation of major, colonel, and general conferred high status.

Technically, the delegates appointed all of the commissioned officers from ensign on up. However, the militiamen themselves agreed upon candidates, and the legislature, doubtless informed by the local representatives (for we find appointments delayed until the deputies arrived), simply confirmed the selection. It intervened in the rare cases of dispute and a few instances of incompetence, but for all practical purposes the officers were chosen by the men. Once elected, however, they ordinarily served until they died or retired, the latter occurring frequently since the obligations were considerable. The long terms meant that the choice of ensign was crucial. He won promotion to lieutenant almost automatically when that person moved up into a captaincy, a slow process except during wartime. The immigrants, men born before 1620, averaged over fifty when they attained that rank. The series of wars or other factors lowered the starting age to about forty-seven for cohorts of 1680-1710, and for those born after 1710, down to forty-four.[1] A long time for a young man to wait! Indeed, as we will see later, representatives in the lower house of the legislature were younger by nearly seven years, though one might have expected the opposite, given the requirements.

Higher officers, from major on up, received their commissions from the legislature, being therefore colonywide rather than local elections and so requiring a broad reputation to attract extensive support. Nevertheless, the delegates scattered their favors widely. The large,

[1] See Appendix 9A.

320

important towns such as Hartford and Fairfield received more than their share—nearly half of the total—but one out of six lived in a recently settled community and ninety-nine officers came from forty-three towns. Curiously, they won appointments when no older than the captains, doubtless because the legislature was free to jump the able young men without waiting for a death. Their ability or influence is also suggested by attaining other high positions.

The third group of leaders held political power. They included the towns' officials, members of the legislature, and judges, of which the first two were selected by the voters and judges by the delegates. We here concentrate on the last two groups, leaving the first, and most numerous, to the specialists.

Just how many men could vote has caused a heated argument. Apparently almost any man attending the town meeting voted for local positions. In most of these, as in the case of committee members today, the problem lay in finding someone competent who would serve, not in choosing among contenders. The same was true for important jobs requiring special education, such as the treasurer and clerk. The moderator, an honorary rather than a powerful post, went to someone skilled, willing, and estimable. The key positions of selectmen rotated among a wide range of people, the pool containing those of proven competence, integrity, and extensive friendships. These qualities most often coincided with long residence in the community, old family connections, church membership, economic success at least above the subsistence level, political experience, and age. Students investigating these variables find fairly high correlations but always exceptions, and none, taken singly, becomes a cause. Rather, as Edward Cook has shown, each forms part of a perfectly reasonable, though complex whole.[2] We have touched upon it in discussing the life cycle. The young single man would own little property and depended upon his family or an employer for support. Whether he should be allowed to vote is arguable, but he clearly was not yet fitted for office. As soon as he married the situation changed fundamentally: it was that act that transformed his role in the town. He proved his stability, his membership in the community; he would not drift. With this went property, certainly enough to meet the usual voting requirements, but it was status that came first. He often joined a church and held a minor office, for an average town needed several score of unpaid public servants. Fifty such divided among one hundred taxable polls meant nearly one for each married man over thirty. Another ten years, and his competitors di-

---

[2] Edward M. Cook, Jr., *Fathers of the Towns* (Baltimore: 1976).

minished: some died, others proved incompetent, a few left. For any important post, youth alone would disqualify at least sixty out of a hundred adult men, old age or disability would take another ten. There remained perhaps thirty eligibles for the dozen or more major positions. Since most of these rotated often, the average selectman serving for only five years or so, our candidate might suppose that if he lived long enough he would have a better than even chance. Thus a man who provided well for his family, behaved honorably, and served the town creditably, would reasonably expect a high office, unless indeed the influence of family or political oligarchy prevented it.

The suffrage requirement for voters electing the town's representatives also eliminated those with little property, again primarily the young single sons, the migrants, and the failures. Each town chose two delegates every fall and spring, potentially four individuals each year. If we counted everyone who served we would tally a long list. Between 1700 and 1719 Glastonbury and Middletown each sent fourteen men, Simsbury eleven, Hartford nine, and Windsor ten. However, many of these lasted only for a term or two, and we will here concentrate on those reelected for at least three years beyond the first.[3] These men received only a small per diem that covered their expenses but did not offer a pecuniary inducement. The beginning farmer or craftsmen, who would not have qualified anyway, could not have left his family, while older members of those occupations might leave a son in charge but would have no financial reason for attending. The advantage probably lay in the excitement and prestige. Professionals and businessmen, of course, could use the position to help obtain favors or another appointment.

The voters also chose the assistants, who formed the upper house of the legislature, the supreme court (all became judges upon election), and an executive branch, since one served as governer, another as lieutenant-governor, and the rest as councillors. They were addressed as "honorable" in contrast to the delegates who earned no title of respect at all, except during the early decades when they were addressed as "mister." Election as assistant came after service in the lower house sufficiently notable to attract a colonywide following, since the candidates won by a general vote. Reelection followed almost, though not quite automatically and ended by death or retirement. The group was small and distinguished, the closest thing to an aristocracy that Con-

---

[3] My list thus includes everyone in Connecticut who served four or more terms up to 1750, though I have data on property only for those who left inventories. The answer to the question of whether men who served shorter terms differed is no.

necticut produced. Its power, however, was limited by the lower house and the possibility of defeat.

The legislature chose all the justices (at first called commissioners) who provided the colony's judiciary. Each county contained a number varying and increasing with its population. These men presided as individuals over minor local cases and collectively over more important questions. Since in Connecticut most disputes came not before the town meeting or the church but the courts, the justices were extremely important, superior to everyone except the assistants (their fellow judges), and perhaps the ministers. They and they alone could place an "esquire" after their names. This job brought not only prestige but a good income. For it some knowledge of the law was really essential, though in the early days the colony did not contain enough educated men for it to become a rule. It also required the good opinion of the delegates, who, however, followed local preferences. Because of these requisites, appointment generally came late in life, and the median age of the justices upon taking office was five years higher than the delegates', though still less than the captains'. The job did not require their full attention, and many served as deacons, delegates, or militia officers in addition to part-time careers in farming or another occupation.

The final two types of leaders belong to a different species in that nobody elected or appointed them, and, indeed, perhaps they owe their existence as leaders to the historians rather than to their contemporaries: namely, in modern terms, the economic and social upper class. We here define the former as those owning £2,000 worth of property in cash (dividing real estate nearly in half after 1750), and adding a few from the tops of tax lists. The figure is low, but not for Connecticut where, if we raised it, many towns would lack a member. We will comment particularly on the wealthiest men who owned £5,000.

Large propertyowners appeared among the first settlers of Connecticut, the origins therefore lying in England, and a few of these established dynasties. Examples from the Hartford region included Leonard Chester, George Gardner, Giles Hamlin, Richard Lord, John Robbins, John Talcott, William Whiting, and Henry Wolcott. Later immigrants with capital continued to immigrate such as James Richards and George Stillman, while others made money in the colonies, joining such children of the first settlers as retained their fortunes. Thus before 1700 every part of the colony contained families rich by local standards, such as the Burrs and Golds of Fairfield, and the eighteenth century added more. Most of these men earned or retained their positions through trade, although other paths to wealth existed and they often diversified. To what extent they attained or confirmed high status by officeholding we will discuss later. For the moment we will observe that these early settlers did not necessarily form part of the great "Puritan" migration but became leaders regardless.

Finally, we can attempt to identify a social elite. During the seventeenth century the title of "mister" elevated certain men above the common run, being used when they bore no other title. The origin remains unclear. Undoubtedly some men carried over from Europe certain claims to social distinction such as a family of gentry rank. Others earned the title by serving as a delegate, since no other preliminary word existed to identify them. Where that does not apply we may find economic achievement as in the case of Richard Bryan, a Milford merchant, or education, like Windsor's schoolmaster John Branker, or a foreigner with a claim to status, like Caspar Varlett from France. Thus also Mr. William Hooker was Thomas's grandson; Samuel Stone, though a goldbrick and sot, received a "mister" as a minister's son; and Nicholas Auger was an early doctor as well as a merchant. Some simply remain mysteries, but testify to the importance of social status. After 1700, in a significant shift, the word gradually lost its value through two changes: either everybody or nobody obtained it, depending on the source.

The other title of social prestige was "gentleman" or "gent.," used sporadically, almost capriciously, often apparently on demand. I found only one instance of it in the New Haven area, where it was used by Reverand Nicholas Street of New Haven (1603-1674), most likely reflecting his father's "esquire." The Fairfield district also furnishes one— Richard Blackleach (1654-1731), a trader who carried along the title when he immigrated as a young man of property. The shortage of early New London probate records prevents any certainty, but I saw only three, given to the French entrepreneur and ship's captain René Grignon in 1715, the Reverend Samuel Whiting of Windham (1670-1725), and Lt. John Slap of nearby Mansfield in 1742, with what justice I know not. Indeed, the northern part of the colony produced most of the "gentlemen," perhaps owing to some subversive influence out of Massachusetts. We find there Abraham Adams of Suffield (1687-1769), of a good Northampton family, and Ens. Simon Kendall (1724-1770), of the same town, apparently without reason. In addition, John Bulkeley, already "honorable" and "esquire" from being an assistant and a captain as well, added this one, or so reads the Colchester probate record in 1753. No other member of his distinguished family did so. Finally, the first John Robbins of Wethersfield (d. 1660) probably came by the term legitimately as son of a large landowner in England. It is surely significant that his prominent sons and grandsons did not claim it. We conclude that the title of gentleman was an anachronism that did not long survive the kind of society Connecticut's people created. Their leaders used titles, but they came to represent personal achievement rather than inheritance.

Such terms as "establishment," "aristocracy," and "standing order" commonly describe the colony's upper class. If these mean that a limited number of families dominated the rest in the ways suggested by the words—in politics, religion, and society certainly, economics and the military less clearly—then their picture is false. Those who provided leadership for Connecticut certainly possessed great influence and in a few areas considerable authority; however, not only was that power limited but the personnel were subject to change. Overall, almost two out of five leaders, at any given time, did not belong to families of leaders. At least two out of three of their mothers were, so to speak, commoners, and they themselves selected wives of the same sort in the same ratio. They seldom owed their position to influence from the female side. Access to positions of leadership did not become more restrictive except that the society of the first generation was unusually mobile and later ones were less so. At first, well over half came from ordinary families; we do not know precisely how much over but 60 percent is a fair guess. After that the proportion declined to and stabilized at one-third until the mid-1700s, when improved opportunities in religion, the military, and commerce raised the figure to the overall 40 percent.[4]

The details vary with the type of leader. Since deacons, captains, and deputies were chosen by the townspeople, or segments of them, these men were most likely to have belonged to ordinary families. That was also true of the "social" variety, at least those with the title of "mister." The members of these four groups, who contributed more than three-fifths to the total leadership, belonged to principal families only a little over half of the time (if we include those of unknown origin, as we probably should). On the other hand, assistants, the military officers holding the rank of major and above, and the esquires, constituting one-fifth of our leaders, belonged to the important families two-thirds of the time. These were chosen by colonywide electorates. The family background of ministers came closer to the local type of leader than to the more general variety, while the economic upper class, like the principal officials, often started life with the presumed advantages of a prestigious father or mother.

Offhand, there seems little reason to suppose that a congregation

[4] See Appendix 9B.

would consider a deacon's ancestry in his selection. Money would have nothing to do with it, since the churches drew their support from taxes, though a few people left bequests in their wills. And, in fact, only 2 fathers of the deacons out of 332 belonged to the wealthiest class without some other qualification. Deacons reached that office late in life, certainly when more than fifty, with ample time to earn their selection. That the position came from merit rather than family is attested by the fact that only four were the sons of ministers even though the deacons were, so to speak, in the same line of work. If merit decided the issue, as the evidence strongly suggests, then we can use the social origin of deacons as a benchmark, a standard, namely, that in colonial Connecticut the church members selected half of their principal officials from among the leading families of the community, presumably because these families, taken collectively, embodied superior attributes. Or, to state the reverse hypothesis, half of the men chosen for positions such as that of deacon will come from ordinary families. The question arises as to how many select families existed within the community. I do not know how to set about answering that unless we accept as evidence the fact that among men who lived long enough to obtain high office, arbitrarily defined as sixty, 20 percent succeeded. Of course, the community contained many more families who, if added to the total, would lower the proportion, but can we really admit to the population in question men too young for eligibility? However this may be, the 50 percent furnishes a starting point.

This half comes mostly from the male side, though one-tenth owed their relationship to a mother or a wife and another tenth had good backgrounds on both sides. The proportion probably changed a little over time but not much. The principal type of father, aside from the ordinary man, was a deacon himself. However, a substantial number were captains, so we can conclude only that the spiritual qualities of a father were more appropriate, if transmitted, than military talent. The fathers held no higher military office, rarely served as assistants, and seldom as justices, but they had often become delegates. Thus the fathers, like the deacons themselves, belong to what we might call a sort of lesser gentry, insofar as they ranked above the average, and the deacons had moved parallel along the social scale or one step up. While some came from the best families, on the whole their origins were simply respectable.

The particular characteristics of the deacons appear also in that almost two-thirds never held any other high office. Throughout the extensive Hartford district, even through the Revolution, none seems to have served as an assistant, only three rose above the rank of captain, and ten, scarcely 7 percent, became justices of the peace. Rather more attended the House of Delegates but only one out of five, certainly fewer than one would expect, given their merit. As we will discuss later, the deacons were usually farmers and not wealthy enough to hire substitutes during their absence, so that the combination of their private affairs, the church, and ordinary town offices would fully engage them.

With the captains, we move up a notch. Only about two out of five came from ordinary families, they owned half again as much property as did the deacons and more often held higher office. Out of 543 captains who died before 1789, we know the parentage of all but 41, most of the latter being early immigrants or generally obscure. Among those we know about, 56 percent came from leading families as defined by the father or mother and another 5 percent had married women of that origin. The proportion diminished over time—that is, relative mobility increased even after adjusting for the early unknowns; this may reflect the demand created by eighteenth-century wars, especially the conflict of 1756-1760. In the male line they drew more heavily from families of deacons than did deacons from them, suggesting that becoming a captain was a step up socially. Not far from half succeeded military fathers. The rest of the fathers resembled those of the deacons. Like them, captains came from families of the local gentry or the simply respectable, and almost never from the wealthy class. Evidently the economic elite did not send sons into the army as was usual among the English aristocracy, probably a result of partible inheritance in the New World.

The captains as a group had improved upon their fathers' status but most of them proceeded no higher. Half held no other office, again excepting local politics. A few, as we know, became deacons and a few more won promotion to a higher military rank. About one-fourth served as delegates, usually before the captaincy, and the legislature appointed one out of eight a justice. A handful achieved the colony's highest honor as an assistant.

The captains' age at taking office decreased over time. Men born outside the colony in the early years, before 1620, had already lost some years getting started and averaged well over fifty. After that the age at captaincy averaged forty-nine until the men born after 1710, when forty-four became the median, surely a result of the Seven Years' War.

While the captains may have outranked the deacons, the advantage was minor. The desirable qualities for the two offices differed so much that comparisons seem out of order; as we noticed, a man rarely held both. The slightly greater achievements of the captains in other fields, especially as deputies, may have reflected an unexpected value judgment on the part of the people, or more likely the captains possessed certain qualities of leadership, the capacity to govern in times of danger, that the community found valuable in other posts.

The men with social titles seem to have come from the same background. Most of them, the "misters," immigrated early in the seventeenth century, ancestry unknown, which probably means ordinary or at least below the gentry. Of those we do know, 64 percent came from leading families, a proportion higher than that for deacons and captains, but the unknown group if included gives the much lower boundary of 46 percent, with a probability of about 50. Such fathers as belonged to the better sort scattered over the spectrum about evenly divided between the local group, deputies, and higher officials. A third of the misters earned the title by serving in the legislature, a few others held miscellaneous posts of consequence, but over half had none at all, sometimes leaving the reader puzzled about their merit. Obviously the people at the time respected them for qualities now often obscure. In any case they contributed a small proportion of the towns' principal men.

Unlike the foregoing types of leaders, the deputies performed on a colonywide stage and confronted problems more extensive, probably more important, than local church or militia affairs, and they were responsible to all the voters of the town rather than a specialized part. This presumably elevated the qualifications for their office and narrowed the pool of candidates. During the seventeenth century that pool, insofar as it depended upon family status, evidently fell far short of the demand. Of those whose family we know, nearly 60 percent came from the usual reputable origins, but the number about whose family we remain ignorant is so large that as many as 56 percent may have come from ordinary backgrounds. A fair average is half. After that matters settled down, at least from our point of view, for we can identify all but 4 percent of the parents. The proportion of men who gained their election without family advantages then declined to 36 percent for those chosen between 1690 and 1740 and to one-third thereafter. If we agree that the deacons set the par at 50 percent, then family made a difference of some sort, slight in the seventeenth century but thereafter to the extent of perhaps one-sixth of the deputies who might not have obtained their office had they not benefited from family influence, training, or prestige.

By "family" we have meant one that was headed by any type of leader. If for the moment we narrow the definition to those in which the head was a deputy, then the proportion of delegates born to the office, so to speak, shrinks to just over a quarter.[5] Of the other fathers of deputies one-third had served as militia officers, half of these being delegates; one-sixth as deacons; and 9 percent as justices, mostly also delegates. In addition, 10 percent were ministers.

If the deputies owed some of their success to their father's training and example, that helps to explain the breadth of their own activity. Captains, as we saw, held other office, but over half remained just captains, excluding town positions. In contrast fewer than 10 percent of the delegates remained so limited. One-third became or had already served as justices and almost half held a military rank, from ensigns on up. One out of eight was a deacon. These positions followed election to the legislature and perhaps owed something to it. More likely, however, the man of ability first earned the approval of his neighbors by performance in politics beginning with local tasks, because there one need not wait for a death or resignation. Meanwhile he was proving himself in the militia or among the congregation, moving up as the vacancies opened and his own merits won appreciation. Whereas the church and the army required special training or ability, serving as a deputy did not, but only a capacity to obtain election and reflect the people's interests, so that deputies drew from the broadest spectrum and might hold the greatest variety of leadership positions.

Justices of the peace, the "esquires," came slightly more often than the delegates from leading families, the boundaries being 71.4 percent of those known and 65.3 percent out of the whole group. The fathers represented the entire gamut of eligible citizens. Of those whose offices we know, over one-fifth had been themselves justices, one-third served as deputies, one-fifth as captains, and nearly one-fourth as either deacons or ministers. Since the office required legal knowledge it is perhaps surprising that one-third came from families that provided no such background and probably owned no appropriate books, so that the pool of technically qualified candidates must have fallen considerably short of the demand, especially since lawyers were rare. During the seventeenth century the people overcame that difficulty by getting along with only a few.

The importance of this office eventually rivaled that of the ministers. Whereas turnover among deputies was common, the justice, once chosen, almost always retained the judgeship until he resigned. Therefore, as in the case of captains and deacons, the justices had to await a vacancy unless growing population increased the number, and their

[5] However, among our deputies half produced a son who succeeded to that office.

329

average age at taking office fell between that of the deputies and captains at about forty-six years, declining from over fifty for those born
before 1650 to forty-three among men born after 1700. Some of them
held no other office but five out of six did so, most often as a delegate
(nearly half), frequently in the militia (almost a third), and occasionally
as deacons.

One might suppose that the social origins of the ministers would
average the highest, above even the justices, but they did not. Instead,
they very closely resembled the captains and the deputies, the overall
proportion of Reverends without family connections being almost average for the entire leadership class—42 percent. The data here includes all the ministers of the colonial period, totaling 366.[6]

Let us first notice changes over time. Of those born in the eighteenth century, one third of the total number, 70 percent of those
whose origins we know came from prominent families, half being the
sons of ministers. The parentage of 20 percent is unknown or uncertain, and if all these belonged to the ordinary folk then the proportion
falls to two-thirds. This compares with the probable 50 percent for
the deputies during the same period. The number of men from good
families among the latter thereafter rose to two out of three, but for
the ministers the reverse occurred. Among those born after 1700, fewer
than half came from above-average families. Put differently, the proportion of ministers lacking any known advantage of birth rose from
about one-third to one-half, an increase of 50 percent. This change
clearly reflects the diminished role of class in the colonies compared
with the mother country, where one can assume that a minister inherited gentry rank with property enough to afford a university education. Connecticut contained fewer well-to-do families at the top and a
college degree was available to young men of ordinary, though not
really humble means. Moreover, by 1740 the degree had become un-
necessary for the preachers in some "separate" churches and the addition of a few more such men of lowly origin accounts for the final
decline.

Overall, then, 40 percent of the ministers were not the sons of leaders. Of those who were, exclusive of the few whose mothers supplied
the lack, the largest group had ministers as fathers. Actually one would
expect this as a rule, but it was true of only two out of five, the proportion remaining stable over time. Deacons and captains supplied
about the same percentage, one out of six for the former, one out of

---

[6] Frederick Lewis Weis, *The Colonial Clergy and the Colonial Churches of New England*
(Lancaster, Mass., 1936). Of those born in the colonies the percentage is 41.6 (N = 352).

five for the latter. Surprisingly few were the children of the colonywide upper class or of members of the legislature. Even if we add deputies, assistants, justices, and major or above, less than one-fourth of ministers belonging to leading families came from this highest background, fewer still of those engaged in politics; and, of course, the proportion shrinks even further if all the ministers are included of whatever origin, to just over one out of ten. One is tempted to write that if Connecticut contained a "standing order," ministers did not form part of it, at least by inheritance.

They usually did succeed in marrying well, but only 60 percent of the time. About one-fourth of their wives were daughters of ministers and one-third belonged to other leading families. Considering the fact that most of them were college graduates with a high probability of economic and social success, one would have expected them to select their wives from the top, especially since they seldom married before obtaining a church; yet so many looked outside the upper class that they clearly felt no compulsion to do so, and we could as easily argue that they sought brains, good looks, and character, with a probability that those qualities would appear most often in the better families in the actual ratio of three to two. Equally probable is an association between their own background and that of their wives. The proportion of ministers of ordinary rank rose over time, as we saw, from roughly 35 to 40 and then up to half, while that of their wives kept pace almost exactly. In sum, ministers did not form a uniform social species but included men of varying background, just as they differed intellectually.

The two highest-ranking groups of leaders consisted of those militia officers above the rank of captain, selected by the legislature, and the assistants, chosen by the voters. Both required a colonywide reputation of the kind best achieved through family connections and holding conspicuous office, in addition, of course, to proven ability. Both therefore belonged to families characterized by leadership. In the case of the military men that commonly meant fathers with military experience. A little over two-thirds came from leading families, not far from half being military. These men almost always served the colony in other capacities, commonly as justices, deputies, or even a few assistants. The last, who in most colonies were called councillors, drew their membership even more from the same experienced pool. They had themselves served as deputies and upon election they became judges, but they did not become deacons or, naturally, ministers. These two highest groups might reasonably be called an "establishment" if we recognize that one-third originated outside of any such group and that the total number of individuals involved was too small and too dependent upon popularity for their appointments to have constituted an aristocracy with power. Moreover, as we will see presently, they did not interlock significantly with the economic upper class, so as part of an establishment they left a good deal to be desired.

Those men who left over £2,000 (cash) when they died (before 1775) included fewer than one-third who had achieved their wealth without help from family connections. To be exact, among those we know about 27 percent were self-made and if we add all those whose origins we do not know, the proportion would reach at most one-third. In this case, however, some of the unknown group had immigrated, probably with capital, so the true figure for vertical mobility is under a third. If we examine only their economic background, not more than 30 percent of the total had inherited wealth, for the very good reason that few Connecticut citizens owned estates above £2,000.

The fathers of our wealthy class, then, consisted of the following elements: ordinary citizens, three out of ten; wealthy but without any office of leadership, fewer than one in ten; wealthy and also holding such office, one out of eight; officeholders lacking large property, one-half. Only ten of the fathers were ministers and four had served as deacons, fewer than 10 percent of the total. The military provided nearly twice as many, justices the same, and politicians even more, as many, in fact, as the wealthy group but still fewer than the fathers who held no office and did not belong to the economic upper class. We certainly do not see here a concentration of inherited wealth nor a consolidated aristocracy from which almost all men of property descended.

The economic upper class, in addition to originating partly from ordinary families, often did not enter the society's non-economic leadership. Thirty-seven percent held no post of honor, though a few others received a "mister" or a lesser military title. Among the officeholders religion once again took a back seat with four ministers and seven deacons. Thirty-seven percent held the rank of captain or above, 30 percent sat in the legislature, some as assistants, and 21 percent served as justices of the peace. To some extent, therefore, they did intersect with other types of leaders, but if one subtracts those who held no more than the local offices of captain or deacon, then barely half interacted at a colonywide level. Wealth did not automatically result in office while office rarely meant wealth.

To summarize the question of mobility, every species of leader was recruited to some extent from the generality of people, the degree varying from a little over half in the case of deacons down to one-third for the highest officers and the wealthy men. Among the factors contributing to this was the inability of the leaders themselves to produce sons who could succeed them. If the legal or value system had created a hereditary aristocracy in which at least one son always succeeded to the title, the colony's upper class would have supplied enough members, for it averaged not far from three sons per leader. Even those who died after 1760 still left 2.6 each, down two or three tenths but still adequate. But those dying before 1740 produced but one *successful* son, and thereafter even less (0.76, N = 96). In general, fewer than one-third of the sons of leaders became leaders themselves. If the number of openings had increased as rapidly as the population, the success rate would have had to double, if not more. Actually the number of positions did not keep up with the growth of population, but still required the leaders to furnish more than one heir apiece. The growth rate of ministers in the colony averaged less than two per year, and of leaders themselves the increase was just about the same, slower by 50 percent than the population growth but of course faster than the leaders' children were filling them. The deficiency, common to upper classes, helped to maintain an open society. For the Connecticut boy of quality there was always room at the top.

We next turn to the economic characteristics of the leaders, beginning with their occupations.[7] Since the eligible men were generally over forty years old (except ministers) and reputable, they were never laborers at the time of their selection. They must be able to leave their work entirely for some hours (deacons) or days (the rest), again ex-

TABLE 9.1
Occupations of Leaders (Minus Ministers)

	Probated Estates		Occupation of Eligible Decedents	Ratio of Leaders to Eligible
	N	%		
Lawyers	54	5.3 ⎫		
Doctors	13	1.3 ⎬	4	3.0
Officials	54	5.3 ⎭		
Traders	148	14.5	6½	2.2
Artisans	117	11.5	26	0.4
Artisan-farmers	83	8.1	7	1.2
Farmers	552	54.1	56½	1.0
Total	1,021	100.1	100	

[7] For the data on this and other characteristics see Appendix 9D.

cepting the ministers whose occupation coincided with the position. Also, aside from justices and ministers, the duties brought no direct, certain monetary reward, not even expenses in some cases. Finally, most leaders needed special training, the ability to communicate effectively, and often education, preferably in college, but at least in reading, writing, and keeping accounts, often much more (justices).

All of these considerations eliminated most craftsmen. Those who did serve had larger incomes and farms so that their families would not suffer by their absence. Farmers were also at a disadvantage. Those who held office were the richer ones and frequently with a supplementary income—hence the contribution of artisan–farmers. The traders furnished more than their share in the commercial towns such as New London where they formed most of the qualified men, but not in the country villages because local shopkeepers could not leave. Finally, the professional class supplied leaders in a proportion far in excess of their numbers—indeed, including ministers, almost six times their percentage in the pool according to age. Nevertheless, there were so many farmers in the appropriate age group, and enough with the other requirements, that they furnished half of the leaders.

The leaders' personal wealth varied with the community that they served. Along the south shore the people could draw on the owners of fertile farmland as well as the merchants and professions of the old, diversified towns. There, the median value of the personal estates left by these men ranged from £200 to £300 and in the New London area one-third owned £500 worth. At the opposite extreme, in the northeastern district of Windham, the median was £150 and only one of eighty-nine was worth £500. The overall average was one-sixth. The fact emphasizes what we have already learned, that the colony as a whole lacked an economic upper class numerous enough to supply the necessary number of leaders and the people were obliged, if indeed they did not prefer, to draw upon the skills of men with quite modest properties.

Table 9.2 shows the distribution for the colony during the entire colonial period. Column two shows the proportion of leaders leaving personal estates of various values. Those with under £50 had retired, but most men owning less than £100 truly had small properties. They were especially numerous in the hill towns of the interior. The third column furnishes the distribution for all men and the next, the proportion at each level who became leaders. Thus, those with estates of £100-199 comprised 27 percent of all decedents and exactly the same percentage had served as leaders, but the owners of large properties provided several times as many leaders as their numbers warranted.

TABLE 9.2
Distribution of Leaders' Personal Wealth, 1650–1775 (cash)

£	(1) N	(2) %	(3) Distrib. of all estates	(4) Col. 2 ÷ col. 3	(5) Distrib. of fathers 40–59	(6) Col. 2 ÷ col. 5
1–49	69	6.6	32.0	0.2	16	0.4
50–99	163	15.6	28.0	0.6	31	0.5
100–199	284	27.1	27.0	1.0	34	0.8
200–299	183	17.5	7.0	2.5	9	2.0
300–399	126	12.0	2.5	5.0	4	3.0
400–499	56	5.3	1.0	5.3	2	2.6
500+	167	15.9	2.5	6.4	4	4.0
Total	1,048	100.0	100.0		100	
Median £	204		£82		£105	

SOURCE: Estate inventories.

The wealthiest group, with over £500, were thirty-two times more likely to reach the top than those with under £50. However, since most men with small estates would not have been eligible because of youth, these data prove little. The next column focuses on the personal property of the relevant pool, and the last one shows the relationship between that and column two. It remains true that the poorer men attained high rank far less often than their numbers warranted. The dividing line occurred at £200, a sum that provided a sufficient estate to free a man for other tasks, impress his neighbors, or influence them, depending upon one's interpretation. They became leaders four times as often, proportionate to their numbers, as men with £50 to £100. The odds then level off until the top group, which was twice as likely to provide leaders as the owners of £200.

Thus men of small property did appear among the colony's most important men but far less often than their frequency in the eligible population. Those owning between £100 and £200, a sum that we established earlier as comfortable for an older father, furnished leaders in due proportion. Men of greater property were overrepresented by two to four times. Property mattered, yet was far from dominant. Only 16 percent of the elders owned more than £500. The median of £200, twice that of men forty to fifty-nine, also means that half of the colony's "better sort" had less than that; they were well-off but far from wealthy. Property, office, and status were associated but the relationship was suggestive rather than fundamental.

The leaders' standard of living is best judged by their household and

TABLE 9.3
Value of Leaders' Consumer Goods

	N	%
Poor (under £20)	35	3.9
Subsistence (£20–29)	65	7.3
Subsistence plus (£30–59)	205	23.0
Comfortable (£60–119)	339	38.1
Well-off (£120–99)	173	19.4
Luxury (£200+)	73	8.2
Total	890	99.9

personal goods. We would expect them to possess more than the average for fathers with adult children because their offices made demands on them for travel, entertainment, and style. The amount of £120 would certainly allow for living close to luxury, given Connecticut's characteristics, and for purposes of comparison we add another level at £200. Table 9.3 interprets their situation. The men with consumption articles below £20 and many in the next level were old, but they did include a few bankrupts and other poor individuals. Almost all of our leaders lived well above subsistence and the general median of £85 makes them well-off, as one would expect.[8] The surprising feature is the failure of one-third to achieve the comfort level and the fact that only a small proportion lived in luxury, indeed a rather subdued luxury since the leaders by definition included the wealthiest men.

Since Connecticut remained primarily agrarian and even those men not engaged in agriculture depended on it indirectly, the acres owned and the value of real property are important for describing the leaders. Appendix 9C contains the details, and here we simply state the generalizations. Most of them owned substantial farms. Indeed, in the New London area the median was almost 280 acres and overall it coincided with Windham's 178. This far exceeded the amount necessary for a profitable farm, and many of these men retained extensive undeveloped tracts.

The smallest properties belonged, as one might expect, to older men, though some of the townspeople had only a home lot. The desirability of a forty-acre farm shows in the increased frequency at that point. Most impressive are the number with tracts over 200 acres, and one-

[8] The median varies geographically as before from about £60 in the Windham district and £90 everywhere else. The highest proportion with more than £200 were in the trading towns.

sixth owned plantation-sized estates of 500. Since half of the leaders were not primarily farmers the importance of landownership to these men is clear: five out of six, regardless of age, owned a real farm and exclusive of retired men the true proportion may have been one out of ten.

The same generalizations apply to the value of their real property. The general median was just over £400, which would consist of the 178 acres averaging about £2 each, a house, barn, and often an additional structure such as a shop.[9] Once again we find 6 percent of the men without any such property and a slightly large proportion with under £100 worth, but even more owned estates exceeding £1,000. The largest number, almost a fourth, held between £500 and £1,000. Just one out of thirteen had £2,000 in real property, yet the leaders included the richest men in the colony, the justices of the peace, the members of the upper house of the legislature, and the principal military offers. Thus by this criterion too the leaders included almost no really rich men compared with most agricultural societies, concentrating around a respectable but relatively moderate median.

Two other species of property deserve attention: books and slaves. One would expect the leaders to value and purchase books and they did so, many enjoying real libraries. The median of something over a pound's worth is clearly too low, because almost all of the men whose inventories contained none were elderly men who surely had owned some when they were younger, and besides we have references in wills to books given that do not show up in the inventories. The right-hand column of Table 9.4 excludes them and shows that the true median was nearly £2. Ten pounds' worth certainly meant a couple of hundred

TABLE 9.4
Value of Books Owned by Leaders

	N	%	% of owners
None	72	8.4	—
Under £1	210	24.4	26.7
About £1	189	22.0	24.0
£2–4	211	24.5	26.7
£5–9	75	8.7	9.5
£10–19	49	5.7	6.2
£20+	55	6.4	7.0
Total	861	100.0	100.0

[9] This excludes ships.

volumes and is respectable. Obviously, few of these men were great readers, but almost all of them did own at least a Bible.

We saw earlier that slaves were uncommon in Connecticut except in a few prosperous towns along the Sound and among certain sorts of people, usually nonfarmers. We might suppose, however, that men at the top of the status order would certainly buy at least one. Actually, outside of the New London and Fairfield districts half of the leaders had none at all. In New Haven two-thirds did not, nor did three-fourths in Hartford and nearly four-fifths in Windham. This reinforces the conclusion that a slave had not become a necessary article of conspicuous consumption even for a man of property nor a servant essential to his wife. Overall, two-thirds of the leaders owned none, 15 percent had just one, 6 percent two, 8 percent three or four, and fewer than 5 percent had as many as five, these last including merchants who had imported slaves along with other trading goods. Thus the existence of a large staff of unfree servants, that symbol of an aristocracy, was missing in Connecticut, along with a big library, thousands of acres, and mansions finely furnished. Her leaders were men of the middling sort.

We turn now to a more particular description of the colony's principal men, examining first the leaders of the town and church, then those of wider importance. The deacons, as we have seen, came from respectable families, most of whom were farmers of moderate properties. The deacons themselves continued to farm and prospered, but seldom belonged to the economic upper class. If we include farmer-artisans, three out of four were farmers, a proportion actually higher than the norm for their age. Most of the rest were craftsmen, so that only 4 percent belonged to the intellectually prominent professionals and just 5.5 percent engaged in trade, only a third as many as among the leaders generally. One is tempted to associate this preference with a value judgment favoring honest toil, productive work, and so on, or to conclude that professionals and traders lacked religious enthusiasm, but they may just have been busy.

The church members certainly did not elect deacons for the money they might contribute. Their personal wealth in the probate records, while twice the general median, was well below that of other leaders. Only 8 percent owned over £400. But few were really poor, most of whom had retired, and they clustered around the very comfortable but far from luxurious median of £150.

So also they owned less consumption goods than their social equals by about one-third. Their median of £59 is just on the border of comfort for the older fathers, though well-to-do for a grandfather.

Practically none lacked the necessities but few, especially given their prestige, lived at our luxury level of £120 and only three individuals owned above £200 worth. Far more could have afforded to do so, and this seems clearly a matter of choice: they disapproved of immoderate spending.

They had nothing against buying land, however, and as men with some extra money who were disinclined to waste it on high living, they acquired substantial farms. Only one in six owned less than the familiar forty acres and these were elderly or nonfarmers, commonly artisans. The median was a very comfortable 140 and for the farmers among them a full quarter-section. Well over a third owned above 200 acres. This meant that they were buying more than they needed. The purchase brought them quite close to the median of the leaders generally both in acres and in the value of real property. Once again, very small and very large estates were uncommon.

Finally, we inquire whether they spent some of their extra income on books or servants. The answer is, yes on the former, up to a point. Over 90 percent owned at least one book, obviously a Bible, prayer book, or psalmbook, a proportion even higher than that for the leaders collectively. However, they almost never had more than the £5 worth that might qualify as a library—only 4 percent against 21 percent for all leaders. The median was a pound's worth. As to servants, they might hire but seldom bought any, and when they did, a single one sufficed. If we can assume that anyone with £200 in personal wealth could afford one, then about half of the potential buyers made the purchase. Alternatively, if we assume that £60 in consumption goods was ample, then anyone with, say, £80 could have bought a servant, which yields the same result. Perhaps this represents a moral judgment; it certainly confirms the conclusion that the deacons spent carefully and practically, and preferred to work rather than to purchase a laborer.

For illustrations we select four fairly typical men. Deacon John Hubbard of Middletown (1692-1753) was a farmer of average property. His father, Nathaniel, died at the age of eighty-seven, having given away most of his estate to seven daughters and three sons, of whom John was the second. John married Elizabeth Stow, the daughter of a farmer who died in 1722 with an inventory of £228. John and his wife had ten children when he died, at least two of whom had married. He left £102 in personal estate consisting of the usual farmer's possessions: a Bible and some other books, typical livestock, seven acres of rye still on the ground, a lot of hay, some bees and geese. His consumption goods totaled £54, which he probably needed for that family. Hubbard owned a house (£45), barn (£10), a seventeen-and-a-half acre home lot at £6 per acre, nine acres of upland noted as part of the home lot at £4.10, two acres of orchard worth £30, and thirty-eight other improved acres, the total therefore being sixty-seven acres appraised at £326, a higher value than the average, nothing spectacular but a good solid farm.[10]

Nathaniel Newell of Farmington (1704-1753) did have a family advantage: his father was an ensign and his older brother Daniel served as the minister in Middletown. His mother and his wife were both members of the reputable Hart family. The elder Newell's farm, still intact, contained 130 acres, ranging in value from £8 per acre for meadow down to £1.10, probably woodland. Nathaniel also owned twenty or thirty acres of undivided rights. His personal property totaled £204 of which £121 consisted of consumption goods, featured by £20 in clothing. He also owned a Bible, fourteen other books, and seven pamphlets, all valued at only 18 shillings, and the unusual sum of £13.26 in money.[11]

Deacon William Douglas's father was also a deacon and a deputy who moved from Boston to New London some time after 1645 and died there in 1682 at eighty. Ours enters the story primarily because, dying at forty-four, he left some children under age who, he wrote, should be taught to "read and write and siffer [cipher] well," and the four youngest, all boys, should be put out to good and pious families to learn good trades.[12] His farm in Plainfield, valued at £400 (around £300 cash) probably covered 150 to 200 acres. Douglas's will refers to a share in a vessel and his inventory includes a small amount of shop goods, also the "apparel of a servant that is dead" at £1.16. He owned the usual books and livestock and a less usual £177 in debts receivable, more than balanced by debts payable. The whole inventory totals £600 cash of which £60 was in consumption goods.

Finally, Deacon Eliasaph Preston of Wallingford (1643-1707) began without any known advantages. He was the fourth of five sons of William (1591-1647) and his second wife Mary (Robert) Seabrook. The deacon's first wife is unknown, the second and third belonged to average families. He owned a farm covering 384 acres in Wallingford but how much of this was improved we do not know, perhaps not much, for he lived at a time when Wallingford was a large frontier community. Even his three-acre meadow lot was valued at only £3

[10] Middletown district probate records, 1:23-26.
[11] Hartford district probate records, 17:7-8.
[12] New London probate records, B:282.

country pay. He also had a ninety-six-acre division worth £10. He had planted three acres of wheat and eight in rye and owned rather few farm animals—a yoke of oxen, three cows and three other cattle, a horse and mare, six sheep, and seven pigs. He and his wife and five children shared three beds. The consumption goods of £54 would seem adequate, though his own clothing took up £10 of this. The entire estate came to just £275, but that land would double in value almost at once. Preston's attributes that led to his election do not show in the probate records or his relationships. They clearly involve his own character and virtue, and these personal qualities rather than property or family probably account for most of the deacons.[13]

Captains resembled the deacons in their local sphere of activity, the fact that many lacked family connections, and their moderate economic status. However, they did own somewhat more property and generally enjoyed a higher standard of living along with slightly superior prestige.

The two groups were almost identical in occupation. Three out of four of both types of leaders came from farm families. Few of their fathers belonged to the professional class and less than 10 percent had engaged in trade. The captains' personal wealth exceeded that of deacons by one-third with a respectable median of £200. An even smaller percentage owned under £50, two-thirds of whom were elderly. The difference between the two appears primarily at the upper end of the scale, since nearly a third of the captains owned more than £300 as compared with one-sixth of the deacons, and the same ratio applies to the well-to-do men with £500.

The captains invested more of this surplus personal wealth in the form of consumption goods with over £80 worth and a particularly large concentration between £60 and £120, within or above our comfortable range. One-fourth owned even more—twice as many as in the case of deacons. They also owned more land, though the difference between the two was less. The typical captain had 173 acres or, excluding those with none, 189. Very few had under 40 and the majority ranged from 120 to 600. The number of large landowners with over 500 acres exceeded the deacons' by half. Their total real wealth was a third more than the deacons', and this contrast extended along the whole spectrum of real estate. This difference in wealth between the two types of leaders so similar in family background and of equal responsibility in the community probably arises from three or more

[13] New Haven district probate records, 3:97; Donald Lines Jacobus, *Families of Ancient New Haven*, 9 vols., 1922-1932, reprinted in 3 vols. (Baltimore, 1974).

circumstances. First, during the seventeenth century military service occasionally won a reward in the form of land grants. Second, the captains sometimes profited from their responsibility in supplying the companies. Finally, business acumen and executive ability probably characterized captains, whereas the qualities one sought in a deacon might not absolutely eliminate but would not necessarily include these capabilities. One can imagine a threadbare deacon but not a shabby captain.

The distribution of books differed little, few having none and even fewer many. On the other hand, the captains were much more inclined to buy a servant, more than a third owning at least one. Perhaps this simply reflected their greater surplus income. Following our guess that anyone with £60 in consumption goods could readily purchase a servant or slave, then only a third of the deacons who could, did, while more than half of the captains with money enough bought one. This suggests that economic considerations cannot account for the difference: captains preferred to own a slave where deacons preferred not to own one.[14]

Again we furnish a few sketches of captains nearly average in their characteristics and who did not hold another major office. Capt. Samuel Marshall was born in England sometime before 1630, probably about 1627 to judge from his date of marriage. We know nothing of his ancestry. He married a daughter of Lt. David Wilton (ca. 1605-1677), who moved to Northampton and left a small estate to his daughter, the only surviving child. Marshall had died two years earlier during King Philip's War. One of his five sons became a deacon. The captain's estate, valued at £632 (cash), included 130 acres of improved land and about 240 more of unimproved, some of it in Westfield. He left £177 in personal wealth, principally the usual livestock, tools, and crops. Of consumption goods he owned £96 worth, filling a small house. The parlor contained the best bed, surely for himself and his wife, and a trundle bed; the chamber over it had two featherbeds and two others, and the chamber over the hall held still another. Probably the eldest daughter, at eighteen, enjoyed her own little hall chamber, and the baby girl had the trundle bed, leaving six other children with four beds in the parlor chamber.[15]

Capt. Daniel Hubbell of Stratfield (1691-1736), on the other hand, belonged to a family quite prominent in local affairs. His father, Lieu-

[14] Again Appendix 9C supplies details. In this case there were 245 deacons and 369 captains.
[15] Hartford district probate records, 3:148, 4:26.

tenant Samuel (1657-1714), a shopkeeper, left a good property including two or three hundred acres to be divided among his five sons. Daniel's uncle, Lieutenant Richard, had served as deputy and his cousins included two captains, a deacon, and a minister. He himself became a farmer and a glazier, acquired a 102-acre farm and a 73-acre division, personal wealth of £194, and consumption goods valued at £60 not counting a silver tankard, but including a Bible and some other books.[16] Quite similar was Capt. Matthew Marvin of Norwalk (ca. 1703-1745), who also improved upon his father's rank of lieutenant, perhaps helped by his maternal grandfather, a deacon. He married an ensign's daughter and became a prosperous farmer with 126 acres and a personal estate of £154. The inventory informs us of his Bible and twenty-one books worth 22 shillings cash, and it also itemizes his livestock (£122) and crops, a mixture of hay, corn, oats, flax, wheat, and rye, worth £26.[17]

Finally, Capt. John Warner of Middletown (1708-1761) represents a slightly different type in that his father was also a Captain John (1671-1743), of a family that included a number of captains and deacons. Warner left a valuable 130-acre farm with a new house and an older one, a barn, a cowhouse, and a quarter interest in a sawmill. The land had already produced 110 bushels of wheat, 70 of oats, 20 of rye, and 14½ of barley, and 70 bushels of wheat remained on the ground, all valued at £48, besides which he owned the normal farm animals. His estate totaled £1,115, of which £277 was in personal wealth, consumption goods forming £117 of it. The possession of almost £3 worth of silver to display and £5.10 in money identifies him as a man of substance, a little (but only a little) above the average for a captain.[18]

The third group of locally chosen leaders consisted of the delegates or deputies. These resembled the captains very closely, and, indeed, they overlapped since many men held both offices. Certainly they drew from the same pool. The deputies more often were professional men, especially lawyers or public officials during the eighteenth century, and they included fewer farmers. Like the captains, few owned either small or large personal properties. The median in consumption goods was identical at £82, almost none except the aged failing to achieve a level of living well above subsistence. They owned the same number of acres, though the delegates included a few more with really large es-

---

[16] Fairfield district probate records, 8:360, 5:284.
[17] Fairfield district probate records, 9:270, 371.
[18] Middletown district probate records, 2:122.

tates. The deputies had more books, the median being close to £2, surely because the task of legislating for the colony required more information than commanding a militia company. Finally, slightly fewer had bought servants.

Ens. William Goodrich derives his interest for us both because he had average property for a deputy, and founded a line of leaders. Goodrich was the second son of an English clothier, after whose death he immigrated, arriving in Wethersfield in 1635 when quite young; thirteen years passed before he married. He left eight children when he died in 1676 including four boys, among them a future lieutenant, a captain, and a colonel. His four girls married well. In the New World Goodrich acquired an estate of £640 including at his death over sixty acres of improved land, seventy-eight more in wood, a fifty-acre unimproved tract, and another piece valued at £80, which could be anywhere from ten acres to several hundred. The year's crop of "corn," the meaning of which is uncertain, was worth £35, along with winter corn (wheat) on the ground and hay. He owned typical livestock, "husbandry tackling" and carpentry tools, about £9 in money, and £1 worth of books, while his consumption goods totaled £86. The long delay before marriage suggests that he did not bring any considerable property with him and that he acquired this good estate on his own.[19]

A year later Deacon John Moore died in Windsor in his middle or late sixties. His father Thomas, an obscure man, had died in 1645. John immigrated to Dorchester in 1630 and became a freeman the next year. His only son, also a deputy, achieved the higher status of justice. Moore became both a farmer and a craftsman, his will referring to a shop, a bake house, an assortment of tools, and timber for wheels. His improved land consisted of forty-nine acres, perhaps plus a river lot, forty-five in woods and upland, twenty in Simsbury, and thirty-six far up the river in Deerfield, in all 150 acres plus the lot. He pastured the usual animals and had harvested corn, rye, peas, oats, hay, a little wheat, and more than enough apples for four barrels of cider, collectively worth £15. Books and a basket came to £3 and his consumption goods to £80.[20]

Deacon and Deputy Nathaniel Chapman of Saybrook serves as a balance to the above men who lacked family advantages. Chapman (1653-1726) was the third and youngest son of Captain Robert (1616-1689), who immigrated from Hull and left three sons, all leaders, by

---

[19] Hartford district probate records, 3:175. His livestock consisted of a yoke of oxen, thirteen other cattle, four horses, thirteen sheep, and £12 worth of swine, probably fifteen to twenty animals.

[20] Hartford district probate records, 3:195.

his wife Ann Bliss. Our deputy himself produced a minister (Reverend Daniel of Fairfield). Chapman left a good estate of £797 as did his eldest son, who died the same year at age forty. The deacon-deputy owned a homestead with its buildings worth over £300, which surely means 30 acres, and over 100 other acres of improved land, plus 120 of lesser value and two rights; his son had 190. He also possessed, as one would expect, an exceptional amount of livestock: two yoke of oxen and a pair of steers coming along to replace one of them, six cows with two calves, nine other cattle, four horses, five pigs, forty-six sheep, and fourteen lambs. His books came to £2 and the consumption goods a very satisfactory £122. Substantial but not rich, of good though not prominent family, he typified the upper half of the deputies.[21]

Ministers resembled the captains and deputies in a general way, but with several striking variations. Their median personal wealth exceeded both, being over £200, but was peculiarly concentrated around that figure, half of them owning at their death between £100 and £300. Poverty was virtually unknown but so were estates over £1,000, and fewer left above £500 than did either of the two secular groups. They had an additional £24 in consumption goods of which all but £8 consisted of books. They almost always lived comfortably, a considerable majority were well-off, and some even achieved luxury. Only one in twenty captains possessed consumption goods valued at £200 but one out of seven ministers did so.

On the other hand, they acquired less real estate. Few fell below the twenty acres that would supply food and firewood, but in their case any deficiency would be met by the society. About one-fifth had a small farm of 40 to 80 acres and a similar group owned 200 to 500, with a median of 120. Anything above 60 acres or so surely exceeded their own needs and the surplus represented either inheritance from parents or wives, or purchases. One in five possessed over 500 acres, a larger proportion than any of the men discussed thus far, and it seems clear that the acquisition of land did not belie their religious conviction. The median value of this real wealth, however, fell considerably short of the captains and the delegates, suggesting a larger proportion left uncultivated. Again there were two modes, one between £100 and £300 (37.7 percent), the modest but adequate properties, the other between £500 and £1,000, the large estates (23.7 percent).

What distinguished the ministers above all was their books, valued at £17, almost always over £5 and sometimes ten times as much. We

[21] Guilford district probate records, 2:108.

can identify two groups. The ministers who did not inherit property or status, and who therefore had to assemble their own libraries, averaged under £10 worth apiece, and seldom over £20, while those from leading families owned more than twice as many.

Finally, exactly the same percentage owned slaves and servants as did the deputies, fewer than the captains. They rarely had more than one, and only three are known to have bought as many as five. Why so few bought slaves, if a need existed, or if need existed why any minister spent the money, remains a puzzle. The age and sex distribution follows that of Connecticut's slaves generally: three to two adults over children, the same ratio of male to female, and 50 percent more adult men than in the white population. One factor lies in the concentration along the south coast from Saybrook to Fairfield, which contained over half of the slaveowning ministers, and another little group in Middletown and Hartford, together accounting for three-fourths of the total, suggesting religion plus economics. The owners possessed above-average properties and in some cases we can see a need for a servant, free or slave, such as the childless man, the household with young children, or when all the children had left; but why the ministers found a slave preferable to one of the local lads or girls we do not know.

Samuel Stone (1602-1663) was one of the first-generation ministers. He had graduated from Cambridge (in 1623) and settled in Hartford. At his death he left £226 in personal property, of which an impressive £89 consisted of books. That still left almost £100 in consumption goods. The inventory describes his house: a parlor, a hall with two beds, a kitchen, and a study were the principal rooms. Above the parlor, hall, and kitchen were chambers, each with a bed, and another bed was in the garret. That not only provided six beds for his son (who died a drunkard) and three daughters, himself, and his wife, but one left over, perhaps that in the garret for a hired hand. In addition to the home lot he owned twenty acres of meadow and another ten or more in woodlands, certainly adequate.[22]

Reverend Roger Newton of Milford, another early settler, had better luck with his children, producing a captain and through him a series of leaders. His wife, the daughter of the Reverend Thomas Hooker, deserves equal credit. Newton, another Cambridge man, had probably reached seventy when he died in 1683 with an estate still valued at over £500 cash even though he had already endowed three of his eight children. The inventory lists five featherbeds and a trundle

---

[22] Hartford district probate records, 3:4-6.

bed—perhaps a daughter had claimed hers—and itemizes his books, mostly theological but with an Ovid, worth £35. The acreage of his farm is not specified except for fourteen acres of meadow at £49 cash. With this evaluation as a guide we can guess the whole at 130 acres. The consumption goods totaled a very comfortable £145. Also interesting is the debt of £35 owed by the town for his salary.[23]

Seth Pain (1702-1753) represents the self-made man among the ministers. The sixth son of John of Braintree, Massachusetts, Pain graduated from Yale at the age of twenty-six and obtained a church in far-off Stafford, probably marrying a Windham girl, for he had a small lot there. He also acquired a sixty-acre farm, an additional six acres probably in woods, and a house. The total estate was only £210, the personal property just adequate, and the £31 in consumption was rather low; but the children were all still small so they lived safely above subsistence, the farm supporting a good supply of livestock. Pain owned fifty-one books worth £2.4, less than a shilling apiece.[24]

We close with Ephraim Woodbridge of Groton (1680-1725). He was the third son of Reverend John of Wethersfield and Abigail Leete, daughter of the governor. His older brothers became ministers at Simsbury and West Springfield (his grandfather had been the minister in Springfield proper), and of his two sons who lived to maturity one became a successful doctor and the other, entitled "captain," was the father of another Reverend Ephraim. Our Ephraim married into one of Groton's leading secular families, the Morgans. He left an estate somewhat below average, especially as to consumption goods; but the inventory did not include his clothing and his wife probably claimed some household articles, for otherwise the property was comfortable. The acreage of his home lot is not given, but judging from the value it included twenty acres or so in addition to which he owned thirteen other acres and a third of a gristmill. The books, at £40, consisted of perhaps a hundred bound volumes and some in paper, interesting because of their variety: six volumes of Henry's *Annotations* (£13.10), ten "doctor physic" books, thirty-three schoolbooks, a lawbook, seventeen volumes of the history of Europe, six more on history, five miscellaneous, and £7 worth dealing with divinity.[25]

This diverse group of ministers accurately represents their basic characteristics. They were the most learned men of their communities, admired and influential. Their societies relieved them from financial

[23] New Haven district probate records, B:69, 104.
[24] Hartford district probate records, 16:284-85, 333.
[25] New London district probate records, C:104.

worries to concentrate on preaching and ministering to the congregation. Enough were born into ordinary families to prevent them from becoming a separate class, yet their colonywide dispersal, the college education most enjoyed, the books that they shared, and their occasional meetings enabled them to provide not only religious but intellectual leadership for all of Connecticut's people.

The justices of the peace and other judges, entitled to the "esquire," owned even more property than the preceding leaders. While farmers plus farmer-artisans still contributed half, that was a smaller proportion by far than the deputies, captain, or deacons; and fewer artisans attained that office. Instead, one-fourth were professional men, principally lawyers and officials—by which we mean that they earned their living primarily as judges—and the rest were traders. The income derived from three sources: inheritance, occupation outside of their legal functions, and the fees of their offices. The combination raised their economic position to a high one for the colony. The median personal property, at £275, considerably exceeded the level we considered "well-off" for the largest families and more were rich than fell below a subsistence-plus level. A justice of the peace was, like the minister, almost guaranteed a comfortable living. The same applied to the median for consumption, the considerable majority ranging from £60 to £200, with as many even above that than owned under £40. The latter were principally older men for whom even £20 was sufficient.

They added to this substantial wealth large farms, both under cultivation and undeveloped tracts. Their total median acreage came to 235, considerably above the other groups thus far considered, and one out of five had acquired over 500, almost as many as owned less than 80. The real estate exceeded £500 in value with again few small properties and one-quarter owning over £1,000 worth. This wealth led almost half to purchase a slave or servant, and nearly a quarter owned more than one. Finally, although they could not rival the ministers in books they averaged £2 worth. Over 90 percent had some, and more of them owned large libraries than anyone but ministers. Thus the justices, like the ministers, formed a large part of the educated class in Connecticut, deriving offices, property, and status at least in part from that advantage.

Capt. Gershom Clark, Esq., of Lebanon (1697-1747) typifies the justices. He succeeded his father, Captain William, to the office. William's father William, born in 1609, had immigrated to Dorchester in 1638 with his wife and from there moved to Northampton, where he became a lieutenant and served in the legislature, dying at the age of eighty-one. Captain William, also a deputy, the last of six sons, was born in 1656 and moved to Lebanon about 1700, marrying the daughter of Elder John Strong. He died at sixty-eight leaving five grown sons, of whom the third was Gershom. William had left 403 acres at his death, by which time all of the sons had married. With Captain Gershom the line of leaders ended. He operated the inherited farm valued in the inventory at about £430 cash, probably around 140 acres, and another £300 worth in four lots, which could mean anywhere from 100 acres on up to 600. He was raising livestock: the inventory notes that three fat hogs sold for nearly a pound each (weight therefore about a hundred pounds apiece) and three fat sheep had brought 10 shillings apiece, twice the average price. He also owned two yoke of oxen, six cows, and sixteen other cattle. The consumption goods of £116 featured the books he had given to his only son, plus some in Latin, Greek, mathematics, and religion, and an "interest" in the "Philogrammatian Library," the whole valued at £9.[26]

Capt. Asahel Strong of Farmington, who died four years after Clark, began with a simpler background but ended among the elite. His father Asahel (1668-1739) was a respectable farmer and maltster who left a property of £375. Perhaps his wife, the daughter of Deputy and Deacon Stephen Hart, brought exceptional ability, for her brother Thomas became a deputy, captain, and justice. Strong's younger brother, also a deputy and justice of the peace, attained the rank of colonel and married a minister's daughter. Asahel himself found an equal in Ruth Hooker, daughter of John, Esquire. As to property he remained almost exactly average for the rank. The 136 acres of improved land are itemized, beginning with the five-acre home lot surrounding his "mansion" house, barn, and malthouse. He also owned seventy-three acres in undeveloped land, all of which totaled £762. His £268 worth of personal property included a fine herd of cattle and £7.15 in books. These consisted of a Bible, three lawbooks and a clerk's guide, one on military matters, one on arithmetic, a dictionary, ten history books, twenty-four others, and fifty-one pamphlets; he too owned a right in a library. An addition to the inventory tells us of fifty-eight bushels of wheat supplementing earlier items of a hundred bushels of oats and twenty-eight of corn, these collectively probably forming a surplus for sale worth £18. Incidentally, he owned tools for cooperage, carpentry, and reed-making (for looms) in addition to the malthouse.[27]

Finally, Capt. Samuel Couch of Fairfield (1670-1740) also owned typical property but made his way by himself. The youngest of three

[26] Windham district probate records, 3:445.
[27] Hartford district probate records, 16:23.

sons of Simon (d. 1688), a farmer, he married a young widow, Edrea (Thomas) Hurlbut of Woodbury, who bore him five sons, none of them distinguished. His neighbors elected him both captain and a deputy at age forty, and he became a justice thirteen years later. Couch still owned about 129 acres of improved land when he died, judging from the values, plus another 120 undeveloped at Redding, where at least two of his sons settled, and a large tract in the same town. The money for these purchases must have come to some extent from his office, for the farm was good but not exceptional. He owned only four books: a Bible, a lawbook, and two others, combined worth £1. The consumption goods totaled £62, just comfortable. Couch's career illustrates the opportunity afforded by the colony, and perhaps at the same time the limits imposed by the lack of family inheritance or connections.[28]

Property increased with rank, and the majors, colonels, generals, and assistants owned more of everything. They also came more often from leading families, as we have seen, and only a minority were farmers. We will distinguish between the military and civil officers while stressing the strong resemblance between them.

In both cases these highest of all leaders normally owned farms that supplemented some other occupation. Two-fifths were professionals, lawyers in particular furnishing assistants; and the men we are terming public officials, the military men. One-fifth engaged in trade. Farmers and a few farmer-artisans supplied one-third but plain artisans very rarely served in such high positions. The assistants were even less likely than the military officers to be farmers or artisans, since nothing in the careers of such men would prepare them for positions requiring both information and technical ability. Traders and lawyers, on the other hand, and those who had customarily held important political positions, did qualify. Also, selection required that the candidate be widely known as well as respected, which gave an advantage to those serving conspicuously or traveling widely, as did the merchants and justices.

Their large property came partly from inheritance, from their occupation before and after taking office, and from the offices themselves, as we discussed earlier. The military men had the advantage in this, apparently because many of the assistants did not try to accumulate wealth; the position may have demanded more time for less pay. The difference, however, was small. The officers' median personal wealth was £350, that of the assistants who did not hold high military rank, £275, of those who did, just short of £300. As usual the estates

---

[28] Fairfield district probate records, 9:36.

clustered between £100 and £300, but a significant percentage owned more than £500 and almost one-fifth of the officers left over £1,000.

The surprising thing about their consumption goods is the low median compared to what we expect from men of the highest status— only a little over £100. Just two of eighty-four inventories list more than £400 worth, plus three over £300, though far more could certainly have afforded to live in luxury. Indeed, almost one-fifth did not even grant themselves comfort, most of whom had not retired but lived simply, as it seems by choice. The vast majority enjoyed life's amenities, with houshold articles not only useful but pleasurable and valuable. They lived well, but not expensively. So also, few acquired the landed estates typical of their contemporaries in colonies to the west and south. Just 13 percent, perhaps a few more, owned a thousand acres. On the other hand almost all the rest, among those still active, had a farm above 120 acres, the median being nearly 300. The median value of real wealth reached almost £700, the military men in this case owning a little more than the assistants. Again, however, one is struck by the scarcity of really large properties, only 12 percent leaving more than £2,000 worth. No doubt at the height of their incomes the proportion would increase, but even if we elevate all of the retired men to the highest level, which is absurd, the figure would not exceed one in five.

Both sets of high officials owned for the period a respectable number of books, the median of £3 second only to the ministers' libraries. Only 4 percent of the inventories contained none, and these probably incorrectly. At the other end of the scale, 15 percent owned over £10 worth. Assistants greatly exceeded the officers in this respect: their median was the same, but the officers almost never had invested as much as £10 whereas more than a fifth of the assistants did so.

The greatest difference between the two groups of leaders lay in their purchase of slaves. One is tempted to generalize that the officers bought slaves rather than books, but actually all of these men could have doubled or tripled their libraries without affecting their ability to buy laborers. Occupational differences may have had some influence, since a slave might benefit a farmer more than a lawyer; but the difference overwhelms any such explanation. Only a fifth of the assistants who did not double as officers owned any, whereas half of the officers had one or more. The figure for the entire set of these leaders is 36 percent possessing slaves or servants, obviously not counting free laborers. Since economic, occupational, or family factors seem inadequate to account for so great a disparity one is led to conclude that some characteristics of high military rank, lacking among the assist-

351

ants, disposed the officers to buy a slave. A possible clue may lie in the composition of the slave force. The officers preferred adult men even more than most Connecticut buyers, a fact that suggests the use of personal manservants or possibly field hands. On the other hand the assistants, excluding those also officers, actually owned more children than adults, and mature males formed fewer than one-fourth, which indicates household help—both articles of consumption, but with quite different values implied.

Two members of Stratford's Gold family introduce these interlocking groups of leaders. The father of Nathan (ca. 1620-1694) was a yeoman, and we do not know his early history. He may have had a wife before marrying the widow of Edmund Harvey, a trader who died in 1648 leaving a small property. Thus Gold seems to have reached the rank of judge in 1656, assistant the next year, and major in 1673, on his own. At his death he left an excellent estate for the time and place totaling £280 in personal wealth and £1,177 in realty. The latter consisted of two houses and at least 150 acres of improved land plus as much more unimproved (the quantities were not given). He was raising grain and livestock as usual, with an assortment of tools amounting to £20, had £14 in cash and silver plate, two Indian servants, and books valued at £3. His four daughters married quite well, and his only son, Nathan (1663-1723), became the deputy-governor, a captain, and chief justice. Nathan the second married a Talcott, one of Hartford's first families, and the combination produced, in the male line, John, Esquire, and Reverend Hezekiah. Nathan improved upon his father's estate, leaving £578 in personal wealth and £2,032 in real estate, the latter consisting of 130 acres improved and 1,400 unimproved. He shifted from Indian servants to black slaves—a man, boy, and girl, of whom the last, says the inventory, "lives on" bed and bedding worth about £2. He had the same collection of tools (cooper, joiner, turner, glazier, farmer, a sawmill and a malthouse), books valued at £4.10, now mostly on law, more silver and more cash. Both owned a little over £100 in consumption goods, moderate given their economic position, and it is notable that the younger Nathan, with a larger family and twice as much personal property, actually had less.[29]

Major and Judge Moses Mansfield of New Haven (ca. 1640-1703) was another self-made man. He was the second of two sons of Richard, who left a small property in 1655, and Gilian Drake. Mansfield's

[29] Ibid., 4:179, 6:161, 174; for the family, see Donald Lines Jacobus, *History and Genealogy of the Families of Old Fairfield*, 2 vols., 1930; reprinted in 3 vols. (Baltimore, 1976), 1:228-31, 371-73.

first wife was the daughter of Henry Glover, whose property totaled only £200 at his death in 1689, and on or after 1685 he married Abigail, daughter of Thomas Yale. The Yale connection sounds important, but Thomas was an ordinary farmer, leaving £336 in 1683, and was an uncle, not the father, of Elihu. Mansfield became a deputy in 1676, assistant in 1692, and major two years later. He sired eight children, of whom the oldest son, educated at Harvard, died young. The second, however, became a justice and the third a deacon. Mansfield had given some of his property when he died, leaving an estate of about £700. He then owned a farm of thirty-eight acres, a home lot, sixty acres of less value, and between thirty and eighty acres more. His personal estate of £232 included a good supply of livestock, the usual grains, and a very comfortable £113 worth of consumption goods. Probably he had once owned more than that. He had three good beds, enough for himself and wife, one single daughter and a teenaged boy, but the six married children would have required more, which one guesses had gone to the four girls.[30]

We conclude with another seventeenth-century man of fairly typical characteristics, Major and Assistant Samuel Mason of Stonington (1664-1705). Mason was the oldest of three sons of Major and Governor John of Norwich (1600-1672). He himself left no sons to pass on the sequence. Mason's inventory lists £641 in real and £288 in personal property. The former consisted of 150 acres of undeveloped land, a town lot, the house lot, and an island valued at £600, which, if it was improved, translates to 200 acres. Presumably on the island he pastured an excellent herd of eighty-three cattle and thirteen horses. He owned £20 worth of clothes and armor, four lawbooks, ten on dentistry, four on history, and a couple of others, totaling twenty for £5 (lawbooks were expensive then, too). The consumption goods came to £98, ample for four daughters. Mason, like the others we have described, really had quite a small estate, considering the importance of his offices.[31] Other men owned much more, and to this economic upper class we now turn.

The wealthiest men in Connecticut's society, less than 10 percent of the leaders and under 1 percent of the people, formed a varied conglomerate rather than a uniform class. Almost every occupation contributed. One-third were farmers and an additional 4 percent doubled as farmer-artisans. Two out of five derived their incomes from trade, generally as import-export merchants. The remaining fourth were di-

[30] New Haven district probate records, 2:317.
[31] New London district probate records, 1:319.

vided about equally among officials, lawyers, ministers, and artisans. The last, however, were really manufacturers, entrepreneurs like the merchants. In modern terms we would classify them as businessmen, 47 percent, farmers, 36 percent, and professionals, 17 percent, but they overlapped, as we have seen, the farmers often earning money from other investments and the others owning farms.

This economic aristocracy did not always own large amounts of personal property. A few of the farmers did not even have £100 worth, and one-fourth left less than £500. Just one in five possessed the £2,000 that would qualify them as wealthy by general colonial standards, and the median was £900. Judging from consumer goods the situation also permits interpretations in either direction. On the one hand, nobody lived less than comfortably (a few exceptions being attributable to old age or a fluke of the inventory) and 37 percent had the £200 that meant luxury. But that is not a really impressive sum. Presumably all of these leaders earned enough to afford a high standard of living, yet the median was a moderate £160 and only eighteen individuals out of ninety-eight had £300 worth; not a soul owned household goods worth £500.

Real wealth better shows why these men deserve their place in this chapter. Even though three-fifths were not primarily farmers only three owned less than 80 acres and almost all had over 200. The median was 700 and more than a third held 1,000, very large estates in New England. Obviously some of that land consisted of unimproved tracts, especially in the properties before 1730 or so, but the average value, after allowing for the price increase, was over £2 per acre. The largest properties belonged to Zachariah Tomlinson of Stratford, who left 2,406 improved and 750 unimproved acres, which his appraisers evaluated at £10,333 in 1771, and John Chester's £11,698 for 1,686 acres in the Wethersfield area.[32]

The wealth of these men did not translate into large libraries. The median was £3, not much above that for the leaders as a whole and far below that of the ministers at £17. Indeed, only one out of ten equaled such a sum. The best we can say is that they all did have *some* books, which is not saying very much given their incomes.

So also, more happily, they did not always invest in slaves. Once more an interpretative line can run either way, for one could observe that two out of five did have at least one, a high proportion for the colony. But by definition all these men owned at least £2,000 worth

---

[32] Land values are multiplied by 0.6. The actual inventory price was over £3 per acre. Tomlinson's and Chester's holdings are not adjusted.

of property, cash value, at their death, so that everyone could have afforded a slave or indentured servant. In the southern colonies and the northern cities everyone who could, did. In Connecticut, however, three out of five bought none at all and only eleven of our group, less than 10 percent, owned five or more. Slave owning, then, was not automatic even with the rich. It did not serve as an invariable symbol of status nor as an economic necessity. These men undoubtedly had household servants, but they hired free girls just as they contracted with free men and boys for work in the fields or personal help. The rich farmers were more inclined to buy servile labor than the other wealthy men, and, when they did so, to buy adult men, so that nearly half owned an unfree field laborer, but even they averaged just one apiece. Three out of five traders and professionals bought one, the former averaging 0.79 men each and the professionals 0.57. The last, indeed, owned about as many females as males and nearly as many young as old. Thus most of the rich men, if they relied on slaves at all, probably bought a maid for housework or a personal manservant, and the expenditure formed an insignificant part of their wealth.

Alexander Allin (ca. 1663-1708) immigrated to Windsor from Scotland in 1689 and entered into trade, probably through Boston and possibly with two brothers who remained in Scotland. We do not know his parentage. He married Elizabeth Cross, the daughter of a small farmer. They had three sons and a daughter of whom the eldest, Alexander, became a wealthy merchant and landowner; we lack an inventory. The elder Allin's estate, reckoned (says the appraisor) with silver at 8 shillings the ounce, came to a little over £2,000. He had bought about 400 acres, half of it improved, and owned two warehouses and a shop. The personal estate included £12 worth of books, and he also had books for sale as part of his "stock," a considerable sum in debts receivable, and £120 or so in money, jewelry, and silver plate, but no slaves. His will left bequests to the church and a school. Whether he had been a poor boy we do not know, but he certainly had made good.[33]

Colonel and Deacon Samuel Gilbert (1712-1772) on the other hand, belonged by birth to the colony's upper class. "Marshal" Jonathan, a trader and innkeeper of Hartford, married the daughter of Elder John White and started the family fortune, leaving an estate of £1,740. The most successful son was his fourth, Captain Samuel, an innkeeper who married into the Rogers family of New London. Among his sons were Captain Nathaniel of Coventry and Captain Samuel (1688-1760), a

---

[33] Hartford district probate records, 7:199-204, 12:231-32.

large landowner. The latter's first son, our man, was born in Lebanon, lived much of his life in Hebron where he married a deacon's daughter, and died in Lyme, New Hampshire, leaving an estate of £2,451 in personal and £2,839 in real property. The inventory includes only a small quantity of consumption goods but he must have once possessed a good deal. He owned a male slave (£55), a large quantity of debts receivable, and a substantial amount of land, notably farms of 250, 123½, 105 and 65 acres, all with houses (the first identified as "white"), each given to a son, averaging £4 per acre. For himself he had purchased land in Lyme, where he was just starting to farm. He was, in short, a creditor and large landowner.[34]

Our final example comes from the Burr family of Fairfield. The immigrant, Jehu, of unknown parentage and wife unknown, died without an inventory. He had served as deputy and earned the title "mister," so joins our lesser leaders. A daughter married a captain and all of the sons became prominent: Lieutenant Jehu, a deputy; Major John, an assistant; Nathaniel, a deputy; and Mr. Daniel. Of these, the first paid one of the top assessments and acquired 294 acres, though his inventory was just £745. The second also prospered but did not achieve wealth, the third left no inventory, and Mr. Daniel remained a prosperous but ordinary farmer. The reader may recall that Fairfield, though possessed of some excellent land, developed rather slowly until the depression lifted toward 1700.

Lieutenant Jehu (1625-1692) married as his second wife the minister's daughter. Of their children, two daughters married into the Wakeman and Gold families, already noted. The two sons who survived to marry were another Mr. Daniel, who acquired over a thousand acres and left an estate of £3,309, and Major Peter. Daniel we will not follow, but remark that his sons included Deacon Stephen and Reverend Aaron of Princeton. Major Peter (1668-1724) graduated from Harvard and served as assistant and of course a judge. He accumulated over 200 acres and left an estate valued at £3,429 of which £1,369 was in personalty. Most of Burr's land was highly developed and included three farms. His consumption goods of £287 consisted of rich household furnishings, itemized in the inventory, and £10 or so in books. He specialized in wheat, apparently to the extent of twenty acres; and in livestock, owning eighty head of cattle, some of which he had fattened quite successfully for the market, thirty horses, and 240 sheep. He had purchased five slaves: a Negro man and his

[34] Colchester district probate records, 4:101-120.

wife; "Mingo"; another woman "Moll" who was worth more than the other three combined; and a Negro girl of equal value.[35]

The major left two sons and two daughters. The second son, Gershom, owned a respectable property but achieved no distinction. Thaddeus (1700-1755), however, became a justice of the peace and more than doubled his father's economic success. His land covered 2,913 acres of which he was using 378. He too raised both livestock and grains, and he owned a similar group of slaves: a man, "wench," girl, and child. The consumption goods exceeded £200. These featured fourteen pictures, twelve maps, and a library valued at only £3.2 but containing nine volumes, sixty pamphlets, and twenty-nine magazines, with the *Spectator*, Cato's *Letters*, Euclid, and Locke. Over half of the personalty was in the form of debts receivable. The estate certainly deserves admiration—only three in the county exceeding it—but one cannot call the man truly rich; one of the wealthiest and most distinguished families in the colony had just £14 worth of clothing even at age fifty-five, and invested most of his capital in land, not in conspicuous consumption. The four slaves, at £67, equaled only one-twelfth of the value of his land and half as much as his cattle.[36]

We must not leave Connecticut's leaders with the Burrs imprinted on our memory. Instead, let us summon ten of them to a major's spacious farmhouse, in Milford. None of these is elegantly clad and four wear the common clothes of men who work with their hands. The major's slave girl helps his wife, and if we were meeting in the homes of several of the others we might find a local daughter hired as a house-servant. The major himself owns 300 acres, half improved in one way or another, including the home farm inherited from his father, the local country "squire."

Another prominent family has two representatives present: the elderly minister and his son, a deputy. The Reverend himself came from another town where his father, a prosperous farmer, had served as the respected longtime moderator of the town meeting and a frequent deputy like his grandson. Another family combination consists of the present justice and his father. The judge is, like the minister, a college man and a well-to-do lawyer. He and the minister own the town's only considerable libraries. His father, who continues to serve as deputy now and then, came from an ordinary farm family and rose both economically and socially. Two brothers form a fourth family, the sons of a respected blacksmith and captain, one succeeding his father and

[35] Fairfield district probate records, 6:168.
[36] Ibid., 11:352.

the other, not an officeholder, prospering through trade sufficiently to equal, in that respect, our host the major. Finally, four of those present did not enjoy any inherited advantages: the deputy already introduced, father of the justice; the second of two captains and one of the two deacons, both plain farmers though with special qualities; and the other deacon, the town's miller. Our group, with four men unrelated to any of the principal families and including two artisans and four farmers, did not form a separate upper class by inheritance or wealth, nor did it constitute an establishment, standing order, or elite, but was in Jefferson's words the town's *natural* aristocracy, rising in part with the help that established families can offer, in part due to their own worth, and in either case holding their positions with the consent of the community.

Age at Taking Office by Cohorts

	Year of birth	21–29	30–39	40–49	45–59	50–54	55–59	60+	N	Median
Deputies	1600–1619	2	17	14	9	10	5	6	63	44
	1610–1629	2	18	9	2	0	0	1	32	38
	1630–1639	2	14	4	1	7	2	0	30	39
	1640–1649	2	6	9	23	11	1	4	56	47½
	1650–1659	2	13	10	12	6	4	2	49	45
	1660–1669	2	15	15	11	5	3	0	51	42½
	1670–1679	1	15	13	10	2	2	0	43	42
	1680–1689	5	14	10	5	0	0	0	34	38
	1690–1699	3	12	14	5	2	1	1	38	41
	1700–1709	6	12	8	2	2	2	0	32	39
	1710–1729	1	7	12	1	1	0	0	22	41½
Captains	1600–1619	0	1	2	1	4	4	7	19	57
	1620–1629	0	3	2	5	7	0	2	19	49
	1630–1639	0	1	6	1	2	2	4	16	49½
	1640–1649	1	1	0	16	9	5	2	34	49
	1650–1659	0	2	3	5	6	7	4	27	52
	1660–1669	0	9	8	13	7	3	1	41	46½
	1670–1679	0	4	10	14	13	3	4	48	48½
	1680–1689	2	5	11	10	10	3	1	42	46½
	1690–1699	0	8	16	24	7	3	1	59	47
	1700–1709	2	12	20	22	15	5	0	76	47
	1710–1719	0	9	19	14	6	6	0	54	44½
	1720–1729	0	9	12	8	9	2	0	40	44
Justices of the Peace	1600–1619	2	3	3	2	2	3	3	18	47½
	1620–1629	0	2	1	1	1	0	4	9	52½
	1630–1639	2	5	1	0	3	5	3	19	52½
	1640–1649	1	0	4	9	6	2	4	26	49
	1650–1659	0	4	5	2	6	2	1	20	47½
	1660–1669	3	6	5	2	3	1	1	21	42
	1670–1679	0	2	10	5	6	1	1	25	45
	1680–1689	0	1	6	7	3	0	0	17	47
	1690–1699	0	5	11	10	6	1	0	33	44½
	1700–1709	3	9	9	7	5	3	0	36	43
	1710–1719	1	7	5	4	3	4	0	24	44
	1720–1729	1	5	7	1	4	3	0	21	42½

APPENDIX 9B

Social Origin of Leaders

SONS OF FATHERS WHO WERE LEADERS

Fathers	Deacons	Captains	Deputies	Ministers	Justices	Majors & up & Ass'ts.	Economic leaders	% leaders born of econ. leaders
Deacons	40.7	15.5	9.8	19.2	9.8	6.2	4.3	0.9
Captains	27.1	43.6	12.6	16.4	10.5	17.5	18.1	2.2
Deputies	11.0	6.4	36.1	2.3	19.6	13.4	5.3	3.1
Ministers	3.4	6.4	10.2	40.1	13.1	14.4	10.6	3.3
Justices	0	9.5	8.5	7.3	22.2	15.5	14.9	5.8
Major & up	0	3.0	4.9	4.0	3.9	10.3	1.1	5.9
Assistants	1.7	3.0	10.2	4.5	11.8	11.3	8.5	3.1
Economic leaders	7.6	1.9	2.9	2.8	3.9	3.1	34.0	21.8
Social leaders	8.5	10.6	4.9	3.4	5.2	8.2	3.2	4.9
Total	100.0	99.9	100.1	100.0	100.0	99.9	100.0	
N	118	264	246	177	153	97	94	

Father-leaders	35.5	48.6	48.0	53.4	59.1	58.8	60.3	
Mother or wife	9.3	7.6	6.4	2.1	6.2	3.6	5.8	
Ordinary	45.2	36.3	32.3	40.4	27.4	23.6	24.4	
Unclear	1.5	1.1	2.3	0	1.9	1.8	0.6	
Unknown	8.4	6.4	11.1	4.2	5.4	12.1	9.0	
Total	99.9	100.0	100.1	100.1	99.9	99.9	100.1	
N	332	543	514	337	259	163	156	TOTAL: 2,306
Mobile of known	45.2	39.2	37.3	42.0	29.6	27.5	27.0	37.5
Plus uncertain	53.1	43.8	45.7	44.5	34.7	37.6	34.0	43.8
Probable mobile	40	41	41	44	32	31	30	41

NOTE: Among the categories across the top, deacons are exclusive of captains, captains exclude deputies; deputies includes those who were captains, justices includes all who were esquires; assistants includes deputies since all were; economic includes all wealthy.

Leaders' Age at Death

	Deacons	Captains	Deputies	Ministers	Justices	Majors and up	Assistants	Economic leaders
21–29	0	0	0	3.2	0	0	0	0
30–39	0	3.0	1.8	6.1	1.6	3.4	1.6	5.0
40–49	10.3	11.5	4.2	8.7	9.1	11.9	10.9	11.5
50–59	14.9	21.8	12.0	17.5	18.7	13.6	14.1	28.0
60–69	21.7	27.6	19.8	23.0	25.7	37.3	39.1	28.6
70–79	28.6	22.7	42.5	24.8	30.0	18.6	23.4	20.3
80+	24.6	13.3	19.8	16.6	15.0	15.2	10.9	6.6
Total	100.1	99.9	100.1	99.9	100.1	100.0	100.0	100.0
N	175	330	167	343	187	59	64	182

Leaders' Age at Death

For the benefit of those interested in the ages and life expectancies of various types of people, I supply data on these leaders. They consist of two groups: those who acquired their positions when relatively young and those who generally did so in the forties.

If the misters and gentlemen, the economic upper class, and the ministers had inherited their status or wealth we ought to find about 15 percent of them dying before they reached age thirty, minus something for a relatively sheltered life, and another 15 percent in their thirties at death. Actually none of the first two died before age thirty nor did the expected proportion appear in probate records during their next decade. Therefore we conclude that both the titles and the wealth had to be earned. In the latter case, a man of large property would as we know divide his estate, so that even an only son would inherit at most two-thirds if his mother lived, as she almost always did, and only one-third, if he had two sisters. Some succeeded in recreating the property or in establishing a new fortune during their forties, but judging from the age distribution most men did not acquire our minimum of £2,000 until age fifty. At that point they could expect fifteen more years. (N = 182. Inventories through 1789, no change in life expectancy over time.)

So also the men with social titles of respect did not receive them automatically but had to earn, or confirm them by some accomplishment or behavior pattern, in their case apparently during their forties. For some reason an abnormal number died then so that their life expectancy at age forty was eighteen years and at age fifty, twelve years.

Many ministers did obtain their appointments while still in their twenties and a few died then, but only 4 percent. Their median age of death at sixty-five reflects in part the date of their selection in the middle twenties rather than at age twenty-one, and because others never became ministers and so do not enter our pool. More statistically accurate are the median ages at death of sixty-seven for a man of forty and seventy years for a man of fifty. Both of these compare favorably with the life expectation of the population at large.

The other leaders reached their positions later in life and therefore the age structure was skewed upward. None died in the twenties nor did any deacon before thirty. The age of death for captains was the youngest of this group at sixty-five, not because they received the position first but because of wars. However higher-ranking officers only survived another year. Then came the justices at age sixty-eight, with both deacons and deputies (including assistants) at no less than seventy-one. If we assumed that all these men won their selection by age fifty, then we could state their expected age at death from that point as follows: captains, sixty-eight; justices, seventy; deputies, seventy-two; deacons, seventy-three. Later age at taking office probably accounts for the difference between these and the economic leaders, who died at about age sixty-five.

APPENDIX 9D

Leaders' Property

Personal £	Deacons	Captains	Deputies	Ministers	Justices	Majors & up	Assistants	Economic leaders
1–49	12.7	6.8	7.1	2.5	2.3	0	1.8	0
50–99	18.4	16.3	16.6	17.4	10.7	3.9	3.5	0
100–199	37.1	27.1	29.5	26.4	26.6	17.3	22.8	4.0
200–299	16.3	18.7	18.6	24.8	14.0	23.1	24.6	5.6
300–399	7.3	13.3	11.2	15.7	16.4	13.5	8.8	10.3
400–499	0.8	4.9	3.1	5.8	6.5	5.8	10.5	7.1
500–599	6.1	9.5	9.2	6.6	12.6	17.3	17.5	27.7
1,000+	1.2	3.5	4.7	0.8	10.7	19.2	10.5	45.2
Total	99.9	100.1	100.0	100.0	99.8	100.1	100.0	99.9
N	245	369	295	121	214	52	57	126
Consumption								
1–19	6.9	2.6	3.9	3.0	1.1	0	1.8	0
20–39	20.2	15.5	13.8	8.0	12.4	10.9	7.4	3.1
40–59	23.6	17.1	18.9	5.0	14.6	8.7	7.4	3.1
60–119	36.5	40.3	36.2	44.0	36.2	37.0	35.2	29.6
120–199	11.3	19.4	23.6	26.0	23.2	23.9	27.8	27.6
200–299	1.0	3.2	2.8	12.0	9.7	13.0	14.8	18.4
300–399	0.5	1.9	0.8	2.0	2.2	4.4	3.7	14.3
400–499	0	0	0	0	0.5	2.2	1.9	4.1
Total	100.0	100.0	100.0	100.0	99.9	100.1	100.0	100.2
N	203	310	254	100	185	46	54	98

Acres	Deacons	Captains	Deputies	Ministers	Justices	Majors & up	Assistants	Economic leaders	All
None	4.8	7.4	7.6	5.7	5.2	2.0	5.6	0.9	6.0
1–9	2.4	1.9	0.4	2.9	1.0	0	1.8	0	2.4
10–19	1.9	2.2	2.4	4.8	1.6	4.1	1.8	1.9	2.6
20–39	6.8	3.8	6.0	8.6	4.1	2.0	1.8	0	5.1
40–79	17.4	10.9	12.0	19.0	9.8	4.1	1.8	0	13.3
80–119	12.1	11.5	7.6	8.6	5.7	2.0	5.6	1.9	9.4
120–199	17.8	18.6	16.3	8.6	16.6	16.3	18.5	3.7	15.8
200–499	27.0	29.5	30.0	21.9	35.2	49.0	33.3	19.6	28.4
500–999	6.8	10.3	11.2	9.5	9.8	12.2	9.3	35.5	10.4
1,000+	2.9	3.8	6.4	10.5	10.9	8.2	20.4	36.4	6.6
Total	100.9	99.9	99.9	100.1	99.9	99.9	99.9	99.9	100.0
N	207	312	251	105	193	49	54	107	1,278
Median	140	173	174	120	220	290	250	683	176
Median with	152	189	210	155	235	290	300	700	192

Real wealth, £	Deacons	Captains	Deputies	Ministers	Justices	Majors & up	Assistants	Economic leaders
None	5.3	6.5	6.2	5.3	4.6	2.0	5.2	0.8
1–49	6.2	2.8	2.7	3.5	2.3	2.0	3.5	0
50–99	5.8	3.1	7.3	5.3	5.7	4.1	3.5	0
100–199	15.6	10.5	12.0	18.4	6.9	8.2	8.6	0.8
200–299	15.1	12.2	14.3	19.3	12.0	6.1	12.1	0.8
300–399	14.2	10.2	9.3	8.8	5.1	4.1	6.9	0.8
400–499	8.0	10.5	8.9	7.9	10.3	6.1	6.9	1.6
500–999	20.4	26.3	23.9	23.7	28.6	36.7	27.6	9.6
1,000–1,999	8.0	14.2	12.7	6.1	16.6	20.6	12.1	40.0
2,000+	1.3	3.7	2.7	1.8	8.0	10.2	13.8	45.6
Total	99.9	100.0	100.0	100.1	100.1	100.1	100.2	100.0
N	225	353	259	114	175	49	58	125
Median £	325	446	383	289	530	700?	600?	1,880

Continued

Slaves and servants	Deacons	Captains	Deputies	Ministers	Justices	Majors & up	Assistants	Economic leaders
None	82.4	63.3	67.7	67.7	57.5	48.9	73.7	34.2
1	8.8	16.1	14.4	19.2	17.1	25.5	8.8	15.8
2	2.9	7.0	6.6	5.1	9.8	6.4	7.0	11.7
3	2.0	4.7	5.4	5.1	7.8	4.3	5.3	11.7
4	0.4	2.8	3.1	0	2.6	0	0	11.7
5+	3.4	6.0	2.7	3.0	5.2	14.9	5.3	14.9
Totals	99.9	99.9	99.9	100.0	100.0	100.0	100.1	100.0
Leader's occupation								
Farmers	65.1	65.3	57.4	—	44.2	30.9	25.0	32.2
Farmer-artisan	10.2	10.5	9.8	—	5.0	5.4	3.3	4.1
Artisans	14.9	11.0	9.5	—	7.0	5.4	8.3	7.4
Lawyers	1.9	2.5	5.1	—	11.6	13.2	20.0	5.0
Doctors	0.4	0.6	1.8	—	2.0	1.8	1.7	0.8
Officials	1.4	1.4	5.1	—	11.6	20.0	21.7	5.8
Traders	5.6	8.8	11.3	—	17.6	18.2	20.0	39.7
Other	0.4	0	0	—	1.0	5.4	0	5.0
Total	99.9	100.1	100.0		100.0	100.3	100.0	100.0
N	215	354	275		199	55	60	121

TEN

Conclusion

Connecticut's white society began in the 1630s as an emigration from Massachusetts and to a lesser extent from England. The settlers justified their removal as an extension of the great "Puritan" diaspora and acknowledged a desire for more land. The prospect attracted, not a cross-section of the settlers in the Bay colony, but a mixture of youthful families and young single males who displayed as much enthusiasm for dividing the land as for establishing churches.[1] The average age was scarcely over thirty; men outnumbered women at least two to one; and the great majority had neither property nor social status.

About half of the young bachelors and a fourth of all the men either died very soon after their arrival or continued their dispersal, generally out of our sight. They could not become farmers or craftsmen without skill, tools, and capital, and lacking certainly the last and probably all three they had to work for others; indeed, some had arrived as servants. Their prospects seemed gloomy, what with too many Indians, too few women, and no quick fortunes in sight, so they left. Their departure benefited the colony since the economy did not require a surplus labor force and poor, restless, sex-starved, unhappy young men menace everybody else. Besides, that cut in half the excess of males over females and permitted most of those who remained to marry, if they waited a few years.

The exodus recorded the colony's failure to achieve economic growth. During the first few years newcomers brought in capital and a demand for food and services such as the building of houses and the clearing of land. That flow became a trickle in the early forties with the end of the Puritan migration from England, and the people could find no substitute for that economic stimulus. They did produce a surplus from their farms and woodlands, which aggressive traders such as Richard Lord marketed all the way from the northern fisheries to the Chesapeake plantations and presently to the West Indies. These activities prevented bankruptcy except for individuals, but could not forestall a

---

[1] For an example of varied behavior patterns see Christopher Collier's account of early Saybrook and Lyme in George J. Willauer, ed., *A Lyme Miscellany, 1776-1796* (Middletown, Conn., 1977), 9-28.

broad economic decline. Thus the price of oxen remained as high as £16 (pay) per yoke into the early 1650s because of their scarcity and then dropped to £12 in a dozen years. Horses reached their maximum value of £10.7 at the same time followed by a catastrophic fall that ended at £2.7 by 1680.

The continuation of that decline owed something to the absence of immigration but above all followed the price of West Indian sugar. The early settlers there produced their own food. During the 1640s they began to concentrate on sugar culture and to import food, thus helping the Connecticut farmers, but by the 1670s sugar prices were dropping sharply. That market reached bottom in the late 1680s. King Philip's War, injurious though it was, did not affect this particular aspect of the economy and the low point coincided with that of the West Indies. We can see retrospectively that better times lay ahead. Land values were rising in the older towns, while new villages appeared along the frontier. The Glorious Revolution seems not just a political settlement but the start of a new prosperity. The last half of the seventeenth century, however, fixed the colony in a mold that allowed for some variation but no fundamental change for the rest of the colonial period. It would never again attract large numbers of poor young men nor prosperous older ones; it would neither collapse nor flourish, but could provide an economic cushion for a stable middle class.

The failure of Connecticut's very first social order, then, was cause for celebration. The presence of men with capital and ability guaranteed survival, but so many poor, nomadic, unskilled workers in their late teens and twenties had created unrest, great class distinctions, and economic inequality. The early demise or departure of a quarter of the population encouraged a stable family life and left behind a people with enough skill and capital for their modest necessities, even after the wealthiest among them left for home or suffered financial losses. The upper class that remained still held positions of leadership but their high status was modified in several ways: they had to get along with few servants, could not aspire to a genteel level of living, and shared high office with men entirely lacking in family connections and large estates. The first generation of leaders, immigrants all, did include some men of good background but probably not much over a third, at most two out of five, so that well over half of the colony's principal men, sitting side by side in the churches, legislatures, and selectmen's meetings, were ordinary folk by birth whom circumstances now made uncommon.

Moreover, geography tended both to level fortunes and to elevate the poor. The failure of New Haven's mining industry closed that avenue of wealth. The fur trade never amounted to anything and the natives did not provide material for *encomiendas*. Without any possibility of a large favorable balance of trade, the settlers had to become as self-sufficient as possible. Fortunately, many if not most of them knew how to raise livestock and grain crops, to which they added fish, game, and corn; and a surprising proportion possessed craft skills so that not far from three out of ten became part- or full-time artisans. Land, of course, cost almost nothing. The immigrants brought tools with them, but had to wait some years for oxen to come down in price and for their sons to grow strong, since few could afford hired labor. By the middle 1600s, however, the cost of oxen was declining and the women had produced an adequate supply of relatively cheap labor. This development enabled young men to move easily from farm laborers or low-income crafts into agriculture, very nearly eliminating any exploited permanent class of the laboring poor at the same time that the potential exploiters failed to appear. If, on the one hand, the mean value of the people's wealth declined from its originally high level, so did inequality, with the share of the top 10 percent falling from close to half to less than 40 percent, indeed, in the case of real estate to only one-third by the end of the century. The reduction in mean wealth fortunately did not affect the standard of living except perhaps for the largest propertyowners, for it was their misfortune that dragged down the mean. Instead, the standard of living increased over time, and although we can hardly call Connecticut's people prosperous, nine out of ten lived above the subsistence level either by virtue of their own earnings as heads of households or by living as dependents among such families, and nearly half in the same way enjoyed comfort.

By the 1670s, then, the social structure of Connecticut had crystallized into its permanent form. From the point of view of occupation, about a third of the men, excluding the teen-agers, provided the labor force—more or less skilled, dependent upon a parent, an employer, or (rarely) a master for a wage or for room, board, and clothing. The largest number of these were local boys living at home plus a few with neighbors. Migrant freemen and servants formed a much smaller group after the first hectic years, and the rest consisted of married men just starting out, older ones who had failed to achieve independence, and a few elderly "retired" grandfathers. Farmers exceeded the laborers in number, totaling 40 percent if we define the farmer as deriving his principal income from that vocation. Since the average age at marriage was twenty-five now that the sex ratio had equalized, some of the farmers' sons could begin that work even before they had reached thirty, but the cost of buying sufficient land, tools, livestock, and buildings meant that most farmers were older. Indeed, their median age exceeded forty, and, of course, men continued to work on the land all their lives whereas most laborers soon ceased to be such.

Over one out of five men were craftsmen, a proportion made necessary by economic circumstances. These skilled workers included far more young men than did farmers because they needed much less land and livestock, indeed, at first none at all; could learn their trade more quickly; and might require less expensive equipment. Their median age was only thirty-four, seven years less than that of the farmers, and whereas the latter generally remained in that occupation, some of the artisans moved out of their craft into agriculture. Thus among men in their forties and fifties 60 percent were farmers but fewer than one-fourth were artisans. This shift occurred because certain crafts, while easily mastered, earned a bare subsistence, so that the workers acquired land as soon as they could, and even those with more remunerative specialties sometimes became primarily farmers. This occupational mobility involved some farmers' sons who inherited insufficient land and who therefore became artisans, and meant that as many as one out of seven or eight of each new generation changed occupations. During most of the colonial period farming attracted more young craftsmen than the reverse, but the proportion of artisans remained stable and may have begun to rise before 1775.

The remaining men became professionals or engaged in trade, both increasing in number over time. Until 1700 the colony contained almost no doctors or lawyers, very few men who earned their living by public office, and not over one minister per hundred men—some towns actually got along without one for several years at a time. After 1700, with the geographical expansion and boom years, the number of professionals increased and by the end they formed 3 percent of the total. Traders, like ministers, arrived with the first wave and (if we can infer from inventories) 4 percent of the men entered that field, principally as retail shopkeepers. That finally reached 7 percent as ships' captains in particular multiplied during the late colonial period.

The increase in the proportion of professionals and traders came at the expense of farmers and records the end of agricultural expansion within the colony. At the same time the number of laborers rose until they equaled the farmers. This increase did not reflect a greater slave population nor immigration but rather the absence of cheap unimproved land, so that the boys had either to emigrate, as many did, or to wait a few years longer until land became available within the colony. How many years we can infer from the age structure: the percentage of laborers rose from 23 to 32, most of which increase took place within the twenty-year-old group, while the proportion of farmers, declining from 45 to 32, involved primarily the loss of men in their twenties and early thirties. Clearly farm boys now had to continue as wage laborers for three or four more years, and since they did not postpone marriage that meant some additional young families with properties close to subsistence, a fact that we found on the tax lists. This change did not mean a universal decline in wealth or property since the young couple ultimately had as good a chance as before; but it certainly must have caused discontent and doubts about the future.

Connecticut's society was also characterized by the status order usual in western Europe, but here different in degree, permanence, and composition. We may suppose that among the first settlers those entitled to deference in England expected to transport their prestige along with other belongings, and in fact this did occur to some extent. The early documents contain various titles indicating rank, notably mister, gentleman, honorable, and esquire. But these words gradually lost their original significance. Instead they came to denote an office held or function performed, in the way that Reverend signified not someone to be revered but the man who delivered the sermons and otherwise served the community at their behest. Mister most often identified a deputy to the legislature or another official, esquire became limited to a judge or J.P., and honorable meant a member of the council. Gentleman, however, identified nobody and so vanished from Connecticut in the same way that sir and lord, lacking a practical utility, disappeared. Status therefore soon lost its Old World origin and developed tabula rasa, pragmatically reflecting the way in which Connecticut's people regarded one another, but now uncertain and shifting in the absence of a fixed hierarchy of respectful terms.

At the bottom of this new social order were the "inferior" or "lesser sorts," especially the servile, and those lacking any permanent attachment to the community, migratory rather than settled, and almost always poor, such as sailors. These did not own productive property and therefore either depended entirely upon an owner or earned wages, typically low and temporary. They could not vote or hold office and occupied a lowly place in church, but the towns hired them in time of war. A considerable cut above them came the unmarried sons of the farmers and craftsmen. They, too, lacked political rights nor would they usually enjoy full membership in a church, but the parents would have seen to their baptism and many completed the process during the Great Awakening. Also, they lived in the community and so shared in their family's status and standard of living. Finally among those near the bottom of the social order were the older men who had not succeeded in achieving financial independence and remained wards or relatives of the town, forgiven their taxes and supported as needed. Half of these were single and most could earn at least a part of their necessities.

This last group included no more than 8 percent of the older men, one out of a hundred of the whole adult male population, and they with the slaves constituted the only permanent "proletariat," since the situation of all the others might improve. Obviously these two had nothing in common. The rest of the men of comparatively low status also consisted of two different groups: young migrants, mostly though not all free, and resident sons. The first varied greatly in number over time and place but probably exceeded 5 percent of the men only in the port cities, which might contain twice that number. About a third remained mobile, making at least one additional move before settling down, sometimes outside the colony. Some of them died still young and single. The rest generally married, and of those who became family men, over half succeeded in exchanging low status for a higher, the others becoming part of the older poor group mentioned above. Thus the young wanderer would see, in any town, a few respectable men who had once been outsiders and laborers, too, and seldom would view himself as a hopeless outcast except perhaps in a city such as New London, and then only during bad times. As to the local sons, they belonged as we said to the community, not to any class. If their fathers left them poor and underage, one out of four would remain poor and probably of low status, but not over one in five who lived to be forty failed to overcome his humble origins. If their fathers could provide decently for them, then obviously they fared even better, rising at once when they married and settled down.

The category or class called the "middling sort" began at marriage. Other factors established a different lower boundary marker: ships' captains often attained the rank while still single as did some ministers, and we have rare instances of important men who remained unmarried, such as Deacon Thomas Allyn of Middletown (1604-1688) and Wethersfield's Gentleman John Robbins (1649-1699). But for almost all men, marriage elevated their status for several reasons. First, they either achieved or declared an intention of achieving independence, becoming heads of households. Second, they usually obtained or would soon earn a sufficient property to support a family. Third, they demonstrated stability as residents of the community, no longer migrants or restless lads. Fourth, some of them joined the church with their new wives. Finally, they could now vote and hold office—become citizens of the town and colony. They became valuable members of society, useful men who would no longer be sent off to war as expendables, and respectable.

This middle group, which in Connecticut included three out of five of the men, consisted by definition of small and medium-sized propertyowners, almost all of whom worked for themselves. Practically every craftsman belonged here as did nearly every farmer. They shaded imperceptibly into the top level of men whom we have called the leaders. These occupied the important positions, civil, religious, military, economic, and social. They did not form a separate, distinct, or permanent class. During the seventeenth century the title "mister" usually, though not invariably, distinguished the men of education or high position who lacked some other title, but when that word lost its meaning nothing replaced it. We therefore cannot discover major political officeholders (other than the assistants) without looking hard for them, nor can we identify men of wealth without records such as inventories and then only by ourselves deciding when someone belongs: they themselves do not say. Finally, nothing reveals a social elite unless we invent one, set its distinguishing marks, and select a name for it.

These principal men drew to some extent from the families that carried status from England or acquired it by their contributions to the colony, but two out of five entered from the middle group, especially the prosperous and capable farmers. The professionals and traders contributed more than their numbers would predict, the craftsmen fewer. While some sons of leaders undoubtedly had a head start because of their environment, education, property, and inherited capability, they had to compete with their neighbors and enough failed in this competition that they left vacancies. One of the clearest proofs of an open society lies in the fact that very few men less than forty years old joined the leaders. There was nothing automatic about the process. Regardless of background, except for a few individuals in the earliest years, all ascended a testing ladder or, in the case of the economic group, had to reestablish the divided fortunes left by their fathers or create a new one. At any given time about 7 percent of the men belonged to this highest rank. However, the opportunity for eventually reaching it was much better than seven out of a hundred because the odds improved greatly with age. They were a hundred to one against the young, and twenty-five to one against the young fathers in their thirties, but those living to sixty had one chance in four.[2] As a final

[2] All this comes from actual counting of the probate population and translating to

373

point in support of this argument for labeling colonial Connecticut an "open society," the leaders had not selected their wives exclusively from their own kind, but often had chosen women of the middling sort. Thus the native-born upper class never became separate from the rest of the people and, if anything, the trend was in the other direction during the final decades.

The people of Connecticut thus differed greatly in status at any given moment, with many at the bottom, a few at the top, and a majority occupying various intermediate positions, but as with Bellamy's coach the personnel constantly changed. Those at the bottom who lived long enough to marry commonly progressed into the middling ranks, while these in turn moved steadily up, in a few cases eventually to the top, passing some who slipped downward as well as those who never advanced, but primarily occupying the positions vacated by death or old age.

Let us recapitulate the economic implications of this life cycle. The "average" Connecticut lad married at age twenty-five. Some, of course, did not marry at all, especially during the early years when too few women lived in the colony, even though they became brides several years younger than their daughters. Also, the outsiders, especially slaves but white servants and migrants as well, frequently failed to find wives, and so those who became free moved on or married late. A few natives of the town also remained single but very few; even lads orphaned without much property became husbands and fathers after only a year's delay. As long as they served another person or lived at home they owned very little property although they enjoyed a good standard of living. Inventories include little but their clothing unless they were credited with the share of the family estate that they would have inherited had they lived. Assessment lists either omit their names and charged the father with the extra poll or show them as the possessors of nothing but their "heads," the body below which presumably produced an income, along with perhaps a horse or a cow and a couple of acres.

In order to marry they needed, of course, a place to live. Apparently this did not present much of a problem, because for the first few years the couple could survive in a single room with a lean-to, cheap and easily constructed. They did not need plumbing, electricity, glass windows, a hot-water heater, or any heating system other than a fireplace.

the living. The seven men would, in our hypothetical town of a hundred men, consist of the minister, two deacons, a captain, two deputies, a justice, and a couple of well-to-do individuals, with some overlapping.

Outdoors a shed would serve. All these buildings were makeshift, quickly replaced or incorporated into a larger dwelling. The bride contributed the household articles and the groom brought tools, livestock, and land, varying with his occupation, the family's property, and his own savings or purchases on credit. Normally the farmers among them would begin with less than forty acres of land, only half of which would be improved, below par for a family but enough for the moment. Their consumption goods would at the least permit a subsistence-level standard of living and, indeed, one very close to comfort, given their modest needs. This level was reached by the first generation born in the colony and remained stable over time.

As long as the children remained at home the cost of living rose for the average family at the rate of between £4 and £5 per year if they wished to live decently. Fortunately, most parents remained alive and the father's earning power, presently supplemented by that of his teenagers, exceeded that minimum, creating a surplus for the children as they married. As a rule this extra income over and above that needed for the added household goods—a couple of pounds a year for young fathers, up to £20 for older men—was invested in land, totaling (again on the average) as much as eighty acres. Moreover the men, taking them collectively, actually continued to save at a reduced rate of about £5 per year until well into the sixties, by which time most of the children were provided for; but this varied greatly. The process continued without any change throughout the colonial period.

Overall, the increased wealth of each older generation precisely balanced the small properties of the younger, so that while no net gain occurred over time neither did a decline. Of the numerous poor men at a given time, some died, others left, a majority married and became propertied, so that when a given cohort reached its forties fewer than 8 percent still remained poor (varying from two to thirteen with the business cycle). Another 20 percent just subsisted. The proportion of both declined gradually as men entered their fifties. If one survived to become a grandfather he generally ceased to save any money (some did but more did not); however, his needs diminished as the children left and as he no longer had to purchase land or other assets for them. Therefore, the grandfathers lived even better than when they were younger.

The "retired" men, despite their fewer needs, slipped back a little even into dependent poverty. In most cases this meant only that the elderly couple had given away their home to the children and now lived with one of them, though a few may always have been poor. However, this was a small group. About a third of the retired men, at the subsistence level or less, required some help, but since not more than two out of five grandfathers had retired and since grandfathers themselves numbered less than 12 percent of the men, this category of semi-dependent men constituted only 1 or 2 percent of adult males. During the colonial period, then, the economic lower class was not numerous enough, too varied in its composition, too well cared for, and too transient to constitute any threat or probably to create any awareness of class, except perhaps during the two major periods of depression and the short one of the 1760s, and perhaps also in the principal port towns as these increased in size toward the end of the colonial era.

The details of this process and the distribution of wealth differed with occupation and place of residence. Each occupational group had its lower economic class—the traders their peddlers and sailors, professionals their teachers, craftsmen their apprentices and journeymen, farmers their field hands; and these always owned little property. Otherwise, men in trade and the professions earned the higher incomes, farmers came next, and artisans last, though every economic level existed in each. Traders accumulated more money than anyone else, with merchants at the top and shopkeepers below them. Few active ships' captains owned estates above the average though many became well-off eventually. The most successful entrepreneurs diversified and retained their position as owners of the highest mean personal property, though not the highest median—there were too many hazards for that.

Although nobody could rival the richest merchants, the professional men led in median incomes, lived more comfortably, and more often achieved high status. The teachers generally became ministers or obtained another good position while the doctors either prospered with age, moved to a town with a clientele able to pay high fees, or changed fields. The lawyers, ministers, and officials possessed even more consumption goods than our requirement for the well-off and their estates contained more land than the farmers'.

The distribution of property owned by laborers, traders, and professionals considerably affected that of the colony as a whole, but that of the craftsmen and farmers established the basic pattern, because they were by far the most numerous and because their level of wealth remained stable over time. The proportion of craftsmen in the general population and the income of the several varieties of artisans changed very little. Shoemakers, tailors, and weavers began their practice as young men, often those sons whose fathers could not provide them with land. Only a few of them, serving the upper class of the larger towns, prospered from their skill, and the rest switched into farming or another craft. The other artisans resembled the farmers in their property and standard of living. They usually acquired land unless they lived in a commercial center and specialized. Some furnished leaders for their society, especially the millers, tanners, and others whom we termed manufacturers. As such they intersected with the large land-owners and wealthier traders just as did the coopers and smiths with the farmers. Thus artisans never formed a distinctive class either in status or in property, differing from one another as much as they resembled the farmers and traders and intermarrying with or descended from both.

Finally, farming retained its economic significance as the principal occupation in Connecticut. Men of all wealth classes were farmers but in general very few became really rich and few remained poor. The fact that the general distribution of property, the level of inequality, the value of consumer goods, and the standard of living varied so little resulted from the continuity in the farmers' fortunes. Each depression was succeeded by a boom. Thus after 1750 rising land prices and improvements almost doubled the value of the farmers' real estate while leaving that of their personal wealth undiminished.

The history of that final quarter-century poses some problems. The key fact is negative: no decline occurred, but an actual gain if we regard the greater wealth in real property as a genuine enrichment. To some extent it took place because farmers (and others) began to add various buildings and either to construct better houses or to enlarge the old so that the value, as recorded in estate inventories, increased. Primarily, however, the price of the land itself doubled as compared with 1700. Some of this rise occurred because fewer vacant tracts remained within the colony and because greater demand for the limited supply of the best-quality soils increased the price of meadow, for example, by 50 percent, but the principal reason lay in "improvements," the transformation of woods and uplands into income-producing orchards, pasture, and arable land. If we accept these changes as additions to the collective wealth of the colony, they translate into a per capita growth of between 1 and 2 percent annually, depending on when one wants to start it.

A common interpretation of New England's agricultural history stresses the idea that rising land values deprived more and more men of land so that the increasing wealth of a few actually implied a per capita decline. This did not occur in Connecticut. Instead, young men delayed entrance into agriculture for a few extra years, remaining artisans or laborers, and some farmers' sons who normally would have stayed on the land went into trade, a profession, or a craft. Above all the rate of emigration out of the colony increased starting with those born during the 1730s. For these reasons we find a rise of five years in the average age of farmers (measured by age at death) and the entire resident population also aged, not because of any increase in the life expectancy but due to a loss of men in their twenties and thirties. This emigration registered at least as much the superior attraction of excellent cheap land becoming available elsewhere as declining opportunity in Connecticut.

Connecticut's towns differed from one another rather less than was true of other colonies. They included no dominant seaport; instead, commerce was scattered among many trading centers as in New Jersey and North Carolina. Neither did Connecticut contain a region characterized by large-scale staple-crop agriculture with its accompanying propertyless labor force. Even in the areas of good soil, farms rarely exceeded two hundred acres and produced a diversity of crops and livestock. Moreover, the colony's farm laborers consisted principally of native-born whites who were residents, seldom migrants and rarely servile. The same was true of the non-agricultural workers as well. Even towns with the best land and the largest agricultural surplus did not depend upon slaves, who acted as household or personal servants as often as they did as field hands. Furthermore, the centers of commercial farming also contained many craftsmen and traders, diversifying rather than specializing. Finally, Connecticut lacked the religious and cultural variety of colonies such as Pennsylvania and New York, nor was it settled by disparate peoples as were the Carolinas or in separate sections like New Jersey. Relatively, sectional harmony and cultural uniformity prevailed despite occasional political differences.

We can, however, identify a few distinctive regions and sort the towns into several species. The strip of land along the Sound contained some good soil and was relatively warm with a long growing season and a large number of sheltered harbors, each with an agricultural hinterland along a river. New London had the most extensive foreign trade, but Fairfield, New Haven, and Milford also became significant centers of commerce. These contained skilled craftsmen who specialized more exclusively as population increased. Stamford, Norwalk, Stratford, Branford, Guilford, and Stonington belonged to the same species but in lesser degree. All of these towns included many farmers. During the eighteenth century some towns near, though not on the coast, with the same good soils and climate, also flourished. The Connecticut Valley formed a separate region with Hartford as its principal commercial and political center, and Middletown's commerce later came to rival that of Hartford. The rich soil of the upper Valley benefited other towns that could develop crafts and support traders and professionals.

As one moved north from the Sound and away from the great river valley the climate becomes colder and good soil scarcer. Thus the towns in present-day Windham, Tolland, and Litchfield Counties, with adjacent communities to the south, did not produce as much surplus wealth and many remained largely self-sufficient. Agricultural discontent centered there and in similar communities for related reasons, and toward the end of our period·they exported more people than commodities.

Connecticut's communities, ranging from populous urban centers like New London and Hartford down to scattered farms and hamlets, differed in social structure and the distribution of wealth in ways so obvious that we need only sketch them. At one extreme, those two towns and others like them contained not only prosperous traders but a concentration of professional men such as lawyers, doctors, and public officials and also well-to-do manufacturers. These formed a large upper class both of status and wealth, contrasting with numerous laborers, mostly sailors and apprentices. In addition an unusual number of slaves lived there, primarily acting as household servants. Such towns were also distinguished by the presence of fine houses and exceptional personal wealth in consumption goods, books, debts receivable, and trading stock. A few leading families owned much of this property and of the real estate as well.

At the other extreme, of course, men of real wealth were scarce in the upland villages. There, the laborers consisted of local boys plus a few white migrants, and most of the men were farmers or craftsmen of the middle rank, living in plain houses simply furnished, and with rather more debts owed than owing. One is tempted to applaud a society of yeomen farmers with an equal distribution of wealth and few class distinctions, but they had to forgo any chance of acquiring large property or leisure or learning, and the trading towns and westward roads filled with their sons, for whom the home town offered little prospect of improvement.

In some ways the most desirable place to live was in the more prosperous farming areas. These did lack the variety and excitement of urban communities but they offered security, opportunity at least for the local boys, and very likely a longer life expectancy. The higher concentration of wealth reflected the superior quality of the land and residents achieved, by middle age, a level of comfort rarely available to the people of poorer rural areas. For Connecticut one might formulate a novel rule: the higher the level of inequality the more comfortably the majority of the people lived, median wealth rising with the mean.

The benefits of such a social order depended upon the ability of the younger generation to advance economically and socially so as to equal, on the average, the success of the older. In Connecticut, as in other societies, some men failed—because other people so ordered, as in the case of slaves, or as a result of initial poverty combined perhaps with community prejudice that outsiders faced, or from private misfortunes. We have seen also that two long periods of depression lowered the level of wealth and opportunity so that good times were by no means eternal. Nevertheless, taking the colonial period as a whole, the residents created and preserved a society in which two-thirds of the men could earn a decent living, more than ample to support families, and most of those who did not were still young and enjoying the higher standard of their parents or guardians. Among the older men only one in twenty remained eternally poor while four out of five were able to help get their children established on secure careers. One out of the four, as we have seen, would eventually beome a leader and well-to-do. Some young men failed to succeed their fathers nor did newcomers always find equality, but most of those who failed had died too young. Even the poor orphans and migrants, if they lived to age forty, joined the respectable middling sort nearly three times out of four. Since even the sons of well-established farmers retained their property and full status only slightly more often at the same age, Connecticut offered a decent chance to its young men.

How can we account for this favorable environment, which lasted even to the end of the colonial period, especially since some other students have found a long-term decline? To begin with, the colony produced all the food it needed and sold a surplus: during the Revolutionary War it sent large quantities to the army. The people imported wheat during the later seventeenth century due to wheat blight, and perhaps even after the southern districts renewed production of that grain the northern may have been forced to buy some (we do not know); but if so that was due to a preference for white bread, not a shortage of grain. Secondly, the craftsmen were numerous enough and the farmers skilled enough as general handymen that the people could live at the same level of comfort right down to 1776.[3] Third, new

---

[3] Although the estates left by craftsmen did not increase, they may have produced articles of superior value for sale outside the colony, and thus helped to account for the greater number of merchants.

towns came into existence through the 1740s and farmers continued steadily to transform undeveloped land into tracts sufficiently improved, if not for tillage, then at least for orchards, rough pasture, and as a source of wood. These improvements account for about half of the increase in land values. Fourth, the soil does not seem to have lost its fertility, such as it was; yields per acre of the familiar cereal crops did not decrease, indeed, our data suggests the reverse. Livestock did not decline in quality, and horses more than doubled in value between 1700 and 1760. The farmers used their land more intensively and diversified, introducing new crops such as onions, potatoes, and flaxseed. Fifth, growing economic diversification meant that each new generation would shift occupations in response to opportunity, particularly from farming into trade and the professions. Population growth accounted for some of this, but wars and international trade enabled farmers to find markets outside the colony.

Sixth, the values and laws of the colony encouraged an open society with moderate rather than large fortunes. There was no incentive to amass great wealth, since it brought neither a title nor any deference beyond that of other successful men, such as ministers; nor did lavish hospitality, building great mansions, supporting numerous servants, or buying rich household furnishings win particular applause. Men acquired hundreds rather than thousands of acres and an estate in five figures was almost unknown. Also, the only way a man could prevent the fragmenting of his property among his heirs was to avoid leaving children at his death, or just one, something seldom accomplished. Even an only son, with two sisters and a mother still alive, could lay claim to no more than a third of the estate. The normal expectation was still less. Each generation therefore had to start, if not from the bottom, then at some distance down the ladder. The level of inequality of wealth and status did not increase and the names of men at the top rotated. The standing order kept walking away.

Finally, men at the bottom or doubtful about their prospects could always leave, and did so. The effects of the depression during the late 1600s were mitigated by emigrations to New York and New Jersey, while that of the 1730s and 1740s would have been more severe without the founding of new towns both in and beyond the colony. Once again, after the French and Indian War the movement resumed both north and west on a large enough scale to slow the rate of population growth and reduce the proportion of young men. The considerable geographical mobility thus did not take the form of a movement from country to city, as in Europe, so great as to create an urban proletariat, but from both country and town into sparsely settled or even unoccupied land. Perhaps if emigration had diminished after 1765 the colony's prosperity and standard of living might also have declined; but as matters developed it did not. Connecticut ended as it had begun: a land of plenty for some and of sufficiency for most people.[4]

[4] Whether Connecticut was overpopulated in 1775 remains doubtful, and I think it was not. The colony contained 4,820 square miles, each square mile of which might be divided into eight eighty-acre farms. If families consisted of five persons, then the 36,560 farms would support 192,500 persons; and if half of the families lived on farms, which is pretty close to the mark, then Connecticut could contain 385,000 people without overcrowding. The eighty acres allows for some leeway in the form of land not good for much except wood, and we assume that parts of the colony would sustain a larger number of farmers in compensation for poorer areas, but let us subtract one-third for bad land as Congress did in the Northwest Territory. In that case the land would support over 256,000 persons at a time when 200,000 resided there. All this assumes no changes in existing technology or in any other factors such as expanding outside markets. Even as matters stood, one can make a better case for the "pull" of opportunities in other areas than for internal "push" factors in the colony as a whole, though obviously some of the poorer towns would indeed push out more than the usual proportion.

BIBLIOGRAPHICAL ESSAY

Several bibliographical aids guide the researcher through the large quantity of unpublished and the smaller amount of published sources. The microfilm index to the collection of the Church of Jesus Christ of Latter Day Saints lists most if not all of the second type and microfilms of the former, notably probate court records, deeds, and church records. Branch libraries have the index and will obtain individual reels. The Library of Congress and the New York Public Library, among others, have published catalogues of their genealogical and local history collections. Major university and other libraries commonly own at least one such.

Christopher and Bonnie B. Collier have assembled a full annotated guide to the *Literature of Connecticut History*, published by the Connecticut Humanities Council (Middletown, 1983), and Bruce C. Daniels furnished a critical discussion of "Antiquarians and Professionals: The Historians of Colonial Connecticut," in *Connecticut History*, 23 (1982), 81-97. The secondary works most apt to be missing from libraries are the pamphlets of the Connecticut bicentennial series, edited by Glenn Weaver. These cover the revolutionary period but overlap with the colonial.

Since readers can easily find these secondary accounts and the familiar published primary ones such as the *Colonial Records* and the newspapers, this essay will mention the unpublished materials forming the core for this book. These are almost all located, sometimes on microfilm, in the Connecticut State Library, Hartford.

Of particular importance were the tax lists and probate records. The library contains most of the former still in existence though a few good series remain in town collections. There is a guide to them but no name index. An index does exist to the probate court materials but only to the name of the decedent. The researcher therefore must note the names of spouses and relatives, including children, in order to identify the individual and to determine his or her stage in the life cycle as well as the characteristics of the family and the fates of the children—details that required the negligent writer to reread many hundreds of manuscript pages.

If one wishes to learn more about the people of the probate records or those on tax lists, several other collections are available. First, the so-called Barbour collection of town vital records are now on microfilm. Next, another card index covers gravestone inscriptions and obituaries in newspapers. These furnish at least the place and age at death. A third index extracts names from church records, for example, baptisms or acceptances by societies. Finally, all of the deeds are on microfilm. These preserve the conveyances of land including original grants by the town or proprietors and later divisions as well as subsequent transfers. Anyone conducting really intensive work in local history, which this is not, would find these essential. I used them only for particular purposes, for example in tracing the careers of poor young laborers and orphans. The deeds are arranged by town with an index of grantor and grantees for each town, but not including the many other names they contain. Genealogists read right through them!

If none of these yield the necessary information, or perhaps as the very first step, one can consult the genealogies. The State Library owns most of those covering Connecticut families both in book form and in manuscripts. They vary greatly in value just as do histories, but some are enormously useful; Jacobus's two big multivolume works on Fairfield and New Haven I would call magnificent. His belong to a genre called town genealogies, which commonly form a sort of appendix to town histories, but in his case are separate publications. The most efficient procedure in reconstructing the population of a town is to consult such a work first and vital records second, then either the other indexes or the genealogies of the individual families. I have not attempted in the footnotes to cite all the sources for every person mentioned.

I did not consult three bodies of primary sources: town and church records except for some that are published; the records of courts other than probate despite their undoubted valued for social history; and the unpublished colonial records of the government. These are so enormous in quantity as to defy anyone working so generally as I, especially since indexes are almost entirely absent. Their use by historians in the future should transform our understanding of early American history.

Library of Congress Cataloging in Publication Data

Main, Jackson Turner.
Society and economy in colonial Connecticut.

Bibliography: p.   Includes index.

1. Connecticut—Economic conditions. 2. Wealth—
Connecticut—History—17th century. 3. Wealth—
Connecticut—History—18th century. 4. Connecticut—
History—Colonial period, ca. 1600-1775. I. Title.

HC107.C8M35   1985   330.9746′02   84-42892
ISBN 0-691-04726-X (alk. paper)

*Jackson Turner Main is Professor Emeritus of History at the State
University of New York at Stony Brook. He is the author of many
books and articles in American history, including* The Social
Structure of Revolutionary America *(1965),* Political Parties
Before the Constitution *(1973),* **and** Connecticut Society in
the Era of the American Revolution *(1978).*

DATE DUE

DEMCO 38-297